SONG HONGBING

CURRENCY WARS II
The Power of Gold

Song Hongbing

Song Hongbing (born in 1968) is a young economic researcher who emigrated to the United States. He worked there as a consultant for the American pension funds Freddie Mac and Fanny Mae that will disappear during the financial crisis of 2008.

货币战争②金权天下

CURRENCY WARS II
The Power of Gold

Translated from Chinese and published by
Omnia Veritas Limited

www.omnia-veritas.com

© Omnia Veritas Ltd – 2021

All rights reserved. No part of this publication may be reproduced by any means without the prior permission of the publisher. The intellectual property code prohibits copies or reproductions for collective use. Any representation or reproduction in whole or in part by any means whatsoever, without the consent of the publisher, is unlawful and constitutes an infringement punishable by copyright laws.

PREFACE 13

CHAPTER I 16

GERMANY: THE BIRTHPLACE OF INTERNATIONAL BANKERS 16

Who's the international banker? 17
The War That Stopped 20
Old Bleichröder: Rothschild's Agent 23
Oppenheimer: The Financial Overlord of Cologne 26
The 1848 Revolution and the Banking Rescue 30
The Rise of Bismarck 33
Bleichröder: Bismarck's Private Banker 35
The Danish Crisis: Bismarck's Unexpected Opportunity 38
The Prussian War: A Test of Golden Power 41
Parliamentary liberals: obstacles on the road to German reunification 44
Privatization of the Cologne-Minden railway: a source of wealth for the Austro-Prussian war 46
Why the Austro-Prussian War came to an abrupt end 50
"The Battle for the Popularization of the Law: 10,000 gold taels at the sound of a cannon. 52
5 billion francs war payout: the banker's "big pie" 56

CHAPTER II 59

THE UK: THE HEIGHTS OF GOLD POWER 59

Francis, the founder of the Baring dynasty 60
The Netherlands: the pinnacle of commercial capitalism 62
The Hope family: Baring is the richest man in Europe 65
"Red Top Businessmen": Gold Power in Power 66
Transatlantic network of people 69
Louisiana Financing: The Most Amazing Financial Case Ever Made 71
The Anglo-American War of 1812: The Baring Family in and Out 72
France's Post-War Payout: Baring Promotes to Sixth Power in Europe 75
French public debt contracts: a feud between two men 78
Rothschild is finally the king 81
Financiers and Politicians 85
The Suez Canal: Rothschild's Financial Blitzkrieg 87
Saving the Bank of Baring 90
Golden Cross 92
Enter China 95

CHAPTER III 98

FRANCE: THE CESSION OF GOLD 98

The Swiss banking family behind the French Revolution 99

Banque de France: The Return on Investment of the "Coup of 18 Brumaire" 102
The Monopoly is Broken: The Rise of the Jewish Banking Family 105
Revolution in Financial Innovation...107
Credit Mobilier: The Challenge of Pereire 110
"Both a liar and a prophet." 113
Bank of France: strategic high ground to defeat Pereire............................117
Crimean War..122
Catholic Bankers: The Third Force..125
The evolution of gold power: from ownership to control 126

CHAPTER IV 130

THE UNITED STATES: THE "CIRCLE OF THE GOLDEN POWER" 130

Seligman: From small businessman to international banker....................131
August Belmont's "Federal Reserve" 133
New York's High Society 135
The king of national debt, Seligman. 139
Seligman shakes Finance Minister..143
Seligman: America's Rothschild..146
"Seligman: the true "father of Panama" 151
The Age of Schiff 156
Schiff and the Russo-Japanese War..162
New Circle and Old Circle 165

CHAPTER V 170

A TURBULENT EUROPE 170

An unquenchable longing: to return, to return to Zion...............................171
The German banking family: the fire of hope for a return.........................172
The Palestinian Dilemma 176
Siege and Rise: The Strategic Competition of Yingde 178
Hamburg-America Line: The Battle for Maritime Hegemony....................179
Max Warburg: The Economic Czar of the Future...181
Berlin-Baghdad Railway: Germany's Strategic Corridor Against Siege 184
Agadir Incident..186
The Balfour Declaration and the Bankers' Dream 189
Treachery: The Contradiction of the British Ruling Elite and Zionism.......192
Economic weapons and the Versailles Agreement 196
The "independence" of the German Central Bank in 1922: the "eye of the wind" of the super-inflationary hurricane 199
The "currency war" that overthrew the Weimar Republic 201
Schacht's Battle for the "Ground Rent Mark"...204
The Dawes Plan: Supporting the Beginning of Germany...........................208

CHAPTER VI 212

HITLER'S "NEW DEAL" 212

"Cynical Hitler" 213
Feder: Hitler's financial mentor 216
Brewpub Riot: Hitler's Fame 219
Hitler was hit in the waist by the god of wealth 222
Circle of friends of the leader of the Third Reich 227
The Haavara Agreement 229
Schacht: the intermediary of international bankers 231
The Great Game of Chess 236
Social power platform in Nazi Germany 239
The economic system of Nazi Germany 244
Hitler's "New Deal" 246
Hitler's first fire of the New Deal: Nationalization of the Central Bank ... 247
"Federity": Germany's Lincoln Greenbacks 249
"Financial innovation" saved the German economy 253
Rothschild and Hitler 255
Hitler's power play 258

CHAPTER VII 261

BANKERS AND INTELLIGENCE NETWORKS 261

The KGB's "Cambridge Five" 262
"The Fifth Man" 264
The Circle of the Apostolic Council 266
Philby's father 271
Kim Philby and Victor Rothschild 273
"The Cambridge Five" penetrated British intelligence 275
Between Sumerian and American, the two sides of the same coin 277
Core Confidential 279
Victor's Price: The Secret Exchange of Atomic Bombs for the Establishment of the State of Israel 284
"Target Patton" 289
Donovan's Origin 292
OSS - "Oh So Social" 294
The motive for Patton's murder 295

CHAPTER VIII 297

THE RULING ELITE AND THE "INVISIBLE OLIGARCHS" 297

The mysterious crash of Korean Air KAL007 298
The Diamond Empire and the Elite Fathers 302
The Lodz Club, the "Whampoa Military Academy" of the British ruling elite 304

    "Milner Group" 308
    German policy of the "Milner Group" is based on two core points 311
    "Anglo-American power bloc" 313
    The Foundation: The Invisible Rothschild of Wealth................................315
    The Chicken Soup of the Heart says: the more you give up, the more you have 319
    The Rockefellers, the "family down the road" 322
    Leverage and wealth control 326
    Congressional Inquiry 330
    Foundations, elite groups and governments 333
    Foundations and the education system...337
    Public opinion shaping...338
    World government: the goal of the "Anglo-American power bloc"..........340

CHAPTER IX **345**

    AFTER THE FINANCIAL TSUNAMI..345

    Greenspan: Engineer of the economic machine 347
    The Korean War made Greenspan an overnight success.......................351
    Ayn Rand: Greenspan's Spiritual Director..353
    Who is the Hand of God?...356
    Ayn Rand's Pseudo-Proposition 358
    "If Hercules strikes"..361
    Gold: the ideal currency for the elite 363
    The distorted dollar and the "debt lagoon"...366
    The Future of the World Economy: 14 Years of the "Great Depression"...371

CHAPTER X **375**

    BACK TO THE FUTURE...375

    On January 1, 2024, the world single currency is launched 376
    The single currency: the end of history 380
    The crisis has come at the right time 387
    The fate of money and the fate of nations 392
    The Perfect and Deadly Combination: World Single Currency = Gold + Carbon Currency 399
    End of the Dollar 402
    "The world under Hercules" 405

    ACKNOWLEDGEMENTS AND REFLECTIONS 408

    AFTERWORD...411

OTHER TITLES **413**

PREFACE

On June 11, 2009, at 2:41 a.m., "The Currency War 2 – The Power of Gold" was finally finished. Since the completion of "Currency War" in the summer of 2006, we have been working on collecting information for this second volume. Over the past three years, we have carefully combed through the connections between all the major banking families in Germany, England, France and the United States for more than two hundred years, and their links with wars, revolutions, coups d'état and crises in various countries, beginning in 1723 and ending in 2024, involving many important historical events in Europe and the United States and the financial operations behind them, to arrive at a map of the connections between the "17 major banking families" of the world.

In more than 1,000 days and nights, reading hundreds of family histories, economic histories of various countries, all kinds of documents, maps, magazines, newspapers, online articles, etc., the total reading volume exceeded 50 million words, an average of 50,000 words per day, finally completed this work that is now too much to think back to. During the days of 2009, he averaged no more than four hours of sleep per day and worked overnight for eight consecutive weeks.

I self-evidently think that *Currency Wars 2 – The Power of Gold* is more than 10 times as informative as the first book, with as many as 200 characters with surnames, and I believe that people who read the first book should not consider it a waste of time after reading the second one. The logic of the two books is perfectly self-contained, a large number of historical facts corroborate each other, and many of the major historical enigmas will have a rational and unifying logic to support them.

There is a major research blind spot in the Chinese theoretical community when it comes to studying the workings of Western society, and that is to ignore the human connections in Western society. Any society is made up of people, and the study of society should be people-centered, especially the key minority groups that play a significant role in a society. A thorough understanding of these people's network of relationships is an important basis for a proper understanding of Western society.

In fact, the structure of any human society is a typical pyramidal one, with a critical minority of people gradually moving up through the social structure due to their own intelligence and diligence, and in some cases through violence and fraud. When they have sufficient financial power and influence, they will in turn consolidate and expand their vested interests by changing the rules of the game and creating a ruling elite with interlocking interests. If the power pyramid structure of Eastern societies is based on regimes, the Western pyramid of domination is a chain of very hidden debts that hold the various strata of society firmly together. In Western societies, creditors have dominant power and debtors are in a dominated position, and the main function of the state apparatus is to protect and reinforce the reliability of this chain. In the West, whoever is the biggest creditor is the ultimate lawmaker of the game, and central banks, controlled by international bankers since the 19th century, are undoubtedly the biggest creditors of society as a whole, with the rest of society, including governments, being their debtors. From this perspective, the West today is actually a financial powerhouse controlling government decisions.

China is increasingly becoming a major power with global influence. China's new generation of strategic thinkers must have a broad global perspective and a deep historical perspective in order to form a long-term and practical national strategy. The premise of any strategy formation is that it is necessary to determine who is the primary strategic opponent, that a strategy without an opponent does not become a strategy, and that a strategy based on the wrong primary opponent does not become an effective strategy. A comprehensive and thorough understanding of the historical origins and connections of international financial power groups is the cornerstone of a correct national strategy for China.

This book will comprehensively describe the formation, development, exclusion, conflict, alliance and checks and balances of the major financial power groups in Europe and the United States over a period of 300 years, systematically analyze the operation and decision-making mechanism of the dominant forces behind the scenes in the world today, and for the first time unveil the mystery of the "international banking family club" that rules the world. The book presents the subtle relationship between the financial powerhouses that dominate the world today in a panoramic and three-dimensional manner, with exciting stories, vivid language, a broad financial perspective, a broad historical perspective, a deep theoretical foundation and solid historical data.

It is a vast network of international contacts that has so far been almost entirely unknown to the Chinese, with the financial industry at its core, intertwined with government agencies, oil consortia, military-industrial complexes, biopharmaceutical groups, strategic intelligence systems, national armed forces, news media and lobby groups, judicial and legislative bodies, borderless organizations, vast foundation systems, think tanks, religious groups, secret elite groups and other key social forces. It is the compass for a proper understanding of the frequent financial crises, wars and conflicts, revolutionary riots, upheavals and coups d'état, religious hot spots, global agendas, geopolitics, great power relations and international organizations in the world today.

Due to the large span of time, complex relationships, twists and turns of historical events and my limited theoretical knowledge, errors and omissions are inevitable.

Author.

Beijing, 20 June 2009

CHAPTER I

Germany: the birthplace of international bankers

Since the 19th century, 17 major international banking families, represented by the Rothschilds, with the Netherlands, England, France and Germany as their birthplace, have gradually spread to Russia, Austria, Italy and the United States, eventually forming a backbone of financial contacts with far-reaching implications for the world today.

International bankers are a critical minority in a world of enormous energy, and the way they think and act largely determines the fate of humanity. In the past two hundred years, these families have been very powerful on the world stage, and the vast and complex network of human relationships formed by these families at the core of Western society has played a major role in the development trajectory of human history and the formation of the current world pattern. Some families have fallen in the midst of the rising and falling tides, but most still exert an important and even critical influence today.

The Chinese are by no means unfamiliar with the human history of power, but they are far from familiar with the human history of wealth, so let's begin this twisting journey of discovery in Germany, the most internationally banker-intensive country of origin.

At the critical moment of the Austro-Prussian war, Prussian Chancellor Bismarck insisted on abandoning the warplane under the threat of resignation and jumping from a building, when the Prussian army was in a good position to capture the Austrian capital, Vienna, in one fell swoop.

Behind the abrupt end of the war, we will see one international banker after another, Rothschild, Bleichröder, Oppenheimer ... and behind these figures, there is a well-connected, deep-rooted, vertically-connected family financial network. They were born to each other, working together while fighting and setting up a trap.

This ubiquitous, omnipotent network of gold power essentially manipulates, controls, and determines the intricacies of Europe's national domestic diplomacy, wars and revolutions, regimes, and intrigues. From the rise of the iron chancellor Bismarck, the process of German reunification, the revolution of 1848, the Danish crisis, to the Franco-Prussian War and the Franco-Prussian War, there is no doubt that this powerful network of golden power is inextricably linked. History also plays out in a thrilling way as it turns its hands to cloud and rain.

Who's the international banker?

Since the 19th century, 17 major international banking families, represented by the Rothschilds, with the Netherlands, England, France and Germany as their birthplace, have gradually spread to Russia, Austria, Italy and the United States, eventually forming a backbone of financial contacts with far-reaching implications for the world today. As the wave of the French bourgeois revolution swept across the continent, religious and feudal kingship declined, the old social domination blocs fell apart and the emerging bourgeoisie quickly filled the social power vacuum. In the course of the explosive expansion of railways, metallurgy, mining, military industry, machinery, communications and other industries resulting from the Industrial Revolution, when successive wars broke out as a result of the imbalance of power of the European powers, international bankers perceptively seized the great historic opportunity to raise large sums of money rapidly through the financial markets for industrial expansion and wars between nations, gaining great and amazing wealth while also exerting great influence on the course of history.

The power of wealth is reflected in the erosion of power, the desire for power, and the control of power. International bankers have progressively controlled the channels of world capital and credit flows in the process of docking capital supply with demand, and have developed a set of rules of the game.

Today's Chinese are familiar with the concept of "channel is king", and if even Wal-Mart's channel control and commodity bargaining power in the area of commodity distribution has been memorized by many entrepreneurs, then the social influence of monopolistic control over the channels of capital and credit flows that everyone in society needs is far from being matched by Wal-Mart.

From their humble beginnings in society, international bankers have grown from a position of subordination to the powerful and elite in each country, gradually gaining great economic power and control over the capital and flow channels of each country, gradually taking control of the industrial and commercial systems and creating interlocking interests, which then begin to influence national policies for the greater good. They are increasingly integrated with the interests of the powerful and elite, using the temptation of money that is difficult to resist, and increasingly dominate the selection of politicians from the appointment of government officials to presidential elections, from the formulation of economic policies to the formation of foreign strategies, from the operation of strategic intelligence systems to the promotion of military generals, from the formation of elite groups to the influence of public agendas, from the management of media publication "self-regulation" to the sway of social information sources, from the education of cultural preferences to the shaping of ideology... After more than two hundred years of evolution, the Golden Power has gradually completed the historical transformation from germination to growth, from influence to monopoly, from the front office to behind the scenes, becoming an invisible dominant force in Western society, overriding the legislative, executive and judicial power, completing the transformation of Golden Power dictatorship.

Such a high-energy group of international bankers includes:

- The Rothschild family, the "big brother" of international finance for over 200 years.
- Bleichroder, the Berlin banker who was a confidant of Germany's hardened Chancellor Bismarck.
- The Oppenheim family of Cologne, Germany.
- The Warburg family (Warburg) of Hamburg, Germany.
- The Seligman family (Selingman), Wall Street bankers of Bavarian origin in Germany.
- The Schiff family (Schiff), of Frankfurt, Germany, who became superstars in the United States.
- The Schroder family (Schiff), which started in Hamburg, Germany, and later grew to London and New York.
- The Speyer family (Speyer), which started in Frankfurt, Germany, and then emerged in the United States.

- ➢ The Mendelsohn family (Mendelssohn), the oldest banking family in Berlin, Germany.
- ➢ The Baring family (Baring) of England, who became famous with the Rothschilds in the 19th century.
- ➢ The Hope family (Hope) of Amsterdam, the Netherlands.
- ➢ The Fould family (Fould), relied on by the French royal family.
- ➢ The Mallet family (Mallet), a French family that has been a director of the Banque de France for a century.
- ➢ The Pereire family, founders of the Crédit Mobilier in France, who challenged the Rothschilds.
- ➢ The Mirabeau family (Mirabaud), the titans of Swiss bankers.
- ➢ The Rockefellers and the J.P. Morgan family, originally from the Rothschilds, who have rapidly become the dominant financial forces in the world through the rise of the United States.

It turned out to be the Rockefellers and the Morgan's who quickly became the dominant financial force in the world today through the rise of the United States after the Roche family.

International bankers are a critical minority in a world of enormous energy, and the way they think and act largely determines the fate of humanity. Where they come, there is prosperity; where they abandon, there is recession and depression. They are able to stimulate massive wealth creation in society in the process of turning hands into clouds, and they are also able to grab huge amounts of money in the operation of turning hands into rain.

In the past two hundred years, these families have been very powerful on the world stage, and the vast and complex network of human relationships formed by these families at the core of Western society has played a major role in the development trajectory of human history and the formation of the current world pattern. Some families have fallen in the midst of the rising and falling tides, but most still exert an important and even critical influence today.

The world is changing new every day, but human nature is constantly repeating itself. How greedy and fearful human nature was of wealth thousands of years ago, how obsessive and cursed it was of power, is still true today. The human beings' desire for freedom but suffer from it, their pursuit of fairness but selfishness, their desire for good but their inability to reject evil, whether it is the political game in China's "twenty-four histories" or the money and power schemes in Western history, are constantly repeating the essence of humanity. This is where it makes sense for us to grasp the future by studying history. All phenomena that occur in human nature today can find precedent in history.

The Chinese are by no means unfamiliar with the human history of power, but they are far from familiar with the human history of wealth, so let's begin this twisting journey of discovery in Germany, the most internationally banker-intensive country of origin.

The War That Stopped

> "In the last two hundred years of its history, the Rothschilds have focused on two major events: war and revolution. Whether it is a war or a revolution, the warring parties are bound to make substantial financing in order to carry out large-scale and organized violence."
>
> Niall Ferguson.

At dawn on 3 July 1866, a force of 35,000 men was silently advancing rapidly through the rain curtain at the fortress of Konigrecs in the village of Sadova in Bohemia (now Czech territory). A young, angular face filled with tension, excitement and anticipation. These lads of the Prussian Elbe knew that they were about to attack 200,000 Austrian-Saxon allied troops. With the enemy outnumbered, all they could count on was the First Prussian Corps of 85,000 men, commanded by Prince Frederick Charles, attacking from the other side at the same time. In accordance with the strategy of General Helmuth Karl Bernhard von Moltke, Chief of the Prussian General Staff, the attack should have included 100,000 troops of the Second Corps, led by the Prussian Crown Prince, the future Kaiser Wilhelm II, but the manoeuvre was not carried out because the corps was stationed beyond the reach of the telegraph signal and could not receive orders in time.

Due to the excessive haste, the Prussians' Elbe Corps did not extend its line of attack sufficiently, and its fire crossed the First Corps' path of attack and the situation was for a time very chaotic. By 11 a.m. the Prussian attack was halted under heavy Austrian counter-shock and intensive artillery fire, and the reserves were engaged in an already intensive frontal attack. Had the Austrians made a determined cavalry charge at this point, the Prussians might have been driven from the field. But the overly cautious Austrian commander, Marshal Benedek, let the cavalry hold their troops in place. The two sides stalemated on the chaotic battlefield.

Just as the Prussian army was about to be defeated, Otto von Bismarck, the Prussian prime minister who had been with Mauch, suddenly noticed that a line of tree-like objects was moving a few kilometers east of the battlefield. Mauch picked up the telescope and observed for a moment, then said excitedly to King William I, who was beside him, "His Majesty has not only won the battle, but the war as well." It turned out that just as the Prussian Elbe and the First Corps were engaged in a bitter battle with the Austrian army, a courier travelled more than 30 kilometres to deliver the King's imperative orders to the Crown Prince, and the Second Corps immediately began to move northwards, the "moving trees" that Bismarck saw. At 2:30 p.m., the Second Corps attacked the Austrian defensive zone to the north. The Austrian defense line disintegrates. Marshal Benedek ordered a full retreat at 3 p.m. But the Prussian offensive was so fierce that the Austrian First Army could only launch a cavalry counterattack to support the artillery and to cover the retreat of friendly neighbouring forces. The operation resulted in 10,000 casualties within 20 minutes, and the First Army was nearly crippled. But the counterattack bought time, and nearly 180,000 Austrian troops managed to withdraw from the gap before being completely surrounded. In the Battle of Sadua, the Prussian side won a decisive victory, and 10 days later, the Prussians closed in on the Austrian capital, Vienna, and captured the fortress of Frosloff, only 6 km from Vienna, with the capture of Vienna and the conquest of Austria just around the corner.

At this point, something strange happened, and the soon-to-be victorious King William I of Prussia, Prime Minister Bismarck, and General Mauch, Chief of General Staff, suddenly quarreled at this moment. Mauch, from a soldier's point of view, of course, wanted to seize this rare opportunity to take the already isolated city of Vienna in one fell swoop. However, Chancellor Bismarck made an effort to "pour water into the boiling wine", insisting that the attack on Vienna be abandoned and that the military advantage be taken to sign an armistice with Austria as soon as possible, which would be a great success as long as the aim of excluding Austria from the German family was fulfilled. When the king wouldn't budge, Bismarck shed hot tears, threatened to resign as Prime Minister of Prussia, and even intended to jump from four stories. The quarrel lasted until late at night, when the king finally and painfully promised to give up the attack, but to record the circumstances in the National Archives "to prove how helpless and compassionate he was".

Later, Prussia signed the "Undercity League" with Austria without ceded land and Austria withdrew from the German Confederation. However, Bismarck gave up the opportunity to attack Vienna in order to expand the results of the war under extremely favorable circumstances, and the matter became an unsolved case in the history of the world war.

Why did Bismarck resolutely prevent the approaching Prussian army from marching into Vienna even under the threat of resignation and jumping from a building, against the will of the Holy Spirit? Secondly, although the Prussians won a decisive victory at the Battle of Sadua, they did not destroy the main force of the Austrian army, and the 180,000-strong Austrian army managed to break through the siege and retreat to defend the capital. As a brilliant strategist, Bismarck had a more long-term vision.

In fact, Bismarck didn't call himself a brilliant strategist; he was just a lucky adventurer. Just four years later, in the Franco-Prussian War, Bismarck insisted on forcing the defeated France to cede the provinces of Alsace and Lorraine and pay a huge war payout of 5 billion francs, thus inserting an ever-painful blade in the hearts of the proud and proud French, and making France commit itself to the arms of Germany's real future strategic opponent, the British. Germany did not have to deliberately humiliate the French, thus leaving room in the future to exploit the Anglo-French conflict for the strategic purpose of Germany's rise to world power, but Bismarck's shortsightedness saw Germany as creating a formidable and unconquerable enemy and prompting Anglo-French alliances to besiege Germany's rise to power in Europe, and Germany's disastrous defeats in the two later world wars were linked to Bismarck's reckless strategy of the year.

In fact, there was another reason behind Bismarck's war that came to an abrupt end under the city of Vienna. That is, by the time the Austro-Prussian War reached its seventh week, Bismarck, who was approaching the limits of his financial mobilization capacity under the city of Vienna, was powerless to keep the war going. To understand the situation of the Prussian army at that time, we must expand our horizons to the historical process of the Prussian rise to power, to observe the crucial role played by financial forces, and without understanding the financial forces behind the wars and revolutions, we cannot really see the whole picture of history.

Old Bleichröder: Rothschild's Agent

Germany is at the point of connection between the East and West of Europe, and Berlin in particular is at the geographical centre of Europe and a transport hub. Merchants from north to south and east to west converged on Berlin, creating a situation where all the currencies of Europe were concentrated in Berlin. From the beginning of the Roman Empire, Berlin was the center of currency exchange, and after Napoleon occupied the area, the demand for currency exchange became even stronger.

Old Bleichröder was called Samuel, and his main business was to buy and sell local government bonds, earning a spread in the process of buying and selling. Around 1828, the Bleichröder family began a business relationship with the Rothschild family. Since the Rothschild family was at the height of European financial power, it was this kind of business partnership with the "big names" that made the Bleichröders family stand out from the rest of the Berlin bankers, and after 1830, the Bleichröders family began to receive regular commissions from the Rothschilds, while the oldest banking family in Berlin, Mendelssohn, was gradually marginalized.

Coordinated by the unified command of the Roche family, Bleichröder sought arbitrage opportunities between the financial markets of London, Paris, Frankfurt, Berlin, Vienna and Naples by buying low and selling high. As the prices of various bonds and currencies in the European market can vary slightly from city to city, the key to arbitrage using geographical spreads is to obtain accurate intelligence and seize the right moment. The financial industry has had a very high demand for intelligence from the very beginning, and indeed modern international intelligence agencies are based on the early international banking family business intelligence delivery system. The most advanced intelligence system at the time was undoubtedly the Rothschild family's courier system, whose coverage, speed, confidentiality, accuracy and sophistication far exceeded the official systems of governments.

The Bleichröder family had a strong desire to have access to the Rothschild family's network of intelligence couriers as early as the 1830s. They were doing business in Berlin, and it took six days to receive correspondence from Paris to Berlin, and if it took only five days to get through Roche's intelligence network, that one day difference would mean huge business benefits. The Rothschilds have gradually incorporated the Bleichröders into their own intelligence system based on years of inspection.

In 1831, the Bleichröders became the faithful agents of the Rothschilds in Berlin, who constantly passed on to the Rothschilds information about various aspects of Prussian internal affairs as well as financial markets, such as the political attitudes of the five European powers, such as the King of the Netherlands, towards the newly created Belgium, and the attitude and position of Tsarist Russia towards the Polish rebellion. The Bleichröder family also reported on the spread of the plague in Europe, as well as the dynamics of the 1848 revolution in Berlin, and repeatedly secured the gold and bonds purchased for the Rothschilds.[1] The various types of intelligence gathered and transmitted through Bleichröders, which were continuously fed into the Rothschild family's European intelligence system, helped the Rothschild family to take advantage of information asymmetries, thus influencing the domestic and foreign policies of European countries in a broad and deep way, and also benefited greatly from the financial market transactions throughout Europe.

Berlin's financial market was small in the 1830s and 1940s, and the most active financial product was railroad bonds. The Prussian government, in an effort to "attract capital" to the outside world, drew the attention of international bankers such as the Rothschilds to railway bonds and tried to attract the Rothschilds to invest in the Prussian railway industry. In the course of the investment, the Rothschild family's influence in Prussian industry grew considerably, gradually becoming directors of several railway companies.

In 1836, James Rothschild of Paris took over as head of the family when Nathan, the head of the Rothschild family's Bank of England and head of the entire family, died. In the early days of Bleichröder's defection to James, the two sides were on completely unequal footing,

---

[1] Niall Ferguson, *The House of Rothschild*.

and Bleichröder had to cede a lot of benefits to be allowed to join the privileged financial network of the Rothschild family. At the time James did not treat Bleichröder well and often hammered Bleichröder not to overlook the interests of the Rothschild family. This warning actually meant that the Rothschild family wasn't very happy with their cooperation and had been trying to find new agents and partners.

In order to maintain this special channel with the Rothschild family, the Bleichröders had to sacrifice their own interests frequently, especially during the major crisis in the German financial markets in 1840, when the Bleichröders lost their commissions in exchange for orders from the Rothschild family. Years went by and the cooperation still didn't satisfy the Rothschilds, so much so that the Bleichröders sometimes not only didn't get a commission, but even had to pay back some money in order to maintain their business relationship with the Rothschild family.

The affiliation of the two parties can be glimpsed in a letter written by Bleichröder Sr. to the Rothschild family. In this letter, Semio recommended his 17-year-old son Gerson to Baron Solomon Rothschild of Vienna.

> "Allow me to express my gratitude to you with all my heart and deepest love. Over the years, I have been honored by your generosity and kindness, as if a grain of dust had been picked out of a cloud of sand. You are a noblest and most well-meaning nobleman. I can't thank you enough for putting me in such an important position in a large family. As long as I live, your portrait will remain in my heart and mind until the end of my life, and I will always be completely faithful to you, my benefactor. Now I ask you to be able to pass on your love and care for me to my son."[2]

In the mid-19th century, the industrial revolution was expanding rapidly in Germany and Berlin's financial markets were entering an era of unprecedented prosperity, fuelled by industrial development. At this point, the most important asset for the Bleichröders remains their long and strong business relationship with Rothschild. This model of cooperation was further cemented during Gerson's time in charge of the Bleichröders family. At the same time, Gerson began to construct his

---

[2] S. Bleichröder to Baron Anselm Solomon, 17 Nov. 1839.

own centers of power. He formed a large community of interest with numerous other Jewish bankers in Berlin, penetrating extensively into metallurgy, railway construction, and other industries. Their main partner at the time was the Oppenheimer family of Cologne.

Oppenheimer: The Financial Overlord of Cologne

In 1834, Abraham Oppenheimer married Charlotte Dreyfus, 23, a granddaughter of Rothschild Sr. From then on, Abraham had a wealthy and powerful father-in-law and uncle – Amschel, who determined Frankfurt's fiscal policy, Solomon, who held the keys to the Austrian treasury, Nathan, who dominated the financial city of London, Karl, who controlled Italian taxation, and James, who conquered the banking industry in Paris.

The Oppenheimers, who were able to marry the daughter of the Rothschilds, were certainly not mediocre. The Oppenheimer family belonged to the highest class of Jews, the "Court Jews", and in 1789 Abraham's father, Solomon Oppenheimer, at the age of 17, founded the Oppenheimer Family Bank in Bonn, which later moved to Cologne. Solomon, who was young but had been following his father's footsteps in the financial market for many years, was acutely aware that the feudal aristocracy had gradually lost control in the era of the rapid expansion of the emerging bourgeoisie's financial power.

Any dominant social group will inevitably create a fractured situation of power struggle as its control over various other social groups decreases. In Chinese history, from the decline of the Zhou Dynasty to the rise of the five hegemons of the Spring and Autumn Period, from the disintegration of the Eastern Han Dynasty to the formation of the three kingdoms, from the internal struggle of the Jin Dynasty to the Five Hu chaos, from the end of the Tang Dynasty to the domination of the clans and ten kingdoms of the Five Dynasties, every decline in control is bound to form a power vacuum, at this time the external and internal emerging forces are coming in, is bound to form a subversive social reconstruction. So it is in the East and so it is in the West. Capitalism, with the pursuit of profit as its core value, has been expanding in late 18th century Europe and has cracked the feudal aristocracy and religious theocracy that used to bind all sectors of society, and the traditional power structures of declining societies have crumbled. The power of money will quickly creep up through the cracks in the social structure and the ruins of the collapse of power, and they will be hooked and netted, climbing up the walls and seams, flourishing and eventually overshadowing the sky.

The young Solomon Oppenheimer decided to move from the traditional court lending and money exchange business to the emerging business of government bond underwriting and cross-market arbitrage. By 1810, the assets of the Oppenheimer Family Bank had reached 1 million francs, placing it among the top banking families. The ambitious Oppenheimer family was determined to emulate the Rothschild family's successful model, which eventually grew into a vast financial empire. To that end, Solomon did not mind using any means to achieve his goals. On 18 March 1814, in a letter to his partners in Amsterdam, the Rothschilds warned them of Oppenheimer's methods.

> *"We are glad to see that the currency shipped to you from our James place (Rothschild branch in Paris) and Oppenheimer in Cologne is just what you need. The latter will also pass through our cousins to deliver a sum again. But pay special attention to everything the Oppenheimers send that needs to be carefully examined; they are very greedy and don't always play by the rules, so care must be taken not to give them orders with no upper limit, or the profits will be all theirs."*[3]

In 1813, he married his 15-year-old daughter to Benedict Fould, son of the Fould family, a prominent Jewish banking family in Paris, France, and it was with the support of the Fould family that the later French Emperor Napoleon III ascended to the throne. Through the ties of marriage, the Oppenheimer family extended their influence into the French capital markets. The two families of the bride and groom jointly contributed 60,000 francs to establish the famous House of B. L. Fould & Fould-Oppenheim.

In 1815, after the disastrous defeat at the Battle of Waterloo, France faced even harsher reparation terms than at the Paris Peace of 1814, especially Prussia, which had been repeatedly conquered by France in the past, demanding war reparations of up to 170 million Taylor (Prussian silver, 1 Taylor = 3.54 francs). It would have been a great deal of business to pay this large sum of money on behalf of the

---

[3] Michael Sturmer, Gabriele Teichmann and Wilbelm Treue, *Striking the Balance – Sal. Oppenheim jr. & Cie. A Family and a Bank*, 1994, p. 37.

agent, by which time the Rhine region of Cologne had been adopted by Prussia as the Rhine Province. Oppenheimer, a New Prussian, rushed to contact his recently married French in-laws, Fould, to work together on the big deal. With the assistance of his French in-laws, Oppenheimer pulled up the old Berlin banking family, Mendelssohn, and in 1818 finally got the big bill of 52.5 million francs paid by the war reparations agent.

The Mendelssohn family in Berlin is one of the oldest Jewish banking families in Berlin. The world-renowned 19th century composer, pianist and conductor Felix Mendelssohn is a direct descendant of this family. His grandfather was the famous German philosopher Moses Mendelssohn, whose banker father, Abraham, once flirted with the idea that "I was the son of a famous father and later became the father of a famous son."[4] The Mendelssohn Family Bank became the designated Royal Agent Bank of Tsarist Russia around 1850, responsible for underwriting large amounts of Russian treasury bonds in the European market until the outbreak of World War I.

On 4 November 1818, Oppenheimer reached an agreement with the Commission of Liquidation of the victorious country, which raised 52.5 million francs in Paris within 14 days and paid it to the Commission of Liquidation at Aachen, with a 0.75 per cent fee for fund-raising, exchange, transportation and guarantees, which amounted to a huge income of nearly 400,000 francs. For this business, Oppenheimer also invested all his movable and immovable assets. The business was done beautifully and reaped praise from all sides. In the eyes of the traditional Prussian bankers, this fee was not much, for they imagined that the raising of such a large sum in such a short period of time, and the delivery of silver coins, would be a tedious and complicated project of man-feeding and armed escort, not realizing that, after the establishment of an international network of bankers and contacts, the fund-raising of 52.5 million francs was simply not enough to be distributed in the French capital market under the control of Jewish bankers, and was no less contested than the short-term financing notes and medium-term bills that are so popular in the Chinese interbank market today. It was so simple to transfer a bill of exchange between Paris and the Bank of Cologne for such a large amount of cash, that

---

[4] Sebastian Hensel, tr. Carl Klingemann, *The Mendelssohn Family 1729–1847*.

Oppenheimer and others made 400,000 francs with ease and pleasure. The backward Prussian banking system was deeply shaken by the emerging network of financial contacts.

The Oppenheimer family's influence on the European capital markets flourished after their marriage to the Folds. In 1826, Oppenheimer's business and the Rothschild family were inextricably linked. At this time Solomon Oppenheimer maintained close commercial intelligence almost daily with the Rothschilds of Frankfurt, Vienna, Paris, London and Naples. With the development of tourism resources in the Rhine region, travel to the Rhine became a fashion in the British upper class. These tourists from the wealthy side are reluctant to carry too much cash. The Rothschilds then partnered with Oppenheimer to open a letter of credit in the English Rothschild family that would allow cash to be drawn at the Oppenheimer family bank in the Rhine region, and the relationship was further strengthened.

In 1834, Abraham married Charlotte Befes, and on his subsequent honeymoon, he traveled to visit his uncles and grandparents. In a letter to his most powerful uncle, Nathan Rothschild, Abraham humbly mentions.

> *"Your Highness the Baron, until two years ago you used to refer all your clients to Cologne, but recently through no fault of our own we have lost your clients, which has caused us great distress, As recently as I was fortunate enough to marry your niece to give me access to your asylum, I do not presume to speculate whether you will be able to restore the former relationship between our two families, and give us a higher priority than the Schaffhausen family. I will also make you a preferred choice for our family partnership. I hope my request will be accepted by you. I have the honor to pay you the highest tribute."*[5]

Since 1830, the Oppenheimer family and the Hansemann family joined forces to finance the railroad and shipping industry and to establish a new joint-stock company to invest in the Rhine railway project. Due to the high rate of industrial development in the Prussian region, the entire region is strapped for funds and almost all industrial companies have reached the limits of their credit. Abraham sensitively

---

[5] Michael Sturmer, Gabriele Teichmann and Wilbelm Treue, *Striking the Balance – Sal. Oppenheim jr. & Cie. A Family and a Bank*, 1994.

seized the moment and began a strong push into credit insurance for businesses and investments. With the cooperation of the Rothschild family, Abraham established the world's first reinsurance company.

In 1842, Abraham Oppenheimer established strong business ties with the prominent Jewish bankers of Berlin, the Bleichröder family, who later played a major role in the German reunification process. Since then, the Oppenheimer family's network of contacts in Europe has been tentatively laid down as an international banker with a dominant position in Cologne, a leading role in Prussia, and an influence that cannot be ignored in France, Austria, Italy and England.

The 1848 Revolution and the Banking Rescue

The period around 1830 was an important turning point in the recent history of the world, with the spread of the Industrial Revolution from Britain to the European continent accelerating significantly. Countries such as France, Germany and Austria have entered a whole new phase of economic development. The process of industrialization, on the one hand, has led to the unprecedented development of mining, textiles, machinery, railways, ships and other industries, and, on the other hand, has created a large number of winners for the industrial bourgeoisie and, at the same time, an even larger number of losers, namely, the dispossessed peasants forced into the cities by the loss of land, the workers working in extremely harsh conditions, the unemployed craftsmen and the urban poor class. With feudal authoritarian forces waning in their grip, the winners of the industrial revolution, dissatisfied that their political power did not match the growing economic power, demanded more power from their rulers. At the same time, the losers of the industrial revolution have long been resentful of the tragic realities of life, including the strong resistance of Jews to more than a thousand years of religious and social discrimination, and these powerful forces of agitation have converged on issues such as civil rights for full equality and violent revolution. Beneath a seemingly booming industrial landscape, a sudden storm is brewing.

From 1845 to 1847, there were three years of natural disasters in many European countries and famine in large areas. Poor agricultural harvests, soaring food prices and declining sales of agricultural products have led to a reduction in the size of agricultural credit and a decline in employment. At the same time, European industry began to stagnate from 1840 onwards, especially as the rate of railway construction largely lost growth and industrial credit tightened. The two forces of austerity combined to create the economic depression of 1848 in many parts of Europe, and the stability created since the end of the Napoleonic wars in 1815 has been fractured by the enormous pressure of economic contraction.

After observing the widespread capital crunch in various European capital markets, Abraham Oppenheimer already foresaw a major crisis.

In February 1848, the stock market in Paris, France, collapsed and the long-awaited revolution finally broke out. The resentment of the people and the impulse of the bourgeoisie to seize power prompted a volcanic eruption of social grievances, and on 26 February the Fould family in France sent word that the revolution appeared to have succeeded and that the Second Republic might be successfully established. In March, the wave of the French revolution began to hit Cologne, and the revolutionaries asked Abraham Oppenheimer to negotiate with the government as their representative, which Abraham refused without even thinking about. In fact, the Oppenheimer family had an unusual connection to the revolutionaries, as Abraham's third brother, Dagobert Oppenheim, was directly involved in financing revolutionary agitation, and in the summer of 1842, after graduating from Marx University, he worked as editor-in-chief of the Dagobert Oppenheimer-funded Rheinische Zeitung, often bombarding the Prussian government with heavy artillery.

The real estate market in Cologne collapsed and Schaffhausen Bank had a payment crisis due to over-investment in real estate. Oppenheimer didn't invest much in real estate. In the tradition of international bankers, who are rarely involved in real estate investments because of an extreme aversion to illiquid assets, on March 29, Schaffhausen stopped making payments to 170 clients and more than 40,000 workers. Terrified depositors rushed together to collect their money, the Bank of Schaffhausen was no longer able to pay and the bank's survival was at stake. If the Schaffhausen Bank collapses, the entire banking system in the Rhine Province will fall apart, so it is the kind of bank that is too big to fail (Too Big to Fail).

Once the Schaffhausen bank falls, there will also be serious problems for the Oppenheimer family, with whom they do business. The Colon-Minden railroad, funded by the Oppenheimer family, is cash-strapped and needs half a million Taylor's in cash, while the

Oppenheimer Bank needs the same amount to get through. Abraham's brother Simon, who presided over the family's railroad business, wrote to Abraham on April 3,

> "I have superb confidence in your abilities, and I feel that you will succeed in getting us at least half a million Taylor from the government for a year or more."

Three days later, Simon sent more bad news:

> "My dear Abraham, today Colon Minden spent another 3,000 Taylor, and Dagburke they say they need more money tomorrow." On April 10, having not yet received the good news from Abraham, Simeon was anxious: "We are in a very peculiar situation, and Hansemann (the Prussian minister of finance) would have given way. We're the largest, and currently almost the only bank still in operation in the Rhine province, and it's in the government's interest (to bail us out), and everyone would agree that protecting a company like ours is a very wise choice." On April 11, Simon again urged, "I hope that the Almighty will bless the fruit of our hope which was ripe yesterday, and that Hansemann has made a decision to provide us with the sum of half a million Taylor. Dear Abraham, you must be sure that we must have this money if we want to sleep soundly every night."[6]

On April 1, Abraham had personally gone to Berlin to ask his old friend Hansemann for a government credit of 500,000 Taylor against real estate and stock to save the Schaffhausen Bank, at which point saving the Schaffhausen Bank would mean saving himself. After two weeks of back and forth, Hansemann decided to reach a compromise between the creditors and the bankers, and in order to achieve this, money had to be asked of Berlin. The Berlin side was reluctant to give money at first, and Abraham threatened that the importance of bailing out the banks was not simply a question of saving the liquidity of individual banks, but of whether the revolution could be contained, a major political question of the survival of the Prussian government. He concluded that unless bank credit is restored, the existing social order banks will collapse. The Prussian government was so alarmed that it immediately set up a crisis coordination committee, with Hansemann on the government side and Abraham on the bankers' side, to agree on specific ways to rescue the Schaffhausen Bank. An agreement was soon

---

[6] Ibid.

reached to transform the Schaffhausen Bank into a joint-stock bank and the first joint-stock bank in Prussian history was born. This was actually part of the financial reform policy that liberals and Abraham had been advocating for the government to implement since 1830.

To put more pressure on the government, Abraham even threatened that unless a timely bailout of the financial crisis could be achieved, the Rhineland's secession from Prussia would be inevitable. Apparently, Abraham raised the bailout bank to the heights of national sovereignty, a killer move made while the Prussian government was too busy calming social unrest to bother him. At this time, the Prussian government's primary approach was stability over all, with the view held by Abraham and Hansemann and others that "political stability presupposes financial stability" prevailing. All of this was actually a strategy long ago orchestrated by people like Abraham and Hansemann, whose goal was a top-down revolution in finance and politics. Through social unrest and political chaos, Abraham finally achieves his dream goal.

At the beginning of May, Oppenheimer received a bailout of 500,000 Taylor from the Prussian government, and the Prussian financial system began to undergo major changes.

If we compare this history with the financial crisis now underway and the U.S. government's bailout, we find that with a few minor adjustments to the chronology and name, it could simply be published directly on the front page of the Wall Street Journal today. It is entitled "Banking rescue and financial reform: finance minister and bankers agree on goals".

Human nature repeats itself over and over in history, and this time is no exception.

The Rise of Bismarck

If the unification of Germany could not have been achieved without Bismarck, Bismarck's success could not have been achieved without the Jewish banker behind him, Gerson Bleichröder. Bismarck's position in German history is similar to that of Qin Shi Huang in Chinese history, both of whom accomplished the unification of the country with tenacity and iron-blooded means, leaving an indelible mark of prominence in history. There are more than 7,000 different monographs on Bismarck in Germany, and his achievements and failures have been thoroughly analysed and studied by the German historical community. But the influence of the vast financial powerhouse behind Bismarck's policies is almost completely ignored in this sweatshirt literature. In Bismarck's own three-volume biography, which mentions the Bleichröder family only once at the death of Kaiser Wilhelm II, the influence of Jewish bankers on German politics seems to be a research blind spot.

In fact, Bismarck's correspondence with the Breiszlauer and Rothschild families numbered in the thousands throughout his political career, and throughout his career he provided the Rothschilds with almost daily information on changes in German politics, military movements and financial markets.[7] From these communications, we can accurately judge that without the strong financial backing of Bleichröder and Rothschild, Bismarck could hardly have gained a foothold in German politics, let alone accomplished the great task of unifying Germany. For more than a hundred years, Bleichröder has been drowned in the dustbin of history, and his reexcavation will authentically restore the significant influence of long-neglected financial forces in German history.

Bismarck was born with a golden spoon in his hand, belonging to the Junker class of landowners. From a young age, he was ambitious, and it was this innate superiority that gave Bismarck his unique personality, as many of the social positions and riches that were unattainable in the eyes of the common man were readily available and easy to him. He was hot-tempered, quick-tempered, bold and tough, tough and rude, even a bit headstrong.

Bismarck was ambitious and had a keen interest in politics. At the same time, he, like other Junker nobles, had a great desire for money. His main purpose in owning money was to gain a position without scruples, using large sums of money to satisfy political ambitions and lust for power. If one day he finds himself bored with a political career, he will be able to withdraw from politics with ease, free from economic influence and restraint.

Since Bismarck entered politics, his appetite for money has grown, and he has had less and less time to manage it himself. So he had to use

---

[7] Fritz Stern, *Gold and Iron – Bismarck, Bleichröder, and the Building of the German Empire*, 1977, p. 21.

the Jew's sensitivity to money and talent for wealth management to assist in private money management and achieve wealth accumulation and growth. In the process, Bismarck adopted a pragmatic attitude towards Jewish bankers, who by nature were not particularly fond of Jews, and even believed that Jews should not enter public government institutions, and that what he had to ask of Jews was their superior financial ability, and that he relied to a large extent on these shrewd Jewish banking families to add to his personal wealth.

The great power vacuum created by the European revolutions of 1848 gave Bismarck great scope for growth, fueled his political ambitions, and further contributed to his characteristic realist attitude. In the wave of revolution, Bismarck finally chose his direction to become a staunch royalist. Bismarck was convinced that Germany must eventually move towards unification, and that this process must rely on the strength of a strong monarchy. He believed that democracy would only lead to weakness and laxity, and for this ultimate purpose, he had to be a staunch defender of the king. In 1851, in return for these words and deeds, Frederick Wilhelm IV appointed Bismarck as Prussian delegate to the Congress of the German Confederation in Frankfurt.

From then on, Bismarck officially became a public figure and took to the stage of history.

Bleichröder: Bismarck's Private Banker

> *Gerson Bleichröder was both a private banker to Bismarck, the first Chancellor of the German Reich, and a banker to the German public. He has reaped great benefits with skillful sleight of hand and patience. The Rothschilds were his role models and secret allies, but he was even more of a man who went his own way and realized his values.*
>
> —Fritz Stern.

Bismarck came to Frankfurt in 1851 and soon attracted the attention of Amschel Rothschild, the head of the Rothschild family, which was then sitting in Frankfurt. At the time, Amschel, the oldest of the five Rothschild brothers, was in his eighties. Bismarck was extremely impressed with Amschel from his initial acquaintance, and often imitated Rothschild's accent for his wife when he returned home, including the use of Jewish accents and grammar to express German. He had a very strong impression of the Rothschild family's great wealth and power, and was also happy to meet the Rothschild family.

Whenever he was invited by the Rothschilds in the future, he was always flattered to be invited. He once described Amschel Rothschild in this way:

> "He was a very old Jew, with tons of gold and silver, with many, many plates of gold and knives and forks. Since Amschel had no descendants, despite being wealthy, he had no descendants to inherit. He was more like a poor man in a palace of luxury, surrounded by countless people who were cheating and scheming to get his money. His relatives, who surrounded him in order to inherit his wealth, actually had no genuine love or gratitude for him."[8]

Bismarck was industrious and learned, desperately yearning for power and wisdom, and his ambitions and aspirations in politics soon caught the eye of both Amschel and his stepson, Meyerkar. The Rothschilds were particularly fond of grooming political upstarts, and they often prided themselves on being a boon. Throughout the recent history of Europe, the Rothschild family has chosen to raise a number of political stars. Rothschild is convinced that Bismarck will be a very worthwhile potential stock to invest in. In addition to Bismarck, the Rothschilds chose Benjamin Disraeli, who would later become Prime Minister of the United Kingdom; the Rothschilds also chose the Earl of Rosebery, who had three major life aspirations in his youth: to win the Derby Race, to marry a super-rich woman, and to become Prime Minister of the United Kingdom, all of which he eventually got. The Rothschilds were the ones to discover, cultivate and grow into the heavyweight politicians that have influenced the entire history of the world.[9]

Although Nathan Rothschild once claimed that he had "controlled the issuance of currency in the British Empire", the old aristocrats of Europe still have a deep-seated contempt for Rothschild and other Jewish bankers emerging "mega-money". However, in specific cases, the nobility also had to succumb to the power of money. Bismarck held a similar mentality, both exploiting and despising the Jewish bankers.

Bismarck first arrived in Frankfurt and soon began a rather cozy honeymoon with the Rothschilds, but it wasn't long before an unusually

---

[8] Bleichröder to Baron James, 21 Feb. 1863.

[9] Niall Ferguson, *The House of Rothschild*.

heated argument broke out with the Rothschilds. It all started when Austria, then the head of the German Confederation, was often arbitrary and disrespectful of the Prussian government, while Bismarck was an extremely sensitive and powerful man who, as a diplomat, could only submit to the political will of the Berlin side, but who was often furious about the arrogance and details of the Austrian side. In 1852, Austria and Prussia had a not-so-serious conflict over the German Confederation. The German Confederacy had a small fleet at the time, was poorly funded and difficult to sustain, and desperately needed a sum of money to pay the crew. Austria asked the Rothschild family directly for a loan of 60,000 guilders, despite the firm opposition of Prussia. Rothschild was in a sense reluctant to fund this fleet, but he was nonetheless willing to follow the orders of the Habsburg dynasty. The incident greatly enraged Bismarck and heatedly quarreled with Amschel.

The Rothschilds, even though they were rich, were inevitably rats in the windbox and were in a difficult position during the contest between the Prussian and Austrian governments. These feudal ruling aristocrats still viewed the Jews from their bones as an inferior subordinate group, and from the historical circumstances of the time, money did not solve the problem of the inferior political status of the Jews.

Even after the big fight, Bismarck's anger has not completely subsided. He felt that the Rothschilds were closer to Austria than to Prussia, and in his anger he began to reject the Rothschilds' invitations, while at the same time persuading the Prussian government to use the Bestman Bank, a rival of the Rothschilds, as the official bank of the entire Prussian government. Unfortunately the Prussian treasury was not as impulsive as Bismarck and they did not replace the Rothschilds. The main reason for this is that Rothschild's position is essentially irreplaceable. The Prussian government knew by heart that only the Rothschilds could provide decisive help when money was really needed. After such a quarrel, the Austrian ambassador left Frankfurt in indignation, and Bismarck thought he had prevailed in the struggle. As the saying goes, no fight, no deal. Bismarck also weighed in on his opponent's weight in his encounter with the Rothschilds.

In 1853, Bismarck supported the government's proposal to make the Rothschilds of Frankfurt the official bankers of the Prussian government. Not only that, but he went on to ask for the award of the Red Eagle of Prussia to Sir Meyerkar (Amschel's stepson). With the relationship repaired, it is a much more realistic and close layer than before.

In 1858, the Prussian Crown Prince (later Kaiser Wilhelm I) appointed Bismarck as ambassador to St. Petersburg, and before leaving Frankfurt in March 1859, Bismarck specifically asked Meyer Karl Rothschild to recommend a reliable banker for him in Berlin, and Bismarck insisted that the private banker responsible for his personal finances in Berlin must be Jewish. For various reasons, he believed that only a Jewish banker would have sufficient talent and ability to help him achieve his goals in financial management. The real reason behind this was that he wanted to continue his special and close relationship with the Rothschilds through this path. So the Rothschilds formally recommended Gerson Bleichröder as Bismarck's private banker.

By 1861, Bleichröder had become an extremely influential Jewish banker in Berlin. Although there were several older banking families in Berlin at the time, such as Mendelssohn, and these older families were superior in size and depth to Bleichröder, the Bleichröders, with their close business dealings with the Rothschilds, quickly rose to become "rising stars" in the Berlin banking industry. In other words, among the many banking families, the closer the relationship with Rothschild can be maintained, the better the chances of whoever is able to be the best in the market competition.

The Bleichröder family quickly stepped into the role after becoming Bismarck's private bankers. All of Bismarck's salary and other income was handed over to the Bleichröder family bank, while Bismarck managed the payment of his private debts, set up and operated bank accounts overseas for him, and was responsible for the management of Bismarck's assets, which were not large at the time.

From this point on, Bismarck and the Bleichröder family began to correspond closely. Like the Rothschilds, all banking families are super-sensitive to political news and market intelligence, because behind this information lies a wealth of business opportunities. The Bleichröders did not ask Bismarck for any monetary reward; all they sought in return was political information and some insider information.

The Danish Crisis: Bismarck's Unexpected Opportunity

Money and food is behind any war, and whoever has the greater economic potential resources is more likely to win the ultimate victory in the war. The first thing Bismarck encountered in the historical process of unifying Germany was the money dilemma.

When William I succeeded to the throne in 1861, the first obstacle he faced was a liberal-held parliament. Since the French bourgeois revolution at the end of the 18th century, the liberal ideology, with democracy at its core, has swept through Europe, and especially after the 1848 revolution, the influence of liberals in Europe has become even more profound, even to the point of violence and bloodshed in an attempt to completely break down the feudal, authoritarian social power structure. In Prussia, a country with a more conservative ideological tradition, liberals both aspire to the French and British model of democracy and fear from the bottom of their hearts the bloody revolution that France has experienced. This is the most fatal weakness of the Prussian liberals, who remain, from the bones, earthy nationalists, and are merely cloaked in the skin of the liberals.

William I inherited a Prussian military tradition, and his years of military service led him to take an extra interest in building his army. He was the most determined minority to suppress the European revolutions by force in 1848, opposing any political compromise. In 1862, William I finally made up his mind to make the controversial Bismarck Prime Minister and Minister of Foreign Affairs of Prussia, after the army reform bill was blocked by Parliament. In his inaugural address, Bismarck put forward the famous iron-blooded theory, saying, "The great problems of our time cannot be solved by speeches and majority resolutions; that is the mistake we made in 1848 and 1849; (these problems) can only be solved by iron and blood." Bismarck at the same time gave William I a shot in the arm: "Since we are going to die sooner or later, can we not die more decent... His Majesty has no other way to go but to strive!" Bismarck has since won William I's firm support for his policies.[10]

At the heart of the military reform bill is the strengthening of the regular army and the weakening of the National Guard. The bill extends the period of service in the regular army from two to three years. The ostensible reason for congressional opposition is that military spending is excessive, and in its bones it is resentment of the National Guard's demotion. In the Prussian military establishment, where the core of the

---

[10] Holborn, *Modern Germany*.

regular army was the feudal Junker aristocracy, and the National Guard represented the emerging bourgeois power of the urban middle class, the strengthening of the regular army inevitably resulted in the further strengthening of the Prussian authoritarian power, something that the liberal parliament was deeply afraid of. Their tactic was to refuse to approve the government's budget and get Bismarck dead in the neck on the money issue. Bismarck showed no sign of weakness and immediately threatened to adjourn Parliament and rule without it.

The Danish crisis erupted at a time of stalemate between the two sides. In March 1863, the king of Denmark wanted to include the disputed territories of Schleswig and Holstein on the Prussian frontier, which immediately stirred Prussian nationalism. Although these two areas were governed by Denmark under the Treaty of London of 1852, their sovereignty remained with the German Confederation. The gloom of war began to loom over Prussia.[11]

For Bismarck, this is a once-in-a-lifetime opportunity. He will use the war against Denmark to significantly weaken the liberal opposition at home and consolidate his power. At this point Bismarck needed a victory in the foreign war too badly. Analyzed strategically, Bismarck's approach is calm and old-fashioned. In order to achieve his goal of defeating Denmark, he had to rope in Austria. To this end he cleverly proposed that Schleswig be placed under Prussian rule and Holstein under Austria, which readily accepted. At the same time, in order to pacify the interference of other European powers, Bismarck made a gesture of support for the Treaty of London and the preservation of the existing European order to appease Britain, France and Russia.

Bismarck's political manoeuvring and diplomatic skills in the Danish crisis were at their best, and the Prussian military machine had more than enough to deal with Denmark, but what disturbed Bismarck most was the fact that his huge war costs had not been met, that Parliament was stubbornly opposed to his domestic and foreign policy, and that it was impossible to pass his war budget.

---

[11] Eyck, Erich, *Bismarck and the German Empire*, W. W. Norton & Company. (1964).

The Prussian War: A Test of Golden Power

Bismarck's only hope was to bypass parliamentary budgetary constraints and find another way to finance the war. He pinned his main hopes on his own private banker, Bleichröder. Bleichröder had close ties to the hand-and-eye Rothschild family, who not only could solve the huge financial problems, but also had extraordinary influence over Napoleon III of France. In the war against Denmark, Napoleon III's neutrality was the key to success or failure.

At this time, Bismarck, flanked by Bleichröder, had been quietly observing a series of upheavals in Prussian politics, contemplating how this major political change could be used to great economic advantage. In terms of personal good and evil, Bleichröder, as a Jew, leans more towards liberal ideas. In fact, the Jews constituted an important force in the 1848 revolution for their own fair power. But as a banker, his judgment must be absolutely rational, even cold, and he must choose interests!

Through daily correspondence with the Rothschild family, a steady stream of commercial market information and political-military intelligence on the Berlin side flowed to James Rothschild in Paris... On 1 May 1863, Bleichröder revealed in an intelligence alert to Rothschild that the Danish crisis had resulted in

> *"our Minister (of Finance) had planned a loan of 50 million Taylor for naval construction, but (the Danish crisis) reduced the loan to 30 million Taylor, mainly for port defense in the Baltic Sea... (Bismarck) revealed that the Danish events could lead to serious complications, but that there would be no action for three months, since military preparations were not yet complete".*[12]

From May to November 1863, Bismarck's war preparations were under intense pressure for money. After repeated negotiations with Rothschild, Bleichröder finally made an offer to Bismarck in November. Bleichröder's proposal was simple, Prussia could sell state owned assets for financing. They were interested in the rich reserves of coal mines in the Saar region, which were mainly under the control of

---

[12] Fritz Stern, *Gold and Iron – Bismarck, Bleichröder, and the Building of the German Empire*, 1977, p. 32.

the Prussian government, and Bleichröder proposed to sell them to the Rothschilds of France. In fact, as early as 1861 there were rumours that the Rothschilds were willing to pay 20 million Taylor for the coal mines in the Saar area. Bismarck had long known that Napoleon III was also interested in the coal mines in the region, and Napoleon III even made a direct show to Bismarck that if France was to remain neutral in the Prussian War, it would have to trade the Prussian Sal coal mines.

In a letter to Rothschild on December 7, 1863, Bleichröder revealed that the government was about to present a budget of 10 million Taylor to Parliament, which might reject it. Two days later Bismarck decisively proposed a budget of 12 million Taylor for the war in Prussia. The Prussian treasury at the time had 21 million Taylor available for the war against Denmark, but Bismarck, out of a prudent assessment of the war expenses, considered that the money must be kept in case of unforeseen circumstances, and on 22 January 1864 the Parliament rejected Bismarck's request by a narrow margin of 275 to 51.[13]

Bismarck had to find another way to find money. At this point, the Frankfurt banker Raphael von Erlanger came to Bismarck's door in the hope of offering a loan of 15 million Taylor. The incident angered the Rothschild family, the Erlanger family, originally under the Rothschild family, which had grown on its own to become one of the Rothschild family's main rivals and had risen into the international bankers' ranks. The Rothschild family had always hated the betrayal of their own disciples, not to mention the fact that the Earlanger family had often dragged the French Foulds and Pereire families to steal business from the Rothschild family.

James Rothschild is up in arms about this, berating Brexler for his ineptitude. Bleichröder hastened to assure that Parliament was firmly opposed to any lending to the government by private banks without Parliament's approval and authorization, and that "Erlang's approach to government lending had been completely rejected."[14]

The war against Denmark was officially launched by the Austro-Prussian forces on 1 February 1864, and on 3 February, after meeting

---

[13] Ibid, p. 39.

[14] Bohme, *Deutschlands Weg*, Chapters 2 and 3.

Bismarck, Bleichröder again warned Bismarck, on behalf of the Rothschilds, not to accept the loan from Erlangen. Rothschild even asked Bismarck to smear Erlanger in the Prussian press. Bismarck rejected this excessive request, but assured that the Prussian government would carefully consider cooperating with Erlanger. Bleichröder then made a new proposal to Bismarck to mortgage the amount of loans that Parliament had once approved for railroad construction, financing them at a certain percentage discount to the bankers, who in turn sold the full amount of the bonds to investors.

In the first week of the war, Bismarck's anxieties about the funding of the follow-on war outweighed his concerns about the situation, the expenses of the war clearly exceeded his projections, and without follow-on funding, Bismarck's army might only be able to support it for another two months or so. By then, if the war had not ended, Bismarck would have been caught between the indiscriminate bombardment of Parliament and the gloating ridicule of the European powers. It is no exaggeration to say that the name Bismarck will become the laughing stock of Europe, and he himself will henceforth retire from the stage of history.

In early March, when the Prussian bank reached a secret agreement with the Erlanger family, Rothschild was outraged and again called Bleichröder incompetent, and on 14 March, Bleichröder wrote back swearing that "Bismarck had no knowledge of this and was deeply troubled by this act". Bismarck pledged to condemn the finance minister in charge.

Of course, Bismarck wasn't a light to save gas either. Seeing the contradiction between Rothschild and Erlanger, he consciously and unconsciously exaggerated Erlanger's potential threat in order to get the best possible loan from Rothschild on the best terms as soon as possible. He applied the wisdom of international politics to the financial aspect, playing the trick of "money for money" is really clever. In the end, Bismarck got war financing at 4.5 percent interest, and Rothschild got a lucrative financing agent's fee.

On April 18, 1864, Prussia achieved a decisive victory. But the war's expenses also created a serious crisis, and "throughout the summer of 1864 Bismarck was troubled by the liquidity strain caused by the Prussian War." The war had cost a total of TTL 22.5 million, and the fiscal surplus of TTL 5.3 million in previous years and the funds raised by the Prussian government of TTL 17 million had been exhausted.[15]

Through the war, Bismarck finally realized the importance of money, especially at critical times when politicians are often forced to make major compromises with bankers. The Prussian War broke out around the same time as the American Civil War, and in a commentary on the war and Lincoln's assassination, Bismarck said, "There can be no doubt that the division of the United States into two weaker confederations, North and South, was settled by the financial powers of Europe long before the Civil War broke out." "He (Lincoln) received authority from Congress to borrow by selling the national debt to the people, so that the government and the country jumped out of the foreign financiers' trap. When it dawned on them (the international bankers) that America would escape their grasp, Lincoln's death would not be far off. Lincoln's death was a great loss to the Christian world. No one in America may be able to follow in his great footsteps, and the bankers will regain control of those who are rich. I fear that the foreign bankers with their high-handedness and cruelty will end up with America's enrichment and then use it to systematically corrupt modern civilization."

Bismarck's words should have been heartfelt.

The Prussian War was Bismarck's first major victory and achieved the effect of killing many birds with one stone. One is to use rival Austria to achieve its own strategic goals, two is to divert Austria from its allies and three is to silence domestic liberal opposition.

Parliamentary liberals: obstacles on the road to German reunification

In 1815, the Napoleonic Wars ended. After the collapse of the Holy Roman Empire, numerous German states formed the loosely organized German Confederation and Austria became the leader of the German Confederation. Since the European Revolution of 1848, the idea of German unification has been twofold: the establishment of a great Germanic empire, encompassing all Germanic regions, including

---

[15] Fritz Stern, *Gold and Iron – Bismarck, Bleichröder, and the Building of the German Empire*.

Austria, a multi-ethnic empire; and the establishment of a small Germany, excluding Austria, with Prussia as its core. Bismarck, out of practicality, went the little German route.

After the end of the Prussian War, Austria became the main obstacle to Bismarck's ambition to unify Germany. To achieve this strategic goal, Bismarck still adopted the strategy of using foreign warfare to forge a domestic consensus and force the parliament to cede power and consolidate its position within Prussia. On the diplomatic front, Bismarck saw an opportunity for Italy to resist Austrian rule and establish a strategic alliance with Italy. At the same time, France was tempted by the great interest of the coal mines of the Saar region to keep Napoleon III neutral. Bismarck also used the Russian-Austrian dispute in the Balkans to gain Russian understanding. Finally there was the attitude of Britain, which was insensitive to the potential for a change in the balance of power on the continent, and although Britain did not want to see Prussia unify Germany, Austria seemed to have a better chance of winning in the light of the situation, not to mention the inertia of thought that had been created by the Napoleonic era to contain France, and Bismarck thought that Britain would not be satisfied with the Austro-Prussian war, but would not be fiercely opposed either. After Bismarck's operation, by the summer of 1864, Prussia had more friends than Austria and fewer enemies than Austria.

At the moment, it was the money that worried Bismarck the most. The Prussian treasury had been badly wounded by the Prussian war, and years of financial surpluses had been wiped out with the war's ashes, and Bismarck felt it most directly in its astonishing ability to devour wealth. War, in fact, is fought with money and food!

From 1864 to 1866, Bismarck was scrambling to do two things: to do his best to get every penny for Prussia for war preparations, and to do his best to prevent Austria from raising money for the war on the European financial markets. Bismarck's strategy was to drive his opponents to extinction financially, dragging down Austria's national power under the threat of war. Austria's financial situation is indeed worse than Prussia's, which has long been depleted and on the verge of bankruptcy as a result of years of exhaustion in suppressing nationalist riots in the Balkans and elsewhere. Neither side is willing to publicly show financial embarrassment, both are secretly raising funds behind the scenes, ready to strike out in a big way.

What drove Bismarck the most crazy was that Parliament, as before, rejected all his budgets and declared that the Government did not have the right to use public funds without parliamentary approval, otherwise it was unconstitutional and government ministers were fully responsible for it. Bismarck issued a strongly worded response the same day, characterizing the parliamentary opposition as "traitors" who obstructed the king's foreign policy and objectively had the effect of collaborating with the enemy. In fact, Bismarck knew that many of the parliamentary liberals were inwardly gloating over the Prussian victory in the Prussian war, and that his accusation of treason was a deliberate attempt to stab these people in the face of their self-esteem, thus prompting them to change their tune. Nor are the fanatics among the parliamentary liberals vegetarians, and some have attacked Bismarck for cheating the parliament and the king. Bismarck, on hearing of this, was furious and immediately demanded a duel. The entire Berlin political scene was shocked to learn that duels are a mixture of bravery and recklessness, that once they begin, there is no possibility of backing down or of discouraging a fight, and that the probability of death or injury on either side is extremely high. If the Prussian Prime Minister died in a duel, the whole situation in Europe would have changed suddenly. This Bismarck was a very irascible man, who had 27 dueling fights as early as his college days, and had an incredible amount of guts. Bleichröder and others hurried to dissuade privately, and even Rothschild, who was far away in Paris, was concerned about the duel. While the final showdown was dissuaded, Bismarck's anger and anxiety over Parliament's rejection of the government's budget grew by the day.

Bismarck was too eager for money, and without it, his ideals could only be dreams, and his dreams would eventually fade into fantasy.

Privatization of the Cologne-Minden railway: a source of wealth for the Austro-Prussian war

In 1865, the scales of war and peace hung a little above the direction of the flow of credit, and in July Bismarck's long-awaited war funding finally came into view. This is the privatization of the Cologne-Minden railway.

The Cologne-Minden Railway was one of the first railway lines to be built in Prussia, designed in 1833 and completed in full in 1859, becoming the hub of the Prussian railway system. The railway project was originally built to transport coal from the Ruhr region cheaply to industrial production sites. Bleichröder played a key role in the financing of the Cologne-Minden railway, becoming a director of the railway company and a banker who financed the company. Considering that the railway transport system can transport large numbers of military personnel and materials in future wars with high efficiency and low consumption, the nationalization of railway companies is the main direction of development of the company. In fact, the Cologne-Minden railway was from the beginning a major public infrastructure project led by the Prussian government. The Prussian government purchased $1/7^{th}$ of the original shares outright and guaranteed the railroad bonds at 3.5% coupon interest for TTL 14 million. In 1854 the Prussian government, influenced by the free market economy, suspended the nationalization process until 1870, when it was determined whether to continue, depending on developments. However, the government's guarantee of interest on the railroad bonds is still in effect, and the $14 million guarantee is locked up in a dedicated account and unavailable.

Bismarck's war preparations for Austria required a total of some 60 million Taylor, and the burden of raising such astronomical war costs fell on the shoulders of Bleichröder. In fact, as far back as December 1862, Bleichröder, after careful calculation and much deliberation, had proposed the controversial privatization of the Cologne-Minden railway. The central part of the scheme was that, instead of the government's huge purchase of the railroad's shares in 1870, which put a huge strain on the finances, the Prussian government, at the expense of renouncing nationalization, could immediately receive a compensation from the railroad and, at the same time, renounce its guarantee of interest on the bonds, and could immediately liquidate part of the 14 million Taylor margin.

As soon as it was introduced, it was opposed by many people who saw the Brexler-Lauder programme as a way of making the railway company's shareholders, including Brexler himself, profiteers at the expense of the Government's long-term losses. In this scenario, the government would lose a total of T$30 million in various entitlements in return for T$10 million in compensation and T$14 million in available margin. The Cologne-Minden railway is a very profitable project for the government to invest in, and the privatisation programme will provide the government with emergency funding in the short term, but at the cost of selling good assets at a discount of less than 50 per cent, and losing the right to future long-term earnings, which is not a good deal for the government in any case.

When the time came in 1865, things changed dramatically. Bismarck's ambition to unify Germany was overwhelming, and there was little else to be done to prepare for war against the behemoth that was Austria. That's why international bankers love war, and when governments are forced to do so, they will sell quality assets at unusually low prices, when the opportunity to make a fortune arises. When international bankers reach a certain level of power, they stimulate nationalist sentiment, stir up national antagonism, promote massive government arms investments, inflame potential contradictions, induce the war process, and then step forward to handle the war payouts in a dignified manner. International bankers will always receive high fees for their services, as long as there is a large amount of money passing through their hands. Where there is a flow of money and credit, there is an investment banker.

On July 18, 1865, the Prussian government signed a contract with the Cologne-Minden Railway Company. The end result was that the government relinquished its power to nationalize the railroads and was compensated with 13 million taylor, with the first payment of 3 million taylor in cash, due October 1, 1865, and the second payment of 2.705 million taylor in cash, due January 2, 1866, with the remainder compensated by the railroad issuing new shares. In recognition of Breislauder's credit, Bismarck entrusted Breislauder with the business of transferring the funds involved in the treaty between Prussia and Austria. The transfer of 2.5 million taels was made to the Austrian Rothschild, and Bleichröder was kind enough to pocket 1% of the "management fee".

When the financial resources were not forthcoming, Bismarck prepared another hand for a diplomatic solution, and the negotiations went on for a long time. When Bismarck learned that the government contract with the railroad was officially signed, he immediately took a diplomatic hard line against Austria. On the day the contract was signed, Bismarck immediately sent a telegram to the Prussian crown prince: "At the Regensburg conference, His Majesty resolved that the financial means for a full war start and a year's war were available, amounting to about 60 million tales." A week later, Bismarck's Secretary of War, Roon, said in a letter to a friend,

> *"We have enough money to give us greater diplomatic freedom, and we can mobilize all our military forces for an all-out war if necessary. This strengthens our position, and we can force Austria to accept our reasonable demands, thus enabling both sides to avoid unnecessary war. Where does the money come from? Without breaking the law, the rearrangement was achieved through the Colon-Minden railroad."*[16]

The Austrian side soon realized that the financial arrangements for the Cologne-Minden railroad were an emergency arrangement for the start of the war and that the Austrian side was still far from being ready for war and began to soften its position in the diplomatic negotiations. On the other hand, Bismarck, after the initial euphoria had cooled, also gradually realised that the Cologne-Minden railway was still quite some time away from being funded, and judging by the feedback from Brexler's contacts with international bankers, the situation was not good. The transfer of the Taylor 9 million claim between the Rothschild family and the Minden Railway stalled when the parties could not agree on a price. With the war funding conundrum hanging over his head like a sword, Bismarck was once again on fire, and the one thing he was most anxious to know was when the money would come in.

At this point Bismarck's firm determination to go to war also began to falter and he had to seriously consider the possibility of a diplomatic solution.

On August 10, 1865, Bismarck divulged his shake-up: "We still need time to raise funds and keep France neutral... In the meantime, we can preserve our honor while keeping the option of war." Bismarck's judgment likewise influenced his private investment decisions, and he commissioned a message to Bleichröderder: "If I still have bond investments in my investment account, which I cannot know here now, he should not have sold them (the Minden Railroad) simply because of premature war worries."[17] Bismarck's conduct is, by today's standards, suspicious of using insider information to invest and reap illegal benefits.

In this atmosphere, Prussia and Austria reached the Gastein agreement, with Prussia administering Schleswig and Austria

---

[16] Roon, *Denkwurdigkeiten*, p. 354–355.

[17] Rohl, "Kriegsgefahr", p. 102.

administering Holstein, and both parties continuing to share sovereignty. But both Prussia and Austria knew full well that the agreement was only a delaying tactic, and they were waiting for a major breakthrough in the issue of war funding.

Why the Austro-Prussian War came to an abrupt end

In February 1866, Bleichröder's efforts to raise funds to buy shares in the Cologne-Minden railway on the European market were met with a general boycott by the international bankers, led by the Rothschilds, who believed that the funds would be used by Prussia for war and that peace was the "common ideal" of the international bankers; in mid-February, Bleichröder's secret letter to Rothschild mentioned in code language that the government might be considering the sale of the Saar coal mine, and rumours circulated in the market that Rothschild and Oppenheimer might be buyers. Apparently, blocking the sale of the Minden railway shares in anticipation of the change of hands of the Saar coal mine meant that the international bankers found the potential gains from the mine even greater, and the Prussian government would certainly be reluctant to sell the Saar coal mine again if it allowed Bismarck to get enough money through a smooth transfer of railway shares.

The money problem did not progress substantially, while preparations for war escalated, and on 28 March 1866 the Prussian army began to prepare for war on a large scale, and at the end of March, with no hope of finding a buyer privately, the Prussian Ministry of Finance began a public sale of shares in the Cologne-Minden railway on the market. On 8 April, Prussia announced its military alliance with Italy and the stock market plunged. Rothschild's instructions to Bleichröder were to throw out all of Law's bonds in Berlin as soon as war was about to begin. By this time, Bleichröder had already sold off the Rothschild's bonds in a big way, with the result that the Rothschild's were furious because, according to their thinking, they would never start a war until Bismarck got substantial money, so an alliance with Italy did not mean that war was about to start.

Bleichröder clearly made the mistake of sinking his teeth.

Rothschild said in his letter, "There is no evidence that you are protecting our family's interests and we would like to hear an explanation for your dumping of our bonds. Our telegram to you this morning states that we do not accept your recent sale (of bonds)." On April 18, Bleichröder rushed back to explain that the bond sale had been halted altogether because of the recent easing of relations with Austria.

In May 1866, the Prussian general mobilization began, and the cost of bringing all nine legions into a state of readiness was 24 million taylor, and increasing by 6 million taylor per month.[18] On 18 May, in the midst of a serious shortage of funds, the Prussian government was forced to announce the establishment of a public credit agency and the provision of unsecured credit of 25 million Taylor, while at the same time repealing all decrees restricting high interest rates and seeking to attract private capital for credit. Even so, the credit crunch has not eased, with the finance minister lamenting that he no longer has enough money to wage war, not even to cover his expenses two months later.[19]

Towards the final hurdle before the outbreak of the war, Bleichröder's Cologne-Minden railway scheme played a decisive role. After all attempts to raise money had failed, the Prussian Treasury was bitterly determined to commission Bleichröder and Hansemann to form a syndicate to buy the railway shares. The equity buyout was priced at Tk110 and the market traded at Tk117, with bankers other than the two of them trying to take advantage of the government's financial woes to push the price down to Tk105. The government could not accept such a low offer and decided to sell in batches. If the fighting goes well, stock prices will climb all the way up. It is also a risky move, in case the war goes badly, the government will face the pressure of both depleted funding and plummeting stock prices. But Bismarck was determined to take the risk!

As a result of the government's renunciation of nationalization and the release of the loan's interest guarantee, 14 million Taylor's locked-in guarantee was immediately obtained, and it was this money that sustained the war for the next seven weeks, in addition to the funds from the sale of the Cologne-Minden railway shares for general military mobilization. By the time Bismarck's army came to Vienna, the money was already less than 3 million taels, and with 180,000 Austrian troops

---

[18] Michael Sturmer, Gabriele Teichmann and Wilhelm Treue, *Striking the Balance – Sal. Oppenheim jr. & Cie. A Family and a Bank*, 1994.

[19] Ibid.

still stationed in Vienna, Bismarck would be the most unjust politician in history if he could not force Austria to surrender within two weeks.

Bismarck's abrupt end to the war made him triumphant in this great gamble on the fate of Germany and his personal destiny!

The Battle for the Popularization of the Law: 10,000 gold taels at the sound of a cannon

The loser of the Austro-Prussian War was Napoleon III of France, who watched the rapid rise of Prussia under his watch. Instead of receiving any substantive "compensation for neutrality" as a result of Bismarck's strategic deception, France was taunted and ridiculed by Bismarck in the case of Luxembourg. Napoleon III's mistake in alienating Austria was the same as King Huai of Chu who was lured by Zhang Yi to break diplomatic ties with Qi by "offering 600 miles of land to merchants".

Britain, which had always played the game of parity of power, was not as sensitive as it should have been to the dangerous prospect of Prussia emerging as Britain's greatest challenger to the unification of Germany. Britain was still overlooked by the bluff-loving Napoleon III, who overestimated the strength of the Second French Empire. The Suez Canal, built by France in 1859, was completed and opened to navigation in 1869. Britain saw this as a direct threat to the Middle East and India under its rule: to cut the line of communication between the British mainland and the Indian colonies would be to cut the backbone of the British Empire, which the British imperialists could not tolerate in any case. So the strategically short-sighted British government used Prussia as a counterweight to France and gave the green light to Prussia to unify Germany. British concerns about France trumped concerns about German unification.

Tsarist Russia's relations with Britain and France have been lukewarm since the crushing defeat of the Crimean War. It was ostensibly neutral, but in fact supported Prussia in its fight against France in order to reap the benefits of the fishermen and to avenge that year's slap in the face. The sluggish and closed-minded Czar was concentrating on fanning the flames in the Balkans, not taking full advantage of Prussia, a former anti-French ally and dozens of small, loose German Confederate states, and thus sowing the seeds of future defeat.

Austria, newly defeated and on the verge of financial insolvency, is no longer able to support France in its retaliation against Prussia.

Rather than being a great strategist, Bismarck was a fortunate adventurer whose fortune lay in the strategic negligence of his opponents and the lightning-fast rise to power that he himself did not expect. After the end of the Austro-Prussian War, only Bismarck knew that the unification of Germany could not be achieved without defeating the powerful France. A war on popular law will be inevitable.

The fuse of the Franco-Prussian War was the so-called "Ames Telegraph", in which a Prince of the Prussian Hohenzollern family was elected heir to the Spanish throne at the beginning of July 1870. Napoleon III ordered the French ambassador to Prussia to protest on the pretext that France could not tolerate threats on both the east and west flanks. At the time, William I was recuperating at the Ames spa, when he indicated to the French ambassador that the Hohenzollern family could consider relinquishing their right to the Spanish throne. Napoleon III, however, did not rest, and ordered the French ambassador to find William I to give him a written assurance. William I promised to return to Berlin to negotiate the matter again, while sending a telegram to Bismarck. On receiving the telegram, Bismarck redacted some of its contents, making it a telegram from William I refusing to negotiate with the French ambassador, and published it publicly in the newspapers, and on 19 July 1870, Napoleon III declared war on Prussia under the pretext of being insulted.

And at this point France did not even have an ally.

As a major contributor to the Pu'ao War, Bleichröder's position is not what it used to be, and he has gone from being the younger brother of the Rothschilds to an equal partner. Bismarck's reliance on him outweighed his reverence for the Rothschilds, and shortly after the end of the Austro-Prussian War, Bismarck resolutely transferred the entirety of his private account from the Frankfurt Rothschild Bank to the Bleichröder Bank.

Just ten days before the outbreak of war, Bleichröder inquired about the possibility of war in a confidential letter to Bismarck, and cunningly mentioned the investments in Bismarck's private account. In the letter he asks.

> *"On my part, I do not believe that extremely serious political circumstances have arisen, so I have not sold the assets in your*

> account, If I am wrong in my judgment, and you think many unpleasant events are about to occur, I beg you to give me a timely warning."

As it turned out, Bismarck did not dare to be lax when it came to the profit and loss of Bismarck's personal wealth, and the next day a reply arrived, but in the name of Mrs. Bismarck, which was.

> "He didn't think anyone else would suddenly go on the offensive against us because the Spanish vote didn't go anyone's way. But he felt that perhaps at some point the anticipation of war would be stronger than it is now, so it might be a good idea to sell the railroad shares, and he would need the money here anyway."

Upon receiving the reply, Bleichröder immediately understood that war was about to begin. The next day, he immediately sent this valuable piece of information to Rothschild in Paris: "All offers fall fast." At the same time, he instructed traders in various European markets to dump all of his various assets, some of which were even sold at a loss. Bleichröder couldn't care less at this point.

One result of the Austro-Prussian War was that the Prussian constitutional crisis ended and Bismarck's government was granted a considerable degree of financial freedom, and on July 21, 1870, the Prussian-dominated North German Confederate Parliament approved a war credit of 120 million Taylor.

In the early days of the war, the stock market situation in Berlin bordered on panic, with even quality stocks like the Cologne-Minden railroad falling by 30%. The Prussian government, in an emergency sale of 100 million Taylor's first war bonds, tried to get rid of the underwriting channel monopolized by the bankers and offered them directly to the market on the condition of 5 percent interest and 88 percent discount, while the bankers' offer of 85 percent discount was rejected by the government. "This is a ridiculous condition under current market conditions," Oppenheimer stressed in a letter to Brexit. As a result the sale suffered a huge failure and the bond sold for only 60 million Taylor. In fact, the root of the problem is that bankers cannot earn underwriting fees if the government sells directly, so they resort to a collective boycott. This point once again shows the power of "channels as king" in the financial markets.[20]

On 1 September 1870, the French and Prussian sides engaged in a general battle at Sedan, and the French army was again defeated. The following day, Napoleon III surrendered with 100,000 French troops, and on September 4, the Parisian workers staged an armed uprising to overthrow Napoleon III's rule.

After the Battle of Sedan, as many as 300,000 French prisoners were taken into Prussian captivity. Keenly aware that this was a great opportunity to make money, Bleichröder volunteered to take on the "responsibility" of paying the monthly living expenses to the POWs. To him it was a sure-fire lending business, and in the future whoever represented the French government would have to pay the principal and interest on this huge loan, which would be part of the war payout. Bleichröder was not afraid of the French cheating, for as long as the Prussian army did not receive war reparations, it would not leave French soil. And the French army has been completely dismantled, and there is no way it can rise again in the short term.

As war approached and broke out, daily commercial correspondence between Bleichröder and Rothschild in Paris became increasingly difficult, and later direct contact between Berlin and Paris was forced to be redirected via Brussels and Amsterdam. As usual, Bleichröder reports on the Berlin market. Prior to the Battle of Sedan, Bleichröder urgently informed Rothschild to sell their holdings of Cologne-Minden railroad shares as soon as possible, and Bleichröder then sold 1,250 railroad shares for Rothschild at 128 Taylor, which was 95.72 Taylor in July. After 15 September, contact was broken off and Paris was besieged and Rothschild was trapped on 20 September. It wasn't until February 1871 that it was reconnected. During this period, Roche in Paris could only occasionally pass on information by means of balloons, and on 5 October the Prussian army expropriated the Rothschild family's estate of Ferrier to become the command of William I, Bismarck and Prussian Marshal Mauch. It was here that the famous "Ferrier meeting" took place, and the French Foreign Minister tried unsuccessfully to persuade Bismarck to sign the peace treaty.

---

[20] Ibid, p. 176.

At the end of October 1870, the Prussian government learned the lesson of the last time and appointed Hansemann to form an underwriting group to sell the 20 million Taylor II loan in London and Berlin. With the Prussian army's quick report, the price of these loan contracts rose, the government was soon able to foreclose some of the pledged lines of credit, and finally the interest rate on the war bonds was fixed at 5 per cent for a period of five years. Huge sources of war money were flowing to the Prussian armies on the French front, and on 30 November the bankers followed up their efforts with another successful issuance in England of a 92-fold loan of 34 million Taylor, with an option to issue a further 17 million Taylor. And at the same time, although the British began to sympathize with unlucky France, French bonds were barely selling in England, and on the invisible front of finance, France failed again.

On 18 January 1871, King Wilhelm I of Prussia was crowned Emperor at Versailles and the German Empire was proclaimed; on the 28th, an armistice was signed between the two belligerents and a preparatory peace treaty was signed on 26 February. By this time, the Franco-Prussian War was over, and the total cost of the entire war in Prussia was 22 million Taylor.

5 billion francs war payout: the banker's "big pie"

Bismarck's army began to rest, but the international bankers were even busier. The war reparations business of up to 5 billion francs is a huge business that everyone salivates over, and if a 1% overhead charge is charged, that alone is a 50 million franc pie!

By November 1870, when the war was under way, Rothschild of Austria offered Bismarck his services to Prussia to collect future war reparations from France. Of course, Oppenheimer and other international banking families have competed for their services. Bismarck sought the advice of Bleichröder, who, of course, wanted to take it for himself, and Bleichröder volunteered to come to Versailles on February 7, 1871. He got the two big orders he wanted most, to raise 200 million francs for war reparations in Paris and to arrange for the coordination of war reparations throughout France.

On the amount of the war reparations, the French Government of Tigre envisaged 5 billion francs, but Bismarck took a piece of paper and wrote down 6 billion francs in a flash! Teiyaer jumped up in a flash like a dog that had taken a bite. The two men began to argue violently. One of the other reasons for Bismarck's fury at France's opposition was the sudden intervention of the British side, which asked Bismarck to put a stop to it. Thiers argued that excessive war reparations were neither fair nor realistic, and that France could not take out so much money. Bismarck was thunderous and unforgiving. Finally, Thiel suggested that Rothschild be asked to intercede. When Rothschild appeared, Bismarck turned all his anger on Rothschild, and all those present were astonished. Rothschild is indifferent and still insists that 5 billion francs is a "sustainable" amount of compensation. Later Bleichröder mentioned the matter in a letter to Kaiser Wilhelm II, who was also very unhappy with Bismarck's deliberate rude behaviour.

The fury was unshakeable, Rothschild's position in the international financial markets was unshakeable, and without accepting his terms there was no hope of raising sufficient war reparations in the European markets, the Prussian army would have to remain indefinitely in hostile France, all the daily expenses of supplying the army were rapidly increasing, and discontent with Bismarck was rapidly accumulating within Prussia and in the European countries. After weighing the pros and cons, Bismarck had to accept Rothschild's offer of 5 billion francs. What the French government in Tigray couldn't handle, the Rothschild family immediately took care of.

On May 10, 1871, Germany and France officially signed the Peace of Frankfurt. The treaty provides for the payment by France of 5 billion francs for the cession of all of Alsace and most of Lorraine.

Immediately afterwards, the French side began to prepare the first 2 billion francs of war reparations bonds, with interest rates set at 5 per cent, and a German underwriting consortium, headed by Bleichröder, was established with the participation of the Oppenheimer, Warburg and other families. The resulting bond issue was a huge success, oversubscribed up to 14 times. The total reparations were completed ahead of schedule and remitted by the Rothschild family bank directly to the Bleichröder and Hansemann banks, and in 1872 the second war reparations bond of 3 billion francs was oversubscribed 13 times, with the Oppenheimer family underwriting alone 490 million Taylor, of which they themselves held 74 million. The reparations went surprisingly smoothly, and in the summer of 1873 the war reparations, which amounted to a staggering 5 billion francs, were completed. German troops began to withdraw from French territory. The powerful fundraising capabilities of modern financial markets were completely unimaginable in the past. Whereas war reparations in the Qing Dynasty tended to come directly to the poor common people in the form of taxes, the West offered an investment opportunity to the rich by way of bond investments. Different ideas create completely different effects.

In this process, international bankers play a dual role. They act as problem solvers on the one hand, and problem makers on the other. They provide both sides of the war with a comprehensive package of war solutions, from the listing of arms companies, the issuance of arms bonds, operational financing, to the issuance of national war bonds, post-war underwriting of reparations bonds, transfer of reparations funds, national reconstruction financing and other operations. In war, where the government is costless, it is the perfect opportunity for bankers to acquire state-owned assets on the cheap. There is a Chinese saying that says it all: once a cannon goes off, gold is worth 10,000 taels! Regardless of the outcome of the war, international bankers on both sides are equally profitable.

Or did Napoleon see through it: money has no fatherland, only profit in the eyes of bankers!

CHAPTER II

The UK: the heights of gold power

Since the rise of commercial capitalism in the 16th century, Britain has taken advantage of the timing, location and people to take full advantage of overseas trade and colonial expansion, rapidly accumulating huge amounts of wealth. With the rise of industrial capitalism, represented by the watt steam engine in the 1870s, the productivity of England was greatly increased, and the establishment of the Bank of England in 1694 was a major event in human history, as English bankers finally discovered the secret of credit, expected to become an important part of money. Backed by a strong material production capacity, Britain's financial energy is highly magnified. The credit revolution, the industrial revolution and commercial capitalism were fully integrated, and wealth creation reached unprecedented levels of astonishment, finally creating a sun-rising empire that was as powerful as ever in human history.

The nineteenth century was a critical historical period in the development and growth of international bankers, whose rise to power in Britain, France, Germany and the United States followed different patterns. Of these, the UK is the most special case. Because of the strength of private capital, the development of the textile, metallurgical, coal, shipping, railway, machine-building, and military industries of the pre-industrial revolution depended largely on private bank investment and domestic capital financing, and Britain still had a surplus of capital in addition to supplying and meeting the capital needs of the industrial revolution. With the exception of large amounts of UK and foreign public debt financing needs, the capital needs of international bankers are not strong for domestic industrial development. Despite the relatively laxity of UK company law, overcapitalisation has led to the relatively slow development of joint-stock banks, and private banking remains the dominant force in the UK financial sector, with its matching secrecy becoming a core tradition.

Hiding behind the curtain of secrecy are 17 British private banking families that have controlled the Bank of England throughout British history, even after the nationalization of the Bank of England in 1946. Prominent among them are the Baring, Rothschild and Schroeder families. They control the financial channels of bond issuance in Britain and even in Europe and the United States, monopolizing the direction of the flow of world capital and credit. After acquiring vast wealth, they gradually began to influence government decisions on foreign and domestic affairs. They privately stirred up national disputes, heavily supported the military industry, financed wars with bets from both sides, stirred up coups d'état with their hands, and managed war reparations from inside and outside. Their interests can also conflict. They each embrace political spokesmen, compete with each other for large projects, and in extreme cases they face off in the financial markets.

Where there is money there is a game of interest, where there is more money there is a power struggle, and where there is harnessed power there is more money.

Francis, the founder of the Baring dynasty

The Baring family has more seniority than the Rothschilds, and while the Baring banks were in London to finance the European powers, the Rothschild family was still playing a small business of gold coins in Frankfurt. The Baring family, as Christian bankers, is one of the few international bankers, but the earliest and most influential, and their pioneering model of a modern multinational banking network later became the object of imitation by the Rothschild family.[21]

The Baring family originated in North Germany, and its earliest recorded ancestors lived in Groningen, where they were heavily influenced by the Christian Lutherans, most of whose descendants were Christian Lutheran ministers and government servants, and began to do business in the generation of John Baring. John moved to Exeter, England, in 1717 and married the daughter of a wealthy local merchant in 1723, beginning the legendary journey of the Baring family.

---

[21] Byron, *Don Juan*, 1821.

It was Francis Baring who really brought the Baring family forward. Throughout the 18th century, Europe's increased penetration of the Indian subcontinent, Southeast Asia and the Far East, combined with the booming markets of the New World in North America, led to a boom in Europe-centric international trade. With a huge demand on the one hand, a booming commodity manufacturing capability on the other, and a ready sea transport industry, but a lagging financial sector serving the entire international trade process, Francis decisively moved the family business from the traditional manufacturing and trading sectors to the financial sector. He set up separate operations in Exeter and London, where he supported each other and pioneered a new business model that spanned trading, industrial and note business. This model was only replicated by the Rothschilds on a European scale 25 years later.

But Francis's bold transition to finance was not a smooth one, and his decision was met with fierce opposition from the Exeter side of the family. Due to differences in business ideas and conflicting interests, several brothers of the Baring family had to sign a separation agreement in 1777, with Francis taking ownership of the London branch of the family business. London was then fast replacing Amsterdam as the world's financial centre, and Francis led the Baring family as they began to make their way onto the historical stage.

After the split, Francis is looking to throw off his arms and make a big splash in the financial sector. The changing international situation, however, does not seem to favour the ambitious Francis. The victory in the American War of Independence not only diminished the military might of the British Empire, but also nearly destroyed the British economy, with imperial trade plummeting for a time and the Exeter branch of the Baring family hit hard, and by 1790 it had almost disappeared. Francis's London branch was also spared, thanks to his wife, the heir to the former Archbishop of Canterbury, and her management skills, which helped him to survive. Mrs. Barring kept the cost of running the house to £800 a year, and thus Francis lamented after his wife's death:

> "If, in those difficult years, the cost of running the house would surely have reached £1,200 a year without my wife's care, then I would have been doomed."

The family business got on track after the crisis, with profits rising from £3,400 in 1777 to £10,300 in 1781 and a record £12,000 in 1788.

The company's capital stock was only £19,452 at the beginning of the American War of Independence in 1776, and had grown to £43,951 by the end of the war in 1783.[22] By 1780, the family's important branches were spread across the British Isles and continental Europe, with one each in Exeter, London, St. Petersburg, Cartagena in Spain and Leghorn in Italy, in addition to two branches in Amsterdam, the world financial centre of the time, and a financial network linking the flow of money, logistics and information throughout Europe was already taking shape, and the clouds of the future Baring financial dynasty were now over Europe.

The Netherlands: the pinnacle of commercial capitalism

Before the rise of London, Amsterdam was the financial centre of Europe. The Netherlands, which had its beginnings in eastern trade, competed with Portugal for the dominance of eastern trade with a strong shipbuilding presence. From 1605 to 1665, Dutch shipyards were fully utilizing machinery and building ships at a fairly rapid rate, almost building a ship a day. The Netherlands had a total of tens of thousands of ships, accounting for three quarters of Europe's shipping volume by tonnage, and most of the world's trade freight was carried by Dutch merchant ships, known at the time as the "coachmen of the sea". The total number of seafarers in the Netherlands amounts to 250,000. By comparison, Portugal has a fleet of only about 300 ships and a total of only 4,000 seafarers. After 60 years of commercial competition and armed conflict, the Netherlands finally defeated Portugal in the second half of the 17th century and took control of the Cape of Good Hope, making it a hub for East-West trade. At its peak, the Dutch East India Company had 15,000 branches and traded half of the world's total trade. With more than 10,000 merchant ships flying the Dutch tricolour cruising the world's four oceans, the Netherlands became the centre of the commercial capitalist world.

The explosive growth of Dutch trade created a great demand for financial services and in 1609 the world's first national bank, the Bank of Amsterdam, was established.

---

[22] Philip Ziegler, *The Sixth Great Power*, Alfred A. Knopf, 1988.

An important reason for the establishment of the Bank of Amsterdam was to regulate the financial industry, which was very chaotic at the time. At the time, two major circles existed in Amsterdam's financial industry, a group of Jewish bankers migrating from Antwerp and a group of indigenous bankers with Christians at their core. The Jewish bankers were mainly engaged in their traditional housekeeping skills: currency exchange, note discounting, deposit taking and lending, and one of the major problems in these operations was the wide variation of interest rates and the confusion of management.

> *"The main reason for the establishment of this institution (Bank of Amsterdam) was not to provide credit, but to prevent unscrupulous and proliferating currency exchange and excessive speculation in the discounting of bills, thereby providing an efficient and stable exchange discounting service (for trade). The key point for her (Bank of Amsterdam) is its publicly owned nature rather than a privately owned or managed institution."*[23]

In the more than one hundred years since its establishment, the Bank of Amsterdam has greatly contributed to the development of Dutch trade, consolidated the country's position as a world trading centre and created unprecedented prosperity and wealth in the Netherlands. A number of mega-rich families have sprung up with them, the Hoper family being a prominent representative.

The Hope family, whose ancestors were Scottish traders, later operated shipping, warehousing, insurance and credit businesses in Amsterdam and Rotterdam, the Netherlands, mainly in Rotterdam where they paid to organize the emigration of the laity to the New World and to run the Amsterdam slave trade. In the former, the Church pays 60 guilders for every member of the laity who moves out, while in the latter, the treatment of slaves during the sea transport is disastrous, resulting in an average mortality rate of 16 per cent. Throughout the Seven Years' War (1756–1763), the Hoper family made a fortune from this speculative business.

After the Seven Years War, the Hoper family entered the field of international finance, arranging government loans for Sweden, Russia,

---

[23] Stephen Zarlenga, *The Lost Science of Money* (American Monetary Institute 2002).

Portugal and Bavaria, leading the Anglo-Dutch syndicate to underwrite these national debts, from which Hoper himself took a commission of 5 to 9 percent. The family also focused on lending money to West Indian planters, getting sugar, coffee and tobacco in return, which were then sold in the Amsterdam market. Because of the large loans given by the Hope family to the Portuguese royal family, the Portuguese licensed Hope to operate the Brazilian diamond trade, thus making Amsterdam the center of the European diamond trade.[24]

The Hoper family's most important client was the Russian empress Catherine the Great, who, likewise because of the large financing loan Hoper gave to the Tsarist government, granted Catherine the exclusive right to import sugar from Russia, as well as to represent the European trade in Russian grain and timber. Through their commercial and financial operations, the Hopes became almost the richest family in Europe at the time, and their influence not only controlled the Dutch East India Company and the West India Company, but also formed an Anglo-Dutch syndicate with their major British allies to influence the political and foreign affairs of European and American countries with financial power.

From 1779, Henry Hope was the head of Hope & Co. and in 1786, Adam Smith dedicated the fourth edition of his masterpiece, The Wealth of Nations, to Henry Hope.

> "I didn't originally make any changes of any kind in this 4th edition. Now, however, I find it my duty to give thanks to Mr. Henry Hope of Amsterdam. It is thanks to this man that I was able to obtain some unique and extensive information on such a very interesting and important subject as the Bank of Amsterdam. Before he helped me, the account information of the Amsterdam bank was not satisfactory to me, even incomprehensible. This gentleman's honorable name is so prominent in Europe that whoever receives such information from him will be honored beyond measure. My vanity makes me very anxious to give thanks to Mr. Henry Hope, so that I may have the honour of attaching it to the latest revised edition of the clumsy work, as the best advertisement for it."[25]

---

[24] Schama, S., *Patriots and Liberators, Revolution in the Netherland 1780–1813.*

[25] Adam Smith, *An Inquiry into the Nature and Causes of the Wealth of Nations* (4th Edition).

Being able to establish a business relationship with the Hope family meant a pass to wealth and power in European banker circles at the time. Francis Baring is one of the lucky ones.

The Hope family: Baring is the richest man in Europe

Francis' cold appearance, quiet disposition, and adherence to integrity gradually gained him great credibility in the financial world, and his business made great strides in the Napoleonic Wars. By 1771, Francis had been appointed a director of The Royal Exchange Assurance, which in turn had close ties to the Hoper family, and it was this position that opened the door for Francis to work with the Hoper family and was an important opportunity to develop himself.

The Hoper family was attempting to open up the UK market with a bond issue, and Francis took the opportunity to move quickly to put the Hoper family's £15,000 bond issue in order, and the two families have been allied ever since. Commenting on the matter, French banker John Mallet said:

> "The Hope family is struck not only by the enthusiasm and execution shown by Baring, but also by its excellent reputation and abundant resources. From that moment on, the Baring family became one of the Hoper family's important friends."

By 1790, William Hope apologized for the delay in writing to Francis due to his busy schedule:

> "My dear sir, our correspondence is as intimate as family correspondence, and indeed this intimacy is based on the fact that you have treated us in the same manner."[26]

Thereafter, whenever anyone from the Hoper family visited London, they always stayed at the Baring home. By 1796, the Hoper family partners were married to Francis Baring's daughter, and the union of the two families marked the final formation of the Hoper-Baring alliance.

In January 1794, Henry Hope wrote to Francis:

---

[26] Philip Ziegler, *The Sixth Great Power*, Alfred A. Knopf, 1988.

> "I feel that England and Holland have always been friendly and in the same spirit, and that I have stayed in England (at Baring's) as at home."[27]

However, a year later, developments confirmed Henry Hoper's statement, when the French Revolutionary Army entered the Netherlands in 1795 and the Hoper family fled in haste and took refuge in London. Under the operation of the Baring family, the British Royal Navy sent gunboats to escort them. Francis' son, Alexander Baring, was ordered to remain at the Hoper Bank office until the French boots sounded in Amsterdam, when he was evacuated and returned to London.

By the signing of the Peace of Amiens in 1802, the war in Europe was temporarily over and the Hope family was ready to return to Amsterdam to resume their business, and in 1802 the family bank was finally reopened, while most of the capital remained in the hands of the Baring family. By this time Alexander had arrived in the United States, and against the will of his father, Baring, he was reluctant to return to the Netherlands to work with Hope. Subsequent developments proved that Alexander did have foresight. Soon the war in Europe resumed and the French drove into the Netherlands again, and the Hope family's wealth in the Netherlands suffered a major loss. By 1813, the Hoper family had been reduced to nothing, and Alexander, the new head of the Baring family, took over the Hoper family business for just £250,000, only considering the close relationship between the two families did not completely annex the Hoper family estate. The Hope family continues to exist as Baring's main trading partner, under the wing of Baring. The Hopes were then no longer an independent financial force, and the two were essentially two in one.

"Red Top Businessmen": Gold Power in Power

While business has grown by leaps and bounds after its alliance with Hope, Baring has begun to turn its attention to politics. In 1786, Francis wrote to the Marquis of Lansdowne (former Earl of Sherborne): "I am chiefly concerned with three things: the family estate, the public affairs, and the East India Company..." By this time his eyes were set

---

[27] Ibid.

on the colonial enterprise of the British Empire in the East, and he was acutely aware of the unlimited business opportunities that lay there.

In a letter to Henry Dundas, Secretary of the Navy to Prime Minister Pitt in 1787, Francis argued the merits of a commercial treaty with the Netherlands:

> *"It would be of great benefit to our country that the Netherlands, as a trading nation, could help to expand the market for our products in India. This is in addition to the strong political support that can be given to my country, since our two countries share the same fundamental philosophy and complementary interests. In the case of my country, the primary interest is the perpetuation of the empire itself, followed by the interest of trade, while the Dutch interest is equally important, the monopoly of the East Indies and the interest of trade. The fundamental interests of the two are not in conflict and are economically complementary, and a strategic partnership should be maintained."*[28]

The letter is ostensibly in the national interest, and the special interests of the Hope-Baring alliance implicit behind it have been made clear.

And it was John Dunning who really brought Francis into politics. Dunning, then chief barrister of the Duchy of Lancaster, was a close friend of Colonel Isaac Barre, who had been Prime Minister Pitt's chancellor in 1782, and the three had formed an intimidating triumvirate alliance with the Marquis of Lansdowne, Prime Minister Pitt's chancellor of the Exchequer.

A big reason Dunning helped Francis enter politics was that he was already in a debt trap and unable to pay, and from 1783 onwards Francis paid him a huge debt of £5,000 a year for six years.

Under the operation of the troika, British Prime Minister Pitt has made Francis his guest of honour, listening to his views on the Senegalese slave trade, Turkish diplomacy, Gibraltar's military presence, customs reform and other issues.

The Baring family's ploughing through the political arena has finally paid off. Their close relationship and mutual trust with

---

[28] Ibid.

government ministers has led to a big cake of government contracts often patronizing the Baring family. Baring was entrusted with the task of providing logistical support to the front line, and the Marquis of Lansdowne was able to secure a better supply of food for his troops. In 1780, the British government tried to find a banking family to finance its North American war effort, preferably with its own resources or those of its clients and outside investors, to take on war bonds. It was a high-risk, high-reward business, and Francis jumped at the chance to take on the underwriting business, earning £19,000 on North American war bonds between 1780 and 1784. The number seems small, but it is enough to satisfy the appetite of the government and to establish a good image with the British government. The Government knows and trusts Baring, they like Francis and respect his abilities and always feel as if they owe him something. This feeling will help Baring get more government contracts.

The late 18th and early 19th centuries saw frequent wars in England, huge military expenditures, and a dramatic rise in the national debt issue. This made banking families such as Baring rich in underwriting war bonds, earning £190,000 in 12 of the 16 years from 1799 to 1815 as lead underwriters of British treasury bonds. The Baring family's reputation reached its zenith in the Financial City of London, with countries issuing public debt coming to its door.[29]

In March 1797, at the height of the war against France in Europe, the Prince of Brazil of Portugal came to London seeking to raise £1.2 million. He intends to use the profits from the Brazilian diamond and snuff business as collateral for the loan, and if these collateral are not enough, to add "the rich island of Mozambique". Francis was interested, but sought Prime Minister Pitt's advice first. Pitt replied that he was not enthusiastic about the loan "at a time of great difficulty for Portugal"; however, he would not object if Baring were to finance it as a private company, but there would be no official support. Considering Pitt's opinion, Baring had to pass on the opportunity.

In 1801, the Portuguese were in desperate need of large sums of money to pay for the huge war expenses, and the question of loans resurfaced. This time Prime Minister Pitt left office temporarily and

---

[29] N. Baker, *Government and Nick Leeson Contractors: The British Treasury and War Suppliers* (1971).

Francis decided to leave the government alone. Francis told his son-in-law and Hoper family partner Pierre Labouchere: "At this eventful time of year, we shouldn't be talking to ministers about Portuguese loans, and as you know, those ministers are mostly clueless about international financing."

Under Francis' direction, Pierre Loebchelle and George Baring were sent to Lisbon to negotiate the details of the loan cooperation. The two men rode a donkey cart all the way to Lisbon, then found the negotiation process itself as difficult as their bad journey. Pierre Loebchelle complained that the Portuguese "kept changing the text of the negotiations, and it was all text that I didn't understand, and it just made me dizzy". By 1802 several more Jewish bankers had arrived in Lisbon to join the battle for the contract, but George Baring reported that "these Jews, though formidable enemies, need not be overlooked; they are too poor to pay the price we can", and the contract eventually fell to the Baring-Hope consortium, with Baring underwriting 5 million guilders.

After making the money, the old Baring began to seriously consider the need to become a "red top businessman". The poor reputation of the banker has always given the public the impression of a mean-spirited businessman, and only by becoming a politician can one become a member of the ruling class and can build the foundation of the family business on a solid foundation of honour. Having made up his mind, Francis spent £3,000 through the operation, was unsurprisingly elected to the House of Commons, and, for the next 150 years or so, his family retained their seats in Parliament.

Transatlantic network of people

Francis had an early insight into the future importance of the American market, and as early as 1774 he entered into a business partnership with Thomas Willing and Robert Morris of Philadelphia, Pa. Thomas Willing later became chairman of the first privately owned central bank in the United States, the First Bank of the United States, and Robert Morris was one of America's most famous banking families and one of the main architects of the American nation. These heavyweight connections played a key role in the Baring family's later business development in the United States.

At the end of the 18th century, the chaos caused by the French Revolution caused the Baring family to temporarily shift its focus of business to North America, and in 1795, David Humphreys, the American minister in Lisbon, was desperate for money to negotiate with the North African Berber regime (North African pirates) for the free navigation of American merchant ships in the Mediterranean. The United States Government asked the Baring family to issue a 6 per cent national debt worth $800,000, and a month later the Baring family raised $200,000 for the United States, relieving the Minister of Lisbon's urgent need. Rufus King, then U.S. Minister to Britain, wrote specifically to Baring in this regard, congratulating him on his "generous disposition and skill in helping Hafez to succeed in such an important operation". and said:

> *"I have written to our Minister of Finance to inform him of your deeds, and will ask him to join me in assuring him that the Government of the United States will keep a good impression of the important role you have played in this matter."*[30]

At the time, the conflict between the United States and France was on the verge of erupting, and the Baring family contributed $45,000 to acquire 10,000 smoothbore guns and 330 cannons for the United States, which at the time was enough to equip a large army. By the end of the 18th century, the Baring family was not yet a designated European agent of the U.S. government, but always went to Baring whenever Americans needed to raise money from Europe.

Baring thought that the US stock market would be a safe haven for European investors in the event of instability in Europe caused by the French Revolution, and organized a major push into the US stock market by British investors. By 1803, foreign investors held half of the total market value of the U.S. stock market (about $32 million). British investors invest in U.S. stocks and the U.S. remits dividends to the U.K., creating a tight transatlantic financial network, with the Baring family at the central hub of the network.

Thomas Willing had been a loyal ally of the Baring family since 1790, becoming the family's financial agent in the United States. By this time, Baring had become the official agent of the United States Government. U.S. Ambassador to the United Kingdom Rufus King told

---

[30] Ibid.

Baring that the U.S. government had decided to appoint "a family of British banks of first class honour and stability" as agents to regularly "give substantial financing to the Continental Conference" and to fund U.S. diplomatic missions in various countries. In 1803 the Barings were officially appointed financial agents of the United States government in England.

Louisiana Financing: The Most Amazing Financial Case Ever Made

The Baring family has done more than anything else in the history of world finance to finance the amazing purchase of Louisiana by the United States.

The Louisiana region, between the Mississippi River and the Rocky Mountains, stretches from Canada in the north to the Gulf of Mexico in the south, and covers an area equal to the sum of the 13 states that now make up the Midwestern United States. Historically, Louisiana had been a French colony, ceded to Spain after losing the Seven Years War, and in 1800, when the Napoleonic Empire was in full swing, Spain had to return the colony to France. The U.S. government fidgets at the thought of a powerful French army on its doorstep. Britain proposed to the United States that the colony be conquered by Britain first and that the land be given to the United States when the war in Europe had subsided. This proposal simply terrifies the Americans more than the French Army that is about to appear. So President Jefferson sent an envoy to Paris to test the whispers of Emperor Napoleon to see if he could sell part of Louisiana to the United States. To the great delight of the American mission, His Majesty the Emperor intended to sell the entire colony of Louisiana to the United States. With the general direction set, all that was left was bargaining, with France initially holding out for $15 million and eventually settling for $11.25 million.

In fact, Napoleon had an unspeakable affliction. At the time, Napoleon had sent 20,000 people to invade Haiti and was desperate for money to regroup. In April 1803, the United States and France signed a peace treaty, and the United States easily acquired about 2.6 million square kilometers of land (equivalent to 3.85 French) for less than $5 per square kilometer.

The question now is, where to find this money? The answer is readily available. It was only through Alexander's efforts that France agreed to reduce the deal price to $11.25 million, after Alexander had mediated as a representative of the Baring family as early as the French and American negotiated the deal amount in Paris. When the deal was finalized, Baring-Hope logically assumed the task of raising funds for the issuance of national debt for the United States Government, with the Hopps taking 40 per cent and the Barings 60 per cent, in the European financial market, at 5 per cent interest. This amounted to a de facto purchase of Louisiana from France by the Baring-Hope consortium, which then resold the land to the United States Government.

In June 1803 the war between Britain and France resumed and the two countries were in a state of military confrontation. Having difficulty tolerating a British bank paying millions of francs a month to its enemies to indirectly help Napoleon prepare for war, Prime Minister Addington forced the Baring family to suspend French payments. And the Barings easily circumvented the political risk by simply handing over the responsibility for payment to their ally, the Hope family in Amsterdam, to execute it on their behalf. By this time, Baring's correspondence with the Hoper family had been monitored and Hoper, in response to a letter from Baring requesting payment to the French Government on its behalf, stated that "we have no objection to the continuation of payments to France and cannot comply with your request (to pay on its behalf)". The two families appeared to disagree, but in reality, Baring knew that Hope would certainly pay France, and Hope knew that Baring was only making a verbal protest on the surface, all for show to the British government. In the end, Hope and Baring made a total of more than $3 million from the Louisiana Purchase business.

The Anglo-American War of 1812: The Baring Family in and Out

In 1806, former U.S. Vice President Aaron Burr was accused of conspiring to dismember the United States, and everyone believed he wanted to bring the country back under British rule. Popular animosity between the two countries rose sharply in the meantime, and the clouds of war hung heavily over both sides of the Atlantic. In addition, the war between Britain and France led to the imposition of a maritime embargo on the European continent, which greatly affected trade between the United States and France. The British Navy also regularly enforces the law in an area less than three miles from the United States coast, which is a clear violation of United States territorial waters, and the United States intervenes and the United Kingdom continues to do as it pleases. The potential for conflict between the two sides is further increased.

Another major cause of the war was the First Bank of America issue. First Bank was the first privately owned central bank in the United States, established in 1791, and the Baring family is one of the major shareholders of First Bank of America. Thomas Willing is precisely the chairman of First Bank of America, and he and Baring have been business partners for nearly 30 years.

When the U.S. government authorized the formation of the First Bank of the United States in 1791, it was only given a 20-year term, and the First Bank's operations would expire in 1811. There was a heated debate within the United States over the formation of the First Bank from the beginning, and eventually opposition opinion prevailed, and on March 3, 1811, the United States government stopped giving the First Bank of the United States a new extension and the First Bank closed its doors. The matter is a huge boost for British bankers, who have a 70 percent controlling stake in First Bank of America. The core interests of Baring, Rothschild and others are seriously challenged.

For the Baring family, this is also a rare and good opportunity. Where there is war, there is opportunity. This is especially true for a man like the Baring family, who is a master of both the British and American sides. With the outbreak of war, the issuance of national debt by the British and American sides was bound to rise. Baring was dominating the bond underwriting business on both sides of the Atlantic at this time, and the moment it was profitable, it could reach the heights of riches in an instant. At the same time, the war is bound to force the economically weak United States into deep debt, thereby increasing its financial dependence on Baring, and how can the war be conducted without money? The U.S. government inevitably eventually gave in politically and agreed to a private central bank operating under the control of British bankers. That's when Baring stepped up to the plate again to be a good person and make a good name for itself on both sides, in both the British and American sides.

In 1812, the Anglo-American War finally broke out. The situation has evolved unpredictably. By the time the war was fought in 1814, the United States was in debt, and $6 million in war bonds, sold in July, sold at a dismal 2 percent discount on the market. Not only was the government finances severely underfunded that year, but there was also no money for the war of 1815. U.S. Secretary of the Navy William Jones exclaimed, "Urgent action must be taken, and fast! Otherwise we will have a situation unprecedented in history, sustaining our Army and Navy with no funds, and fighting an uphill battle." The poor Secretary of the Navy searched every corner of the treasury like a beggar, trying to find the bare minimum to sustain some of the most urgent military defense operations. The recruitment of naval sailors came to a complete standstill because "sailors never get on board without cash".

The situation in the War Department is no better. The Springfield Arsenal has been completely shut down due to lack of funds. Virginia, the "most democratic" state in America, had a soldier's mutiny due to lack of food and pay. New Hampshire's lack of cash to reissue state debt to veterans "has stirred them to hate the government," Troops in other areas claim they will occupy barracks and sell government property at cheap prices if they do not receive their salaries in time. Soldiers have been owed their salaries for as long as 6 to 12 months, and even longer in some areas, and the soldiers don't even get the pitiful $30 a year salary. In many areas, the military has seen large numbers of deserters, and officers not only cannot afford to catch deserters, but can't even afford to advertise locally to report them. Military prisons in New England were disbanded because they could not afford to operate, and New York's field hospitals were long depleted of medicine and supplies. Government and military officials have sometimes had to borrow money from others in their private capacity to meet some of their most pressing expenses.[31]

War is always a giant machine that devours wealth, and it is delusional to want to fight a long war without money. From another perspective, money is again the master of war, both as an end in itself and as a tool to harness it. It is this deep understanding that makes international bankers love war. Not only do they profit from the war, they can also control the government and influence post-war policies to better achieve their strategic purpose of long-term profitability.

During the war, as a British citizen, Baring naturally could not blatantly finance the United States in the London market, though it was

---

[31] Donald R Hickey, *The War of 1812: The Forgotten Conflict* (University of Illinois Press 1990).

nobody's business to underwrite American bonds through their agents in other European cities. Not only did the Baring family actively plan to return to the U.S. market after the war, but they even continued to pay dividends to investors who held U.S. stocks during the war, and in 1813 the U.S. government finally sent a delegation to Europe in July for peace talks with Britain. Thinking that Britain would welcome Russia as a mediator, the Americans rushed to St. Petersburg first.

Francis' son, Alexander Baring, began to whitewash and sell favours to both sides of the Anglo-American government. He acted as coordinator between Gallantin, head of the US delegation, and Castlereagh, the British Foreign Secretary. He told his American friends that the British would never welcome a Russian in the role of mediator, and in his letter he noted that "in a family dispute, the intervention of an outsider can only have a negative effect." Gallatin finally arrived in London in March 1814. Gallatin's son James complained: "I found London much more boring than Paris or St Petersburg, we were not in a popular environment, we were often invited by many people but always felt a little constrained... The only place where we felt really at home and really welcome was in Mr Barring's house."

In a way, it was the Baring family's "love of peace" that finally brought about the armistice between Britain and the United States in 1815. Baring and other British bankers succeeded in making a fortune. The U.S. government succumbed to pressure from international bankers and in December 1815 promised a second privately owned central bank, the Second Bank of the United States. Baring, as it wished, held the lifeblood of Anglo-American transatlantic trade and finance for decades after the end of the Napoleonic Wars.

France's Post-War Payout: Baring Promotes to Sixth Power in Europe

> *Today there are six major powers in Europe: the British, French, Russian, Austrian, Prussian and Baring families.*
> —Prime Minister Richelieu of France.

In 1815, France was defeated and Napoleon was exiled. Under the Vienna Peace Treaty, France had to pay 700 million francs in war reparations and cover the costs of 150,000 anti-French Allied troops in France over five years. "In 1816, the French agricultural harvest failed and the treasury was empty. Unable to gain the trust and support of the domestic financial consortium, the restored Bourbons turned to the British Baring family, the most powerful in Europe at the time, with a view to an early settlement of their reparations to the victorious nation and the speedy withdrawal of the foreign occupying forces in France.

With the support of the British ambassador to France, the Duke of Wellington, and the French Prime Minister, the Duke of Richelieu, grandson of Louis XIV's eponymous Cardinal Richelieu, Gabriel-Julien Ouvrard travelled to London on behalf of Louis XVIII to see the Baring family. This Offred had served as Napoleon's financial advisor and had been thrown in jail several times for unclear accounts. But this man, who was well versed in power change, and who had a close relationship with Prime Minister Richelieu and King Louis XVIII, was by today's standards a standard lout.

Offred told the Baring family that Prime Minister Richelieu and Finance Minister Corvetto had given him full authority to negotiate the loan with the Anglo-Dutch consortium. The Baring family did not take this matter to heart at first, as the "middleman", who had no name and no reputation, was not reliable and therefore did not have a clear attitude.

On his return, Offred added to the story by telling the French ministers how interested Baring and the Hope family were in the matter and very much inclined to agree to the deal. Prime Minister Richelieu and the Minister of Finance were overjoyed. With Overd's long sleeves, the parties made a mistake and began negotiating the details of the loan. At The Tuileries in France, the seat of the negotiations, the Baring and Hope families were surrounded by opponents of the loan, with the Hope family still standing by to listen to the objections, while the Baring family shrugged its shoulders in disdain and went ahead with the loan project. French Foreign Minister Talleyrand, out of self-interest, did not want to see a negotiated agreement, while Louis XVIII himself said he was willing to welcome Baring in Paris.

By December 1816, negotiations had progressed to such an extent that the Duke of Wellington formally wrote to the British Foreign Secretary Castlereagh to inform him that the total amount of French public debt was about 300 million francs (about $12 million), of which the equivalent of a share of £2 million would be offered on the London financial market. The Baring family has the support of leading European politicians such as Austrian Prime Minister Metternich, who have also privately purchased French treasury bonds underwritten by the Baring family. The Baring family, together with its Parisian partner Jacques Laffitte, successfully completed the underwriting mission, raising 315 million francs for the French government in three installments.

During the fundraising process, the French consortium, which had previously been distrustful of the royal family, led by the Baring family, began to support French public debt, subscribing to a quarter of it in the first two instalments and more than half of it in the third. The Baring family was a leader in French finance for a while. The Duke of Wellington, in a letter to his friends, commented:

> "Baring has taken French finances into its own hands, and French bonds are as good as fish in the British bond market. To some extent, Baring almost controls the financial markets of the world. Baring will feel the might of the (such financial) power he has, and will think that any move against him is less likely to be won."

As a veteran of a hundred battles, Wellington's words contained both praise and a warning.

In the whole project of representing the French Government, the anti-French allies were paid, France was freed from the burden of foreign occupation, and the Baring family made a fortune of 720,000 Pound, not only in the form of a huge sum of money, but also in the form of a political position, which was a source of great joy. Not only did the Baring family reap a lucrative commission income, but their reputation far exceeded that of any other banking family. French Prime Minister Richelieu lamented,

> "Today there are six great powers in Europe: the British, French, Russian, Austrian, Prussian and Baring families."

The Baring family's career is at its peak.

As with everything that reaches its peak, the moment of greatest brilliance often heralds the beginning of decline. As the Duke of Wellington said, there are already other banking families ready to stand up against the Baring family's single-handed hegemony in the financial sector. The most powerful and formidable of these rivals was the Rothschild family, which rose to prominence during the Napoleonic Wars. It was the Rothschilds who pulled Baring from the financial throne and replaced it 10 years after the family had reached the pinnacle of its career.

French public debt contracts: a feud between two men

In 1815, the Rothschild family in the Napoleonic war blood and fire experience, using its developed financial intelligence network, in order to learn the results of the Battle of Waterloo earlier than the market time difference, the first big short British bonds, and then after the plunge in the price of public bonds, a large amount of eating, such as the official war report back to London, the Rothschild family has seized the British public bond market in one fell swoop pricing rights, becoming a classic case in the world financial history of war.

The Rothschild family, which had been in power during the Napoleonic Wars, rose rapidly in the European financial markets and by the end of the Napoleonic Wars had the ambition and strength to become the world's financial lord. Rothschild kicked off a battle for financial supremacy that profoundly influenced the world's recent history in his battle with Baring over the French public debt contract.

While Baring is negotiating with the French government to represent the French public debt, the emerging Rothschild family is also active. Using the family's strong and effective sales network of Jewish bankers in Frankfurt, Vienna, Paris and London, they were determined to get a piece of this huge business in the underwriting of French public debt.

Initially the situation seemed more favorable for the Rothschilds. Rothschild provided large loans to the French Bourbon royal family during the restoration of France, and the Rothschild family's old friend, French Foreign Minister Talleyrand, was very important in the Bourbon government, and the Rothschild family's influence on the French dynasty was prominent for a time. But the good times were not long, and with the departure of Talleyrand, a new government was formed in France, headed by the Duke of Richelieu, who was intent on weakening the Rothschilds' position in France. James, the fifth James of the Rothschild family in Paris, was very close to the secretary of Prime Minister Richelieu, who also frequently informed the Rothschild family of the true intentions of the government of some value. However, in the autumn and winter of 1816, the French government gave the business of underwriting public bonds to the Baring-Hope consortium. What makes the Rothschilds even more depressed is that the Baring-Hope consortium has completely excluded the Rothschild family from this big deal.

James, reluctantly, initially sought to join the Baring-Hope consortium for partial underwriting of the third tranche of French government bonds, with the result that by the end of 1817 negotiations had broken down and Rothschild was left with nothing. Outraged, James angrily rebuked Baring for "saying what is wrong with his heart and saying what is wrong with his mind".

After returning to London from Paris, Solomon, the second of the Rothschild family, could not help but "envy" the Baring family's methods,

> "Baring is a real villain. Today he and Lafayette ran to dine with us ... we must keep a close eye on his every move. He is as skilled at using and manipulating influence as we are. Every dignitary in Paris had close ties with Baring... Posso di Borgo, the Russian ambassador in Paris, was on the side of France and was acting under Baring influence... The French Chancellor of the Exchequer was in cahoots with Baring interests, and the Chancellor of the Exchequer was simply one of the most insatiable of ministers."

But James also had to admit in his letter to Solomon in March 1817: "You have advised me not to worry too much about Baring, for no one can cover the sky with one hand. But you don't know how smart they are." A few days later, James met with the Hoper family's son-in-law, Pierre Loebchel, by which time Loebchel had become the de facto head of the Hoper family. James considered Rapochet to be a "kind and intelligent man" and said:

> "I've never seen a man like him. I assure you they are all business experts, and all extremely smart guys. Unfortunately they have developed so strong that others can barely survive."

After repeated efforts, the Rothschild family's share of the French public debt underwritten in 1817 was only a mere £50,000. That's all, Baring said stingyly. At the time, Baring's main partner in Paris was the Lafayette family (Jacques Laffitte).

In a letter to Solomon, James reports that he visited Lafayette: "He promised me that we would never be excluded from the next underwriting of government bonds... Yet I do not believe every word that slips through the teeth of this Frenchman." Over the next few months, Alexander Barin visited the Rothschilds and tentatively offered to give the Rothschilds an equal share of the French national debt underwriting to the Barin-Hope consortium. But towards the end of the year, Baring again euphemistically rejected the Law's with the following, which was used countless times: "We can divide this French public debt equally if my partner, Rebochelle, agrees, but Rebochelle sees himself as greater than a saviour, and wishes to take care of this public debt alone." Rothschild was almost furious, and every betrayal of the Baring clan's treachery was driving the Rothschild family crazy.

Baring also agreed at one point to work with the Rothschild family and its business partner, Lafayette, but then changed his mind and went out of his way to sacrifice anti-Semitism by telling his partners that they were not allowed to do business with Jews without permission. Hearing this news, Rothschild wanted to die and was determined to form an alliance against the Baring-Hope consortium in an attempt to challenge Baring's financial hegemony.

The attitudes of both the Baring and Rothschild families can be seen in several letters recovered from their family files, with Rothschild complaining of Baring's "bad mouth" and "arrogance" and Baring accusing Rothschild of "cheating" and "malice". To be fair, at least some of these mutual accusations are objective evaluations for them.

On May 30, 1818, Baring and Hope obtained a bond underwriting business of 265 million francs; they gave Lafayette a line of 20 million francs, but only 10 million francs to Rothschild. In the same year, the Baring-Hope consortium was awarded a £3 million Austrian government bond. Rothschild was invited to provide financial support, but had no authority to handle the loan itself. James complained: "These people have an incredible arrogance. Yesterday at the Home Secretary's, I was chatting with Besman, and Ray Porcelle and I brushed shoulders without even saying good evening…" and the image of Ray Porcelle as a "good guy" has since been erased from James' mind.

The elder Fourkar in Berlin commented more philosophically on the brother's exasperation:

> *"First we are Jews, second we were not born millionaires, and finally we are in fierce competition with the Baring family. In that case, why ask them to be our good friends?"*

Whoever is right or wrong, in 1818 the Rothschilds were enraged and Baring made a powerful and terrible enemy for himself. Rothschild is about to start taking revenge.

Rothschild is finally the king

For the Rothschilds, the most important thing in 1818 was how to "hurt" the Baring family as much as possible. Of course, the Rothschilds have their own set of skills in the field.

What they did was to start by eating into the market in large quantities of the French public bonds that the Baring family represented, speculating them up in price. Then, on the cusp of the Allied Summit in Aachen, the market suddenly sold off these French bonds in volume, and immediately hit the price of their collapse, the market immediately panicked. At this point, unprepared, the Baring family was forced to buy back these bonds in large quantities to stabilize their price, with the result that nothing could be done. The Baring family almost collapsed due to cash flow constraints. Fortunately, the political leaders at the summit did not want to see the explosive effect that the collapse of the French national debt could have on the situation in Europe, and Metternich and the princes and prime ministers of Prussia and Russia stepped up to support the Baring family politically, since their own wealth was also invested in these French public debts, which Baring represented, and they were only able to support Baring and the French public debts in their own right. The Bank of France has also taken decisive steps to rectify the financial market and curb speculation in the market, which has stabilized the situation, and the price of French public debt has risen steadily again. I don't know who the Lehman Brothers have fallen under today.

But this was only a small test of the Rothschild family's efforts against the Baring family. Their real strategic calculus was that since the Baring-Hope consortium had a monopoly on the underwriting of French reparations bonds, the Rothschild family should seek to become the financial agents of the "sacred alliance" of Russia and Austria. After integrating these three great European empires into their own financial networks, and then organically combining them with the Rothschild family's dominant position in the British public debt market, they would deal a devastating blow to the Baring family's financial networks from both the East and West strategic directions, ultimately excluding the Baring family's power from the middle of the European financial stage.

After 25 long years of war against France, the European countries have all been left destitute and in ruins, and are in urgent need of substantial funds to revive their national economies. As the main force and the main battlefield of Europe's war against France, Prussia, Austria, and Russia, without exception, were all in dire need of substantial financing on the developed Anglo-French financial markets.

As British Prime Minister Disraeli said some years later, "After 25 long years of bloody war, Europe had to get money to keep the peace... France needed a lot of money, Austria needed more, Prussia needed slightly less, and Russia needed several million." At that time, the Baring family, the "sixth power" in Europe, had all its energy and financial resources devoted to the operation of the French repayment bonds and had no time for it. The Rothschild family seized this strategic moment to make a decisive move and entered into contracts with Prussia (1818), Austria (1820) and Russia (1822) to issue huge national debts as agents, firmly integrating this "sacred alliance", which had been in power in Europe for a while, into its own financial network. And the three countries marveled at Rothschild's control over London's financial markets:

> "Rothschild has an incredible amount of influence over all financial business in London. The consensus, and indeed the closest thing to the truth, is that they have complete control over the interest rates on the London Financial City finance exchange. As a banking family, the power they wield is nearly limitless."

In fact, Rothschild's influence over the three countries of the Holy League was so profound and so close that it was alleged that Nathan Rothschild was an "insurance broker" for the Holy League, helping it to put out the "political fire" (i.e. the liberal wave) in Europe. By 1821 Nathan had even received a death threat letter because "his association with foreign powers, and especially his strong support for Austria (Metternich), enabled that government (Metternich) to plot the suppression of freedom throughout Europe".

Rothschild's power has increased dramatically and the position of the Baring family as the "sixth power" is at stake.

It is at this juncture that the commercial quality and enterprising spirit of the entire Baring family declined, and the interests of the main members of the family either shifted to politics or to the literary arts and other vociferous lives. The core of the family, Alexander himself, became less and less involved in the family business and instead turned his main attention to indulging in the landscape, artistic pursuits and the political struggles of the Lower House. Due to the non-Jewish identity of the Baring family, there are more opportunities in traditionally anti-Semitic European politics, which draws much of the family's attention to the political struggle, with a correspondingly lower energy commitment to the financial business. The most important thing for a master to do is to be distracted.

The Baring family's investments have also gone astray. The first was the massive investment in property, which was so deep that the bank's own funds had to be pumped out to support the investment in property, with the result that the Baring investment bank's own capital plummeted from £622,000 in 1821 to about one-third of that figure in two years. Rothschild, by contrast, has more capital and a more widely distributed network of branches to support its investment banking business. And the Baring family's investment in Latin America has suffered repeated setbacks and significant losses, which have also weakened Baring's financial strength.

Another general trend of interest is that between 1809 and 1939 there were 31 investment bankers in the world with over a million pounds of own funds, 24 of whom were Jewish, or 77.4 per cent of the total, and only four of whom were Anglicans, or 12.9 per cent, of whom Baring was one of four. Throughout the 19th century, Jewish bankers started from Germany and quickly pounced on the world, forming the Rothschild family as the core, the English side of the army included the Longhey family, the German side of the army included Oppenheimer, Mendelssohn, Bleichröder, Warburg, and the Erlanger family, the French side of the army included the Fould, Heine, Beret, Walms, and Stern families, and the American side of the army included the Belmont, Selingman, Schiff, Warburg, Lehmann, Kuhn, Leibow, and Goldman families. These families have formed a group warfare posture, with each other's horns and interests interlocking, gradually forming a large and dense financial network, which is increasingly difficult for outsiders to break into. As a result, the Baring family has less and less access to business opportunities in an ocean of investment banking dominated by Jewish bankers.

The decline of the Baring family gave the Rothschild family, which was on the rise, a chance to catch up. And the Rothschilds did seize the opportunity. First, the underwriting of the 6.5 million pound Russian bonds of 1822, which until then had been the monopoly of the Baring-Hope consortium, was taken by the Rothschild family. For this reason, the Baring-Hope consortium accused the Rothschilds of bribing the Russian ambassador in London, Prince Levin, to obtain the public debt contract.

In 1824, when the French government bonds were ready to be issued, the Rothschilds had turned their back on their clients and the Baring family was reduced to a participant rather than a decision-maker. James Rothschild, sitting in Paris, called a meeting of his London cousins, the French prime minister, the Baring family and Lafayette to propose a plan to restructure the French debt, and Rothschild and Lafayette were so distrustful of Baring's intentions that the two added this clause to the supplementary terms of the agreement: if Baring withdrew, the two would take care of this French debt themselves, thus excluding the Baring family from the core circle of dealing with the French debt. In his letter, the Baring partner told Alexander Baring, who was reveling in the political maelstrom:

> *"On the whole the Rothschilds were well-planned, very clever and old-fashioned – but, like Napoleon in wartime, at the first sign of an emergency, they fell into mediocrity like everyone else. I really wish we could get out of their grasp."*

By 1825, the situation was becoming clearer and the Rothschilds were undisputedly the new hegemon of international finance. The capital of the Rothschild London branch in 1825 was as much as £1.14 million, and the corresponding capital of the Baring family was only £490,000, less than half that of the former. And the Rothschild Family Bank has a total capital of upwards of £5 million. With £120,000 left in the Bank of Baring's dividend in July 1825 and a loss of £56,000 a year later, the Baring family even had its second chair in jeopardy – although Baring still surpassed all other banking families except Rothschild in capitalization on the books, the Brown Brothers of Baltimore, New York and Boston in the United States rose at an alarming rate, followed closely by a capitalization of £350,000, and grew faster than Baring. Baring has barely retained its second position and still plays a pivotal role in the field of international mega-credit financing and international relations, but the stage has been turned to Rothschild.

Financiers and Politicians

> *There is no doubt that politics and finance have always gone hand in hand.*
> —Rothschild[32]

After the mid-19th century, as the Rothschilds consolidated their position as the world's financial hegemon and simultaneously began to climb to the pinnacle of power, their influence and role in politics became increasingly apparent. They have formed extraordinary personal relationships with heads of state and dignitaries and have participated extensively and deeply in the decision-making and implementation of state affairs. From the "master" behind the scenes, who does not appear on the stage, gradually evolved into a new force that various parties and political forces do not dare to underestimate, and then became an important object to be fiercely contested.

The Earl of Glanville, the leader of the English Liberal Party, solemnly addressed the Queen, saying that Rothschild represented a special class, whose great wealth, brilliant mind, omnipotent connections, and influence over many seats in the House of Commons could not be ignored, and that it would be best to include them in the nobility as soon as possible, lest they should fall into the Tory camp.

The Rothschilds had an unusual personal relationship with British Prime Minister Disraeli. Disraeli's election depended heavily on the backing of the Rothschild family, a wealthy and rugged gold master. Disraeli has repeatedly praised the Rothschilds and other Jewish tycoons for their loyalty to the Liberal Party. And the British government's overseas expansion and support for the Zionist movement reached unprecedented heights during his reign. Rothschild and Prime Minister Disraeli called each other "my dearest friend" and "the best and most trusted friend of our family".

British Prime Minister Disraeli was also Jewish and had a political career in the British government for more than thirty years. He had known Rothschild since 1838 and had been a close friend of the Roth family, and he was first elected prime minister in 1848, and by 1846 Lionel Rothschild was helping Disraeli to operate the speculative

---

[32] Niall Ferguson, *The House of Rothschild The World's Banker 1849–1999*: Volume 2, p. 369.

business of the French railway. The Prime Minister was a veteran politician and a prolific literary writer, but was extremely unlucky in personal finance, always facing a mess of debt. Thanks to Lionel's help, he helped Disraeli pay back over £5,000 in arrears in 1846 alone.

Rumors have been circulating that Disraeli's personal finances are in dire straits and heaps of debt. And the Rothschild family's moneybags were always following him, taking care of the Prime Minister's debts. To this the Rothschild family gave an official denial and a list of the Prime Minister's own income, especially the manuscript fees he received for publishing his literary works, was sufficient to pay off his debts. Indeed, the Rothschild family, as creditors, should know the Prime Minister's finances best.

In the summer of 1845, Marianne declared Evelina, the six-year-old daughter of the Disraeli family, the sole heir to the entire estate. Mrs. Rowe's Charlotte was flattered and humbly excused herself. But the Prime Minister's wife had already written out her will: "We've long been family." And designate the most beloved butterfly accessory for Evelina to wear.

That's no ordinary friendship.

Disraeli, a devout Jew, considered Lionel a confidant in his religious beliefs, and the two men shared their common political and national views in countless heartfelt talks.

In Disraeli's most famous novel, Coningsby, the male protagonist is recognized as a combination of Lionel and Disraeli, and the hero is a carbon copy of Lionel in terms of his background, profession, religion, personality and even looks.[33]

In addition to Prime Minister Disraeli, another British Prime Minister, the Earl of Rosebery, even became the son-in-law of the Rothschild family when he married Hannah Rothschild, and in 1884, when Rosebery was then the British Foreign Secretary, the Rothschild family's London bank allocated £50,000 from the Egyptian loan it had just issued to Rosebery for his use, and this money went directly into Hannah's account. The Rothschild Bank has become more and more

---

[33] Benjamin Disraeli, *Coningsby, or the New Generation* (Coningsby at Project Gutenberg, 1844).

able to integrate world affairs, national affairs and family affairs and win in one fell swoop.

As a result of the political connections done right, between 1865 and 1914 the UK issued a total of £4 billion in national bonds, of which the Rothschild family undertook a huge ¼ of. With the Bank of Baring before them, the JPMorgan Group after them, and the American Seligman of the same period, the Rothschild Bank's dominance in the world financial markets is unshakeable.

War is undoubtedly expensive for all politicians, and in 1899 the Polish writer and banker Ivan Blach estimated that the cost of a war between the major European countries was about £4 million a day, and in 1902 the famous British economist John Hobson said that no European country could afford to go to war as long as the Rothschild Bank and its affiliates were against it.[34]

The Suez Canal: Rothschild's Financial Blitzkrieg

For Britain, the best route from the Atlantic Ocean to her largest overseas colony, India, is from the Strait of Gibraltar, through Malta to Egypt, and from Egypt to India, an "imperial lifeline" that Britain sees as unchallengeable. As a maritime empire, Britain had to rely on the navy, which in turn relied on fortified overseas bases, which were already well established during the heyday of the British navy in the 19th century. In the Atlantic, there is Felifax and Bermuda in Canada; in the Indian Ocean, Bombay and Trincomalee; in the Pacific, Hong Kong and Esquimat on the west coast of Canada; and in the Red Sea, Port Aden. These naval bases are located at the gateways of the oceans and firmly control important shipping waterways at sea around the globe. But Suez, Egypt, was a key region leading to India, the empire's largest colony abroad, and it was precisely this region that constituted the weakest link in the empire's lifeline.

Egypt went semi-colonial since 1801 when it ousted Napoleon, 1805 when Muhammad Ali came to power and established an Arab empire, and 1840 when it was forced to accept the Treaty of London. During the reign of Abbas I of the Ali dynasty (1849–1854), Western

---

[34] Lewis Samuel Feuer, *Imperialism and the Anti-imperialist Mind* (Transaction Publishers, 1989).

colonial power took advantage of the situation, and in 1851 Britain was granted the privilege to build the Alexander-Suise railway, and in 1854 France was granted a concession for the construction and use of the Suez Canal, and in 1869 the French engineer Ferdinand Le Cypress, with the support of French capital, built the famous Suez Canal, which has since connected the Mediterranean Sea with the Red Sea and greatly shortened the shipping distance from the Atlantic to the Indian Ocean, becoming a golden waterway of great strategic value. With 70 percent of the annual fleet passing through the canal belonging to Britain and 50 percent of British trade with India passing through the Suez Canal, it is no wonder that the Suez Canal was dubbed by Bismarck "the spine of the British Empire".

However, the possibility that this imperial spine could be cut off by Britain's biggest rival, France, is an important reason for the British to be restless.

When British Prime Minister Disraeli came to power, he had commissioned old friend Lionel Rothschild to go to France to see if he could pay for the Suez Canal, but was stopped by the French government.

On November 14, 1875, which happened to be a Sunday, Prime Minister Disraeli made another visit to Law's house. While the guests were greeting each other, the Rothschild family courier sent a confidential letter from the family's Paris branch. Lionel looked at it and told Disraeli that the Egyptian governor, who was in debt and desperate to sell 177,000 shares in the Suez Canal Company, had first made a motion to the French government, but was so unhappy with the French offer and the speed of the response that he was to cash in quickly, the sooner the better.

Disraeli and Lionel realized at the same time that this was a major opportunity. Thinking for a moment, Disraeli only asked, "How much?" Lionel immediately telephoned for an offer from the Parisian side. While waiting anxiously, Disraeli no longer had the heart to taste what he called "the best dinner in London" at Law's. While waiting to get on the brandy, the Rothschild Express arrived again and the other side offered: £4 million.

Disraeli said without hesitation, "We must take the canal." Lionel did not take a positive stance, what he needed was to verify the accuracy of the intelligence again. On Monday morning, the information was confirmed to be correct.

Their first priority now is to get the deal done quickly, without any reaction from other countries, and to do so quickly and with the utmost secrecy. However, Parliament was on holiday at the time and it was too late to reconvene for a lengthy debate. The Prime Minister could not go to the Bank of England either, the "old lady" (Bank of England) was unresponsive and did not have so much cash, and the Bank of England was not empowered by law to lend to the Government during parliamentary holidays. Finding a joint-stock bank wouldn't work either, they'd still have to convene the board and then have a slow, British gentlemanly discussion. If the collection is carried out in the financial market, one is that it is difficult to raise such a large amount of money in a short period of time, and the other is that too much noise can easily get out of the news. Only the Rothschild Bank is fit for this role.

British Prime Minister Disraeli immediately called a meeting of his cabinet ministers at which the subject was to authorize borrowing from the Rothschild family. Disraeli sent his most intimate chief private secretary to stand guard outside the cabinet room, and as soon as a resolution was reached, he came out and said "Yes", and the private secretary immediately jumped into the carriage that had been waiting at the door and dashed off to meet Lionel Rothschild. As soon as the panting secretary saw Lionel, he said, "The Prime Minister desperately needs £4 million, tomorrow." Lionel unhurriedly clips a grape in front of him, eats it up slowly, then spits out the skins and asks, "What does the prime minister use as security?" The answer was, "The British government." Lionel said blandly, "Well, you got the money."

Disraeli reported to the Queen with excitement and excitement:

> "This time France are out, they're out of it. £4 million! Take it out right away! There's only one bank that can do it, Rothschild!"[35]

Rothschild's generosity in making such a quick and generous contribution was certainly not a heroic act, and if the return on the investment did not meet his targets, not to mention a guarantee from the British government, or a pledge from the Queen, the Rothschild family might not be willing to do it. What drove Lionel down in one fell swoop

---

[35] Niall Ferguson, *The House of Rothschild The World's Banker 1849–1999*: Volume 2.

was the interest on the investment: £150,000 for 3 months, equivalent to 15% per annum, which is a quick buck without risk!

What's more, the deeper meaning of the Rothschild's move lies beyond money, and by financing the Suez Canal acquisition, Rothschild has taken a rare step closer to the core of British domestic and foreign policy-making, making the relationship more solid. With this money, the Rothschild family's foreign policy and affairs towards Britain and Egypt were "in good standing". This became a strategic inflection point, as the Rothschild family began to have more influence and involvement in British public policy and affairs than the "politically dominant" Bank of Baring.

Britain was so keen on the Suez Canal project with an eye to gaining total control of Egypt's political economy. And as British power penetrated deeper into Egypt, Rothschild Bank hitched a ride and rolled its financing operations across the board. Between 1885 and 1893, the Rothschild Bank and Bleichröder joined forces, led by the Rothschild London, Paris and Frankfurt institutions, to underwrite four of Egypt's largest national bond issues, totaling nearly £50 million.

Rothschild and other Jewish bankers chose the Liberal Party for their "political stand" and strongly supported its "imperialist" policy of overseas expansion. Britain expanded its power abroad at the end of the 19th century, nourished by the lucrative money of Jewish plutocrats. The Jewish bankers, led by Roche, took advantage of British colonial expansion not only to reap huge economic rewards, but also to put their "gold fingers" into the financial lifeblood of the world.

Saving the Bank of Baring

In the 1880s, South America emerged with a rapid economic development based on and supported by its rich mineral and natural resources (coffee and rubber in Brazil, phosphate and copper in Chile and iron ore in Argentina). Argentina is the strongest of these, and is the only country in South America to do so. All countries in South America are rapidly expanding their industries, and capacity and economic figures continue to set records. British banks, led by the Bank of Baring, hold large amounts of bonds from South American countries. The Bank of Baring holds the most bonds in Argentina, while Rothschild is bullish on Brazil.

In 1888, Nathan Rothschild, who ran the Rothschild Bank of London, began to voice his concerns about Argentina one after another: "The Argentine economy is overheating." "Argentina's real economic growth can no longer support its debt levels." It goes on to predict that "the Argentine capital market will collapse and that the crisis will quickly spread to other countries".

Two years later, in 1890, Argentina's economic bubble burst into economic crisis and its bonds depreciated like an avalanche. The first to suffer is the Bank of Baring. As a result of the dramatic devaluation of Argentine bonds and the sudden and severe withdrawal of deposits in Baring banks by the Russian Government, Baring banks were hit hard, dried up their cash flow and were suddenly on the verge of bankruptcy.

The Bank of England immediately launched a bailout of Baring banks, calling on major banks to come together to rescue Baring. Nathan Rothschild immediately gave a positive verbal response: "If the Bank of Baring goes down, the vast majority of London's financial institutions are going to collapse with it." "We will do our best to prevent a disaster." As the crisis in Baring intensified, Roche London pulled the equivalent of £2 million in capital and £1 million in gold from its Paris branch twice in a month on an emergency basis to help the Bank of England meet its funding shortfall.

With time running out to bail out Baring banks, the Bank of England brought together the banking giants to oversee the rescue programme. Once again, Baring's fate fell to Rothschild. On several occasions, Nathan hesitated during the emergency session, citing the need to "consult with other brothers". After another banking giant, Corey, decided to join the rescue, the Bank of England was desperate and kept pressuring Nathan: "We'll have to go on (to rescue Baring banks) without you." Finally, with great reluctance, Nathan gave his consent.

With Rothschild and Currie Bank leading the way, banks poured money into the Baring bailout, which reached £10 million at the 24-hour deadline and later rose to £17 million.[36]

---

[36] Philip Ziegler, *The Sixth Great Power*, Alfred A. Knopf, 1988.

The Bank of Baring was saved at a moment when its life was on the line.

With regard to the role played by the Rothschilds in the Baring banking crisis of 1890, three questions have been raised by historians: first, was there a "Jewish finger" in that crisis? It is well known that the Rothschilds and the Baring family are the yogis of the financial world, and that they are mortal enemies and strong rivals to each other. Did Neti, who predicted the crisis in Baring even two years ago, pull the trigger on the gun pointed at Baring? Second, what ultimately motivated Nathan to take the lead in saving Baring? Third, why didn't the Rothschild Bank suffer the doom of the Bank of Baring?

Commenting on the first two, Alphonse Rothschild, who runs BNP Paribas, said that the Bank of Baring has essentially become the credit cornerstone for business and the economy as a whole in the UK. Once Baring falls, Britain's credit around the world will be severely damaged. From the point of view of protecting its own interests, the Rothschild Bank finally decided to do everything in its power to save Baring.

On the third question, Rothschild answered that their bond holdings were more in Brazil than in Argentina, and that although the Argentine crisis swept through South America, Rothschild had changed hands and sold most of its Brazilian bonds before the crisis hit. In 1886 Brazilian bonds accounted for only 2.4 percent of the assets of the Bank of London in Roche. Moreover, Rothschild's balance sheet was far better than that of Bank of Baring, and even during the biggest and hottest period of the South American economic bubble, the Rothschilds remained sober and calm at all times, not allowing themselves to be over-indebted, while the hot-headed Bank of Baring was too risky.

In any case, the Bank of Baring was finally saved, but for a long time it was on its last legs and in disarray. Rothschild's century-old rivalry finally fell silent.

The Bank of Baring was finally destroyed by a young 27-year-old trader, Nick Leeson, in 1995. This is an afterthought.

Golden Cross

In the late nineteenth and early twentieth centuries, Britain's massive capital exports were largely driven by the development of the global monetary system, which in the 1870s was transformed from a dual gold and silver to a gold standard and pegged to the pound sterling as the world's reserve currency. The role of the Rothschilds in this major turnaround has always been underestimated.

During the last two decades of the 19th century, the Rothschilds' interest and interest in gold mining grew rapidly, and the vast majority of the foreign bonds they handled during those two decades were in gold standard countries.

After the American Civil War, the Rothschilds and their American agents, August Belmont and the Seligman family, played a crucial role in the process of abolishing the Lincoln Greenback and reusing gold payments.

In the fall of 1874, the Rothschild Bank of London and New York Jewish banker Joseph Seligman joined forces to underwrite $55 million worth of US bonds. Later, JPMorgan and the First National Bank of New York joined in, issuing $25 million in U.S. bonds, of which the Rothschild Bank accounted for 55 percent, and between 1873 and 1877, the Rothschild Bank of London and Wall Street bankers issued $267 million in U.S. bonds. These loans play an important role in stabilizing U.S. finances and lay the groundwork for the future adoption of a gold standard in the United States.[37]

However, in October 1877, the United States passed a bill in the 45th Congress to reintroduce silver as legal tender in circulation. The bill was angrily labeled by Belmont as an "open thief" and a "blind, crazy fool". Under pressure from the Rothschild Bank, the United States had to re-enact that silver coins could only circulate to a very limited extent, and could not be used to pay interest on Rothschild loans. U.S. Secretary of the Treasury John Sherman re-signed a $50 million loan with the Rothschild Bank through the Belmont Bank in 1899, settled in gold coins. This deal became an important turning point in the attempt by the Rothschild family to introduce a gold standard in the United States from 1879.

In March 1893, in order to maintain the convertibility of the U.S. dollar during a period of rapidly shrinking gold reserves, President Cleveland attempted to issue a gold loan of $50 million to $60 million.

---

[37] Niall Ferguson, *The House of Rothschild The World's Banker 1849–1999*: Volume 2.

While the JPMorgan consortium jumped at the chance to join, Rothschild showed great hesitation. Even after Cleveland promised to repeal the Sherman Silver Purchase Act, which had already greatly restricted the circulation of silver coins, Alfred Rothschild was still very unhappy. The Rothschild brothers' negotiating skills were truly remarkable, and they finally made this agreement possible under conditions that ensured the Rothschild family's extraordinary benefits. Law's underwritten $62.3 million worth of U.S. Treasuries at 104.5, which changed hands and sold to eager investors at 112.25 (later rising to 119). The move created the myth of a $6 million profit in 22 minutes.[38] This deal was heavily criticized in the United States and eventually led to the 1896 Democratic presidential candidate being William Jennings Bryan, who favored silver money, rather than Cleveland.

In 1868 only Britain and a handful of British economic dependencies: Portugal, Egypt, Canada, Chile and Australia were on the gold standard. France, Russia, Persia and some Latin American countries use a dual standard system. The rest of the world, including most of Central Europe, is on the silver standard, and 40 years later, only China, Persia and a few Central American countries are still on the silver standard. Gold actually became the standard for the world monetary system.

In the process of transition of the monetary system of the major European countries, Germany in 1871–1873, France in 1878, Russia in 1897, Italy in 1881–1882 adopted the gold standard system, the Rothschild Bank played a decisive role in this process. The Rothschild Bank of London and Paris became, in effect, the second central bank of those countries. The Rothschild network of banks in the international financial market in a large number of credit and currency transmission, countries can only under their dominant gold standard system to avoid the risk of rapid exchange rate changes, its main business – public debt transactions need to maintain free exchange of national currencies, so countries unified under the gold standard system is conducive to Rothschild business. Due to the monopoly of the Rothschild family in the gold market, which indirectly formed the control of the central banks of the countries, the Rothschild Bank in the late 19th century

---

[38] Ibid.

spared no effort to urge countries to achieve the gold standard system, its strategic intentions are here.

Enter China

> *The Rothschilds are unique in that they quarrel with each other, but unite as one against the world.*
> —Charles Dilke, famous British statesman, March 1879[39]

Since 1874, when the first foreign loan contract was signed by the Qing government in China, it has relied on two British institutions for overseas financing: HSBC and Jardine, Matheson & Co. In March 1885, Alphonse Rothschild in Paris heard that Bismarck was "interested in interfering in the Chinese question". Rothschild Intelligence Network quickly confirmed that German Finance Minister David Hansemann had proposed that Rothschild and HSBC represent Germany and the UK, respectively, to share equally the financing of the Chinese government and railway projects. Alphonsus immediately agreed, arguing that "Germany's move into the Far East was long overdue and that it was the right direction". The only problem is that Hansemann wants more than half of the rights in this league. While accompanying the Chinese ambassador in London to Germany, Nietzsche Rothschild urged the British Foreign Secretary to "ensure that British manufacturers are given a fair share of future deals and contracts with the Chinese government".

When Hansemann launched Wilhelm Carl to establish the Deutsch-Asiatische Bank in February 1889, 13 major German banks, including the Rothschild Frankfurt Bank, joined in. Oppenheimer was selected as a delegate for a study tour of the economic situation in China, which was funded by the Rothschild London Agency.

In terms of Far Eastern interests, Britain was on one side alone, with France and Russia competing against it. Despite Russia's growing power and influence in the Far East, Japan finally defeated China in the Sino-Japanese War that broke out in 1894, presenting Berlin and London with an excellent opportunity to join forces. Rothschild and Hansemann are the master planners behind this. Their design: to bring

---

[39] Gwynn, Stephen Lucius, *The Life of the Rt. Hon. Sir Charles W. Dilke*, Volume 1 (Project Gutenberg, 2003).

about the cooperation of HSBC and Waldorf Bank, backed by the British and German governments respectively, to curb further Russian expansion in China. Yet bankers think and diplomats and politicians differ greatly. Some officials in German politics wanted to push Germany to side with Russia and France over Britain, and opposed Japan's annexation of the Liaodong Peninsula in April 1895. Other officials suspect that Rothschild is trying to exclude German banks from the Chinese market. And HSBC is certainly reluctant to give up its traditional monopoly on Chinese government financing. Rothschild and Hansemann's plan did not materialize, and in May 1895 the Qing government announced a loan of £15 million from Russia to pay war reparations to Japan, instead of the multinational loan that Rothschild and Hansemann so strongly recommended. Alphonsus considered it "a bitter pill" for both the British and German governments.

In fact, Russia doesn't have the money to lend the money at all, and it is in debt itself. Russia was able to build the Trans-Siberian Railway to Manchuria, and France got the right to build the railway in China. Riding on this train, in 1896 the Russian banker Rothstein used French funds to establish a new Russian-Chinese bank and also entered into a Russian-Chinese alliance.

Hansemann was anxious and hateful, and Rothschild was even more anxious to take the tantalizing Chinese loan cake into his own hands, so the two men quickly stepped up, prompting HSBC and Bank of Wales to sign a formal cooperation agreement in July 1895. The effort was not in vain, and it was in time for China to borrow a second time in 1898, this time for £16 million. The dilemma came again when the UK government was reluctant to give this loan as a government guarantee, making it difficult to define the UK's share of the loan. In turn, both the British and German governments are uneasy with each other and suspect each other of territorial ambitions against China. At this point a fierce clash erupted between HSBC and Hansemann over access to the railway in Shandong province. The two Rothschild brothers, Alfred and Neti, split up to mediate between HSBC and Hansemann, finally put down both sides' anger in August.

Alfred himself brought all the British and German dignitaries to a dinner at the Rothschild house in London, allowing the German side to speak of its grievances over China in a "friendly, private and unofficial" manner. The HSBC bank there was in a tizzy, accusing the bank of treachery, and Nathan rushed to mediate between Hansemann and the HSBC bank. After a lot of work, in early September 1898, bankers and politicians finally sat together at the London table and agreed on the division of railway rights in China, with the British bankers occupying the line along the Yangtze River, the German bankers controlling the railway on the Shandong Peninsula, and the Tianjin to Qinhuangdao Railway divided equally between the two. The Naive reaffirmed "the German Chancellor's sincere willingness to join forces with the United Kingdom as well as with the United States and Japan in China's commercial interests".[40]

In 1900, Germany sent troops to China after the Boxer Rebellion and Russia took Manchuria directly, and the two sides were looking to rub shoulders again, both looking to Rothschild to spread the word. The Rothschild family, while sending a message to the British government that "the Russians promise not to go to war", brokered a new round of agreements between Britain and Germany on China, preserving the integrity of the Qing dynasty and urging it to "open its doors" to foreign trade. In 1902, Nietzsche and Hansemann organized a meeting of bankers in Berlin to form the Beijing Syndicate (one of the forms of monopoly organization) specifically to address the issue of commercial cooperation in China. On this range of issues, Britain, Germany and Russia regard Rothschild as "the most secure and effective channel of diplomatic communication".

The Rothschild family entered China in the late 19th century as a world financial hegemon and had a profound influence on the country's politics, economy and course of the war, and in 1979, the Rothschild family re-entered China. Only this time, they came "quietly".

---

[40] Niall Ferguson, *The House of Rothschild The World's Banker 1849–1999*: Volume 2.

CHAPTER III

France: The cession of gold

France's industrial revolution was two generations behind Britain's, and the French Revolution and subsequent Napoleonic Wars in the late 18th century hit the French economy hard. Nonetheless, France entered the industrial revolution well before Germany and the United States, in addition to having vast overseas colonial resources in North America, Indochina, Africa, etc., and developed overseas trade. The country's strong savings and capital became the main source of finance in France during the industrial revolution. In the 19th century, private banking remained the dominant force in French finance, with joint-stock banks starting in the second half of the 19th century in unprecedented competition with private banks.

Throughout French history, the major banking families have been divided into two major power groups. On one side were the so-called Puritan bankers, mostly from Switzerland, families that began to rise in the late 18th century and were active behind the French Revolution. When the revolution developed out of their control, they began to support Napoleon's rise to power in order to "restore social order". In 1811, when Napoleon's belligerent policies and dictatorial style of governance went against the interests of the bankers, they began secretly contacting the descendants of the Bourbon dynasty for a restoration. These families include Mirabaud, Mallet, Hottinguer and others. The bankers' power in France and Switzerland continues to this day, with the so-called secret account issue, hotly contested by the U.S. government with Switzerland in 2009, targeting families like Mirabeau.

Another financial power was the Jewish banking families that rose to prominence in the early 19th century, most notably the Rothschilds, Fould, Stern, Worms and others. Among these Jewish banking families, there were also very few who had converted to Christianity, including the Pereire and Heine families. There was also fierce competition within the Jewish bankers, mainly between the Rothschild-centered private banking system and the innovative model of the shareholding system, the French Crédit Mobilier, represented by Pereire and Fould.

France in the 19th century was far more turbulent than England, far more pluralistic than Germany and far more refined than the United States. After all the glory and dreams, failures and humiliations, Jin Kwon broke through the resistance and gradually became the master of the fate of the French Empire.

The Swiss banking family behind the French Revolution

> *"Although I am about to die, I have never committed any of the crimes against me. I forgive those who caused my death, and I pray to God that after my blood is shed, there will be no more bloodshed in the land of France."*[41]
> —His Holiness Louis XVI's last words before the guillotine.

The French Bourbons were still on the periphery of Europe when Britain began to establish colonies in the new American continent in the early 17th century. By the time France wakes up and starts expanding overseas, it will be decades behind Britain. But France caught up quickly, and for much of the 18th century, French Atlantic trade grew even faster than Britain's, thus accumulating valuable raw capital from the later Industrial Revolution era. According to statistics, from 1716 to 1787, total trade in the French overseas colonies increased tenfold.

When the British inventions of the steam engine, textile machinery, mining, pig iron smelting and other technologies came to France one after another, the French industrial revolution slowly took off. Although Britain was the flag bearer of the industrial revolution in Europe and a major technology exporter, France also contributed to the process, such as the invention of Robert's paper machine, whose contribution to the industrial revolution cannot be ignored.

The process of financial reform based on trade and industrial development was interrupted in France by the "financial innovation" scam of John Law (1671-1729) from 1718 to 1720, and terms such as banks, banknotes and shares continued to disgust the French for half a century. For a long time, finance became synonymous with fraud in

---

[41] Alberge, Dalya, What the King said to the executioner ..., (*The Times*, 8 April 2006).

France and the native French largely abandoned the idea of a career in finance. Lacking financial instruments and a strong financial market to back them up, Louis XIV's constant militarism had to rely on harsh taxes and costly foreign debt, which carried interest rates of 8.5% to 10%, twice as high as in Britain.

By the 1880s, the country's debt had already accounted for more than half of its tax revenue, and when the ill-fated Louis XVI ascended to the throne in 1774, he was faced with a mess left by the "Sun King". Louis XVI was by no means a foolish ruler; in fact, he was a gentle and humble man, and on the eve of a social upheaval that was about to break out, his character was weak, his will was not strong, his generosity was not enough to make the people think well of him, and his inability to make the rich and powerful give way was bound to end in tragedy. In a sense, his situation is quite similar to that of the late Ming Dynasty Emperor Chongzhen. With the worsening of the country's finances, coupled with the unreasonable taxation system, the people's grievances and discontent of the aristocrats have become widespread, while the nascent bourgeoisie, in addition to its wealth, has long tolerated the monopoly of power by the feudal aristocracy and religious forces. The three major power blocs of French society: the aristocracy and the traditional power centres of religion, the emerging bourgeoisie and the common people, have focused their anger on the French government, and Louis XVI has been placed on top of a volcano about to erupt.

The French did not value finance, and Louis XVI's growing foreign debt left a vacuum of financial power for foreign banking families in Switzerland, Italy, the Netherlands and Germany. The Puritan banking families in places like Geneva, Switzerland, are among the most prominent. They came to Paris to offer various "solutions" around the debt that had left the royal family desperate. These Swiss bankers, who were so wealthy that they repeatedly helped the royal family to solve urgent problems, were relied upon by Louis XVI and gradually took over the financial discourse and decision-making power for fiscal reform in France.

Louis XVI was in financial difficulties and had to appoint Jacques Necker, a "foreign monk", as Minister of Finance. This Naik, also a Swiss Puritan banker, used his influence in the Swiss banking family circle to raise money to solve a burning problem. The nature of this borrowing is similar to that of some businessmen today who borrow from each other. Since it was near usury short-term financing, the Swiss banking family circle was expecting a quick money investment with lucrative returns, while the expenses of the French court aristocracy were too great for the finances to reverse the deficit in the short term. This can be bad for the bankers, see "fast money" will become "slow money", maybe "slow money" will become "dead money", these people into the is their own lives, not delayed. In desperation, Naik decided to undertake a "shock reform". He first abolished some of the privileges of the court nobles and cut their salaries, and then overhauled the taxation system so that the tax burden was changed from a "man's tax" to a "land tax", and nobles who owned large amounts of land were subjected to heavy taxes. Unfortunately but not surprisingly, this apparently moved the cheese of the powerful. The nobles swarmed to besiege Naik's reforms. In 1781, he published a list of the expenses of the rich and powerful, which immediately shocked French society. The French public, which had been fed by the long-standing liberal ideology of Voltaire, Rousseau and others, immediately blew up its nest, and its anger at the powerful turned into hostility towards the royal family.[42]

Naek also stepped down for being so eager. Since then, France has had four more ministers of finance, and the fiscal deterioration has worsened. Louis XVI had no choice but to reinstate the Swiss banker Naik in 1788. France was already on the eve of a dangerous social upheaval, with the citizens of Paris and the emerging bourgeoisie increasingly at odds with the traditional elite, and a crisis on the verge of breaking out. On the other side, lending bankers have shifted their leverage to the "three parliaments", hoping to seize control of the finances, taxes and government budgets so that they can recover the huge loans. The new French urban bourgeoisie, with its growing wealth in the hands of the emerging bourgeoisie and its desire for power-sharing, had gone from eager to impatient, while the feudal aristocracy and the church were on top, completely ignoring or even hostile to this inevitable trend.

In June 1789, the "three parliaments" in name only were changed by the participants to the "National Assembly", with its own tax powers, and in July the National Assembly changed its name to the "National Constituent Assembly". On 14 July, angry civilians broke out into a revolution and seized the Bastille. In August, the Constituent Assembly

---

[42] George Taylor, review of Jacques Necker: Reform Statesman of the Ancien Regime, by Robert D. Harris (*Journal of Economic History 40*, no. 4 (1980): 877–878).

issued the universally significant Declaration on Human and Civil Rights, and in October, Louis XVI was captured by rioting civilians.

In October, at the urging of the Swiss bankers, the Holy See's law against usury was repealed, and bankers' lending at high interest rates was officially legalized; in November, the Constituent Assembly announced the confiscation of church lands throughout the country; in December, the issuance of banknotes (Assignats) against church lands was announced, and France's finances improved markedly, and bankers' lending finally took hold.

On January 21, 1793, Louis XVI died at the age of 39. He is said to have left a poignant message on the threshold of death:

> "I am about to die, but I have never committed any crime against me. I forgive the man who caused my death, and I also pray to God that after my blood is shed, there will be no more bloodshed in the land of France."

From the outbreak of the Revolution in 1789 to Napoleon's defeat in 1815, with the exception of a brief truce in the middle, France endured 25 years of continuous war. With vast resources destroyed by war, more than five million lives reduced to ashes, industry and commerce withered, and inflation so severe that the French industrial revolution was delayed for nearly 30 years, Britain had developed an absolute strategic advantage over France. From then on, France never surpassed Britain in national strength. The political and economic costs of the French Revolution were undoubtedly heavy and high.

Banque de France: The Return on Investment of the "Coup of 18 Brumaire"

Despite the political and economic turmoil brought about by France's foreign wars and later the Revolution, Paris, the jewel of the continent, remained a magnet for the wealthy and those who aspired to be wealthy in the surrounding countries. France was the birthplace of European emancipation, the gradual reduction of Catholic persecution of other religions and the granting of full citizenship to non-Catholics were irresistible to the Puritans and Jewish bankers who had suffered from religious oppression in Europe. The extreme demand for money from the French royal family and foreign wars created a haven for financiers to take risks as never before. From underwriting royal bonds to supplying the army, from buying and selling church lands to speculating in French currency, from discounting national bills of exchange to revolving British bills, the banking families who profited from this gradually formed what became known as the "Haute Banque" (circle of bankers). Their core members were the Swiss banking families that secretly financed Napoleon's "Coup of 18 Brumaire" in 1799.

The "Jewish Bank" families were generously rewarded when Napoleon came to power. Napoleon gave the financial lifeblood of France to the Swiss banking family by authorizing the "Jewish" family to establish France's first privately owned central bank, the Banque de France, in exchange for coming to power. Throughout the first half of the 19th century, Jewish bankers had a near monopoly on board seats in the Bank of France. The Industrial Revolution played a key role in the expansion of France with the Jewish bankers, who financially monopolized the mining, metallurgy, textiles, transportation, and other industries throughout France.

In the Bank of France's charter, only the 200 largest shareholders have voting rights. The entire Bank of France issued 182,500 shares, each with a face value of 1,000 francs. Of its more than 30,000 shareholders, the 200 shareholders with voting rights are eligible to elect 12 board members. Of the 200 largest shareholders, there are 78 corporate or institutional shareholders and 122 individual shareholders. But a closer analysis reveals that the 200 shareholders, essentially belonging to the same group of people, are the 44 major families that control the Bank of France. And the seats held by these families are inheritable, and in the midst of this three families have remained unchanged for a hundred years, namely Mallet, Mirabeau and Rothschild.

Among the Swiss banking families, the most prominent ones are the Mallet, Hottinguer and Mirabeau families.

In 1557, the Mallet family followed the famous European Reformation leader John Calvin to Geneva, Switzerland, to make a fortune in commerce and banking, and in 1709, Isaac Mallet, 25, arrived in Paris from Switzerland to represent the Geneva banking family in France, eager to find financial opportunities. After more than 70 years of hard work, the Mallett family has become a banking giant in France. Even during the Revolution, the Mallet family bank remained open, and in 1799, his son Guillaume Mallet and other Swiss banking families joined forces to support Napoleon in his "coup d'état". After Napoleon came to power, Mallet was made a baronet by Napoleon and served as the third chair on the board of the Bank of France until his death in 1826. Then his son, grandson, and heavy grandson continued to sit in this cross-chair until the nationalization of the Bank of France in 1936. The Mallett family is the only family to hold the Board of Directors position of the Bank of France from beginning to end, a span of 136 years![43]

The Mallet family is followed by the Hottinguer family, a Swiss Puritan banking family. Jean-Conrad Hottinguer, who arrived in Paris in 1784 as an apprentice in a bank, later opened his own bank and acted as French agent for bankers in Zurich, Switzerland, providing debt resolution and financing services to the French royal family. Hottinguer worked closely with the early leaders of the French Revolution, including the later powerful MP for Talleyrand. During the "Reign of Terror" under the "Jacobin Dictatorship", Hottinguer followed Talleyrand into exile in America and returned to Paris in 1798 to resume his banking business. He was made a baronet for his work in financing Napoleon's coup d'état and was also appointed to the board of the Bank of France. The great influence of the Hottinguer family in the French financial, business and practical circles continues to this day.[44]

The Swiss bankers who later joined the Gothic circle included the families of Mirabeau, Andes, Odiers, Venus and others, most of whom were also on the board of the Banque de France.

The French Central Bank is perfectly capable of opening a Swiss bankers' sorority. The French political system has gone through the changes of Napoleon, Louis XVIII, Charles X, Louis-Philippe and Napoleon III, including the restoration of the Bourbon Dynasty in 1815, the July Revolution of 1830, the Revolution of 1848, the coup d'état of Napoleon III in 1851, the establishment of the Third French Republic in 1870 by Pierre Mirabeau (now President of the Swiss Bankers Association), in the midst of such frequent regime changes, the Swiss bankers actually sat on the board of the French Central Bank and became the financial monopoly, which is really interesting. In particular, the Mirabeau family, whose Swiss branch continues to be

---

[43] Collectif, *Mallet Frères et Cie — 250 ans de banque, 1713-1963* (Presses de Jean Ruchert, Paris, 1963)

[44] http: //en.wikipedia.org/wiki/Baron_Jean_Conrad_Hottinguer

influential to this day, became a representative figure in the Puritan banking family.

At the beginning of the 19th century, these Swiss Puritan banking families gradually built up a vast financial network, and they continued to do close business with the native Swiss banking families, monopolizing the funds and credit of the French banking system.

The German "World War II" embezzlement of Jewish bankers' assets and the United States Government's strong demand in 2009 for Swiss banks to disclose secret accounts should be linked to the century-old civil war of the international banking family.

The Monopoly is Broken: The Rise of the Jewish Banking Family

Another major branch of the Gothic bankers' circle is the Jewish banking family that has been immigrating to France since 1780. They had a late start in France compared to the Swiss bankers, but they were gaining momentum. After the Jewish bankers were granted equal citizenship in the French Revolution, the rise in wealth and social status was so rapid that it gradually created a rivalry with the Swiss banking family.

The Fould, Pereire, and Rothschild families formed the core of the French Jewish banking family.

The Foulds came to Paris in 1784, and their main business expanded from acting as agents for Jewish family banks abroad to operating interest collection on government bonds. Fould began to make his fortune during the Revolution, first by speculating heavily on new paper money issued by the French Revolutionary government in 1790 that was secured by land, and then by actively buying and selling church land, thereby making his first bucket of gold.

Fould was extremely good at pulling strings, and he made strong friendships with many Jewish merchants and bankers in Germany, and became their agent in France. Achille Fould, the elder Fould's son, rose to prominence in the political and financial worlds and continued the family's influence.

After taking over the family business, Asher entered politics and entered the local council as a national representative in 1842. In the revolution that broke out in February 1848, he cautiously supported the revolutionaries and used his financial influence to finance the provisional government that was subsequently formed. Shortly thereafter he published two more pamphlets against paper money. During the reign of Napoleon III, Fould served four times as Minister of Finance and played a leading role in France's economic reforms. Strong conservative tendencies led him to oppose the dogma of free trade, embracing the coup d'état of Louis Bonaparte and the subsequent establishment of Napoleon III's Second French Empire. But he also opposed Napoleon III's excessive attacks on his political enemies, the Orléans family, and resigned as Minister of Finance on 25 January 1852 after the Imperial Court ruled that the Orléans family's property should be confiscated, but was soon appointed Senator and soon returned to the Imperial Court as Minister of State, presiding over the 1855 Paris International Exposition. He resigned again in November 1860, and was reinstated in November the following year, and did not return to his old age until 1867, when he was dying. In the last part of his term, he negotiated a reduction of 300 million francs in short-term loan debts arising from the French invasion of the Mexican War, demonstrating his remarkable talent as a banker and politician.[45]

The Credit Mobilier, which the Foulds created in conjunction with the Pereire family, put strong competitive pressure on the Rothschilds and became a classic battle example of the internal struggle of Jewish bankers.

The Pereire family was one of the most famous banking families in France in the 19th century, alongside the Rothschilds, and was a partner in the Rothschilds' bank. Although fellow Jews, Rothschilds Germanic Jewish origins differ from those of the Pereire, who were Sephardi Jews from the Portuguese and Spanish regions, originally a group migrating westward from the Italian Renaissance. The discounting of bills of exchange was its watchword, and they regarded themselves as superior among the Jews, more noble than those who had migrated to Eastern Europe.[46]

Throughout the nineteenth century, the top of the Pereire family were two brothers, Emile and Isaac, whose father, Jacob Pereire, one of the inventors of sign language, was a translator for Louis XV. The

---

[45] http: //en.wikipedia.org/wiki/Achille_Fould

[46] http: //en.wikipedia.org/wiki/P%C3%A9reire_brothers

Pereire brothers created a new type of joint-stock investment bank, with the Bank of Credit and Real Estate as its core, which controlled not only an important part of the national railway network, but also six gas and tram companies in Paris, two insurance companies, the restructuring of the salt industry, the establishment of the real estate company for the regulation of municipal projects in Paris and the Pan-Atlantic Company, specializing in foreign trade. In addition, the Bank has invested extensively in railway companies in Austria, Russia, Switzerland, Spain and other countries, and has established branches in Spain, the Netherlands, Italy and other countries. Through mergers and acquisitions or financial control, an unprecedentedly large consortium was formed with the Pereire family's Crédit Mobilier at its core, making it a strong rival to the unparalleled Rothschild family on the European continent. From 1852 onwards, the banks and enterprises controlled by this consortium issued stock with a market value of more than 1.5 billion francs a year,[47] and its strong influence on the French and European economies is reminiscent of the Catholic Church in the Middle Ages.

Of course, the most powerful banking family in France in the 19th century was undoubtedly the Rothschild family. In 1830, the Rothschilds abandoned the Bourbons in favour of Louis-Philippe, Duke of Orléans, who took the throne, ushering in the "July dynasty", which had never been more powerful than in France. The Rothschild family's assets controlled by the Bank of France grew from £6 million in 1815 to £14.9 million in 1825, increasing from 1/6 to 1/3 of the family's total assets. In 1836, after the death of Nathan, the core leader of the English Rothschild family, James of France became in fact the new head of the family, with a personal fortune of 40 million francs, the richest man in France, 10 times more than the Hottinguer family and 20 times more than the Mallett family. By this time the Jewish banking family had significantly outpaced the Puritan banker camp.

Revolution in Financial Innovation

In the first half of the nineteenth century, the role of the Banque de France as central bank was not central in the French financial sector, and the influence of private banks largely overshadowed that of the

---

[47] Ibid.

Banque de France, particularly the Rothschild. This situation did not change until the revolution of 1848. With the revolution, the traditional system of social power was destroyed to a greater extent, and a new pattern of power distribution quickly took shape, also in the commercial and financial spheres.

After the revolution of 1848, the Bank of France's paper money issuance rights overflowed beyond Paris and penetrated the important industrial and commercial centres of the provinces. The crisis ended Banque de France's conservative note discounting policy by extending discounting operations to warehouse warrants, government bonds and Three-Signature Commercial Papers, and by authorizing the issuance of 100 franc notes, thus extending Banque de France's influence nationwide. This was followed by the National Discount Bank of Paris, established on March 8, 1848, to provide emergency liquidity to Parisian merchants to stem the tide of mass bankruptcies of Parisian commercial organizations. By 1854 the National Discount Bank of Paris, at the urging of the government, had abandoned its parastatal status and transformed itself into a general joint-stock company, and its activities had shifted from financial services for Parisian business organizations to financial services for foreign trade. In addition to the National Discount Bank of Paris, 76 local discount banks have been set up throughout France, mainly for the benefit of local merchants in the provinces, to discount various commercial paper.

At the beginning of the nineteenth century, the industrialist ideas of the French idealistic socialist Saint-Simon flourished and many French people were deeply influenced by them. Saint Simeon's thought is known for its industrial theory, which envisages the ideal system of the future as an "industrial system". Under the industrial system, industrialists and scholars wielded power in all spheres of society – political, economic and cultural. The sole purpose of society should be to make the best use of the knowledge of science, art and crafts to meet the needs of the people, especially the material and spiritual life of the poorest class, the largest number of people. Everyone is to work, the economy is to develop according to plan, and the individual's income should be in proportion to his talents and contributions, without recognizing the privileges of anyone. In an ideal society, political science would become the science of production, politics would be embraced by the economy, and the rule over people would become the management of things and the leadership of the production process. Because of the limitations of history, St. Simeon saw the bourgeoisie engaged in industrial activity as the same workers or "industrialists" as the workers and peasants, and, hoping for the rationality and goodwill of the ruling class, imagined that kings and bourgeoisie would help the proletariat establish an industrial system and socialism. Saint-Simon also made his own claims for the development of a new French financial sector and the improvement of agricultural operations.

For St. Simonists and others interested in the long-term development of the French economy, large-scale economic construction in France, especially the development of railways, shipping, canals and large industrial enterprises, requires the large-scale establishment of joint-stock companies with limited liability, efficiently mobilizing and organizing the wealth of the entire French middle class and, on the one hand, financing such construction and, on the other hand, returning to the people a virtuous circle of national strength and wealth in the form of dividends and distributions resulting from economic development.

Within the theoretical framework of St. Simon's Industrialism, the innovative idea for the financial sector was the creation of joint-stock investment banks to replace the traditional private investment banking model. Raising huge funds from the public in the form of public issues of stocks and bonds that private banks could not compete with would, on the one hand, free the government from financial dependence on private banks and, on the other hand, give a stronger impetus to the development of industry. Saint-Simon's industrial ideas and assertions of industrialization became the dominant ideas of industrialization in the Second Empire era and had a significant and far-reaching impact on the recent economic development of France.[48]

The expansion of banking power in France and the emergence of joint-stock investment banks posed a serious threat to the traditional private banking power structure in two ways. The Rothschilds' attitude was one of instinctively defending vested interests, firmly opposing such financial innovation, and using all means to stifle the emergence of joint-stock banks. After finally defeating the innovators, represented by the Pereire family, the Rothschild family, in response to historical trends, also set up its own version of a joint-stock investment bank, the

---

[48] Rondo E. Cameron, Mark Casson, *France and the Economic Development of Europe, 1800–1914: Evolution of International* (Routledge, 2000).

Paribas bank, which had a major impact on French economic life in the late 19th and early 20th centuries.

Credit Mobilier: The Challenge of Pereire

From historical experience, many of the theories sound very plausible, but only plausible. Practice never follows the logic of theory, because the person who practices theory, always follows the rules of the game of interest. Therefore, the role of theory in practice can only be truly realized through the rules of the game of interests that are tacitly adhered to by those who conform to the theory of practice.

Napoleon III's superstition in the theory of chattel credit banking was no exception. The Emperor himself was an avid believer in St. Simonism, preferring to make a name for himself as a great social engineer. Long before he came to power in the 1830s, he consulted with his close financial friends, the Pereire and Fould families, on the establishment of a four-pronged system of financial institutions for the implementation of Saint-Simon's industrialism in France.

- Commercial Bank: Banque Nationale Française
- Bank of Industry: Crédit Mobilier
- Mortgage bank: Banque Foncière
- Mutual Banks: Crédit Mutuel for Small Business Finance

At the heart of this is the joint-stock investment bank, the Crédit Mobilier Bank.[49]

In 1852, taking advantage of Napoleon III's vain desire for fame, the Pereire brothers made a strong case to Napoleon III for the benefits of the commercial model of the Crédit Mobilier under the pretext of the St. Simonist idea that "all class contradictions must disappear in the face of the universal happiness that can be achieved by a newly invented social credit scheme". The model is to raise bank capital by selling shares and bonds to the public, and then using those funds to buy shares in the startup industrial companies it wants to grow. The Pereire

---

[49] Ibid.

brothers compulsively touted it as a means of achieving Saint-Simon Industrial Socialism.

This new system of credit invented by the Pereire brothers was enthusiastically supported by Napoleon III, whom Marx sarcastically called "Napoleonic socialism", "from James Rothschild to Isaac Pereire, with such an interesting character as to be both a liar and a prophet".[50] Indeed, the introduction of this credit system has led to rampant speculation, corruption and fraud on the French stock exchange. But in the eyes of the people of the time, it was a great strategic financial system innovation that was well placed to provide capital and credit to the rapidly developing industrialization. Real estate credit banking consists of two main components, the first being traditional banking, including deposit taking, commercial paper discounting, lending and insurance; and the second being investment banking, such as underwriting government bonds and corporate bonds.

In addition to the compulsions of idyllic socialist ideas, the Pereire brothers and the Foulds also resorted to divisive tactics to get Napoleon III to make up his mind as quickly as possible. The great trees beckoned, and the wealth and power of the Rothschild family not only aroused the hostility of the Puritan bankers, but also the jealousy of other Jewish banking families, including the Pereire and Fould families. In his early years, Pereire was a partner in the Rothschild Family Bank, of which the Rothschild family was a mentor in finance. Later Pereire pulled out to go it alone and became increasingly unfriendly to the Rothschild family. Villainism has always been the most abhorrent behavior of the Rothschild family.

Fould, who was part of the same "direct force" that financed the coup d'état of Napoleon III, had the same goal as the Pereire family to financially challenge the position of the Rothschild family boss. When he was French Minister of Finance, Asher Fould solemnly advised Napoleon III:

> "It is absolutely necessary to free your kingdom from the grasp of Rothschild, who has practically replaced your rule."[51]

---

[50] Marx, *The Theory of Capital* (Vol. III), p. 499.

[51] Niall Ferguson, *The House of Rothschild The World's Banker 1849–1999* Volume 2.

Nor is Rothschild a fuel-saving lamp. James Rothschild wrote specifically to Napoleon III in an attempt to shake the French Government's resolve to support the establishment of a chattel bank by stating that, once established and successfully functioning, it would control most of the public wealth and would eventually become "more powerful than the government".

Napoleon III had the support of the Pereire and Fould families, to whom he was of course obedient, and he did believe in the theoretical system of the Crédit Mobilier. Napoleon III did not get along well with the Rothschilds, and James Rothschild neither liked nor trusted Napoleon III. In this case, the Government clearly sided with the Pereire brothers. Since the revolution of 1848, the Pereire and Fould families have been the reigning heroes of the dynasty, and the Rothschild family has tended to be marginalized. Although the Rothschilds had contributed to the rise to power of Napoleon III, after all, they did not have the air of the Bourbon Restoration and the July Dynasty. Add to that the constant drizzle of wind in the Emperor's ears from Pereire and Fould, and James was having a rough time.

Rothschild's backer at the French court was the once very favored General Changarnier. But General Changarnier gradually lost ground with Napoleon III, and throughout 1850 James tried to reconcile Napoleon III with Changarnier while trying to give himself extra points before the President (note: Napoleon III was not yet emperor at that time):

> "The President seems to think that I have misunderstood him, and it seems that I must take special care to keep a low profile before him, and that Fould will not give me a good word."

Napoleon III apparently favored Fould, and was increasingly deaf to the advice of Changarnier and James on foreign policy. Napoleon III was intent on getting rid of Changarnier. James took a bad look and hurriedly transferred the gold in his hand to London. He said without anxiety:

> "I'd rather put all my gold in London and earn a paltry 3% than stay in France, and Napoleon might confiscate my money just because I'm friends with Changarnier. I'm not afraid of him, but watch out for him. It's an extremely politically dirty country."

In December 1850, Changarnier's arrest marked the complete loss of Republican power. James was so smart that he never confused his political inclinations with his commercial interests and immediately saw the wind turn and abandoned the republicans in favour of the imperial system. But after all, the stance was not as firm as that of the likes of Pereire and Fould, more or less seen by Napoleon III as a fence-sitting faction.

In 1852, the Crédit Mobilier, which Pereire and Fould had joined forces to create, was formally established with the strong support of Napoleon III,[52] and has since become a fierce rival of the Rothschilds.

"Both a liar and a prophet"

> *"The inherent dual nature of the credit system is, on the one hand, to develop the drive of capitalist production – to get rich by exploiting the labour of others – into a system of gambling fraud in its purest and greatest form, and to reduce the number of minorities who exploit the wealth of society; and, on the other hand, a transitional form of transfer to a new mode of production. It is this dual nature that gives the major propagandists of credit, from John Rothschild to Isaac Pereire, such an interesting character: both liar and prophet."*[53]
>
> —Marx.

This assessment by Marx is interesting in that he both understands the role of credit as a driver of productivity and sees that this group of people who practice credit theory are, out of self-interest, a bunch of unabashed liars. This passage from Marx is a classic commentary on the correctness of the nature of all financial innovation. Theory is always practiced by people, and those who practice it have their own pattern of interests; how to integrate the goals of theory with the interests of the practitioner is the most important difference between a great statesman and a great thinker.

The Rothschilds and the Pereire are described as representatives of "two types of Jews". The former is typical of the "Northern Jew", "always calm and rational", and the acquisition of wealth and profit is low energy and efficient in a superconducting state. The latter, on the other hand, represented the "Central Jews", who had benefited from

---

[52] Ibid.

[53] Karl Marx, *Central Compilation Bureau, The Complete Works of Marx Engels*, vol. 25, p. 499

France's liberal policy towards the Jews and were therefore more open and mindful of the public interest in their conduct and business, a "heat of the heart" that would bring about a loss of energy and a disturbance of efficiency. In French society at the time, the Rothschilds marked "feudal finance", while the Pereire family represented "democratic finance".

The Pereire brothers quickly completed their bank organization, with Benoit Fould of the Fould family serving as the bank's first president until his retirement in 1854. But the day-to-day work of the bank has been carried out by Isaac Pereire, who serves as vice president. Other members of the board include the powerful Duke of Mouchy, Galliera, Count Andre, Baron F. A. Seilliere, Charles Mallet of the Puritan banking family, and Auguste de Morny, who planned the coup d'état of Napoleon III, the half-brother of Napoleon III.[54]

With this luxurious line-up operating at full strength, the Crédit Mobilier exploded with amazing energy as soon as it was launched. It priced the stock at 500 francs, which went up to 1,100 francs at the opening and 1,600 francs on the fourth day, and touched 1982 francs in March 1856. And dividends rose from 13 percent in 1853 to 40 percent in 1855. Investors in chattel credit banks are all giddy, and James Rothschild's prediction that chattel credit banks are financial disasters sounds more like a joke.

Despite being a joint-stock bank, Crédit Agricole's starting capital size lags far behind that of the Rothschild Bank. While the Crédit Mobilier started with 20 million francs (of which Pereire had a 29 per cent stake), the assets of the Rothschild Bank of France in 1852 exceeded 88 million francs and the combined assets of the branches exceeded 230 million francs. However, from its inception, Crédit Agricole was dynamic, stylish, flamboyant and ambitious, contrasting with the rigour, tradition, understatement and stereotypes of Rothschild Bank.

In a Crédit Mobilier, the bankers are forever surrounded by a group of friends, each with their ears pricked up to inquire as to the movements of the business, whether the old master is to buy or sell. And employees stand on the stairs greeting customers, eagerly inquiring

---

[54] Rondo E. Cameron, Mark Casson, *France and the Economic Development of Europe, 1800–1914: Evolution of International* (Routledge, 2000).

about business opportunities. Everyone is eager to get rich and do whatever it takes to make sure there is no cover-up.

This period was the peak of railway construction in France, and between 1851 and 1856 investment in railways increased fivefold, with more than twice as many new railways built in the 1950s as in the 1940s. With the rapid expansion of the Crédit Mobilier, its competition with Rothschild on the railroad had become white-hot. Credit Agricole soon took control of the three main French lines, while Rothschild held fast to his two original lines. Crédit Agricole holds eight directorships in the various French railway companies, while Rothschild has 14.

Jewish bankers from both camps are locked in a tug-of-war over French railway financing. Napoleon III favoured the Crédit Mobilier, awarding one project after another for financing of railway lines to Pereire. At this time, his brother Mani, who was half-brother of the Emperor, saw the opportunity of the railway and was eager to make himself rich by it, and suggested that the small railway company should be merged into several main lines. James immediately jumped at the chance to climb the Moony line. The French bank Rothschild holds shares in the railway company worth more than 20 million francs, representing 15 per cent of the bank's assets. These shares have appreciated rapidly, encouraged by Mooney's policies. James netted 1.5 million francs in a week in April 1852 "without paying a penny".

The Rothschild Bank of France was at this point in its fortunes, leading the way in the race for railroad financing. The Movable Property Credit Bank, on the other hand, did not show any weakness, creating a standardized "package" of stocks and bonds of various railroad companies with various maturities and conditions, which can be described as the originator of today's structured finance products. Through "financial innovation", the Movable Property Credit Bank has created a large number of new financial products for investment, filling the gap between the bond and stock markets, which immediately attracted countless small investors. The assets of Movable Credit grew rapidly to 60 million francs, directly challenging Rothschild's boss position in railway financing.

More worrying for James was the fact that Pereire was reaching out to France and sweeping across Europe, and on 2 April 1853, Cologne banker Oppenheimer received a licence to open a new bank in Darmstadt, less than 20 miles south of Frankfurt. This is clearly a German rip-off of the Kreditanstalt für Movimobil and is aimed directly at the Rothschild family's Frankfurt bank. The new bank was controlled by Pereire, Fould, Oppenheimer and Crédit Agricole.[55]

In 1853, Pereire went on to establish the Spanish Crédit Mobilier and the Belgian Crédit Mobilier, and in 1854 the Austrian Crédit Mobilier was to be established. Not only that, but Pereire set his sights further afield in Russia.

Russia, deploring the strategic value of its railway network since the defeat of the Crimean War, is determined to build a national railway network, with Moscow-St. Petersburg as its hub, linking the European part of Russia, west to the Polish border south to the Crimean peninsula, with a total mileage of over 4,000 miles and an estimated investment of 1 billion francs. The Great Russian Railway Company was established with an initial capital of 300 million francs to complete this strategic infrastructure plan. Shareholders include the Tsarist private banker Stieglitz in St. Petersburg, Fraenkel in Warsaw, the Baring brothers in London, Hope in Amsterdam, Mendelssohn in Berlin, and rivals of the French Rothschilds, such as the Pereire, Mallet, Fould and Hottinguer families. Its board of directors included 10 Russians (including the chairman of the board, appointed by the Tsar), four directors of the Baring-Hope group and five directors of the Bank of France, among whom Pereire and Fould were both named. As a result, French financial forces, represented by the Movable Property Credit Bank, infiltrated all spheres of Russian political, economic and social life on a large scale and became the main base of the future Russian-French alliance.[56]

In 1856, the French magazine Industry commented:

> "The Crédit Mobilier is destined to extend its influence to the world. Its parent company in Paris, after four years of development, has become a model for learning in French circles, with semis opened outside France in Austria, Spain, Piedmont (Northern Italy), and, once peace treaties have been concluded (referring to the Anglo-French-Russian peace treaty after the Crimean War), it is bound to open semis in Constantinople and St. Petersburg ... (because) all European

---

[55] W. O. Henderson, *The Industrial Revolution on the Continent: Germany, France, Russia 1800–1914* (Taylor & Francis, 2006).

[56] Rondo E. Cameron, Mark Casson, *France and the Economic Development of Europe, 1800–1914: Evolution of International* (Routledge, 2000).

> *countries recognize that the development of production, material progress, is the greatest political interest in the world today... For this, credit is essential."*[57]

And the pro-Rothschild magazine Railways has questioned the estimated European-wide expansion of the Crédit Mobilier, which is expected to cost 1 billion francs, which will siphon off the capital needed for domestic industrial development in France to foreign countries.

Despite the criticism from the pro-Rothschild media, Crédit Agricole has remained unmoved and is expanding its presence in European countries in a big way. Underwriting of Austrian, Russian, Turkish and American government bonds; investment in Belgian, Austrian, Italian and Romanian railways, as well as mortgage bonds from the Netherlands, Austria and Belgium; opening of a sugar refinery in the Netherlands, an ironworks in Prague and even a coffee plantation in Ceylon (Sri Lanka). However, the Bank's greatest achievement has been the establishment of the Dutch-Indian Commercial Bank, the National Railway Operating Company and the Dutch-Indian Railway Company. The most important of these, the Nederlandsch-Indische Handelsbank, has branches in Singapore and Hong Kong and operates as a mixed business of investment banking, mortgage banking, commercial trading, etc. and is considered a sub-bank of the Movable Property Credit Bank.

Bank of France: strategic high ground to defeat Pereire

Whoever can control the central bank will have a strategic advantage over the competition. It was so in the past, and it is so today. The downfall of Lehman Brothers is the result of not learning the lessons of history.

The Bank of France, which claimed to be a financial centre representing the public interest, actually challenged the Bank of France's operations; before 1852, the Bank of France did not grant loans secured by railway shares, and lent at rates of up to 6 per cent. By November 1852, under pressure from the Crédit Mobilier, the interest rate was only 3.6 per cent. The shares of Banque de France held by

---

[57] Ibid.

Rothschild during the same period also depreciated considerably. Rothschild naturally hated the Crédit Mobilier even more. This situation also began to lead to an alliance between Rothschild and the Banque Française.

While Rothschild had bought 5,000 shares of Credit Agricole at the beginning of its creation to observe the market, Pereire was quietly selling. In fact, like all those who are lazy, Pereire knew very well that many of their financial innovations were going to go badly wrong sooner or later, and Rothschild saw it with a keen eye.

On 15 November 1852, James Rothschild, in a private letter to Napoleon III, severely criticized joint-stock banks such as the Crédit Mobilier as "a disaster for the national economy", pointing out that the shareholders of joint-stock banks did not disclose their names and therefore could be irresponsible and had the opportunity to abuse their power to dispose of the people's property. James warned that the new type of banks would "dominate commerce and industry with their huge investments, making rules and laws for the market, and that such laws would go unchecked and overtake competition ... concentrating in their hands the bulk of the nation's wealth ... and that eventually the power of these banks would exceed that of government".[58] At the same time, James told Napoleon that the Caisse des Crédit Agricoles movables was unstable and 'built on the beach' because the bonds they issued paid fixed interest to investors and the bank's own input into the investment was 'an uncertain and unreliable variable'. In the event of a crisis, the banks would drag the economy as a whole "into the abyss". James foresaw that the new type of bank must be under-reserved and that in the event of a crisis, the Government would have to choose either "total bankruptcy" or "termination of the exchange of gold, silver and paper money". These words were not exactly said to frighten Napoleon III, and later proved not to be empty words. Rothschild's evaluation of the Crédit Mobilier could have been published directly on the front page of the *Financial Times* in the aftermath of the financial tsunami under the title "On the risks of financial derivatives", with a change of name and year. Today, the Rothschild family has not been able to survive the global financial tsunami without a fight.

---

[58] Niall Ferguson, *The House of Rothschild The World's Banker 1849–1999* Volume 2.

In August 1855, the Bank of France had to buy 30 million francs of gold and 25 million francs of silver from the Rothschild Bank of France in order to ease its already empty reserves. A year later, the situation worsened and the Banque de France lost its bid to terminate the exchange of notes and gold and silver. The overwhelming majority of bank directors agreed with the proposal, with only Alphonse Rothschild opposed. Between 1855 and 1857, BNP Paribas Rothschild provided BNP Paribas with gold worth 751 million francs, for a total profit of 11 per cent. The symbiotic and co-prosperous relationship between Rothschild Bank and Bank of France has deepened like never before.

In France, too, the support for Belleroy was far from uniform, and under the Rothschild family, senior pro-Belleroy officials of the Banque de France were transferred out of Paris to serve as ambassadors abroad; in 1855, Alphonse Rothschild was elected president of the Banque de France, and the Rothschild became its largest shareholder. The Rothschild family's influence over French fiscal and monetary policy will ultimately determine who is the final winner in the tug-of-war between the Rothschilds and Pereire.

The expansion of the Pereire family continued with the establishment of the Austrian Crédit Mobilier as its main focus.

Isaac Pereire went to Vienna personally to present a package of proposals for the development of Austrian finance and industry, lobbying the Diet and the court to follow the successful French precedent and establish the Austrian Crédit Mobilier and build the railway line from Vienna to Trieste, while a group of Viennese nobles and bankers also advocated the matter and demanded a charter from the court to establish the Austrian Crédit Mobilier. Both Alexander Bach, the former Austrian chancellor, and Baron von Bruck, the chancellor of the exchequer, felt that the Pereire family's proposal would be of great benefit to the economic development of the Empire.

It was at this time that Solomon, the Rothschild family patriarch in Vienna, died, and the Rothschild family was left alone at the Habsburg court. James could not tolerate the absence of Rothschild family members in the new Austrian financial institution, and chose Anselm Rothschild, son of Solomon, to preside over the Austrian family business. As soon as Anselm came to power, the Austrian court was forced to recognize the strength of the financial consortium, which was hostile to the Bank, and the imperial ministers persuaded the two to form a new bank to serve the Habsburg dynasty together.

In response to this proposal, Anselm shrewdly advised the imperial court to restrict the scope of operations of this new institution strictly to the territory of the Habsburg dynasty in order to prevent capital flight and promote the development of Austrian industry in the country. For the Rothschilds, who have semicolons and partners across Europe, such restrictions can be easily avoided, but they are a straitjacket for a movable property bank that is looking to make its mark on the international stage and is desperate to mobilize resources to support its expansion into the wider world.

Isaac had to agree to join the new financial institution on the condition of a substantial reduction of its original capital of 230 million francs. At this point, however, the Pereire family was at the end of its offensive posture due to lack of sufficient funds.

Having taken control of the central bank, Rothschild then decided to launch a strategic counterattack against the well-established Pereire family on the issue of the Austrian Movable Property Credit Bank.

In September 1855, when the Pereire announced their intention to issue long-term bonds, Rothschild used his influence in the French Central Bank to delay and freeze the issuance of 120 million francs of CMA corporate bonds on the grounds of "easing the pressure on the capital markets", further reducing CMA's cash flow. After losing the opportunity to issue long-term bonds, it is difficult for Crédit Mobiliers to continue investing in huge land development projects. Pereire's offense was finally contained.[59]

At the same time, Rothschild encouraged scepticism within the French government about the large amount of capital that Kreditanstalt was putting into foreign markets, finally forcing Isaac to inform the Austrian government that Kreditanstalt could not participate in the newly created Union Credit Bank of Austria, which soon developed into the leading investment bank of the Austrian Empire and one of the largest financial institutions in continental Europe. In the case of the Austrian UniCredit Bank, the Pereire family failed completely.

---

[59] Ibid.

In 1857, as the economic crisis in Europe deepened, railway work suffered greatly, and several of the main lines in Pereire's hands fell into the red, while the lines in Rothschild's hands survived the crisis. The Bank of France has learned from this lesson that it is the "new" bank, headed by Pereire, and not the "old" bank, named Rothschild, that has the fatal flaw.

As railway construction in Europe increasingly transcends national borders, it is moving towards crossing multinational territories. The Rothschild Bank's "international" strengths came to the fore at this time, while the Caisse de Crédit Agricole lost out to the Rothschild Bank's European branches, which were in sync with each other, and after 1857, the Caisse de Crédit Agricole lost out to railroad financing.

After the outbreak of the financial crisis in 1857, the chattel banks became increasingly underfunded and the sources of cash dividends from the large number of listed companies that they had previously held dried up, but instead they needed massive funding from the chattel banks. In the midst of the plunge in asset prices, Pereire was unable to absorb the severe losses caused by the sale of these stocks, and the funds of the Movable Property Credit Bank were rapidly depleted.

Pereire's investment adventures also contributed to its eventual failure, and in 1854, France was awarded a concession for the construction and use of the Suez Canal. Thinking that the opening of the canal would make Marseille the first French port to the East, the Pereire brothers invested heavily in properties near Marseille, accounting for 52 million francs out of the 55 million francs invested in the same period. As a result, the Suez Canal was finally completed in 1869, and the huge sums of money were firmly invested in real estate projects in the Marseilles region, and the Crédit Mobilier became, in a funny way, a "real estate" credit bank.

In 1863, the Pereire brothers proposed to double the capital of the Crédit Mobilier, but the government rejected it. By the time Pereire finally got approval to expand its capital, it was too late, and the shares of Credit Agricole plunged to the brink of bankruptcy. The other financial institutions were reluctant to help, and in 1868 the Pereire had no choice but to seek help from the Bank of France, the "lender of last resort".

This time it finally hit the Rothschild family. As a condition, the Central Bank asked the Pereire brothers to resign and arranged for a former president of Banque Française to become the chairman of Credit

Agricole and preside over the reconstruction of the bank. The Crédit Mobilier has been in decline ever since. Ended his life in the Great Depression of the 1930s. The momentum of the Crédit Mobilier actually lasted only about five years from 1852 to 1857, when the crisis broke out.

Eugène Pereire, son of Isaac, became a central figure in the next generation of the Pereire family, founding the Transatlantic Bank in 1881, now one of the oldest private banks in France, and in 1909, Eugène's granddaughter married the Rothschilds, who eventually became in-laws.[60]

Crimean War

For more than two hundred years, two things the Rothschilds thought would affect their financial empire: war and revolution. Whether it is a revolution or a war, the warring parties are bound to make substantial financing in order to carry out organized violence. Wars and revolutions themselves can shock the original feudal aristocracy and the ruling order of the church, allowing the financial family to expand its influence over politics. The reconstruction period after a war or revolution also requires substantial financing, so that the effect of three birds with one stone can be achieved.

In March 1854, a war broke out that swept through the major European countries.

At first, signs of an impending war in Crimea did not attract the attention of the Rothschilds, and the battle for the "Holy Land" was the fuse of the war. The so-called "Holy Land issue" is the dispute between the French-backed Catholic Church and the Russian-dominated Orthodox Church over the jurisdiction of the churches in Jerusalem and Bethlehem. This was due to the rapid development of Russian power in the Near East from the second half of the 18th century onwards, with the aim of seizing or dividing the declining Ottoman Empire with the Great Powers, taking control of the Black Sea Straits and fulfilling Russia's long-standing aspiration to move southward out of the Mediterranean.

---

[60] http: //en.wikipedia.org/wiki/P%C3%A9reire_brothers

This creates a sharp conflict with Britain and France, which have significant political and economic interests in the Near East.

Any war is an earthquake in the international financial markets that will dramatically change the financial situation of each country and redraw the pattern of interests in the international financial markets. So the Catholics and the Orthodox fought, and the first ones to get angry were the international bankers.

Rothschild fell into passivity at the beginning of the war because of their over-reliance on information received from diplomatic sources. But St. Petersburg was not honest, and until June 1853 repeatedly promised the Rothschilds that there would be no war; in January 1854 the Western allies entered the Black Sea, and James was still unconcerned, and in February, when Bismarck got word that the Russian ambassador had been urgently recalled from Paris, he knew at once:

> *"I thought to myself, 'Who can be most alarmed by this news? My eyes fell on Rothschild. Sure enough, I just handed him the message to read, and his face instantly turned as white as a chalk. His first reaction was, 'If only I knew the news this morning'; his second was, 'Can you talk business with me tomorrow'."*

Lionel, the head of the Rothschilds in London, was also greatly surprised by Russia's move to start a war, already looking down on Russia in March 1854:

> *"A country that is already £800 million in debt should indeed think carefully before entering another war."*

The Crimean War, fought for three years, has put the Rothschild Bank public debt financing business back on top. As a result of the war, the military expenditures of each of the countries involved in the war far exceeded the revenues from taxation, and all countries were forced to issue debts on a large scale and flock to the public debt market.

The Rothschild Bank's situation, which had been dented by the Pereire family, changed immediately. No one can shake the Rothschild Bank's dominance in the international bond market, which they have held for centuries through their deliberate operations. A number of rivals, including the Crédit Mobilier, were unsuccessful in the contest over the issuance of the Crimean war bonds, while Rothschild's old foe, the Bank of Baring, took a dumb loss by betting on Russia, which was ultimately defeated in the vote. This war was fought and the Rothschild Bank basically had the whole cake to itself.

On the British side, the Government had originally scheduled to borrow money from the Bank of Baring. With Baring's money pressed against Russia, it was forced to watch as the Rothschild Bank chewed up the £16 million war loan.

Wartime France was so badly hit by the economy that Napoleon III rushed to stimulate it with a series of interest rate adjustments. The Rothschild French Bank and the Hottinguer family joined forces to strongly support fiscal stimulus in the government's move to rescue the economic crisis, leaving the Pereire out of the picture. So, when the French treasury was given a succession of Dafabetian war bonds in 1854 and 1855, the Rothschild Bank was naturally the first choice. It was only then that Pereire reacted and fought as hard as she could to get Napoleon III. And the French Minister of Finance told Napoleon III that the French domestic market was nearing capacity for war bonds, so France shifted most of its war bonds to London. The Rothschild Bank of London unpacked early and the French bond business fell into place. After all, Pereire couldn't beat Rothschild, who had already planned it, and watched as the French bank and the London bank ate the French war bond feast clean.

Pereire couldn't beat Rothschild in France and hurried to put his hand in Turkey to rob it of its war bonds. But the Rothschild family had taken the lead again and had already sent their agents to Constantinople. Turkey's war bonds also went to the Rothschild Bank of London, and in 1857 *The Times* said, "The National Bank of Turkey is on the verge of becoming another branch of the Rothschild Bank."

Austria was not directly involved in the Crimean War, but it was not idle either, expanding its forces and finally forcing Russia to withdraw from the Danube. Austria did not have time to revel in the fact that its finances were in serious crisis and its currency was falling by leaps and bounds. The Austrian finance minister sent an urgent plea for help to James: "Only you can save us before our currency becomes completely scrap paper".[61] James promised to join forces with other Rothschild branches to save Austria on the condition that the loan originally granted to Fould by the Austrian government would now go

---

[61] Niall Ferguson, *The House of Rothschild The World's Banker 1849–1999* Volume 2.

to the Rothschild Bank, so the duck that Fould had thought had arrived flew again.

The Prussian government's expenses, which had increased by 45 per cent during the war, had long been overburdened. With Bismarck at the helm, the Prussian war bonds all went to the Rothschild Frankfurt Bank. Meyer Karl Rothschild was also awarded the Prussian Red Eagle Medal for outstanding contributions to his country.

Between 1852 and 1855, public spending increased by 42% in Austria, 68% in England, 53% in France and 88% in Russia. The public debt depreciated by 15 per cent in the United Kingdom, 15 per cent in France, 24 per cent in Austria and 11 per cent in Prussia. As the funds for the war gradually became "anemic" and then "cut off", the war naturally could not be fought any longer. The Crimean War is finally over.

Rothschild Bank doesn't really care about winning or losing battles. By the late 1850s, the British, French, Turkish, Austrian and Prussian governments were all financed by one or more Rothschild banks. The Rothschild Bank had once again made old rivals and new rivals whole and extinct during the war, and its position as the lord of the jungle on government bonds could no longer be shaken.

Even in 1857, a year when all banks were unlikely to escape bankruptcy, no Rothschild bank lost money, and the biggest loss was nothing more than a reduction in profit.

Catholic Bankers: The Third Force

The banking family power in France prior to 1870 was roughly two camps of Jewish and Puritan bankers against each other. Among the Jewish banking families, the Rothschild family is the obvious leader. In the middle of the Puritan banking family system, the head was the Mirabeau family. The Catholic banking family did not suffer from religious persecution like the Puritans and Jewish bankers, which contributed to their lack of cohesion.

After the Franco-Prussian War of 1870, a third banking family, the Catholic banking family, was gradually formed in France. This group includes banking families such as Davillier, Lubersac, Demachy, Goudchaux, and Lehideux. However, the third force is actually a less stable force, and they soon split into two factions again. One faction of

Catholic bankers gradually formed an alliance with the Rothschild camp and supported the establishment of the Third Republic; the other was largely allied with the rising heavy industrial complex, whose leading families were Catholic, of which Schneider, the French steel magnate, was the leader. Of these three forces, the Rothschilds are in a distinctly superior position.

The evolution of gold power: from ownership to control

Both the Rothschilds and the Pereire have had strong ties to the government throughout France's history, but their ties to the French real economy have been relatively weak, with little interest in investing in the real economy other than the railways, which have invested a little more. There are two main reasons for this: first, because the demand for capital at the beginning of the industrial revolution was sufficient for France, which had relatively sufficient savings, and the ample supply of capital made the international bankers less profitable and therefore less motivated to compete; and second, because the demand for public debt for government and foreign wars was so great that the profits were both high and guaranteed, an investment in which the profits were both high and steady. In addition, projects in capital-scarce countries with significant rates of return and local government guarantees are also highly profitable and reliable investments. In such cases, the funds of international bankers do not in fact go directly into the domestic real economic cycle, but chase high profits internationally.

In terms of the banks' operating model, the French private banking model was adequate for the limited financing needs of the textile, metallurgical, transport and machinery industries in the early years of the rise of industrial capitalism in France. At the same time, French people who love to save are more conservative in their investment orientation, preferring to buy and sell stable and reliable government and corporate bonds, and are not particularly keen on risky investments like stocks. If they invest in industry, they tend to invest in private and family businesses and are less inclined to invest in the kind of large commercial institutions or companies, so large joint-stock banks have been slow to develop in France, similar to the UK.

However, this situation has changed profoundly with the construction of large-scale railway projects.

The peak period of railway construction in France was from 1830 to 1870, and the construction of railway projects often required large-scale capital operations, and such a scale of capital requirements were far beyond the capacity of the traditional private banking system. The private bank's investment is largely dependent on the savings of a single bank, a banking model that has encountered great challenges in the big industrial era, especially in the rise of railroad construction in the modern industrial system. In order to adapt the financial system to the large-scale financing needs of the late industrial revolution, it was necessary to establish new types of joint-stock investment banks, deposit banks, savings banks, as well as new types of financial institutions, such as a series of insurance companies, which, by pooling the savings of a large number of retail investors and then operating through investment banking, channelled these large amounts of capital into the industrial sectors of the real economy, where the demand for capital is particularly high, generating considerable returns.

Under the new joint-stock investment banking model, the role of the private banker has changed from that of a lender using its own funds to that of a manager mobilizing public funds, a process that is actually very beneficial to the private banker. Once upon a time, because private bankers used their own funds to lend money, private banks' financial control over the industry was glaring and lacked the secrecy to speak of. The new role of asset manager, as it operates on public funds, amplifies the control of social wealth while increasing the secrecy. In this model of asset management, where they do not disclose their identity and operate primarily from behind the scenes, this masterful arrangement of the financial capitalist system effectively insulates the public eye.

Behind this emerging array of financial institutions, the board of directors is essentially the same family of banks. BNP Paribas is a prime example of this.

From 1870 until the outbreak of World War II, France experienced the Third Republic, with the Jewish banking family, headed by the Rothschilds, being the main financial powerhouse in favour of the Third Republic, but the Puritan and Catholic banking families tending to oppose it. The Jewish banking family, headed by Rothschild, gained great wealth by controlling BNP Paribas, France's largest and most important joint-stock investment banking institution, which by the early 20th century had a decisive influence on the economic and political life of France.

By 1931, BNP Paribas, controlled by the Rothschild family, held shares in 357 listed companies in France, and family members and senior executives of the family bank controlled 180 directorships in 120 companies. This control is designed through very subtle financial capitalist techniques, such as the elaborate design of non-voting and multiple voting rights in equity, and the way original directors vote to co-opt new directors, all of which are effective means of achieving control of majority shareholder wealth by a very small number of special shareholders. Again, for example, a privileged shareholder has one vote per share of stock, but only $1/10^{th}$ of the votes per share of stock issued to the public, so operating ensures that the privileged shareholder has actual control over the appointment of the company's board of directors and the operation of the company.

To counteract the influence of the Paribas, the Puritan bankers set up their own joint-stock investment bank, the Union Parisienne, in 1904. From 1904 to 1919, the Puritan bankers combined various financial forces to fight against the Jewish banking powerhouse, with the Paribas at its core. Indeed, the struggle between the Puritan banking system and the Jewish banker system for political and economic power in France contributed in large part to the paralysis of the French political and economic system. In particular, from 1934 to 1938, the rivalry between these two power blocs reached white-hot proportions, leading to a slow recovery from the Great Depression, with the more serious consequence of France's rapid defeat in World War II in 1940.

Looking at the French listed companies, the total number of companies registered on the Paris Stock Exchange in 1936 was 1506. Some 600 of them are super-important companies with a stake in the country's livelihood, and there are also some 200 important unlisted companies, with some 800 heavyweights in the French economy. Of these, the Jewish banking family group controls more than 400, their competitors control more than 300, and only 100 or so are companies that are not controlled or under the control of other forces. In World War II, during the four years of the French occupation by Germany, the Jewish banking family was stripped of its assets, which also included control of listed companies. After the war, of course, all these powers were recovered by the victorious side, and the defeated Germany had to pay reparations with interest.

Including the two major banking families, 183 plutocrats controlled what was then France, the predecessor of the famous "200 families". In addition, the financial family has increased its penetration into politics and the press, and bankers who invest in the press or run their own newspapers abound. All this has had a profound impact on all areas of French political, economic and social life. In addition to pulling in the rich and powerful, financial giants have personally stepped up to the political arena, such as Achille Fould, who was Napoleon III's Minister of Finance. There are not a few banking family agents who have entered politics, such as Pompidou, the French Prime Minister appointed by President de Gaulle in 1962, who was the managing director of the Rothschild family's French bank, and Pompidou was French Prime Minister from 1962 to 1968 and President from 1969 to 1974.

After more than 200 years of evolution, the power of the Golden Power has taken root in France and is too deep to be shaken.

CHAPTER IV

The United States: The "Circle of the Power of Gold"

The most unique thing about American history is that it all started almost from a blank sheet of paper. People who had been deeply persecuted by religion flocked from Europe and elsewhere to this vast and sparsely populated new land, rich in resources, to start their own businesses from scratch. The United States does not have the primitive capital accumulation that has been accomplished in the days of commercial capitalism in England, France, the Netherlands, etc., nor does it have the home base of the infrastructure projects of towns, villages, ports, bridges, highways, etc., that have been created in continental Europe for thousands of years, a market that is almost never able to satisfy its appetite for capital and manpower in extremely high demand.

Three factors, extreme natural resource abundance, severe labour shortages and high capital scarcity, have come together to create a financial ecology that is very different from that of Europe. There is no suffocating feudal hierarchy, no bigoted madness of religious oppression, it is a heavenly paradise for international bankers. Here the Golden Power grows savagely, expands uncontrollably, grows thicker by the day, and shades the sky. From suppression to control, from resistance to acquiescence, from rejection to alliance, from cooperation to obedience, the regime has evolved from lawlessness under kingship to lawlessness under gold dictatorship.

Golden power is a good thing, it uses more temptation than coercion to achieve its ends, it is more concerned with stimulating one's inner desires than merely exerting pressure from the outside, and it emphasizes even-handedness of interest without deliberately distinguishing between enemy and foe.

Throughout the 19th century, a large number of international banking families grew up in the United States, the most dazzling of which were the Jewish international banking families: the Seligman, Belmont, Schiff, Kuhn, Loeb, Warburg, Speyer, Lehman, Goldman, Sachs. One notable feature that these families have in common is that they are all from Germany. If we say that 90 percent of the financial power on Wall Street today is in the hands of Jewish bankers, then these families are the source of their power. Understanding their ins and outs and their interpersonal relationships will enable us to make a basic judgement on the financial tsunami and other international financial developments that are taking place today.

Society is, after all, made up of many different circles of people; after all, each circle is linked by ubiquitous connections of people; after all, it is a circle of people of extraordinary energy.

Seligman: From small businessman to international banker

In the 1820s, the Seligman family, still operating in the Bavarian region of Germany, was the watchdog business of the Jewish banking family of currency exchange. Germany was not a unified country at that time, consisting of more than 30 small confederate states, which had their own monetary system, and it was very troublesome to use the different currencies carried by merchants from the south to the north.

Joseph Seligman, the young prodigy of the Seligman family, helped the adults play underhand at the bank when he was eight years old, and while collecting money he soon discovered that the price of coins varied from region to region. Young Joseph outgrew his years, starting to walk the streets at the age of twelve and gradually growing into a shrewd money changer. His main business was to help out-of-town merchants exchange the gold and silver coins they brought from other regions for local currency, and then sell the purchased foreign currency to local people who were going to travel or do business elsewhere, making a small difference in price. Through the currency exchange business, Joseph Jr. began to learn about the economic information and geography of the outside world, including the exchange relationship between currencies, and gradually developed a keen sense of business.

In the 1830s, Germany began the process of the Industrial Revolution, Bavaria's traditional craftsmen gradually lost their jobs under the impact of the Great Industrial Wave, and the development of local handicrafts became increasingly depressed, and more and more local Jews sailed across the sea to the new American continent to make a living.

In July 1837, at the age of 17, Joseph arrived in New York with $100 sewn into his underwear by his mother, which coincided with the Great Depression of 1837, and the young Joseph began his difficult journey to become an American. The stock crash and recession in New York made it difficult for Joseph to get a foothold there, and he had to walk all the way west to Pennsylvania before he finally landed. He started out as a cashier and made nothing more than $400 a year.

Joseph was a man who paid extreme attention to observing the details of life. While working as a cashier, the occasional rush of many farmers to the town's bazaar in their wagons to buy things caught his attention. He kept a detailed record of every item these farmers bought and their prices while keeping a watchful eye, and went home at night to analyze them carefully. Over the course of a year, he came up with his own business model in which customers would be willing to pay more for the "value-added service" of bringing the farmer the goods he needed to market to them, saving them the trouble of having to travel long distances. The idea was set, and Joseph immediately bought some mirrors, rings, knives, small jewelry, watches, and other small items of high value and light weight, loaded them into his backpack, and began walking on foot between the wilderness villages and towns of Pennsylvania, door to door, selling the goods. His business model proved to be a huge success, earning his first bucket of $500 in less than six months. He hastened to gather his relatives from his old German home, and several brothers began a business career together. Soon, the Seligman brothers teamed up again to open a grocery store of their own and started a sitter business. Longtime salesmanship has honed the Seligman brothers' reed-like tongue, and their famous saying about business is: "It's not business to sell what the customer needs, it's business to sell what the customer doesn't need."

By chance, Joseph met Simmons Grant, then serving in the 4th Infantry Division, at an early age. Grant's garrison at the time was near Seligman's grocery store, and Grant would often sneak up to Seligman's store to buy a few nice pieces of jewelry for his fiancée. Soon, Joseph and Grant became fast friends without words. Who would have thought that this Grant would be General Grant, later the famous

American Civil War general and later the 18th President of the United States.[62]

Joseph's Grocery has been in business for the past several years and has begun to involve simple banking basics, such as taking credit against a customer's credit, buying and selling a few outstanding notes, and even taking some deposits from customers and opening an account for them to pay for the goods.

Joseph was a man who liked to ponder, and in the course of running a grocery store, he suddenly realized that there was a huge difference between buying and selling goods and buying and selling money. In the act of buying and selling goods, a profit is made only when the grocery store is open and the goods can be sold; conversely, if the goods are not sold, they are in a state of idleness that takes up capital, or even in a state of debt. But money is different, money is always active 24 hours a day, and its buying and selling transactions have nothing to do with store opening hours. Because of the interest generated, once the money starts working, it is 24 hours a day, 7 days a week, 365 days a year, without holidays, without rest and without interruption, tireless and never-ending "autonomous perpetual motion". Joseph finally came to the realization that money is the most wonderful commodity that can create more wealth faster.

After 15 years of accumulation, the Seligman brothers have some savings, and the future direction is the subject of debate. After realizing the "money theory", Joseph argued strongly for a move into banking. So the brothers packed up their stops and set out for New York to join a profession that all Jews aspire to – the financial industry. At this point, the grocery store owners themselves could not have predicted that in just over a decade they would be world-class international bankers, profoundly affecting the fiscal and foreign policy of the United States of America.

August Belmont's "Federal Reserve"

Arriving in New York at the same time as Seligman was another figure who has made his name in the history books, August Belmont.

---

[62] Stephen Birmingham, *"Our Crowd" – The Great Jewish Families of New York*, p. 58.

Belmont was also Jewish, three years older than Joseph Seligman, and his life was full of legend.

At the age of 13, Belmont went to Frankfurt as a free apprentice for the Rothschild Bank. He was ill-tempered, rude and debauched, but a gifted financial wizard. Belmont, who first joined the Rothschild Bank as a sweeper, soon became active in proposing various jobs, demonstrating a remarkable talent, and was soon chartered to attend important meetings that only partners could attend. Unfortunately, Belmont, with his wild and completely aristocratic demeanor, often made the Rothschild face unmistakable in public. The Rothschild family, with a keen eye for talent, transferred the young Belmont to Naples, Italy, for management. Belmont was stationed in Havana, Cuba, when he was 21, and soon came to New York to develop as an American agent for the Rothschild family.[63]

With the rapid economic development and dramatic growth of transatlantic trade, New York quickly rose to become the largest trade center in the United States, with wheat, flour, and cotton from the West pouring into New York for export to Europe, and European industrial goods entering the U.S. market in large numbers through here. The unprecedented boom in business and trade has created a huge demand for financial services in credit, financing, discounting, clearing, insurance, foreign exchange, etc. In New York, bills of exchange from both sides of the Atlantic are centrally discounted, lines of credit are intensively traded, and large amounts of capital flow frequently. The New York Stock Exchange, established in 1792, is even older than the London Stock Exchange, where heavyweight American companies are listed and hundreds of millions of dollars of stock change hands each year. All of this drove the financial industry to soar and New York soon became the third largest central city after Boston and Philadelphia.

Unlike the rest of New England, as an emerging city, New York does not have the rigidity and rigidity of the traditional New England bigwigs like Boston, Philadelphia and Charleston. The traditional families did not have a clear advantage in this young city. The mainstream economies of Boston and Philadelphia are essentially monopolized by the older big families, with a tight and stodgy style.

---

[63] Katz, Irving, *August Belmont; a political biography*. New York and London: Columbia University Press (1968).

Two axes, such as the Capote Lowell Lawrence family group in Boston, which controlled the textile industry primarily through finance, and the Lee Higginson Jackson family, which controlled the money market, essentially controlled the economy of the Boston area. Philadelphia, on the other hand, had several large national commercial banks, monopolized by the Hamilton, Morris and Welling families. This trio's control over the U.S. commercial banking system continues to this day.

And in young and vibrant New York, the traditional family does not have a clear advantage. An unprecedented opportunity for finance emerged in New York, the historical source of the many Jewish bankers who came ashore and laid the foundations from which they grew into a decisive financial force in the United States.

Belmont's arrival in New York also coincided with the onset of the Great Depression in the United States in 1837. But Belmont is not on the same starting line as Seligman, who is backed by the vast financial resources of the European Rothschild family. Belmont arrived in New York and shocked the financial world with one fell swoop. At the age of 24, Belmont was sweeping the New York stock market in a frenzy of shorted bonds and stocks. And while a large number of New York's local banks were on the verge of insolvency, Belmont brought them back from the dead with a massive injection of money.[64] After the closure of the Second Bank of the United States by President Jackson in 1836, the private Central Bank of the United States, under the control of the Rothschild family, was again abolished. At this time in the financial crisis, the United States no longer has a "lender of last resort" to save the banking system on the verge of failure, and the emergence of Belmont, in fact, played the role of the central bank to save the financial system, 24-year-old Belmont actually plays a similar function to the Federal Reserve today. In fact, the powerful Rothschild financial empire behind him is the "remote Federal Reserve" that really controls the credit and money flow in the United States.

New York's High Society

Almost overnight, Belmont became a major figure in New York. The magnitude of the funds he was able to mobilize shocked not only

---

[64] Stephen Birmingham, *"Our Crowd"* – *The Great Jewish Families of New York*, P37.

the New York financial community, but also the U.S. government. Belmont immediately became a rising star in New York, appearing at various social events. He speaks both fluent Spanish and standard Italian, as well as French with an odd accent. New York, then considered by Europeans to be rude and vulgar, had not yet evolved a noble taste in life or an aristocratic style, and was not quite sure of the difference between the various accents, which immediately surprised Belmont.

The New York of his time was at a stage when the rich were desperate to find their own niche, and class divisions were forming in the various strata of society. New Yorkers are beginning to focus on their manners, dress, social circles and upper-class pieheads. There are various etiquette classes, such as teaching not to make noise when drinking soup, not to pick your nose in public, not to stare at strangers, not to spit in the open, etc.

It's important to combat spitting. After seeing a play in a New York theater, the woman sitting in the front row often finds the back of her skirt muddled with spit from the back seat. European travelers to New York were simply horrified by the experience, not realizing that New York was a complete barren land and cultural desert with such a chaotic social order and poor manners. New York's high society also laments this.

At this point, Belmont, a European family with a strong Rothschild influence, made a splendid appearance. He was immediately regarded as a model by high society, and his manner of speech, his conduct, and even his accent became the object of a race to emulate by high society men.

Belmont also led the way in New York's social ethos, such as the "rambunctious, indifferent" social attitude he coined, which was widely emulated in New York's upper class. If the dinner invitation is at 7:00, Belmont rarely shows up before 9:00. According to Belmont's aristocratic attitude, showing up to an appointment on time is nothing more than a courtesy to the rude man.

Belmont often had a sensational effect in introducing European aristocratic customs, and duels were his forte, raising popularity and social hierarchy at breakneck speed. Belmont pays special attention to selecting opponents for the duel, who must be from noble families. Belmont once picked the son of the Hayward family of Charleston to challenge, because Hayward had gossiped about Belmont's origins while talking to his girlfriend in a restaurant, and he implied that Belmont was Jewish, which angered Belmont. No one died in the duel – Belmont took a shot to the thigh, but since the dueling opponents were descendants of the Hayward family, the shot was worth the damage. His glowing image in American high society was instantly established, and with the media clamor and curiosity of public opinion, Belmont was quick to brand himself as a perfect aristocrat.

Belmont is doing big and red-hot business in New York. In 1844, just seven years after his arrival in the United States, Belmont was appointed by the United States Government as Minister to Austria. The U.S. government looks at Belmont's origins with the Rothschild Bank and also wants to be closer to the source of capital.

The fact that Belmont was so influential at such a young age certainly aroused great curiosity among all classes of New Yorkers, especially the upper class. Belmont himself was extremely reluctant to talk about his origins and past experiences, so rumors circulated in the upper social circles that he was so favored by the Rothschilds that he might be a bastard son of the Rothschild family.

Belmont, however, in the eyes of the true aristocracy, was nothing more than a newly rich money-burning thug. Fashionable social circles were not upper class, and the real top aristocracy in America was the colonial era lords of the great estates, to whom the Dutch West India Company, the earliest colonial institution in the United States, directly subdivided land on both sides of the Hudson River near New York between 1629 and 1640. This system of feudalism was in a sense similar to the feudal lordship system in Europe, where the family of the lord of a large estate had permanent title to the land and could set up its own courts and administrative bodies to perform certain governmental functions. The person who leases the land will provide servitude and pay taxes to the lord. The American colonial era did not have a kingdom system, no emperor or king. This system of grand manor lordship produced some of the earliest aristocrats in the United States, who to this day remain the oldest large family in the country. The famous heavyweight lords of New York at the time, including the early Vane, Rossrell, Astor and later Kirst and Morris, were among the heaviest families in America.[65]

---

[65] Ibid, p. 74.

Although behind Belmont stood Rothschild, a wealthy man, the little Bey, who was a new nobleman, still looked short of heart and ashamed of himself when he stood in front of these nobles who were the lords of the great manor. These big families hold gatherings of several hundred people in top hotels every year, and an invitation is the identity card of the real "top people". Belmont had never been invited, and he was furious about it. At one point he broke right into the invitation committee and threatened, "I have investigated all your people's accounts and I can tell you with certainty that either I get an invitation to your party this year, or I will make you all disgraced once the party is over." Belmont used a near-threatening tactic to force his way into the big family gathering. Eventually he received the invitation as he wished. But when he went to the so-called gathering place in all his pomp, he surprisingly found no one – he became the only guest invited.

Despite the considerable influence Wall Street bankers have had, it still doesn't work when it comes to integrating into America's top social circles. The matter was so exciting to Belmont that he thought left and right and decided to enter the core family circle through intermarriage. Belmont carefully selected her fiancée, as one picks stocks, wine, or dueling opponents, after rigorous consideration and careful screening of family power and religious background, and finally chose Caroline Perry as her fiancée.

The Perry family itself is not particularly wealthy, but definitely counts as a socialite. What the Perry family was able to bring him was a social status that money could not buy. Caroline's father was a hero of the Mexican War and the famous General Perry who later opened Japan's doors and forced it to sign an unequal treaty. Her uncle was a famous general in the American-British War of 1812. This intermarriage greatly increased Belmont's social status, and Belmont's social status was finally confirmed when the New York core family could no longer laugh at the fact that he was just a rich dirtbag.

The king of national debt, Seligman

> *"Seligman's role in the sale of national debt was even equivalent to the U.S. Army of the North blocking the attack of Southern General Lee at Gettysburg."*[66]
> —W.E. Dudd, historian and United States Ambassador to Nazi Germany

As the head of the Seligman family, Joseph was a perfectionist, his every move, every word, was precisely in place. He has no patience for any waste of time, and is full of ideas in work and life details. Before doing everything, he will carefully consider the order of work, according to the degree of difficulty, time, and intersection, and arrange it precisely. He is able to process many different information and ideas simultaneously and constructs complex plans and concepts in his brain in the form of overpasses. While ensuring a high degree of efficiency and planning in the diverse handling of complex events, he was also able to make the events as a whole uninterrupted and independent of each other. This overpass type of information processing capability is common to many successful people.

Joseph was impetuous in nature, full of energy, physically strong as a bull, and never knew weariness. His demeanor is so intimidating, so authoritative and controlling.

As the Seligman brothers prepared to enter the American banking industry, the United States was in the "age of free banking". From 1837 to 1862, with the abolition of the privately owned central bank, the Second Bank of the United States, a free and chaotic banking era began in the United States where the public was free to apply to open a bank. It seemed that everyone in New York at the time could call themselves a banker and the only requirement was to dress like one.

Having been in the banking industry since 1852, Seligman has been in the traditionally conservative business. At that time, the U.S. railroad industry was booming like never before, the West was in full swing, and railroad and Western concept stock prices were soaring. Speculators pledged these stocks to apply for new loans, which in turn were used to buy stocks, a process that went back and forth, causing the entire New York stock market to continue to rise wildly. At the same

---

[66] Bertram Korn, *American Jewry and the Civil War*, p. 161.

time, the British side eased up on silver, with New York's commercial banks following suit, and in an environment of loose interest rates, money was at hand, consumers were squandering, markets were booming, and investors' enthusiasm for risk-taking was thoroughly aroused.

At that time, New York was filled with the atmosphere of rich families, women climbing the dress luxury, private parties to compete with the class, mansions and mansions, the whole social life is full of extravagance, climbing and showing off. The illusion of bubble wealth generated in the stock market has made New Yorkers forget about the word risk long ago. Shares of railroads on the stock market have risen back-to-back, and even many that are still stuck on the drawing board have seen their shares soar wildly from 25 cents on Monday to $4,000 a share over the weekend. Of course, as with any crazy situation where a bubble boom is unsustainable, all bubbles must end in bursting. With a keen sense of the market before the bubble burst, Seligman sold off all his stocks in time, leaving only a handful of bonds. When the sudden stock market crash of 1857 came crashing down, a large number of New York commercial banks collapsed in an instant, the only one that didn't suffer much damage was Seligman's bank.

However, the recession of 1857 came and went fast. As a result of the discovery of a large gold mine in California in 1858, $8 million worth of gold arrived in New York, equal to the total amount of gold held before the New York banking crisis. Two months later, gold ownership in New York rose to $28 million. Before the crisis, Rothschild lent a total of $10 million to the U.S. market through Belmont, and when he tightened lending, it caused the financial markets to crash. And just a year later, thanks to the influx of gold, the Rothschild family's $10 million loan was easily paid off in one day.[67]

After the outbreak of the Civil War between the North and South, the Seligman family began dealing with the federal government, primarily taking on contracts for government uniforms. At the time, the U.S. government was paying for the Lincoln Greenback, a bond currency issued by the U.S. government itself with an interest rate of 5 percent that could be used directly for circulation. Since the Lincoln Greenback was not backed by gold, and the North had suffered

---

[67] Niall Ferguson, *The House of Rothschild*.

successive defeats in the early days of the war, many were reluctant to accept it. As the scale of the war grew and the U.S. government's circulation of Lincoln Greenbacks grew, Seligman received more and more Lincoln Greenbacks. But he often ran into trouble when he paid various expenses in Lincoln Greenbacks during production. Seligman began to get his head around the idea that he planned to sell Lincoln Greenbacks as bonds in the European market to hedge his gold.

At the time, yields on the European market for the Lincoln Greenback were as high as 7.3 percent, and such high yields led to a widespread perception of a very unstable government situation in the North, with an uncertain battlefield. Seligman mobilized all the contacts he could muster in the European market to help him sell Lincoln Greenbacks. Sales were not very large at first, and then as the military situation in the north gradually stabilized, sales of greenbacks rose. Seligman further promoted greenbacks in Frankfurt, Munich, Berlin, Amsterdam, Paris, London, and other major European markets, and the more the greenbacks sold the more amazing they became the later in the war. As Northern bond holdings rise and the battleground becomes increasingly favorable to the North, European markets are increasingly sympathetic and supportive of the North. After all, no one wants Northern bonds to become scrap paper. Seligman inadvertently became the U.S. government's most powerful diplomatic activist in Europe.

Between February 1862 and June 1864, the United States issued $510 million in Lincoln Greenbacks and a portion of its national debt, of which $25 million was sold overseas, most of which Seligman alone underwrote and contributed to the remainder of the sales. American historians have argued that Seligman was instrumental in the sale of the U.S. national debt and the Lincoln Greenback overseas, even to the extent that the Army of the North held off the attack of Southern General Lee at Gettysburg. In fact, regardless of Europe and the United States, the financial mobilization capacity in all wars is equivalent to the supply of food and grass in ancient wars, which to a large extent determines the warfare capacity of the warring parties. It is a truism that war is always fought with money and food.

So far, Seligman has only been in banking for 12 years from being a grocery store owner! It is said to have created a miracle in the history of international finance. However, Seligman was greatly stimulated during this period, and he witnessed the energy of Rothschild and other heavyweight European Jewish banking families calling the shots in the financial markets and political arena, creating a strong urge to become an international banker. He dreamed of building a financial empire as large as the Rothschilds'.

In 1865 the U.S. government was ready to issue another $400 million in Treasuries, and Seligman had become one of the leading Jewish bankers on Wall Street, forming an underwriting group of the emerging Jewish banking family that had subsequently immigrated from Germany to New York, ready to underwrite $50 million of it, an astronomical figure for Wall Street at the time. For one reason or another, without an agreement with the U.S. government on the underwriting mission, Seligman went it alone to underwrite the national debt, and they ended up selling a record $60 million!

Seligmanton then became a legend on Wall Street, and his reputation in Washington was skyrocketing. While this war accomplished Seligman, it also greatly weakened Belmont's position. President Lincoln had pinned all his bond sales hopes on Belmont, but the Rothschilds were more than happy to see the United States partitioned for profit, so they pressed national bond underwriting discounts so hard that Lincoln turned to the unknown Seligman in the international financial markets. As a result, Belmont's influence in Washington took a big hit.

A smug Joseph was ready to begin implementing his great strategy. Just as General Lee of the South surrendered, Joseph brought his brothers together and began to form the Seligman International Banking Network. His plan is basically a rehash of what the Rothschild family did over 60 years ago. Seligman is ready to build a network of banks centered on the American continent, radiating across Europe. Each brother was sent to a European city; William Seligman, who loved good wine and food, was sent to Paris; Henry Seligman, who had been in Germany the longest, was ordered to Frankfurt; and Ithaca Seligman, the first of the Seligman brothers to meet President Lincoln, was sent to London. Before his departure, Joseph Thousand exhorted him to make every effort to meet Baron Rothschild in order to establish direct business relations. The Joseph of this time, though ambitious and battle-hardened, was still hovering outside the circle of European international bankers.

Seligman shakes Finance Minister

Despite the rapid economic growth and rise of wealthy families after the war, the financial situation of the U.S. government was not good; in 1866, only about $100 million remained in the U.S. treasury, and the public debt had ballooned rapidly to $3 billion during the war. The U.S. Treasury is prepared to issue 10 to 40 years of long-term Treasury debt to pay off short-term debt as the economy is rebuilt. Seligman, a wartime national bond sales star, also took on a large chunk of business in the issuance of long bonds.

Seligman had a good relationship with all three Secretaries of the Treasury during Lincoln's presidency, and President Grant, who took office in 1869, was a close friend of Joseph Seligman's when he opened a grocery store in Pennsylvania. President Grant even spoke privately to Seligman and asked him if he would be willing to take the position of U.S. Treasury Secretary. Joseph, though not in a position to question his ability, was reluctant to make an appearance and politely declined President Grant's invitation. Unexpectedly, George Potwell, the new treasurer appointed by President Grant, later became Joseph's counterpart. Their relationship started out well, with a joint plan and consensus on the Treasury Department, especially the national debt rollover, currency stability, and building the U.S. government's credit abroad. Two of the areas where consensus is critical are, the first being the resumption of the metal money system in the United States and the end of the Lincoln Greenback, and the second being that the war is over, the political situation is stable, and the interest rate on U.S. government bonds is too high at 6 percent.

Note that Joseph, at this time, was not in a position to discuss monetary and fiscal policy with the Treasury Secretary, which shows the depth of Joseph's influence on the U.S. government. For example, the pricing of 6% interest on the national debt, involving more than $3 billion in the price of the huge bond market, the Seligman family as the rule makers of the game, but also a big player in the bond market, in which the conflict of interest is obvious, but unhindered, such a situation has actually continued to this day.

The entire U.S. bond market has to listen carefully for every judgment and clarification the Seligman family makes, because every change in basis points in the massive bond market means success or failure of the business. The Seligman family and the Treasurer reached a consensus that interest on the U.S. Treasury should be set at 5 percent.[68]

But when Boutwell reported the bond issue plan to Congress, the interest was no longer 5 percent as the two men had agreed, but was adjusted to 4.5 percent. Joseph was so outraged that Boutwell, without prior notice to him, lowered the interest rate to 4.5 per cent, a difference of 50 basis points. A furious Joseph strode straight to Boutwell's office in loud protest, arguing that the interest rate was too low and had fallen too quickly, stressing that such a low rate would not sell in the European market. As an underwriter, the higher the interest rate on Treasuries is set, the easier it is to sell, and the better the underwriting fee, the 4.5% interest rate on Treasuries greatly increases the difficulty of selling and reduces the profit margin of the Seligman family, no wonder he is so angry. However, Boutwell is looking at it from the standpoint of the US government, and a 50 basis point drop would significantly reduce government spending, indirectly reducing the tax burden on the entire population and benefitting the nation. As Treasury Secretary, he also had absolutely no obligation to consult with Wall Street bankers in advance. Theoretical to theoretical, Boutwell violated the "hidden rules" laid down by international bankers.

Don't forget, whoever holds the channel of credit and capital flows in the world financial markets is the real game changer! Channel is king in the financial market is even more bloody truth. Joseph, as a broker, dared to storm the U.S. Treasury Secretary's office to make a fuss, which is simply unbelievable to the Chinese, but in the West, where golden power reigns supreme, it's actually normal. Wall Street sets the course, Washington implements the policy, it did in the past and it still does.

Joseph insisted that such a low interest rate on Treasuries would not only not sell in the European market, but would not sell anywhere in the world. But Boutwell's attitude was unshakable, and every 50 basis points saved on the $3 billion national debt was $15 million in government spending, considering that at the time the entire U.S. Treasury was a mere $100 million! Boutwell said coldly, "I've decided

---

[68] Stephen Birmingham, *"Our Crowd" – The Great Jewish Families of New York*, p. 119.

that 4.5 percent interest is very appropriate." Joseph was furious beyond measure and told Boutwell bluntly, "You are a fool, very foolish!"

In support of his argument, Joseph immediately wrote to his brother Henry in Frankfurt, asking him to inquire whether the German bankers were willing to accept Boutwell's offer, while at the same time he ordered another brother, William, in Paris, to find out the reaction of the Paris financial markets. It turned out that the reaction of the Marlette, Mirabeau, and Hottinguer families in Paris was exactly the same as that of Joseph, and that the sale of Boutwell's low-yielding Treasuries was unlikely to be successful in European issuance, with 5% being the bottom line.

But Boutwell still stands by his views and refuses to concede to the international bankers. Joseph, having reached a consensus with the European international bankers, was also adamant that he would not, and began lobbying MPs in an attempt to get them to come forward to persuade Boutwell to stop his "absurd" practices. As a result, Boutwell was enraged. He protested that Joseph had no mandate to interfere in governmental affairs, much less to directly interfere in congressional decisions, and soon the animosity between the two men became public. It is clear that whoever controls access to international financial markets can hold governments to ransom and even confront them directly.

At the time of the stalemate between the two sides, it was the U.S. Congress that compromised, and on July 14, 1870, and January 12, 1871, Congress authorized two issues of national debt for a total of $1.5 billion. The interest rate on this issue is somewhat biased towards Boutwell's scheme, with only 200 million of the 1.5 billion being issued at a rate of 5 percent, which is a saving grace for the Seligman family, and the rest of the interest rate even lower than the 4.5 percent offered by Boutwell, which is only 3.5 percent. This left Joseph traumatized and very depressed, and he felt taken advantage of. In fact, Boutwell's main purpose in seeking Joseph's cooperation was to use Joseph's financial expertise to help him devise a plan, and he ended up making adjustments only to the interest rate at which the bonds would be issued, while still extending Joseph's plan for the rest. As compensation, the Seligman family should get the $200 million bond underwriting business at 5 percent interest, and market participants thought so, as Wall Street's numerous bond underwriters flocked to find Joseph asking to be a distributor.

It did not occur to anyone that the U.S. Treasury Department had given the Seligman family an underwriting credit of only 100 million for 5 percent of their treasury bonds, less than half the 200 million they had hoped for, and in March 1871, William Seligman of Paris, in a letter to a friend, exasperatedly said:

> "I was completely shocked last night by the contents of the telegram that Boutwell had appointed agents in Europe to underwrite U.S. bonds, and in the list of these companies, Seligman was not even among the underwriters. It is the complete opposite of what we believe, that in the present case we are completely played by the government, and we do not know what has caused such neglect of the fact of our existence, and such injustice in this treatment, whether it is because Boutwell has a personal grudge against us, or a lack of confidence in us, or some conspiratorial trickery on the part of the competitors?"[69]

Treasurer Boutwell was also weighing the pros and cons, and after some thought, he decided to let the Seligman family into the underwriting group, but only as ordinary members, without any special treatment. With this "humiliation", the Seligman family concluded that the sale of the national debt would surely fail. Thanks to his deep connections in the international bankers' circle, his "assertion" was fulfilled and the overall bond sales were extremely poor. In the end, Boutwell even had to sell bonds that were not sold outright. This attempt to bypass the financial channels that international bankers so painstakingly operate has been met with a collective boycott by international bankers in the markets, and most of the bonds simply cannot be sold. In desperation, Boutwell had to invite the Seligman family to join two underwriting syndicates in London and New York. The bonds are selling well. Finally, President Grant was pleased to announce that this bond issue established the establishment of U.S. credit abroad.

Seligman: America's Rothschild

During the War of the North and South, William Seligman, who had been seated in Paris, had tried to establish contact with the

---

[69] Ibid, p. 120.

Rothschild Paris Bank, and Joseph himself had traveled to London to try to reach the Rothschild family, but the Rothschild family had kept aloof, and in 1874 Joseph applied to President Grant's new Secretary of the Treasury, Benjamin Brestow, to underwrite a new tranche of national debt issues worth $25 million. Since his predecessor Boutwell's ill-fated issuance of Treasuries, Brestow wanted a strong underwriting group to undertake the issue, and he strongly hinted to Joseph that he wanted the Rothschilds to hang the underwriting group.

However, Joseph had his own considerations and he himself wanted to be another Rothschild. He suppressed his temper and asked politely in return, what was the point of the Rothschilds entering the underwriting corps? He was prompting the Civil War when the Rothschild family refused to assist in the sale of Northern bonds. However, 10 years after the end of the war, the wartime "bad luck" of the Rothschild family was fading in people's minds, and Brestow was still pushing for Rothschild to enter the underwriting regiment.

In desperation, Joseph had to write to his brother: "Now the President and Mr. Brestow are very anxious and very anxious that we do this (national debt) underwriting with the Rothschild family. As they say, if united, no one can compete with a (powerful) combination like ours. But I fear that the arrogant, arrogant Rothschild family will not see us as equal partners." Joseph's concerns were also true at the time. Although the United States was growing rapidly and he had become the best investment banker on Wall Street, Joseph felt short of breath in the face of Rothschild, the boss of international finance.

Rothschild, the hegemon of the international financial industry, has an unwritten practice of excluding Roche institutions from any business that cannot be dominated by them. Treasury Secretary Brestow got in direct contact with the Rothschild family, and the Rothschild family's response was as simple as asking the Rothschild family to do the lead underwriting, so they'd get 5/8 of the share, and then Seligman and some other supposedly reliable bank, could take the remaining 3/8.

When Joseph heard the news, he was a little angry, obviously his own hand in the business, the Rothschild family has not yet established an inch of success, come up to take the lead, how can the world have such a reason! He immediately went to bargain with the Rothschild family. Joseph offered to consider the Rothschild offer if he could add Seligman's name to all the advertisements underwritten, along with Rothschild's name. After all, appearing with Rothschild's name on the underwriting group's advertisements marked the official entry of the Seligman family into the inner circle of international bankers, with great strategic significance, with less money coming second.

Rothschild's answer was simple: no. The Rothschild family didn't even think about advertising, but now that Seligman has brought it up, the issue needs to be made clear. There is no room for manoeuvre in the Rothschild family's attitude, the Seligman family name cannot appear in the advertisement, not at all. At this point Joseph was both exasperated and nervous, and his letter to his brother Ithaca in London said:

> *"If by next week the Rothschilds do not accept that our name is advertised alongside theirs, that is when we are going to escalate the issue and put pressure on the Rothschilds. Because I don't believe that Brestow can ignore us and give such a large loan only to the Rothschilds. While the Rothschilds were able to overtake us in the bid, we could be used by the U.S. government, and the Rothschilds could not."*

Weighing the pros and cons, Joseph thought twice about it and thought that the branding effect and potential commercial value that would be generated if Selligman's name could be juxtaposed with the Rothschilds' name from a reputational standpoint would be so great that it seemed worth a fight. But still, he was heartbroken, hoping to get a little more share. So he made a new offer again, pleading with the Rothschild family if he could get a little more than 2/8, say within a range like 2/8 and 3/8, which is 31.25% to be specific. Such a motherly pestering made the Rothschilds very impatient, and replied that Joseph could, if he wished, take a 28% share of the issue and put their name on the ad, which of course was after the Rothschilds.

After much deliberation, Joseph finally compromised. In his letter to Ithaca, he said,

> *"So far we've been able to at least come out to bid with the Rothschilds, and even though our 28 percent share is a bit small, I've decided to agree."*

It was with such a condition that Ithaca Seligman of London, as the representative of the Seligman family, went to call on Rothschild with awe and nervousness. Ithaca has seen the big world, as far back as 10 years ago, in 1864, when he was a guest of President Abraham Lincoln of the United States. But his mood at this time was more tense and complex when he saw Rothschild than when he saw President

Lincoln. The Baron Rothschild that Ithaca was to see was Lionel Rothschild. He is also a stubborn man who has been in the British Parliament for eight years but has refused to take the oath. Because in taking his oath, he insisted on using the Old Testament and never the New Testament Bible, a practice that went against the tradition of the British Parliament and created a great controversy in the British Parliament. The result of the stalemate between the two sides is that Lionel has been a member of the British House of Assembly for 15 years without saying a word. Lionel's strong character is evident.

Ithaca visited Lionel on a Saturday. According to the kosher rules, no work is allowed on Saturdays. Lionel told the visiting Ithaca, "I am a better Jew than you. Because you have business on Saturday, I don't do business on Saturday." It was Lionel's way of expressing levity. Ithaca looked around the room, and when he saw the pile of papers on Lionel's desk, he replied, "Your Highness the Baron, I think you do more business on this Saturday day than I do in a week." The master moves, until the point.

In a letter to Joseph that evening, Ithaca said that the old Rothschild had been relatively friendly and that the relationship could have been brought closer if he had been willing. Now Ithaca has finally broken the Rothschild ice and entered the core circle of international bankers. When Joseph received this news, he wrote a three-page letter in response, praising the Rothschild family in all their glory. He told Ithaca to make sure Lionel read the letter. In the letter, Joseph throws a half-covered embroidered ball at the Rothschild family, probing that the Rothschild family would be stronger if they worked with themselves in New York than with someone like Belmont. He strongly recommended himself as far superior to Belmont in all areas of ability and talent.

The Seligman family also achieved an unexpected effect after joining hands with the Rothschilds, which was met with great spiritual satisfaction. In his letter to Ithaca, he writes,

> "This time the Morgan and Zogsol families showed great jealousy, on the one hand because we got the deal, and on the other because our association with the Rothschilds made them visibly jealous."

In the fall of 1874, Lionel invited Ithaca Seligman to his office to deliver the news that $55 million in U.S. Treasuries were about to go on sale, and the Rothschild family suggested that the underwriting group should be formed by the three banking families of Rothschild,

Morgan and Seligman. It was also the first time that Belmont took the stage as both a Rothschild and a joint agent of the two Seligman banks. Ithaca agreed without hesitation, which meant that Seligman was henceforth officially among the most powerful financial circles in the world.

At this time, a large alliance of four international banking families – Rothschild, Seligman, Belmont and Morgan – was formed in New York and Europe. This alliance was so successful and so strong that around 1880, the whole of Wall Street was complaining that these bankers in London, Germany basically had a monopoly on the sale of bonds throughout the United States in Europe. Of course, they do have an almost total monopoly on US bond sales in Europe. This is when Seligman began to be known as the "Rothschild of America".

In 1877, Wall Street bankers came to Washington to discuss the abolition of the Lincoln Greenback with Treasury Secretary Sherman, with Joseph and Belmont as the main players. Sherman asked the two to each come up with a plan on how to help the government balance its budget and roll over government debt. The two high men then made their respective recommendations, unanimously advocating the eventual abolition of the Lincoln Greenback.

A week later, Sherman sent a message to Joseph, praising his plan as excellent and the most sophisticated and practical, to be adopted by the government. The heart of this plan is to build a 40% gold reserve for the Lincoln Greenbacks and use the gold coins to pay the interest on the Lincoln Greenbacks. This scheme effectively locked the Lincoln Greenback issue with gold, essentially limiting the government's power to issue money without making a big deal out of it, a clever design. The currency was pegged to gold, which was firmly held by the Rothschilds. The central banks of the countries of the world that have implemented the gold standard are not the final monetary authority, but the Rothschild family, which holds the world's gold minerals, transactions and flows, is their real backer. Gold as a currency has a natural advantage, how to break the monopoly of gold is the crux of the matter.

On 2 July 1881, the twentieth President of the United States, Garfield, who had just taken office, was assassinated in Washington, D.C., and was taken to the White House for treatment, where his condition stabilized for a time; on 6 September, he was taken to Seligman's villa in New Jersey for "fresh air" in order to "escape the heat", and his condition deteriorated; on 19 September, at 10:35 a.m.,

President Garfield died at Seligman's villa, where he stayed for some 13 days.[70]

It is an extremely rare and dubious piece of history that the assassinated U.S. President Garfield did not die in a hospital, nor in the White House, but finally in the home of Seligman. The President of the United States generally should not, and will not, go to a private home for medical treatment; he either stays in a hospital or in the White House, especially in the event of an assassination of the President, where safety is the first priority. This should be an "unconventional" arrangement. President Garfield, like President Jackson, is a staunch opponent of the private central banking system in the United States, while Seligman and other international banking families are clearly the most powerful advocates of private central banking.

Seligman: the true "father of Panama"

After Joseph Seligman's death, his brother Jesse Seligman became the new head of the family bank. With the opening of the Suez Canal in 1869, the idea of connecting the two continents by canal became a reality. A concept of great strategic value ensued – the creation of a Panama Canal in Panama in the Caribbean, linking the Atlantic and Pacific Oceans, which would significantly reduce the distance and time of transportation from the Pacific to the East Coast of the United States. There is no doubt that this vision has great strategic value.

Jesse Seligman was the main force behind the project, helping to set up the French Panama Canal Company to run the project, and Seligman Bank was responsible for the company's stock issuance. The French company at the time was so eager to finance with the Seligman family brand that it spared a one-time payment of $300,000 as a special brand royalty. Panama's underwriting group was soon established in the United States, with Seligman, Zogerso and JPMorgan joining forces as underwriters for the U.S. stock offering. Responsible for sales in France are the French branch of Seligman and BNP Paribas.

With an initial estimate of $114 million to build the canal and a total stock offering of $600 million, the money looks more than

---

[70] Ackerman, Kenneth D. *Dark Horse: The Surprise Election and Political Murder of James A. Garfield*, Avalon Publishing, 2004.

adequate. When the canal was completed, it was placed under the management of the French government. Of course the matter caused a stir within the United States, with many criticizing the project for bringing in European power and control of vital waterways and criticizing Seligman for selling out American interests. On the other hand, the United States wanted to build a canal linking the two oceans in Central America, Nicaragua, years ago. Geographically, Nicaragua is closer to the United States and would be more in line with practical considerations for engineering construction if a connecting waterway were established through Lake Nicaragua. Prior to the economic crisis of 1873, there had been preliminary exploration work being done by American companies, only the crisis brought the entire project to a halt. At this point, the two project programmes are incompatible and become a major political issue.

The Seligman and Morgan families strongly supported the Panama Canal proposal, and parts of the American media began to criticize them for selling American interests to France, while others claimed it was a Jewish conspiracy. Seligman claimed in the New York papers that this was a private project, that it had nothing to do with the State, and that the operation of the company would be well rewarded, and that the machinery and equipment in the project would be purchased from the United States and would ensure the best interests of the United States. Subsequently, the famous French hero de Lesseps was grandly launched as the head of the construction of the Suez Canal. Since de Lesseps was responsible for the construction, the shares of the Panama Canal Company were sold without any problems in France and without any problems in the United States. The initial stock offering was also oversubscribed.

Excavation was about to begin, and de Lesseps decided at first to build a canal of the same height as the sea level so that the locks would not have to be used, which would take about seven years. In 1884, the Nicaraguan government signed a canal treaty with the United States, which, if completed successfully, would result in two parallel canals in Central America. After the canal was dug, de Lesseps soon encountered many unexpected difficulties and felt compelled to build new locks, with a possible drop in the water level between the two sides. He struggled with the locks for another 2+ years, and finally after 9 years of construction, spent $400 million, which is 4 times the original budget. But the canal project is not even 1/3 complete and the whole project is in serious trouble. The French hero was fired home, and the

US Congress began organizing committees to investigate why American investors had spent so much money and suffered so much loss on the canals, while bankers like Seligman and Morgan had made so much money through stock underwriting. The commission investigated and found that Jesse Seligman had intended to place his old friend, former U.S. President Grant, as chairman of the Canal Commission at a salary of $24,000 a year, but Grant declined the position, so Jesse found President Hayes' Secretary of the Navy, Thompson. Thompson resigned as Secretary of the Navy and accepted the job.

The investigation also found that Seligman also entered into various agreements and contracts with numerous machine builders, all of which constitute a conflict of interest issue in a congressional investigation. During the investigation, the senator asked Jesse Seligman why someone like Thompson would be chosen to chair the Canal Commission: "He's not a great financier, is he?" Jesse replied, "No, but he is a great politician and lawyer." The Senator then asked, "You once offered this position to General Grant, who was a great warrior and a popular idol, but he was not a great lawyer or financier, or a great politician, was he?" Seligman replied calmly, "General Grant is a very close friend of mine and I will always take special care of my friend."

Thompson, as Secretary of the Navy, wrote a letter to Jesse a few days after Joseph's death, which Seligman wanted to add to the materials of the investigation. The letter mentions: "During my official tenure I had the privilege of getting to know Joseph's personality better, and my first contact with your family bank was through him in the summer of 1877, when the Navy Department happened to be under my administration. The finances of the Navy Department at his time were embarrassing, mainly in the hundreds of thousands of dollars owed to your family bank, and the number of debts was growing. At that time the Department of the Navy was unable to pay its entire debt, and even paying off most of it was impossible, and the matter had caused great distress and embarrassment to the Government and had had a rather serious effect on the services of the Department. When Joseph Seligman learned of the situation, he immediately recommended that the entire debt be rolled over to the next fiscal year and that the (Department of the Navy) be allowed to continue borrowing. His proposal was very patriotic. I was filled with gratitude and accepted his offer so that our Department of the Navy could get through the most difficult times."

The strip is timely and powerfully written to the rescue of Seligman, who is in the throes of public opinion. Ultimately a congressional investigation found no wrongdoing on the part of Seligman et al, but the matter had a serious negative impact on the Seligman family's reputation and Wall Street's image. So Congress decided to start building the Nicaraguan Canal immediately.[71]

While the two sides were engaged in a heated argument over which line the canal should go, Seligman found friends in Congress, including Senator Mark Hanna – the leader of the committee studying the determination of the canal line. Seligman asked Senator Markhanna to propose that Congress hold off on a decision for now until the report of this investigative committee of theirs is presented. The senator agreed, and Congress agreed to wait a little longer. But the results were so disappointing to Seligman that the Commission's investigation concluded that the Nicaraguan route was entirely preferred. In desperation, the Seligman family found a man named Philippe Bunau-Varilla in Paris to lobby.[72]

Philippe had dreamed of digging a canal in Panama since he was 10 years old, and when he heard that de Lesseps had succeeded in doing so in Suez, the idea grew stronger. When Seligman approached him, Philip agreed to take the job without hesitation. This person later came to the United States and began to give intensive lectures everywhere. Unfortunately, Philip's months of lobbying in the U.S. still didn't work, and Congress still voted unanimously to go the Nicaraguan route in the end. With strong support from Seligman, Philip entered a final critical lobbying effort to try to reverse the Senate decision. Philip was almost frantically lobbying for the advantage of the Panama line, holding multiple impassioned speeches. This passion was so exaggerated that the French Embassy in the United States, thinking Philippe had gone mad, urgently informed Philippe's brother in Paris. His brother rushes from Paris to America and finds Philip utterly unable to calm himself, and, stimulated by the huge sum of money, Philip has entered a state of paranoia.

---

[71] Mellander, Gustavo A., *The United States in Panamanian Politics: The Intriguing Formative Years.*

[72] Ibid.

It was at this urgent and delicate moment that a dramatic change occurred, when Mount St. Vincent erupted. The St. Vincent volcano is in the West Indies and its eruption has killed thousands of people. Two days before that, a supposedly dead volcano, Mount Pili, had also erupted, killing more than 3,000 people. Nicaragua has volcanoes, Panama does not. Philip had a sudden flash of light, as if injected with a large dose of stimulants, and immediately rushed to the post office, where he found a 5 peso Nicaraguan postage stamp in a stamp shop, which showed the scene of a volcanic eruption in a thick cloud of smoke. As soon as he got the idea, Philip bought 90 stamps of the volcanic eruption, affixed them to the letterhead, and sent the 90 stamps to each senator. He noted in the accompanying letter that the image on the stamp was historical evidence of a volcanic eruption in the Nicaraguan region. This is just three days before the final Senate vote. Seligman and Phillip spent their days in anxious waiting. The Senate ultimately voted to favor the Panama line by a margin of eight votes, with Seligman rejoicing. Philip immediately bought more volcano stamps, sent them to all the House members, and soon the House began to adjust its original position.

Before Seligman and Phillip could celebrate, they were faced with a new, more serious problem. Panama was then a Colombian province, and the Colombian government had changed its mind about providing access to the canal. Philip immediately put pressure on Colombia and used a lot of money to lobby Colombian government officials, but the Colombian Congress nevertheless rejected the canal treaty. If Colombia doesn't approve Panama's canal, Seligman will have worked for nothing and all efforts will have been wasted, including the life-saving volcanic stamp.

Nearly desperate, Philip found Seligman lamenting, "We have lost it all and have nothing left, unless we let Panama get away from Colombia, but that would mean a revolution." Jesse Seligman asked Philip rhetorically, how much would it take to create a revolution? Understanding Seligman's intentions, Philip immediately assembled a group of Panamanian separatists to discuss plans for the revolution and set about accounting for its costs. Panamanian separatists insist that they need at least $6 million to pay the local guerrillas. Philip rushed to report to Seligman that $6 million was the minimum cost to break out the revolution. Seligman felt the offer was outrageously high and gave a floor price, $100,000, and it had to be a complete revolution. The Panamanian separatists accepted this clause with gusto.

After getting a promise from the Panamanian separatists, Philip darted back to Seligman's office and, on the desk of his bank partner, drafted the Panamanian Declaration of Independence and the Panamanian Constitution. He then boarded a train from Washington to see President Roosevelt, Sr. as he says in his memoirs, "I told President Roosevelt and asked him to promise me a condition that when the revolution broke out, American warships would appear near Panama to protect American lives and interests. This American interest also includes Seligman's interests. The president just looked at me and didn't say anything, and of course, there was no way the president of the United States would give me such a promise, especially to a foreigner like me. But he looked at me and that was enough for me." In other words, President Roosevelt Sr. had acquiesced in the matter.

When the revolution broke out in 1903, the U.S.S. battleship Nashville did arrive in Panama to monitor the progress of the revolution. The appearance of the battleship Nasivel can be seen as a moral support for the Panamanian separatists on the part of the United States, and to some extent served to threaten the Colombian government to lay down its arms and make Panama independent. This moment marked a great victory for Seligman. The Seligmans, in gratitude for their meritorious servant and friend, have set Philip up with a very interesting job. As a French citizen, Philippe Bonnefrilla was appointed the first Ambassador of the Republic of Panama to the United States.[73]

The international bankers, at this time, have the power to create a major revolution, national division or war for their own benefit. It is in this way that Panama has become so wonderfully independent that, in fact, the Seligman family is the true "Father of Panama".

The Age of Schiff

Jacob Schiff's family was also a Jewish family with origins in Frankfurt, Germany, but his origins were very different from Seligman. The Schiff family can be described as a prestigious family among the Jews. According to the Jewish Encyclopedia, the Schiff family can be traced back to the earliest origins of the Jewish people. The branch of

---

[73] Stephen Kinzer, *Overthrow – America's Century of Regime Change from Hawaii to Iraq*, 2006.

the Schiff family on this side of Frankfurt dates back to the 14th century. In fact Jacob Schiff even traces his ancestry all the way back to around the 10th century BC, right down to the King Solomon genealogy. Schiff and the Rothschilds are very close to each other, and the two families have been friends for hundreds of years; in the late 18th century, Schiff and the Rothschilds were neighbours for a time and owned a multi-storey house together. Jacob Schiff often said, "I admit that although our family is not as rich as the Rothschilds, we are a more orthodox and noble family." The Rothschilds are recognized as an extremely lucrative family, but the Schiff family has produced not only a number of successful bankers, but also a number of outstanding scholars and religious leaders. The Schiff family has a much longer history than the Rothschilds.[74]

Jacob Schiff was by no means a mere mortal, but rather a new generation of Jewish bankers with great ambition, talent, resourcefulness and resourcefulness. He was unusually clear and persistent about his goals from an early age, hiding the excuse of a trip to London from his parents at the age of 18, when in fact he was ready to go on a solo tour of New York when he left Frankfurt. By the time his mother kept receiving his letters from London, Schiff himself had long since arrived in New York. With $500 on hand, Schiff soon found a few like-minded partners and the group decided to start a stock brokerage firm. When it was time to officially sign the agreement, it was revealed that Schiff was not yet of legal age. Later, Schiff's domineering personality prevented him from working with others, and he chose to return to Germany in search of new opportunities.

On his return to Germany, he met the two brothers, Paul and Felix of the Warburg family, who had made a great impression on Schiff.[75] This meeting has far-reaching implications for the future of Wall Street as a whole, and even the financial industry worldwide. In Germany, Schiff befriended Abraham Kuhn. After founding Kuhn, Loeb & Co. on Wall Street, Kuhn returned to Frankfurt out of homesickness. As soon as Kuhn met Schiff, he felt the young man was different and suggested that Schiff come to New York to join Kuhn, Loeb & Co.. So

---

[74] Cyrus Adler, *Jacob Henry Schiff: A Biographical Sketch*, New York: The American Jewish Committee, 1921.

[75] Ron Chernow, *The Warburgs*, Random House, 1993.

Schiff soon returned to New York and officially joined the Kuhn, Loeb & Co. Company. The year was 1873 and Schiff was exactly 26 years old.

Upon his arrival in New York, Schiff was attracted by the booming situation in the United States and the thriving situation in the country as a whole. After the American Civil War, with the great development of the railroad industry, railroad mergers, bankruptcies and reorganizations created great business opportunities for Wall Street, and around 1870, railroad stocks and bonds were the largest market apart from treasury bonds, became the mainstay of Wall Street profits, constituting 85% of the turnover of the entire U.S. stock market, and at the same time, there was great interest and enthusiasm for railroad stocks and bonds in Europe. The sale of American railroad bonds and stocks in Frankfurt, London, Paris, and Amsterdam was a huge success, creating a large group of banker tycoons. The leading man on Wall Street at the time was, naturally, Joseph Seligman, but his investments in railroads had not been smooth.

Schiff scrutinized every step Seligman took in his railroad investments and soon discovered where Seligman had blundered. Seligman was actually completely uninterested in how railroads were produced, why they came into being, how they operated, and in specific operational matters; he only saw them as a means and end to profit. But Schiff was different, Schiff first had to make himself an expert in railroads before investing in them.

Schiff is preparing to enter the railroad industry. He first served as a director of a number of railroad companies and was deeply involved in every detail of the railroad's operations, such as all the processes involved in laying the tracks, rail warehousing, track production processes, transportation conditions, etc. He also liked to ask the staff for advice when he was on an expedition, from mechanics to engineers, from general steam engine coal additions to senior management, and even pipe brake workers, all entering his radar. Schiff asked various questions and took careful notes, trying to understand all the details of the entire railroad transport. Soon Schiff became an authoritative expert on railroads.

It was Schiff's rigorous and pragmatic approach and deep grasp of the details of railroad operations that gave him a professional judgment of what kind of financial instruments and what kind of financial services the railroad needed under what circumstances. Schiff's knowledge of the inner workings of railroads allows him to accurately and effectively translate the financial needs of railroad management operations into investment products for Wall Street, while combining a command of the channels, pace, timing, and fire of various financing instruments, which Schiff has unparalleled strength in railroad finance.

For nearly 30 years, from 1873 to 1900, the railroads completely dominated the financial industry in the United States. Schiff followed this industry leapfrog, gradually transforming Coonrable from a small investment bank to the giant that dominates American rail finance. Even a heavyweight banker like Morgan had to marvel at Schiff's ability, especially his detailed grasp of the combination of financial and railroad expertise.

Another reason for Schiff's success was that he was able to communicate directly and effectively with international bankers in Europe. It is from the huge European capital and the strong support of European international bankers that Schiff's work has been able to flow unimpeded.

In terms of financial influence, at this point Schiff had greatly surpassed his predecessor, Seligman. Although Seligman also invested in railroads, he never understood the business model. Wall Street financiers believe that behind the railroad's business model is actually a real estate business opportunity, and people are more concerned about the land speculation behind the railroad than they are about the railroad. Under the corresponding Act of the United States, the land along a certain perimeter of the railroad line is owned by the railroad company, the land is used for financing, and the financing is completed for the construction of the railroad. So a large part of Wall Street's speculation about railroad stocks and railroad bonds is looking at land development and land investment along the perimeter of rail lines. In a sense, behind the railroad fever is the land development fever. Financiers, including Seligman, don't really care about the railroads per se, they just use them as a hype topic.

And Schiff's view goes even deeper, arguing that the rail line actually opens up a corridor of land that is sold to developers from all walks of life, thus concentrating all sorts of production, processing, and trading activities along the rail line. It is this commercial activity that creates the demand for rail transportation, which pays for the construction and operation costs of the railroad and creates benefits for the railroad. This is the essence of rail finance.

Schiff did four years of research before, during and after his involvement in the Pacific Union Railroad project. By the time Schiff took a keen interest in the line and began to think carefully about it, the Pacific Union Railroad was in a huge debt crisis, with a debt of $45 million to the U.S. government alone, plus a 6 percent interest rate. These unpaid interest payments have accumulated over nearly 30 years, the total length of the line has been reduced from over 8,000 miles to 4,400 miles, and various pressures, including its debt situation, have made the railroad look lifeless and completely unviable. Everyone on Wall Street is watching this project to death. Schiff found Morgan, who by then had become a post-Seligman Wall Street juggernaut. Morgan made it clear that he had no hopes for the railroad and could let Schiff off the hook.

As it turned out later, Morgan made a major strategic mistake. With Morgan's acquiescence, Schiff began a huge mobilization effort and quietly bought stocks and bonds of the Pacific Union Railway. Soon, he found that there always seemed to be an invisible hand blocking his plans. There are always inexplicable events in Congress that delay the project, the media suddenly becomes hostile to the project, and bondholders in Europe are slow to give the green light to the project. Schiff thought over and over again that there was only one person strong enough to put a hurdle in the matter. At first he suspected it was Morgan who was pulling the strings, and found Morgan to ask if he had changed his mind. Morgan said, "Now that I've agreed, definitely let it go and let you do it, and I can help you find out what it is that's blocking this." A few days later, Morgan dug up the man behind the curtain: Harriman. Harriman was a genius in railroad operations, and Schiff agreed to work with Harriman after a bit of a sparring session.[76] But the Pacific Railway project was so large that Schiff soon realised that it would have to draw on European capital to bring the project back from the dead.

Schiff found a childhood friend, a heavyweight who was close to the Rothschilds in London at the time, Sir Ernest Cassel, himself a legendary heavyweight financier. Sir Ernest was primarily responsible

---

[76] Stephen Birmingham, *"Our Crowd" – The Great Jewish Families of New York*, p. 222.

for the liaison and dispatch of funds with the Rothschilds in London and other international bankers.

Joseph Seligman built his career in America from nothing, laying the foundations of Jewish bankers on Wall Street, while Schiff further crafted a vast conglomerate of forces that dominated the American financial world. By joining forces with Sir Ernest, Schiff was able to obtain timely and accurate information on the movements of the financial markets in London and Europe, and in particular on the movement of funds from and to the various major families. It was with the help of Sir Ernest of London that within three days Schiff and Harriman had received $40 million in guarantees and subscriptions from Europe. The Pacific Union Railroad project, which had been dormant for years and seemed destined for bankruptcy at last, has come back from the dead.

By November 2, 1897, the Schiff and Harriman Group officially acquired shares of Pacific Union. The Pacific Union Railroad, operated by Schiff and Harriman, achieved the great success of the largest single industrial project in history up to that time. Not only did it pay off all its debt and interest, it also made an unprecedented $210 million in profits. On top of that, it creates assets of at least no less than $2 billion. It was only at this point that Morgan regretted it, thinking that to abandon the project was to miss a chicken that had laid a golden egg, a strategic mistake indeed.

In 1895, at Schiff's invitation, Paul and Felix, two of the Warburgers, also came to New York to join the Kuhn, Loeb & Co. Company, bringing the Warburgers of Germany and the Schiff family of the United States into a close and powerful union. Schiff's daughter was married to Felix, and Loeb's daughter was married to Paul. The daughter of Wolfe, another partner in Kuhn, Loeb & Co., married Oto Kane, the Kane who was the backbone of the Speer family and later joined Kuhn, Loeb & Co. as Schiff's successor. The son of the Kuhn family married another daughter of the Loeb family. After the quadruple marriage, the Kuhn, Loeb & Co. Company closely linked the Warburg, Schiff, Loeb, Kuhn, Kane, and Wolfe families, becoming the Jewish banking family in Europe and the United States, the most dense network of people, the most talented and the most powerful Jewish banking family group army.

The figures coming out of this group are extraordinary, almost all of them superpowers who can influence international financial markets.

Max, the boss of the Warburg family, is the financial advisor of Germany's William II, representing Germany in the Versailles peace talks, "World War I" after the domination of German finance and financial power, is a director of the Reichsbank, Hitler's "finance czar" Schacht's big brother behind the scenes, from the end of the 19th century to the end of the 1930s nearly 40 years, on Germany's politics, economy, finance have played a huge influence. Paul the Second, the chief architect of the Federal Reserve, one of the decision makers of American finance, is among the most heavyweight bankers in the United States. The elder Felix III, a senior partner at the most influential Kuhn, Loeb & Co. firm of the early 20th century, one of the Wall Street bigwigs. The elder Fritz, chairman of the German Hamburg Metal Exchange, made a secret peace with Tsarist Russia on behalf of Germany in the late First World War.[77] Otto Kane, a leading Wall Street Jewish banker after Schiff, built his mansion on Long Island in 1919 on a 1.8-square-kilometer site with more than 10,000 square meters of living space and 127 rooms, the second largest mansion in the United States at the time. The Kuhn, Loeb & Co. Company under Jakob Schiff entered its heyday.

Schiff and the Russo-Japanese War

When the Russo-Japanese War broke out in 1904, Japan was ambitiously preparing to defeat Russia, but soon found that the Russian army was so strong that Japan was gradually stretched to the limit of its war budget. In order to raise money for the war, the vice-president of the Shogun Bank of Japan, Sir Kiyoshi, came to London to meet the international bankers.

Coming to London, Gao Qiao was Qing's initial intention to ask the Rothschilds for help underwriting Japanese war bonds. The Japanese opened the door to propose a financing scale of 5 million pounds, the Rothschild family does not even bother to roll their eyes. It is important to know that in the underwriting of the Franco-Prussian war reparations bonds 30 years ago, the Rothschild family raised a huge sum of 5 billion francs (about £200 million) in just two years. Although Britain was Japan's largest political and commercial partner at the time, bankers on the London side did not see any possibility of Japanese

---

[77] Ron Chernow, *The Warburgs*, Random House, 1993.

victory in the war, so Japan's financing plans received a cold shoulder in London.

In the midst of depression, Gao Qiao Yes Ching meets Schiff, who is working in London, at a banquet, and Gao Qiao Yes Ching spills his guts to Schiff, who listens while playing his own game. As the American economy grows stronger, the financial power of the United States is on the rise, although Schiff is also the number one figure on Wall Street, but in London even the role of JPMorgan and other characters have to be careful, watching the face of the City of London Financial City bosses to speak, Schiff understands his own weight is still far from the City of London international banker bosses. But Japan is really a new market, and since the big guys can't see it, the Wall Street nouveau riche might still be interested. And unlike the London financiers who thought Japan was bound to lose, Schiff believed that the battlefield of the Russo-Japanese War was far from Russia's economic center of gravity, but under Japan's noses, and coupled with the corruption of the Tsarist court and the decay of the Tsarist system, Japan, which was on the rise, had a great possibility of defeating Russia, so Schiff promised Kojo Isao to help Japan raise money for the Russo-Japanese War in Wall Street. There was another reason for Schiff's willingness to help Japan: the persecution of the Jews by Tsarist Russia made Schiff consider Tsarist Russia a public enemy of mankind, and he even advocated and advocated the overthrow of the Tsar by armed revolution. Anything that would strike Russia, he was willing to help.

At this point, Schiff was essentially single-handedly financing the war for Japan, and under these circumstances and circumstances, Schiff had to rally his former rivals, the Morgan family and George Baker, into a syndicate. After discussion, the Rockefeller Consortium was brought in, and for the first time in Japan's history, it was able to obtain financing from financial markets other than London.

Japan received a total of three massive loans during the Russo-Japanese War, all of which were the work of Schiff behind them.[78] It was the infusion of funds from these three loans that greatly improved Japan's war capabilities and became one of the key factors in Japan's eventual victory in the Russo-Japanese War.

---

[78] Dictionary of American Biography, Vol. XVI, p. 431–432.

Before the Russo-Japanese War, the European and American powers generally believed that Japan was still a small hegemon in Asia, but simply could not be compared with the British, American, German, French, Russian and other world powers. Japan's victory shook European and American powers and gave Schiff a reputation in international financial markets, and his strategic vision impressed the international banker community. King Edward VII of England invited Schiff to lunch at Buckingham Palace, and the Emperor of Japan invited Schiff to lunch at the Imperial Palace of Japan, the highest courtesy of the Emperor of Japan, and no foreigner had ever received such an honor before Schiff. Schiff was a man of new fashions, and while having lunch with the Emperor at the Imperial Palace in Japan, he suddenly proposed to the Japanese official in charge of etiquette that he want to make a toast to the Emperor. The Japanese ceremonial officer, pale with fright, hurriedly and tremblingly dissuaded Schiff from doing so, for such a thing as a foreigner giving a toast to the Emperor had never happened before in the Japanese court, and the Japanese official, fearing the Emperor's misunderstanding, was shocked. Schiff, however, was stubborn, stood up, raised his glass of wine, and addressed the audience: "First, a toast to the Emperor, that he may always be the head of Japan in the hearts of his subjects, in the smoke of war, in the years of peace." After Schiff finished this paragraph, the Emperor seemed to be in a good mood, and the hearts of all the people were relieved.

Schiff was invited as an honored guest to the house of Baron Gao Qiao is Qing, and Schiff happened to be sitting next to Gao Qiao is Qing's 15-year-old daughter. "You should come to America to visit and study for a while," he said casually. Schiff, who is usually serious and has a casual demeanor like he's calling the shots on Wall Street, doesn't take it personally. But the next morning, Kojo was Kiyoshi himself at the door of Schiff's apartment, and after a deep bow to Schiff said,

> *"Though it is an extraordinary thing in Japan for a Japanese girl of such a young age to leave her native country and go on such a long and difficult foreign journey at such a young age. But because you have proved yourself a friend to the Japanese, I have agreed to let my own daughter go with you to New York."*

But he wanted Schiff to understand that he didn't want his daughter to spend more than three years in America. Schiff's casual remark of politeness was actually taken as an order from Wall Street by Japan's most heavyweight banker. Schiff was a man of his word, and he was bold enough to return to New York with Gaucho's daughter, and to send

Gaucho's daughter back at the end of the three-year term as promised. From then on, Japan fell in love with the big money on Wall Street.

New Circle and Old Circle

Prior to 1840, there were only two dozen wealthy families in the United States with assets over $1 million, and no more than five super-rich families over $5 million, and these families were almost exclusively descended from colonial-era lords of large estates. At the time, New York wasn't too wealthy a city, and probably all the other emerging families, except for the Morris family, had to trade to make ends meet. After the Civil War, the U.S. economy went into high gear, and the wealthy emerged in large numbers, with hundreds of families in New York City alone with assets over $1 million. The explosion of new industries such as steam engines, railroads, textiles, machinery, steel, military industry, oil, telegraph, telephone, and other nascent industries brought about by the Industrial Revolution brought the creation of American wealth to a pace and scale unprecedented in human history.

In New York, the families of many of the traditional lords of large estates are facing great challenges as the wealth of the emerging families soars. While these older families have high status and influence in society and are relatively stable in their value identity with each other, their wealth growth has largely kept pace with the expansion of the emerging families. There is a growing consensus among the new aristocracy and the old-timers that the upper class needs to be redefined. The McAllister family in New York pioneered the idea that the traditional aristocracy of New York, and the emerging aristocracy, must achieve great union. If the old nobility was represented by the Morris family, the core of the new nobility was the Vanderbilt family. In McAllister's view, these old and new aristocrats needed to reach a consensus that would form a fixed circle of high society, a circle of wealth, power and noble traditions that would keep the various so-called speculators, the rich and the foolishly rich and the vulgar out of the noble and elegant high society, so as not to pollute and violate the "best part" of society.

The omission of Jews from the so-called "circle of 400" that McAllister and later Mrs. Astor had created sparked a backlash from Jewish bankers on Wall Street. The position of Jewish bankers in American finance, in terms of their wealth, is unquestionable, as the new and old aristocrats of American society admit. But in social circles and among the upper classes, there is still no consensus on tolerant Jewish attitudes due to religious and traditional prejudices. Even to this day, traces of discrimination against Jews can be found in American society.

There are actually different social classes among Jews in the United States. Among the higher Jews were the so-called "Sephardi Jews", a branch that originated in Spain and Portugal and arrived in America around 1654. The Sephardic Jews arrived in the United States even before the Great Manor Lords' families. The cultural traditions of these Jews are not unlike those of the German Jews who came to the United States in the 19th century, and many of their religious traditions and life customs carry on the unique style preserved in the Middle Ages.[79] Sephardic Jews tend to think of themselves as one of the noblest classes among American Jews. They are basically able to identify with each other with the American circle of large estate lords' families.

The second Jewish class is the German-Jewish nouveau riche represented by Seligman, Belmont, Schiff, Warburg, Speer, Lehman, Goldman, Sykes, Guggenheim, Kuhn, Loeb, etc. They all immigrated to the United States from Germany in the 1830s, and most of them, except Schiff and Warburg, did not have prominent families in Germany, often starting from small merchants, then successively began to enter the banking industry in the 1950s, with the rise of the American economy and rapidly accumulated amazing wealth, basically in the period of twenty to thirty years before and after the Civil War, quickly became rich in the financial field, which greatly surpassed the Jewish banking families in Europe.

The U.S. banking system is divided into two schools of thought, one of which is the commercial banking system, following Hamilton's system of financial thought, mainly based on the traditional large families in New England as the core, monopolizing the large commercial banking system in the United States to this day. The other school of thought is the investment banking system dominated by Jewish bankers, especially German Jewish bankers who form the

---

[79] Kaplan, Yosef, *An Alternative Path to Modernity: The Sephardi Diaspora in Western Europe*: Brill Publishers (2000).

backbone of Wall Street.[80] They are centered on note trading, stock listing, and bond underwriting operations. If commercial banks are the source of credit creation, equivalent to the marrow and heart of the human body, which produce and supply blood, then investment banks are the channels that channel capital and credit, like the aorta and veins of the human body, and the capillaries throughout the body. When a privately owned central bank was established, the function of the commercial bank's cardiac blood supply was transferred to the central bank, which was jointly controlled by the traditional large and Jewish banking families, creating a situation of mutual checks and balances. In prosperity, the two factions went about their own business, and the well water did not violate the river water. In times of crisis, they have pushed against each other in an effort to protect themselves, sometimes joining forces to coerce Governments into bailouts. The central bank is the coordinating body for both factions, while the government acts as the buyer of last resort.

The third class of Jews was the Eastern European Jews who immigrated to the United States from Eastern Europe and Russia in the late 19th and early 20th centuries. In New York, for example, the Jewish population in 1870 was about 80,000, or 9 percent of the city's population. By 1907, an average of 90,000 Jews were arriving in New York each year, and most of the Jews in this period were Russian and Polish immigrants. New York's Jewish population was once close to 1 million, or 25 percent of the entire New York population.[81] With the arrival of large numbers of Eastern European Jews, the Jewish community in New York underwent a major split.

The German Jews, who had been despised by the earlier "Sephardic Jews" when they arrived in the United States in the mid to late 19th century, entered the American financial industry and acquired great wealth, gradually forming their own upper-class circle. When large numbers of Eastern European Jews arrived, German Jews had also held strong prejudices against first-timers. German Jews lived in the aristocratic districts of New York, were well educated, well dressed, had wealthy families, and were already aristocratic in their manners and

---

[80] Walter Lord, *The Good Years, From 1900 to the First World War*, New York: Harper & Brothers, 1960.

[81] Diner, Hasia, *The Jews of the United States*, 1654 to 2000.

speech. Eastern European Jews, on the other hand, were more concentrated in the ghettos, coarse in manner, ragged and disheveled, carrying different cultures, with strange accents, and arguing about various ideas, and these people, with different ideas, backgrounds and experiences, flocked together to New York, causing a great shock and disturbance to the traditional German Jewish community.

There is a significant difference between German Jews and Eastern European Jews, and German Jews are extremely unlike new Eastern European Jews: these people litter, spit everywhere, live in overcrowding, speak loudly in public, push and shove everywhere, behave rudely, and even violence, hunger, crime, and other social problems are frequent in the communities of Eastern European Jews. In fact, these "superior" German Jews have the very same problems that they had when they first arrived in the United States decades ago. There were even "anti-Semitic tendencies" among German Jews, who felt themselves to be of German culture, full of the genes of peace, freedom, progress and civilization, and considered themselves to be superior to the Jews. When they spoke of the new Jewish immigrants from Eastern Europe and Russia, the contempt, disgust, and disdain overflowed, as if they were talking about a different race.

On the other hand, Russian and Eastern European Jews quickly discovered that these German Jewish millionaires had also been peddlers of small business start-ups, and that what the German Jewish billionaires could do, they could do. So a large number of Eastern European and Russian Jews tried to emulate the wealthy experience of the German Jews in those days, and began to sell a variety of small goods on the streets of New York, which in turn embarrassed and bored the German Jews. Many Eastern European Jews tried to "Americanize" the spelling of their names in order to be more Americanized, learning from German Jews, and trying to integrate themselves into the circle of German Jews, but they were never successful.

Surprisingly, Russian and Eastern European Jews, with their tragic experiences in the old European continent and their bright visions for the new American continent, created the American film industry – Hollywood – from scratch and brought their "American dream" to its fullest expression in cinema and in the real world. The founders of Hollywood's six founding production companies, Universal, Paramount, Fox, MGM, Warner Bros. and Columbia, were almost all Jewish immigrants from Russia and Eastern Europe.

In the early 20th century, film technology emerged, and Jewish immigrants in New York began to run movie theaters and, in turn, to invest in making movies. Ostracized by the eastern film trust, headed by Thomas Edison, Jewish producers began to emigrate to California, and in 1915 Jewish immigrant Carl Laemmle began his Hollywood career by establishing Universal Studios, the world's first massive movie town. By 1920, five other Jewish studios had been established. In the 1920s and 1930s, Hollywood movies became a mecca for cultural entertainment, with 3/4 of Americans going to the movies once a week.

The "American dream" of freedom, democracy and self-struggle created by Jewish immigrants, the cultural symbols propagated through mass communication channels – movies – in turn gained the approval of the white American middle class and became the dominant cultural consciousness of American society, and Hollywood spread the "American dream" to the world.

CHAPTER V

A turbulent Europe

A deep sense of pride and frustration is woven into the bones of the German people. The Germanic tradition of hard work, rigor, loyalty and discipline has always placed Germany in a position of excellence in modern world history, with a number of stars in science, technology, literature, music, poetry, military, politics and finance. But at the same time, Germany is a rare country in the history of mankind that is full of tragedy, and no country has ever made so many remarkable contributions to human civilization while at the same time causing so much suffering to humanity.

Germany's greatest misfortune was to be geographically pinned down by two European powers, Russia and France, and to have access to the sea firmly choked by Britain. The more it resists and the more it struggles, the tighter the net will be. From the bloody 30-year-long war between the Germanic peoples (1618–1648), which was deliberately provoked by Richelieu in France in the 17th century, in an attempt to achieve the strategic goal that Germany would not be able to rise within 200 years, to the First World War, when Britain, France, the United States and Russia joined forces to destroy Germany's ambition of global rise, to the Second World War, when the four countries once again cooperated to completely crush Germany's attempts to dominate the world, Germany has been reborn three times under the prison fire of destruction, and its vitality has amazed the world.

Societies that start progressing from a backward economic state and accelerate their catch-up with advanced countries have a common mentality. By the second half of the nineteenth century, Germany's industrialization and colonization of the overseas territories lagged considerably behind that of England and France, and German industrial and commercial companies, in competition with their powerful British rivals, mostly wanted the government to implement protective policies with high tax rates and low credit costs. In 1871, Chancellor Bismarck finally completed the unification of Germany. This was an epoch-making event that meant that the balance of power that had held the continent together for more than 200 years was shattered, that the lax and weak Central Europe was suddenly consolidated by a united and resilient Germany, and that British strategic interests were strongly challenged. Britain began to coordinate the rise of France, Russia and other countries to fully besiege Germany on the European continent.

International bankers have taken full advantage of the antagonism and hostility between countries, sometimes even fomenting such antagonism, on the one hand by deriving huge economic benefits from it and on the other by having their own larger strategic agendas.

An unquenchable longing: to return, to return to Zion

In the Old Testament, Zion is the name given by the Lord to those who are of one mind, dwell in righteousness, and enjoy righteousness and peace. Zion is also the name of the place where the righteous people of ancient times gathered, and where God's elect will one day be gathered again.

Mount Zion, located in Jerusalem, Palestine, is also used to refer to Israel and the ancient region of Canaan, which the Jewish nation regards as its ultimate homeland. In the Israeli national anthem, Hatikvah, there are the words "looking into the eyes of the East, looking at the Grange of Zion" and "being a free people, standing over Mount Zion and Jerusalem". When the Jewish Temple of Yeshua was built, the wood was taken from Mount Zion, and prisoners of war captured by the Jews in ancient times were forced to labor on Mount Zion. Mount Zion is seen as a symbol of Zionism.

The Jewish doctrine accepted by generations of Jews from birth tells them that Canaan is "a beautiful land of milk and honey", that the LORD has given it to them to live in, and that wherever the Jewish people are scattered, God has ordained that they will return and that no power will stop them.

It is on the basis of this unwavering conviction and spiritual drive that the Jewish people, through thousands of years of upheaval and suffering, has never changed its mind. There is no ambiguity in their beliefs, there is no room for ambiguity in their knowledge of the world, for them they are "chosen by God" to exercise divine authority on behalf of God, and their accumulation of wealth and authority is not for squandering and debauchery, but all they do is for the glory of God. For thousands of years, they have believed in this, without hypocrisy or exaggeration. Any shaking of one's faith will inevitably lead to the collapse of the entire spiritual world, and eventually the entire nation will inevitably fade into the sea of people. And today, not only do we not see the weakening of the Jewish people, but we see a group of powerful forces rarely seen in history. If there is a genius among Jews, it is inextricably linked to their highly concentrated psychological energy and unquestionable conviction. For the Zionists, who have consecrated Mount Zion as the Holy Land, God's will, Palestine, must also be the final destination of Jewish immigration.

Jewish doctrine also tells people that the road to return is full of hardships, twists and turns and even despair, but that God will give them the power to save and lead and ultimately lead them back to the land of Zion.

The German banking family: the fire of hope for a return

The restoration of the State of Israel is a very large, extremely complex and almost impossible undertaking. After 2,000 years of displacement, it is not easy for Jews to return to the Holy Land, Jerusalem, to rebuild Israel, which before the nineteenth century was in an extremely difficult phase of survival, let alone rebuilding, under the dual oppression of medieval European religious forces and feudal secular prejudices. At this stage of history, the restoration of the country was only a dream; after the 16th century, the Reformation and Enlightenment movement, which was gaining momentum in Europe, finally tore a crack between the heavy Catholicism and the strict feudal autocracy, and the dream of restoration appeared as a ray of hope; at the end of the 18th century, the French bourgeois revolution quickly became a blazing fire sweeping across the continent, and the religious and feudal traditional social power system collapsed, accompanied by the rise of capitalism and the unprecedented expansion of gold power. By the middle of the 19th century, the dream of restoration was gradually translated into practical action, and Zionists began to converge in Germany, where the religious and social environment was relatively liberal.

Throughout the history of Europe, the social existence and status of the Jewish people was divided into approximately three social classes. The first class belongs to the most general Jewish masses, who live in ghettos or in their own unique communities and are oppressed by a variety of political power, religious exclusion and social traditions. The second level is the protected Jew. They may have paid less tax and enjoyed more power similar to that of relocating a place of residence, and these Jews belonged to a group of people who were more valuable to the local government, so they were called protected Jews, mainly because the particular industry they worked in contributed more to the local area. The third class are the more minority Jews, who have a relatively higher social status, mainly due to the fact that they are engaged in certain unique services, such as bankers, who lend to the government of the country in which they are located, and thus have a higher social status. These people were called Court Jews (Court Jews). Wealthy Jewish banking families, like the Rothschilds, were court Jews by background.

Throughout history, the Jewish people have been under a state of exclusion and oppression. A large number of Jews were marginalized, confined to their own communities, speaking their own dialects, dressing in their own distinctive national dress, and obeying religious regulations to maintain special dietary practices. Due to the exclusion of Jews by the dominant religious forces in Europe and the discrimination against Jews by the local secular society, Jews were severely constrained in all aspects of employment, migration, and life, such as the inability to own property, to own farms, and to engage in crafts. This led to Jews being forced into lowly social occupations like money change. The clients of money exchange services are people who travel and do business in various regions of the country and need to exchange foreign money into local currencies that are circulated and accepted in different regions. The Jewish numismatic brokers with its flexible operation, information, fast flow of fast, delicate features, in a variety of numismatic markets between the spread, set the armpits of the furs, extensive contacts, the hard work of customer resources, after thousands of years of accumulation, so that this profession has become an iconic Jewish tradition of industry, to reach the outsiders are not allowed to enter the realm of the door.

In terms of the course of capitalist development, the development of the financial market roughly parallels the four stages of capitalist development, namely commercial capitalism, industrial capitalism, financial capitalism and monopoly capitalism. From the surge in Mediterranean trade triggered by the Crusades in the 13th century and the subsequent Renaissance movement triggered by the rediscovery of

Greek and Roman-era canonical texts from the Arab world, to the discovery of the New World and the Industrial Revolution of the 18th century, the massive maritime trade led to a high degree of commercial development. The purpose of trade is to build a bridge between producers and consumers, and the merchant is the bridge builder. The increase in trade volume has also led to a trend towards a division of labour among the merchant community, with some merchants moving away from the process of purchasing, transporting, warehousing and selling commodities to provide financial services for various aspects of the process, such as the provision of purchase credit, transport insurance, bill acceptances, bill discounting and financial transactions. This specialized division of labour greatly increased the scale and efficiency of trade, and a large group of "merchant bankers", the ancestors of the later investment bankers, emerged. A large influx of Jews into what was then Italy formed an important part of the "merchant bankers".

Around the 13th century A.D., with the Crusades and the development of seafaring trade, there was a great demand for trade and shipping of goods in the Mediterranean region, and Italy gradually became a central distribution point for the flow of people, logistics and information, and wealth rolled in. Commercial credit, based on trade demand, as well as the trading of instruments, also emerged, making Italy the first region to have financial markets and banking services.

For example, when an Egyptian exporter enters into a deal with a French importer for a fur business, the Egyptian needs to obtain financing before the goods can be prepared, or the French buyer has a shortfall in funds and needs to borrow to finance the full amount. At this point an Italian merchant banker appeared as an intermediary in providing loans, charging interest for his lending, and commercial credit was born. When the Egyptians shipped the hides and skins, expecting to receive payment immediately, and the French buyer waited on the other side of the sea for the ship to arrive, not daring to pay out of thin air, both parties were depressed. At this time, the Italians reappeared and developed a new financial instrument, the "bill of exchange", which stated the time and currency in which the French would pay the Egyptians' appointed Italian agent, and the Egyptians were very happy to accept such a means of payment. The Egyptian woke up and suddenly wanted to put his money in his pocket and not wait until the agreed time to withdraw cash, so he could have his Italian agent sell the bill of exchange at a discount to an investor willing to wait for it to mature before withdrawing it. Who wants to accept these money orders? The main thing is intelligent Jews. The Jews obtained money orders for two purposes, firstly, to benefit from investment, and secondly, to circumvent the restrictions of the strict anti-suspendancy laws of the Holy See, since high interest lending could be hidden in the discounting of money orders.

The Renaissance spurred the rise of urban commerce and industry, and Jews came to prominence in trade for their financial prowess. Especially from the French Revolution at the end of the 18th century, the closure of the ghetto (getto) was gradually lifted. Twenty-five years of war throughout Europe and the industrial revolution that began to take shape in Britain spawned unprecedented demand for financing. The Jewish financiers seized this strategic opportunity to move rapidly from the business of numismatic trading and exchange to the financing of royalty and wars, thereby amassing a great deal of wealth and social status and becoming the backbone of the Zionist movement, the most famous of which were the Rothschilds and Warburg families.

Europe's millennium of exclusion and oppression has produced a unique and sensitive Jewish sense of finance. The harsh external environment forced Jews to find their own way of life, which was to constantly engage in all kinds of buying and selling and trading, from currency to commodities, and in the process to buy low and sell high to earn the corresponding spreads, what we call today arbitrage.

Whoever occupies the channel has a huge advantage. After centuries of hard work, the Jews have finally taken firm control of the global channels of capital and credit flows. Their high sensitivity to business intelligence, extensive client contacts, meticulous business acumen and the strong religious cohesion of the Jewish people have made them the only ones in the industry, establishing a solid position that is unshakeable, and perpetuating this advantage and monopoly for generations to come. In recent centuries, financial markets have expanded rapidly in size, depth and complexity are not comparable to those of the past, and capital, credit, and bills have evolved into a variety of securities, until the modern sense of stocks, bonds, financial derivatives, all encompassing and changing with each passing day. The only thing that has not changed is the dominance and rule-making power of the Jewish financial family over the global channels of capital and credit flows. The Jewish financial family comprises the veins of today's world financial system, a complete, solid, efficient, dense and precise network of financial capillaries spread throughout the global economic fabric and deeply embedded in all social levels, from top to bottom. And it is in this vast vascular system that the wealthy blood of the world flows, and all the money that flows through this channel must be subject to various fees.

If the commodities channel is king, then the financial channel is the Taikoo!

It was by laying the foundation of financial channels that the Jewish financial family, with Germany as its first birthplace, steadily accumulated wealth and firmly established its power, which finally ignited the fire of hope for the Great Reich.

The Palestinian Dilemma

Palestine was under Ottoman rule from its incorporation into the Ottoman Empire in 1518 until the end of World War I. For the Zionists, for the Jewish state to be re-established in Palestine, the Ottoman Empire must agree, and for the Ottoman Empire to cede Palestine, there are only two options, the lure of money and the coercion of war.

In Germany, where Jewish financiers were gaining influence and the Zionists were racking their brains around Palestine, an important turning point occurred in the Bismarckian era. Before and after German reunification, Zionism gradually developed a climate in Germany and became a central area of the international Zionist movement. Germany was a paradise for the Jews of the 19th century, and its openness and tolerance became the Garden of Eden for Jews living in ghettos and suffering from the double oppression of religion and feudalism throughout Europe, especially in Eastern Europe. Historically, the sense of Jewish resistance has been strongest in the region of Central and Eastern Europe living under oppression, which is the birthplace of Zionism. Relatively speaking, the rich and lax German Jews were more liberal and kept some distance from the Zionist mainstream. However, there is no essential difference between the two sides in terms of spiritual philosophy.

In the second half of the 19th century, with the reunification of Germany, the strategic goals of Bismarck and Wilhelm II to the east were so clear that the Ottoman Empire in the Middle East became an object with which Germany had to focus. At this point, the Zionists found strategic allies. The basic idea of Zionism was to obtain, with the support of Germany, a pass from the Ottoman Empire, with which

Germany had good relations, for the mass emigration of Jews to Palestine and the eventual establishment of a state. And to convince the German government, their lobbying rhetoric was to establish a pro-German Palestinian Jewish base in the Middle East, a valuable asset and a reliable springboard for Germany's strategy to move east. The temptation for the Ottoman Empire was that the entry of large Jewish capital into Palestine would greatly enhance local economic development and bring considerable economic benefits to the Ottoman Empire, and that international Jewish capital power would be the strongest purchaser of Ottoman national debt. This was naturally very tempting for the Ottoman Empire, which was already on the verge of financial ruin. The greatly strengthened Ottoman Empire, both financially and financially, in turn became a strong strategic ally to the east of Germany, thus adding a significant weight to Germany's balance of power on the European continent. In the midst of all this lobbying, the Jewish strategy was to vote for each other, and both Germany and the Ottoman Empire were tickled to the point where it was impossible not to float. In terms of lobbying talent, I'm afraid the Su Qin and Zhang Yi of the Warring States period also have to sigh at themselves.

Germany's elite had its own considerations, and the growing number of Eastern European Jewish immigrants moving westward in large numbers led to resentment and rejection by all segments of the German homeland. Kaiser Wilhelm II was under increasing political pressure. The problem of the Jews in Germany requires a fundamental solution. If Jews were to be moved to settle in Palestinian areas, it would both satisfy Zionist demands and ease political pressure on anti-Semites at home. Thus a comprehensive consensus was reached between the German ruling class, the Zionists, and the anti-Semitic forces in Germany regarding the intention of Bartholomew II Palestine as a place of Jewish settlement.

In 1893, Germany, the only major power among the European powers to break taboos, began to propose the abolition of Ottoman laws prohibiting further land purchases by Jews in the Palestinian area, and support for Zionism became even more pronounced when Kaiser Wilhelm II visited the Ottoman Empire in the fall of 1898, and his official visit included a visit to Palestine and arranged talks with local Zionist Hazel. In talks with the Ottoman sultan, William II's support for Zionism was quite evident, with gestures of optimism that the establishment of a Jewish settlement in Palestine would spur economic prosperity for the Ottoman Empire. The Sultan, however, opposed the

Jewish option of statehood on the spot. It is also understandable that the Ottoman Empire was a vast and declining multi-ethnic empire, and once the Jews succeeded in establishing a state, and other ethnic areas followed suit, would it not be difficult to clean up the situation? After this negotiation, William II's mind cleared a lot and he felt he had been greatly overlooked. In order not to fall out with the Ottoman Empire, the German government gave up its support for Zionism in diplomacy.

Lobbying for Germany and the Ottoman Empire was unsuccessful, and the Zionists turned to Germany's rival, Britain, expecting to provoke a war between Britain and Germany, dismembering the Ottoman Empire and thus getting Palestine. At the same time, bankers were able to reap windfall profits from war financing, post-war reparations and reconstruction financing, killing two birds with one stone. In World War I, the Zionists successfully lobbied Britain and the United States to support Jewish immigration to Palestine, thereby abandoning Germany and encouraging the United States to declare war on Germany.

Siege and Rise: The Strategic Competition of Yingde

The foundation of British statehood was free trade, an idea first proposed by the Scottish economist Adam Smith.[82] According to the trade theory of classical economists such as Smith, international trade is beneficial to both parties involved. If a commodity is less expensive to produce in another country, it does not need to be produced in that country because it is more cost-effective and advantageous to spend the money to buy it from another country. On the basis of its vast overseas colonies, which hold 1/6th of the world's land, Britain, with its control over the sea, industrial technology, finance and raw materials, under the slogan of free trade, is forcing the unindustrialized countries to open the doors of trade and carry out a wholesome grab of resources and markets, thereby reaping huge profits. The Opium War was an example of British hegemony over the Qing dynasty, and in the first half of the 19th century, Germany's industrialization and colonization of overseas countries lagged far behind Britain and France. The "successful model" of imitation of the British was the dominant one in German economics at the time, but the recession of the British economy in the 1870s made

---

[82] Adam Smith, *The Wealth of Nations*.

the Germans realize the serious drawbacks of the British model of free trade and turn to the infantile industrial protection theory advocated by the German economist Friedrich List.

Lister was a critic of Adam Smith, who noted in The National System of Political Economy that "the cosmopolitan political economy established by Adam Smith, which treats free trade as an ideal, actually serves British interests. Germany wants to build a national political economy that will serve its interests by implementing trade protection."[83] Liszt argued that it was no longer possible for an unprotected backward country to become an emerging industrial country in free competition with powerful industrialized countries, at which point the more backward countries would generally succumb to the dominance of industrial, commercial and maritime hegemonic powers. Asking relatively backward Germany to compete with developed Britain through free trade is tantamount to putting a child in a tug-of-war with an adult. In the face of this reality, if the emerging countries are to be strong, they must protect their "childish industries". The theory of infant industrial protection is based on the tariff system, with tariff increases as a means to achieve a significant development of national productivity, especially industrial productivity.

Germany is determined to develop shipping and railways, implement tariff protection policies for domestic industries and train scientific and engineering talent. In 1871, Chancellor Bismarck finally completed the unification of Germany. This was an epoch-making event, which meant that the balance of power that had been maintained on the continent for more than 200 years was broken, and that the lax and weak Central European region was suddenly integrated into a unified, resilient and explosive Germany. Germany's economic development and the establishment of a new economic model strongly challenged the British approach to statehood and strategic interests.

Hamburg-America Line: The Battle for Maritime Hegemony

German Kaiser Wilhelm II realized that without a strong commercial fleet and naval escort, Germany's economic interests were

---

[83] Friedrich List, *The National System of Political Economy*.

forever at the mercy of the maritime hegemon Britain. Albert Ballin, the German Jewish shipping king, and his Hamburg America Line (HAPAG) played a crucial role in the history of German maritime development, and in 1899 Ballin became president of the Hamburg America Line. Under his leadership, Hamburg American Lines had 175 megaships, a number that exceeded that of any of its continental European competitors.[84] Later, even the German Kaiser Wilhelm II was so overwhelmed by this huge fleet that he often came to Bowling's flotilla for various events. By 1910, Bowling's fleet employed more than 20,000 people and Hamburg became the second busiest port in the world after New York.

In fact, geographically, Germany's decision to develop maritime power in this way is problematic. Because the German coastline is in a very unfavorable posture. To the northwest of it is the North Sea of the Atlantic Ocean, directly facing Hamburg, which is blocked by Britain, and to the north of it is the Baltic Sea, which has only a very narrow access to the sea, and after coming out into the North Sea, still blocked by Britain. With the excavation of the Kiel Canal, the North Sea and the Baltic Sea were linked, but this still did not solve the problem of the German naval access to the sea.

Unlike Germany, which on the one hand blocked Germany's North Sea exports, and on the other hand had free access to the Atlantic Ocean from its west coast, Britain naturally had maritime superiority, while Germany was locked in the Atlantic Ocean outlet.

Germany's strategy of developing giant ships and ocean-going fleets at that time proved to be a great strategic failure by the two later world wars. Germany's huge navy, which had been built up at great expense over 20 years, was largely destroyed in the First World War. In World War II, Hitler's powerful naval forces, with the exception of submarines, played some role, and all heavy warships, including the two unfinished German aircraft carriers, played essentially no substantial role, the fundamental reason being the difficulty of getting in and out of the North Sea.

The maritime geography that Germany faces is very similar to the maritime situation that China faces today. Although China's coastline

---

[84] Ron Chernow, *The Warburgs The 20th Century Odyssey of a Rememberable Jewish Family.*

is 18,000 kilometres long, it appears from the map that the country's oceans are firmly blocked by the First Island Chain, with South Korea to the north, the Japanese archipelago, Okinawa, Taiwan Island, which borders China in the middle, and the Philippine Islands to the south, all the way to Malaysia and Indonesia, and the Malacca Strait. This first island chain locks China's long coastline deadlocked in China's inner sea, with a second island chain not far away.

Back again to 19th century Germany. Pauline became a good friend of William II, who said that he "never thought of Pauline as a court Jew", and in 1891, at Pauline's instigation, William II made a speech in which he said:

> "We Prussians should be taken to the sea, and let them explore the frontiers of the sea and be fruitful, for the sake of Germany, and for your company; it is a matter of mutual benefit, and of the best of both worlds."[85]

In addition to building warships, in June 1895, William II dug the Kiel Canal, which connected the entire Baltic Sea with the North Sea. Such progress reinforced William II's disillusionment with the sea. In William II's mind, a large merchant fleet and a powerful navy were inseparable. Pauling's large HAPAG ships could quickly be transformed into the German Navy's fleet when war broke out.

In 1898 Bowling publicly supported the German naval construction program, when the most powerful promoter of the naval fleet construction program was the German admiral Tepitz, and in 1900 the Reichstag approved the construction of two large naval vessels by legislation.[86] This is a huge business opportunity for Bowling. And of course he didn't forget to mention his forgotten friend, the Jewish banker Max Warburg.

Max Warburg: The Economic Czar of the Future

The development of Germany's vast maritime fleet is bound to involve a great deal of financial expenditure, and German international bankers will reap great benefits in the process. At the same time,

---

[85] Ibid.

[86] Lawrence Sondhaus, Naval warfare, 1815–1914 (Routledge, 2001).

Germany's grand naval strategy was bound to stir Britain's nerves, and Britain's international bankers further multiplied the maritime threat from Germany to strategic heights for the survival of the Empire. The British government's instinctive response was to build a naval fleet on a larger scale, and so the arms race kicked off a financial feast of sumptuous delights. The arms race, on the other hand, is "organized and invisible violence" and must rely on large-scale financing. In this way, the Anglo-German and their allies in Europe, together with the horsepower to expand the military preparations, the international bankers throughout Europe were "full of public debt ecstasy"!

Max Warburg and Alpert Bowling have been friends for over two decades. With the strong support of Bowling, Max was placed on Bowling's board of directors. During the same period, Max joined the boards of several other Bowling supplier companies on Bowling's recommendation, including a group of Germany's largest shipbuilding companies, such as Bromworth. For Bromworth, Bowling was their biggest client, so when Bowling asked to put Max on the company's board, the company couldn't refuse.

Through this arrangement, Max soon became a central figure in German shipbuilding and trade. By 1920, Max and the other partners of the family bank were holding board positions in 80 to 90 large companies and were the leading industrial, commercial and financial players in Germany. With much lobbying from Max and Bowling, Germany's William II was impressed with the prospect of the sea and ready to go big.

In 1893, Max took over as head of the family Warburg Bank. In the span of ten years, the young man who was then the head of the German financial industry had become a giant.

In 1903, at the age of 36, Max was first introduced to Kaiser Wilhelm II by Pauline. The German chancellor at the time, named Blow, felt that Kaiser Wilhelm II needed knowledge of finance to drive financial reform, and suggested that Bowling introduce Max to Wilhelm II for a dinner together.

Bowling conveyed to Max that Wilhelm II of Germany wished to summon him, but gave him only ten minutes to outline the financial problems. Max refused as soon as he heard it, stubbornly saying ten minutes wasn't enough. His persistence allowed William II to extend the reception to 32 minutes. After repeated rehearsals for his appearance before the Kaiser, Max finally prepared a speech of 25 minutes, with another 7 minutes set aside for discussion with William II.

The rehearsal was a success, but the public performance suffered. William II this man was grumpy and extremely capricious. Max had just begun his speech when William II interrupted, "Tsarist Russia will soon be finished." Max replied, "Your Majesty, it won't, Tsarist Russia will not be finished."

Then Max began to explain that it was because Russia had just issued a new loan, paying off the old one, and not increasing the total national debt. Hearing that Max actually contradicted him directly, the Kaiser immediately burst into a rage and roared, "Tsarist Russia must be finished, all the way." After the roar, he waved his sleeve and left to air the helpless Max. Later Max brought it up and joked, "My listeners were supposed to give me 32 minutes, but in the end I only had 3 minutes."

In spite of the "failure of the public performance", William II favoured Max because of his importance. The following year, William II summoned Max again, raised his glass to him, and said he was ready to hear the lectures on financial reform that had been long delayed.

De Kaiser Wilhelm II was a proud and conceited man, and getting him to posture a compromise was no easy task, as evidenced by Max's position in his heart. In conversation, William II reluctantly admitted that it was true that Tsarist Russia would not go bankrupt any time soon. But Max was ungrateful and then interjected, "I have already told His Majesty." William II pounded the table in exasperation, "Are you right every time?" Seeing that William II was about to storm off again, Max immediately apologized, only to be able to give William II a well-prepared lecture on financial reform.[87]

Thereafter, Max and William II met frequently. Max's relationship with William II is different from Bleichröder's relationship with Bismarck. Bismarck was often dictatorial about Bleichröder, but very subjective. William II, on the one hand, was stubborn in his views and on the other hand, "soft-spoken" and easily moved by others. Every

---

[87] Ron Chernow, *The Warburgs The 20th Century Odyssey of a Rememberable Jewish Family*.

time Max thought he had succeeded in convincing the emperor, William II suddenly changed his mind when he heard someone else's version of events.

In Germany at the time, the Junker nobility and the Prussian officer corps were hostile and resistant to the Jews, mainly because of interest. The Junker landowning aristocracy was relatively conservative in its ideology, and their group interest was to protect the price of agricultural products by demanding higher tariffs and keeping out foreign competitors. The shipping companies and the Jewish bankers, who advocate maritime trade, are strongly opposed to trade protectionism. The reason is simple, once trade protectionism prevails, international trade will not be able to do, and they have no market for the large number of financial services business of international trade. As a result, Junker landowners and Jewish bankers formed a sharp and conflicting conflict. There are also parallels with today's disputes in the field of international trade. The main actors in the fight for free trade, lower tariffs and globalization are essentially supranational corporations and international consortia; on the contrary, most of those who oppose free trade and advocate trade protection are national and local forces that would be harmed by free trade. Globalization and free trade are not slogans of theory and principle, they are a matter of naked interest.

Influenced by the strong advocacy of Max and Bowling, William II was hesitant about the sea and ready to make it big. At the beginning of the 20th century, the two major power groups with Britain and Germany at the core of the European continent began a life and death struggle of siege and counter siege, containment and rise of the most intense and bloody scene in modern world history.

Berlin-Baghdad Railway: Germany's Strategic Corridor Against Siege

In 1885, the German engineer Gottlieb Daimler invented the automobile engine using petroleum, which was much more compact and efficient than the bulky and massive steam engine system fueled by coal used at the time. This advanced engine technology could also be used on ships, battleships and, later, aircraft, and oil resources naturally became the center of attention. At the time, oil had not been discovered by Britain and the colonies it controlled, and the eyes of the world were fixed on the oil resources of the Arab region.

In the face of pressure from the sea, Germany had to try to find opportunities for strategic development from the land direction, given the momentary difficulty of overtaking Britain's powerful maritime power. Since the end of the 19th century, Germany has been doing business and investment and opening banking institutions on the Anatolian Peninsula. The Anatolian Peninsula, bordered by the Black Sea to the north, the Aegean Sea to the west and the Mediterranean Sea to the south, is Europe's strategic gateway to the Middle East. Germany's strategic objective was clear: to build a railway artery from Berlin to Baghdad (the "Orient Express" line had previously reached Istanbul) that would link Germany's strong industrial production capacity to the wealth of raw materials, oil, food and vast potential markets in the Middle East, integrate economically and strategically the industrial production and raw material resources of Central Europe, the Balkans and the entire Middle East, and extend political influence throughout West and South Asia, thus opening the sea route from the Persian Gulf to the Indian Ocean. Most importantly this corridor would bypass the powerful British naval control, bypass the Suez Canal under British and French control, and serve as a strategic artery of German security under the protection of the dominant German land forces. Against this backdrop, in 1900 the Warburg Family Bank in Hamburg, Germany, joined forces with Deutsche Bank to begin providing large-scale financing for the rail project.

Clearly, this strategic attempt has made Britain very nervous. Anglo-German tensions gradually escalated.

In 1907, former British Prime Minister Arthur Balfour worriedly told American diplomat Henry White, "Britain will make a foolish mistake if we do not rush to declare war on Germany before the Germans build more transport systems and take away our trade."[88] White was unimpressed, saying, "If you want to compete with the Germans in trade, then you should work harder." Balfour replied: "That would lower our standard of living and make it relatively easier to wage war. Is it simply a matter of right and wrong? It is a matter of British hegemony at stake."

---

[88] John V. Denson, *Reassessing the presidency: the rise of the executive state and the decline of freedom* (Ludwig von Mises Institute, 2001).

Similar to Britain, France and Russia fiercely opposed the Baghdad railway project and did everything they could to prevent its construction. Britain sought to persuade the Ottoman Empire, suggesting it was a German plot to control and destroy Turkey. And France, despite having a local investment interest of 2.5 billion francs, had a directive from the government not to allow Baghdad railway bonds to trade on the Paris stock exchange.

It should be said that the Baghdad railway project was an irreconcilable link in the siege and counter siege struggle between Britain, France, Russia and Germany, and was one of the major causes of the First World War.

Agadir Incident

After the Napoleonic Wars of 1815, Britain has held an undisputed position of world maritime hegemony, firmly controlling the main waterways of the world's oceans.

Churchill's father Randolph was a close friend of the Rothschilds, and British foreign policy was essentially that of the Rothschilds. Rothschild was one of the Royal Navy's foremost advocates and active promoters.

With the advent of the fuel engine, the demand for oil in the navy and all industries was bound to soar, and the Rothschild branch of France quickly joined forces with the Rockefellers in the United States to divide the world's oil resources. The idea that the Grand Navy could not be developed without oil resources was introduced to Churchill by Rothschild. Churchill became convinced that future naval warfare was bound to be heavily oil-powered, that naval construction was to be scaled up and that the pace of renewal was to be accelerated.

In 1888, the Rothschild Bank of England offered £225,000 in shares for the "Naval Construction and Armaments Company",[89] and after making a fortune, was not satisfied, and subsequently advocated the expansion of the Royal Navy's mega-ship project, with a massive

---

[89] Jules Ayer, *A century of finance, 1804 to 1904: The London house of Rothschild* (W. Neely, 1905).

allocation of funds to speed up naval construction to meet the so-called threat posed by the rapid catch-up of the German Navy.

The "Moroccan gunboat incident", or the "Agadir incident", hit right on the head of the gun and gave a direct account of the serious threat posed by the German Navy.

On 1 July 1911, Kaiser Wilhelm II sent a battleship, the Panther, to the British-controlled Moroccan coast to rescue threatened German citizens, which became the most serious incident of Germany's open challenge to British maritime hegemony, shocking the British and the clouds of war began to gather over Europe.

In fact, the whole so-called "Agadir affair" is a complete wreck. The story goes like this: in 1909, Max Warburg met a mysterious young man named Dr. Wilhelm Charles Regendanz. This man is a huge fan of Cecil Rhodes, and Rhodes is not a simple man, as we'll get into later. Regendance claimed that he had prepared a complete plan for Germany's colonization of Africa, arguing that Germany must act decisively. Germany, a newly imperialist country at that time, did not catch up with the feast of Portugal, Spain, Britain, France and other European powers in the first four hundred years of the global division of colonies, very depressed, the country strong and industrially developed but hardly any sphere of influence abroad has always been a disease of the Kaiser and Bismarck, so any plan for overseas colonization can easily stir up the Kaiser's frenzy. Regendance was apparently a young man with "great ideals" and wrote in his diary in 1909: "I must stand in front of the map to see where to get myself a colony."

On 16 June 1911, Max Warburg quickly became acquainted with Regentes and invited him to act as "legal adviser" to the Warburg family bank, which in fact focused on planning for the African colonies. Regendance portrayed southern Morocco as a "fertile land, rich in minerals" and proved that it was a place of core German interests. And in fact, the place is a desert gobi. The Kaiser's initial reaction was fierce opposition, fearing to spark a diplomatic conflict between Germany and Britain and France. At that time, Max Warburg was not with the Kaiser, persuaded the Kaiser that he was going to be yellow, and in a hurry, Pauline, who was favored by the Kaiser, immediately joined in, shaking his lips and finally persuaded the Kaiser. Finally William II reluctantly agreed to send a warship to take a look. Regendance and others were ecstatic.

But the problem was that there wasn't even a single German in southern Morocco at the time. Without the Germans, there is no way to show that German lives are threatened by the local natives, and there is no way to learn from them. As a result, a mining engineer was sent as a "life threatened" German. The man was supposed to reach his designated location on July 1, 1911, but the old man got lost and wandered through the rugged mountains. But this did not deter Germany from issuing a Moroccan alert that the Germans were under heavy fire on the ground, and Berlin warned the Anglo-French authorities that Germany would send warships to the area to carry out rescue operations. When the German warship arrived, the engineer was nowhere to be found. When the exhausted engineer finally came to the shore a few days later, the men on the warship happened to miss him. The engineer jumped up and down and shouted and screamed like a madman in a hurry. The German warship finally saw him, but really ignored him as crazy. As a result, it was not until the night of 5 July that the "precious German whose life was in danger" was brought aboard.[90]

"Immediately after the Agadir affair, Churchill was appointed British Minister of the Navy and vowed to strengthen the navy and protect the hegemony of the "Sunbeam Reich" from German challenges. This so-called "Agadir affair" was deemed by Britain and France to be a deliberate and malicious provocation by the German Kaiser, and the war of words between the two sides quickly escalated. Britain threatened to declare war on Germany, France began divestment from Germany, and the threat of war infected all of Europe.

The young man of unknown origin, Reagan Danes, joined forces with the Warburg family of Germany, the Rothschild family of England and France, and the German shipping lord, Pauline, and others to entice the Kaiser to fall for the trick, intensifying the antagonism between England and France, causing both sides to invest heavily in naval construction, increasing the demand for oil, and financing it through stock and bond issues in the capital markets, thus making the international bankers rich. Beyond that, of course, they have bigger strategic plans.

---

[90] Ron Chernow, *The Warburgs The 20th Century Odyssey of a Rememberable Jewish Family.*

On June 17, 1914, Churchill suggested that the British government should invest in Iran's Anglo-Persian oil company, a pawn that Rothschild had laid out in advance, just waiting for the British government to overbid it. With such an in and out, the Rothschild family was making a fortune again. The company later became known as British Petroleum (BP).

The Balfour Declaration and the Bankers' Dream

In the early 20th century, the British government, through the Anglo-Persian Company, was given the privilege of extracting oil in the new Persian state (i.e. Iran), the only source of oil for the British navy at the time. Therefore, Britain must have a firm grip on the Middle East. Rothschild used his influence in Britain to convince the British government that the future Jewish state would be a faithful ally of Britain in the Middle East. At the same time, the British could hold a firm grip on the Middle East through the Jewish state, thus linking British colonies in Africa rich in mineral resources to the Middle East. It was the Commonwealth empire dreamed of by the British ruling elite, including British Prime Ministers Lloyd George and Arthur Balfour.

In 1914, World War I broke out. Britain gained Arab support for the defeat of Germany, the dismemberment of the Ottoman Empire, and later the hegemony of the Middle East, on the condition that the Arabs in the Ottoman Empire would recognize and support the establishment of an independent state, including Palestine, after the war. But then the shrewd British signed the Sykes-Picot Agreement with France, which dealt with post-war Ottoman territory, behind the backs of the Arabs. In addition to delineating the spheres of influence of the two States, the agreement provides for "international co-administration" of Palestine. Later, in November 1917, Britain issued the pro-Zionist Balfour Declaration, which supported the establishment of a Jewish state in Palestine.

The Balfour Declaration is very interesting in that it is a private letter from Balfour, the British Foreign Secretary, to Sir Walter Rothschild (note: Baron Rothschild, second generation, and uncle of Victor Rothschild, third generation; Chapter 7 will focus on Victor's experience), and commissioned Sir Walter Rothschild to transmit it to the Zionist Organization. The letter reads as follows.

British Foreign Office

November 2, 1917

Dear Lord Rothschild.

On behalf of His Majesty's Government, I have the honour to communicate to you that the following declaration concerning sympathy with the Zionists has been submitted to the Cabinet and has been supported by the Cabinet.

His Majesty's Government is in favour of the establishment of a national home for the Jews in Palestine, and will do its utmost to bring about the achievement of this goal. But let it be clear that the civil and religious rights of non-Jews already in Palestine, as well as the rights and political status enjoyed by Jews in other countries, must not be harmed.

I would be delighted if you would forward the contents of the manifesto to the Zionist Union.

Arthur James Balfour[91]

The Balfour Declaration of the British ruling elite was a brilliant one-shot ploy. First, the European battlefield was at a standstill, and ultimately only by drawing the United States into the war could a final victory be achieved, and the influence of Jewish bankers in the United States would be a vital leverage; second, the world's Jews would fall on their financial side in favor of Britain, which would be essential for a massive and sustained money-burning war; third, to prevent the German-American Jewish bankers from favoring the German position, especially the Wall Street Jewish banking family represented by the German-sentimental Schiff; and fourth, to rein in the attitude of Russia's senior Jewish Bolshevik leadership, which was as much as 3/4 of the way to make peace with Germany.

Whoever can win the support of the Jewish bankers at the time of the stalemate in World War I will be the final winner; and whoever supports the restoration of Israel, the Jewish bankers will support!

Although the United States declared war on Germany in April 1917, but the United States army "warmed up" at home for about a year, but was slow to go to Europe to participate in the war. It wasn't until after the Balfour Declaration in November 1917 that American troops

---

[91] Ronald Sanders, *The High Walls of Jerusalem: A History of the Balfour Declaration and the Birth of the British Mandate for Palestine* (Holt, Rinehart and Winston, 1983).

wandered to the European front in early 1918, which is called No More Rabbits No More Hawks.

On 6 November 1917, with the strong support of the Arab uprising, British troops invaded Palestine and occupied all the territory in September 1918, and in 1920 the League of Nations gave Britain the "Mandate" over Palestine, and in 1921 the British Government, in implementation of the Balfour Declaration, adopted a policy of division and rule, dividing Palestine into two parts: the east, called Jordan, and the west, which remained Palestine, under the direct rule of the British appointed Governor.

After the Balfour Declaration and the British Mandate, Palestinian Jewish immigration grew exponentially. According to statistics, in April 1917, the Jewish population of Palestine did not exceed 50,000; in 1939, it had soared to more than 445,000, accounting for one third of the total Palestinian population, and Jewish immigrants, with their vast capital and skills, and the shelter of the British Mandate authorities, had established numerous cities and industries in Palestine, which had dealt a heavy blow to Arab industry and commerce. The Jews had also established secret armed organizations such as the "Hagana", the "Irgun" and the "Stern Group", thereby increasing the conflict and strife between Arabs and Jews.

Jewish bankers on Wall Street in the United States have supported Zionism from the beginning and are constantly putting pressure on the US government. As early as October 1917, President Wilson expressed his support for the draft Balfour Declaration to the British Government, and on 21 January 1919, at the Paris Peace Conference, the United States presented "proposals for the establishment of an independent Palestinian State" and "the recognition of Palestine as a Jewish State by the League of Nations as soon as the Jewish State becomes a reality", and on 30 June 1922, the United States Congress formally adopted a resolution supporting the Balfour Declaration. At the same time, full economic penetration into Palestine began.

With the strong support of Jewish bankers, the Zionist movement finally took a big step forward.

Treachery: The Contradiction of the British Ruling Elite and Zionism

After the Balfour Declaration of 1917, the Zionist organization, headed by Sir Rothschild, was bent on the hope that the victory of the Allied Powers in "World War I" would open the door to the resurrection of the Jewish people in the land of God's promise in Palestine, but the reality unfolded far beyond their expectations.

From the world view of the British ruling elite, the strategic interests of the British Empire in the Middle East have three pillars: first, to control the rich oil resources of the Middle East region; second, to control the Middle East region as a strategic hub linking the three continents of Eurasia and Africa to ensure that the British sphere of influence is at the throat of India and other Far Eastern colonies; and third, to prevent any other power from controlling the region and thus threatening the aforementioned core strategic interests of the British Empire. Therefore, Britain's inevitable strategy in the Middle East is to keep the region firmly in its own hands, monopolizing all political, economic and military power, and never to allow the emergence of independent sovereign States in the region that are difficult to control, be they Jewish or Arab States.

Thus, after the victory in the war, the British reneged on their wartime promise to the Arabs to establish an independent Arab state and single-handedly brought the region into the colonial orbit under British imperial trusteeship, out of a need to find allies to defeat the Ottoman Empire. Any further adherence to the principles of the Balfour Declaration in such circumstances would inevitably provoke a great Arab backlash and may not necessarily be in the strategic interests of the British Empire in the Middle East. The British Foreign Office, the Colonial Office and the British Trusteeship Authority in Palestine then implemented a compromise approach that encouraged Jewish emigration to Palestine while resisting Jewish statehood. As a result, this approach both upsets the Arabs: why should the place where we have lived for generations be ceded to the Jews, when it is likely that this group will establish a state on our soil? – The Jews were enraged again: the hopes of statehood were dashed, and the treacherous British were clearly crossing the river.

The British Government has had to consider further adjustments to its policy on Palestine in the context of the escalating and conflicting

Arab-Jewish conflict, the local Palestinian population and the British Trusteeship Authority.

In July 1922, British Colonial Secretary Churchill, on behalf of the British Government, issued a statement, historically known as the Churchill White Paper, the main spirit of which included: (1) there was no intention of turning the whole of Palestine into a Jewish national home; and (2) it was necessary for the Jewish community to increase the number of immigrants, but not more than the local economy could absorb.[92]

In October 1930, the British Colonial Secretary, Parsfield, made another policy statement on behalf of the British government, historically known as the Parsfield White Paper. Its thrust, based on the reaffirmation of the principles set out in the Churchill White Paper, places the defense of Arab interests above efforts to help establish a Jewish homeland, declaring that Jewish immigration should be reduced or stopped if it affects Arab employment.

In May 1939, the British Government again unilaterally published the White Paper on Palestinian Affairs, which became known as the Macdonald White Paper because the British colonial minister at the time was Macdonald. Its main elements included: (1) the British government explicitly declared that the conversion of Palestine into a Jewish state was not part of its policy and that (the establishment of a Jewish state) was a violation of its obligations to the Arabs under the Mandate and of its previous assurances to the Arabs; (2) the policy of the British government was to establish within 10 years an independent Palestinian state linked to Britain, with Arabs and Jews joining the new government in proportion to its population; (3) 75,000 Jews were allowed to move into Palestine for five years, after which they could not move without the permission of the Arabs; (4) the British trusteeship authority was given all powers to restrict and prohibit land transfers during the transition period.[93] The Macdonald White Paper was an overhaul of the Balfour Declaration and a major shift in British

---

[92] Martin Gilbert, *Churchill and the Jews: A Lifelong Friendship* (Henry Holt and Co., 2008).

[93] Paul R. Mendes-Flohr, Jehuda Reinharz, *The Jew in the modern world: a documentary history* (Oxford University Press US, 1995).

Palestine policy, effectively abandoning support for the Zionist movement.

It is clear that the change in British Middle East policy 20 years after World War I was a gradual abandonment of support for Zionism, as the leaders of the Zionist movement saw clearly when the Churchill White Paper was published in 1922. The British Empire after the First World War, with the power to defeat Germany, is the sunset before the sun sets on the Empire.

Thus, the strategic choice before the Zionists was clear: in order to rebuild Israel and fulfill God's promises in the Old Testament, they used external forces to defeat the complete geopolitical plate of the Ottoman Empire in the Middle East during World War I. It was then that they decided to do the same thing again, to use outside forces to defeat the intransigence of the British Empire in the Middle East and to rebuild Israel and the "Third Temple" on the ruins of imperial rule in the Middle East.

So who does this outside force choose? The only countries capable of destroying the British Empire were the United States, Germany and the Soviet Union, among which it was inconceivable to provoke a global war between the United States and the United Kingdom sufficient to destroy the British Empire, which Stalin in the Soviet Union could only use but could not control. The country most likely to jump out and strike at the British Empire by force, the closest geopolitically to the British Empire itself and the most convenient for Jewish capital control, is Germany, the defeated country of World War I, humiliated by the Versailles Peace Treaty, with vengeance gripping the country and in desperate need of foreign capital to restore its national economy. It was the Weimar Republic, organized according to Anglo-American liberal political logic, that ruled Germany at the time, a weak Weimar Republic that fit perfectly into the British Empire's strategy of stabilizing Germany without allowing it to grow, a Germany that was not strong enough to bear the burden of forcing the British Empire to make concessions on the Middle East.

Subverting the weak Weimar Republic, rebuilding a strong Germany, and creating a dangerous enemy for the British Empire in order to force Britain back into dependence on the Jewish bankers' moneybags was a strategy that would both achieve the strategic purpose of the Restoration and reap the benefits. However, they did not expect that they would find and raise a more unreliable figure than Stalin, and that Germany would end up strong, but completely out of control. Of course, this is an afterthought.

The imperative is how to subvert the Weimar Republic. The bankers were unarmed and the conditions were far from ripe for another war to be waged immediately in Europe, where the war had just ended, and in 1922 the bankers' only option was to launch a "currency war" to destroy the foundations of the Weimar Republic.

When the international bankers got down to business, it soon became apparent that another force was pushing in the same direction: the emerging financial powerhouse in the United States – the JPMorgan and Rockefeller groups. When the industrial production capacity of the United States in the late 19th century and early 20th century after overtaking the old British Empire, the financial power of the United States also synchronized rapid expansion, originally following the European banker bosses running errands of the little brother, gradually developed their own ambition. "The emperor takes turns to do, today to my home" idea is growing day by day, as early as the "World War I" before the outbreak, the United States emerging elite group began to consider replacing the British achievement of global hegemony of the big business.

At this point, the two forces met and finally found the soulmate, and the strategic goals of both were almost identical, and the tactical steps implemented could be well coordinated. The highest strategic goal of both sides is to defeat the global hegemony of the British Empire, the Jewish bankers want to realize the dream of Israel's restoration, and the American elites want the world hegemon. The "ideal fighter" to achieve this is Germany, and a strong, aggressive Germany is in the mutual interest of both sides. Of course, a tightrope must be put over the mighty German's head beforehand in case Germany bites back. Thus, from the central bank to the financial system, from the industrial conglomerates to the raw material base, must be completely controlled, and then the weak Weimar Republic must be replaced by a strong new Germany in order to be able to implement this "great" strategy.

How can Germany's economic lifeblood be completely controlled? A "currency war" has surfaced. The complete destruction of Germany's monetary system would make all of Germany's assets so cheap it would be easy to control them again.

According to the jargon of stock manipulation, short first, take it on the low; then long, win big profits!

Economic weapons and the Versailles Agreement

Sir Alfred Zimmern of England wrote a 13-page pamphlet entitled The Economic Weapon Against Germany (London: Allen & Unwin, 1918) in World War I. In this book, he mentions for the first time the idea of "economic warfare".[94] Zeman is listed as a key member of the Anglo-American elite organization by the famous American historian Professor Quigley.

The book hits the nail on the head that the Central European powers at war (Germany, Austria-Hungary, Turkey, etc.) are in the midst of a world-wide siege that they cannot, by their own power, break. For the first time in history, the book refers to the idea of "economic warfare" resulting from a massive economic blockade, a possibility that the Germans believed did not exist at the time.

In December 1915, the British Prime Minister mentioned, "Is anyone seriously going to think that we are going to lose this war because of the rubber shortage?" Because Britain and the United States were able to blockade Germany on the European continent and control the rest of the world's sources of raw materials, which Germany could not be supplied with during the war. Germany's preparation for war was based on the assumption that the war would last only a year at most. Apparently the First World War lasted four years, and Germany was very ill-prepared before the war, and did not expect that the loss of maritime control and the massive siege of Germany by the British economic strategy would make it difficult to replenish the huge depletion of raw materials in the war, and thus gradually lose its fighting capacity to the point of final defeat. This is a major new strategic issue for Germany when it first confronts the maritime powers as a continental power.

In his book, Zeman further mentions plans and predictions about the aftermath of the defeat against Germany, noting that what would happen after a normal peace agreement was signed? The lifting of the blockade of German ports was not actually what the Anglo-Americans wanted to do, but without raw materials there would be no employment in German industry; without employment, the large number of

---

[94] Alfred Zimmern, *The Economic Weapon Against Germany*, London: Allen & Unwin, 1918.

demobilized soldiers coming home from the war would create a large unemployed population that would threaten the social order. In contrast, Britain and the United States, because they controlled the supply of raw materials, controlled the process of rebuilding the German economy. Germany will face an overall shortage of goods, and the economic chaos will last for at least three years if one considers the emergence of famine.

As the Anglo-American economic blockade of Germany continued after the war, Germany was bound to experience a shortage of goods, which was not the usual commercial boycott, but an organized and systematic act of state. In fact, the shortage of supplies in Germany was intentionally caused by Britain and America from the beginning. Guided by the economic strategic ideas put forward by Zeman, the Versailles Agreement of 1919 was actually a continuation of the war. As the drafters of the Versailles Agreement, U.S. Secretary of State Robert Lansing, later noted, the Versailles Agreement would not provide a fair peace and would eventually become a tool and instrument of continued war. He had already foreseen "a disappointment, regret and further depression resulting from the Versailles Agreement, the terms of which were clearly unusually harsh and insulting". And the fledgling Anglo-American-led National League "will be a predator in the midst of complex greed".

Lansing's role as the main negotiator for the United States was actually very limited throughout the peace talks, as bankers from various countries, as "advisers" to the negotiators, actually dominated the negotiations. "On May 15, I received a letter of resignation from Mr. Bully, along with letters of resignation from five of our other leading experts who had come together to protest the harshness and injustice of the peace terms. The resignation letter states that they are unanimous that such a provision violates the fundamental principles that the United States defended when it entered the war." Italian Chancellor Francisco also once said: "In contemporary history, the Versailles Agreement will set a very bad precedent, it violates all precedents, all traditions, and the German representative has never heard of such unjust conditions. In the face of famine, material shortages and the threat of revolution, they had no other choice but to sign. In the ancient system of religious law, everyone must have the right to complain, even the devil, and the wicked should have such a right. But today's new national society does not even follow the sacred principles forged by the dark Middle Ages."

The war consumed by the countries of the First World War, which together amounted to three times the total assets of Germany, would eventually force Germany to pay a huge war reparations of up to DM 1.7 billion per year, which would continue until 1988. Schacht also made this comment when he said that the Versailles Agreement was an intentional design, a design that would destroy Germany economically. This clearly fits the ideals of the ruling elite of the British Empire.

Under the influence of the Versailles Agreement, the natural progress of every economy, the action of recovery and the restoration of confidence in every economy, became impossible due to the control of foreign political forces. In the war, the British financing of the war was mainly through taxes, which accounted for 20 percent of the war financing, and 6 percent for Germany. Germany's money supply increased from DM 7.2 billion to DM 28.4 billion between 1914 and 1918, the equivalent of an increase from DM 110 to DM 430 for each German. At that time, the overall price level in Germany, which rose to 234 after the German defeat in 1918, was roughly similar to that of the United Kingdom, if the benchmark value of 100 was taken as the year 1913. The impact of this degree of price increase on the lives of ordinary Germans was effectively hedged by the German government, and wages in Germany at the time rose from a base value of 100 in 1913 to 248, with Germans' wages rising even marginally above inflation. So World War I, although it hurt the German economy badly, did not destroy the German monetary system.

Clearly, for the British ruling elite, they were trying to radically curb Germany's resurgence. A Germany with a so-called "free economy" system cannot really develop and be strong under the economic siege strategy of the maritime powers. A "relatively stable" Germany, with a weak economy, lax politics, and no weapons at all, was in the fundamental interests of the British Empire. As a result, the German monetary system was in a state of relative calm from the end of the war in 1918 until 1922.

However, in July 1922, when the British ruling elite published the Churchill White Paper, declaring "no intention of turning the whole of Palestine into a Jewish national paradise" and thus perfidiously concocting a reversal of the Balfour Declaration's major commitment to the Zionist state, the German monetary system suddenly changed and the hurricane of hyperinflation made landfall without any warning.

The "independence" of the German Central Bank in 1922: the "eye of the wind" of the super-inflationary hurricane

Germany's hyperinflation of 1922 to 1923 is commonly cited in Western textbooks as a classic case of monetary disaster brought about by government control of the monetary system, concluding that only bankers controlling the right to issue money are "responsible" and "safe". In fact, it is the bankers and their manipulated central banks that are really behind the German hyperinflation.

Founded in 1876 as the central bank of Germany, the Reichsbank was essentially privately owned but largely controlled by the German Kaiser and government. The president and all directors of the Reichsbank are officers of the German government, appointed directly by the Kaiser, and are appointed for life. All the income generated by the German central bank is divided between private shareholders and the government, but in a sense these shareholders do not have the power to determine central bank policy. It was a central banking system unique to Germany, distinct from the Bank of England, the Bank of France and the Federal Reserve, and its most prominent feature was that the German Kaiser, as the supreme ruler of the country, always had firm control over the issue of money. Since the founding of the Reichsbank, the German gold mark has had a highly stable monetary value, which has played a major role in the rise of the German economy and is a successful example of a financially backward country catching up with the developed world. Even after Germany's defeat in 1918, the purchasing power of the German mark remained relatively firm until 1922, and German inflation did not differ significantly from that of the victorious nations of Britain, America, and France. It should have been quite rare for a war-defeated country, and one in an extremely miserable position at that, for the monetary policy of the Reichstag to reach this level and effect.

After Germany's defeat, however, the victorious power passed a series of pieces of legislation that completely stripped the German Government of its control over the Central Bank, and legislation was passed on 26 May 1922 that established the "independence" of the Reichstag, freed the Central Bank from the control of the German Government, and completely abolished the German Government's control over monetary policy. The right to issue money in Germany rested entirely in the hands of private bankers, including heavyweight international bankers such as Warburg.

This is the key factor in the occurrence of the worst hyperinflation in modern history in Germany!

As for the cause of this inflation, the prevailing view in the West is that the German government had to print a lot of money in response to the passive resistance of the then German Chancellor Wilhelm Cuno to the French and Belgian occupation of the German Ruhr. It's an explanation that doesn't make sense from every angle. First of all, is the government overprinting money? It's not. The German Central Bank was privatized in May 1922, while the Ruhr problem arose in January 1923, and the excessive printing of banknotes was the work of a central bank under the control of international bankers.

Second, was the German central bank's overprinting of banknotes an attempt to save the fiscal crisis? It's not. It is true that the occupation of the Ruhr region has caused serious financial difficulties for Germany, but not so much that the German Central Bank has resorted to "monetary suicide" to cope with it, nor has it solved any of the problems. There are actually a lot of options for Chancellor Cuno of the German government, who used to be Pauling's managing director at Hamburg American Lines (HAPAG). Max Warburg is both a director of HAPAG and a director of Deutsche Reichsbank, which at this time has an unusual relationship with the most powerful Wall Street firm in the United States, Kuhn Loeb and Co., of which the two Warburg brothers are senior partners, Paul being the actual operator of the Federal Reserve. In such circumstances, whether the German Government was issuing high-yielding special treasury bonds to international bankers or the Reichsbank, represented by Max, was negotiating an "international bailout" to the Federal Reserve, represented by its brother Paul, there was no problem in coping with the short-term financial difficulties caused by the Ruhr problem for more than a year.

Thirdly, the Reichstag overprinted money to pay the war reparations; can the deliberate overprinting of local currency reduce the foreign debt? No way. In fact, the Versailles Agreement had explicitly required that Germany must use gold, pounds and dollars to pay for the war reparations. In such cases, the excessive issuance of national currencies does not help, and the more Indian currencies fall, the more difficult it will be to exchange them for foreign currency to pay off foreign debt. This is in line with the fact that during the Asian financial turmoil Thailand could not repay its US dollar foreign debt by printing the local currency baht.

It was this contradictory explanation that was later proposed by the President of the Reichsbank, Schacht, in his book The Stability of the German Mark, published in 1927. As a traditional liberal economist, he believes that the crisis of hyperinflation was caused by the German government. He argued that the Reichsbank was within its purview, primarily to control inflation, but the Reichsbank found itself unable to make decisions. The view held by the Reichsbank at the time was that any measures and attempts to stabilize the currency would be useless as long as the Ruhr industrial zone remained under French occupation, the total foreign debt of the war remained unfixed, and the German government did not have sufficient financial resources. The Reichsbank went on a money binge to save the German government and they created a new Reichstag that could be supplied to the government for use. Schacht argued that Germany, then defeated in the war, had to resort to the Reichsbank's power to issue money in order to sustain itself. Germany was facing an existential problem, so the central bank had no way to maintain an independent monetary policy.

Schacht's point is actually hard to make for itself.[95]

The "currency war" that overthrew the Weimar Republic

How exactly was the German mark destroyed? In a nutshell, the easiest way to destroy a currency is to issue too much of it. Such excessive currency issuance can be carried out in several ways: first, by central banks themselves issuing excessive currency; second, by private banks creating excessive credit and currency; and third, by currency speculators in the market through massive "naked shorting", which destroys the value of a country's currency while at the same time having the same effect as currency speculators issuing large amounts of currency. Indeed, in May 1922, when the Reichstag fell into the hands of international bankers, three forms of monetary over-issuance emerged simultaneously.

In the first case, the massive printing of money by the Reichsbank is a fact, but not for the government to forgive foreign debt and solve financial difficulties.

---

[95] Hjalmar Schacht, *The magic of money* (Oldbourne, 1967).

Look again at the second scenario, the effect of the money supply from private banks on hyperinflation. In terms of time.

In November 1921, the exchange rate of the mark to the dollar was 330:1.

From January to May 1922, the mark was stable at 320:1 against the dollar.

On 26 May 1922, the Reichsbank was privatized.

In December 1922, the mark was 9,000 to the dollar.

In January 1923, the Ruhr crisis broke out and the value of the mark plummeted, reaching 49,000 to 1 against the dollar.

In July 1923, the mark reached 1,100,000 to the dollar.

In November 1923, the exchange rate of the mark to the dollar was 2,500,000,000,000:1.

In December 1923, the exchange rate of the mark to the dollar was 4,200,000,000,000:1.

In 1923, prices in Germany doubled on average every two days.

By this time the German mark had been completely destroyed. In the midst of the mad sell-off of the mark, there was hyperinflation in Germany. Many private bankers started issuing their own currencies, which may have gold or foreign exchange as backing. The privatized Deutsche Reichsbank, which was printing money at full capacity, could not keep up with the total amount of money issued by the private banks. Schacht made an estimate that about half of the total amount of German money in circulation at that time was issued by private bankers and not official money from the Reichstag. So, private banks' excess money printing accounts for nearly half of the source of hyperinflation.

The third, least obvious but most deadly, was the systematic and massive shorting of the German mark, which led to a dramatic devaluation of the mark, the effect of which was equivalent to the massive printing of money.

The basic working mechanism of shorting a country's currency can probably be divided into several stages, starting with the obvious endogenous problems with the currency. The situation in Germany at the time was perfectly in line with this. After the First World War, Germany needed to use foreign currency for reparations and was clearly under tremendous external debt pressure, and the German mark itself did have a very obvious flaw. This is similar to the situation of the four small Asian dragons during the Asian financial crisis, which was overburdened with external debt and they had to get dollars to pay it off. Under normal circumstances, this problem can be resolved incrementally by the slow and automatic adjustment of the economy. These external debts could be gradually repaid, for example by increasing taxes or temporarily lowering living standards. But when currency speculation occurs on a large scale, concentrated and sudden, it will affect the value of the currency, and this large scale currency speculation, is still considered a legal act. In the process of speculation, speculators tend to end up super profitable as long as they sell a country's currency on a large scale beforehand, and that currency has endogenous difficulties and problems.

What is a shorting mechanism? When currency speculators engage in currency short selling, they don't really own the currency, but rather claim to. As long as there is a significant devaluation of the currency within a certain period of time, they can make huge profits by buying the currency back from the market at a low price after the devaluation, and by smoothing out the "lies" that they "claimed" to have in the first place. In this sense, when a currency speculator is shorting a currency that does not exist and "claims to own" it, he is in essence gaining the power to create it for a certain period of time. These currency speculators are all out at the same time, shorting together on a large enough scale and in large enough quantities and at a time when the country's currency is weak enough that such shorting will have a strong "self-fulfilling" effect, with the end result being a free-fall devaluation of the shorted currency and, in serious cases, a currency panic. And a currency panic would lead to a chain reaction, triggering an instinctive panic among other social classes to sell local currency for foreign currency in large quantities, leading to a larger market shorting exercise.

In such a currency crash, the huge profits earned by speculators are the wealth accumulated over the years by the producers and savers of this country, and social production and economic activity will be devastated. The so-called liberal economists, at this point, will blame all the mistakes on the government's faulty monetary policy and ignore the huge disaster created by the speculators.

In fact, the problems in Germany in 1923 were very similar to those that emerged from the Asian financial turmoil of 1997, with serious inherent flaws in the local currency system and the national economy, high external debt, the influx of foreign currency speculators, mega shorting of the local currency, the monetary system on the verge of collapse, the sharp devaluation of the local currency, inflation that swept away social wealth and destroyed the economic base of the country. The difference is that, instead of curbing currency speculation, the Reichstag is disguised as giving speculators plenty of ammunition; the private banks of international bankers are also adding fuel to the fire by issuing half of the total amount of money in circulation in the midst of hyperinflation.

The reason history is surprisingly similar is that the people who repeat it are the same people. Today's Soros and the international bankers behind him are in the same league as the currency speculators who destroyed the German mark in 1923.

The social wealth of the Weimar Republic was looted in the course of a year. The anger of the German middle class being reduced to abject poverty, the loss of everything and the humiliation suffered after the war have raised the anger in the hearts of Germans into a vengeful mentality like no other. German society at this time was already dry, waiting for just one spark to detonate.

Schacht's Battle for the "Ground Rent Mark"

The German mark's credibility was gone after 18 months of bloodshed, when most people felt a completely different currency was needed from a psychological perspective. This new mark, also known historically as the Rentenmark, was a new currency issued with all of Germany's land and industrial products as collateral, with a total value equivalent to 3.2 billion marks. The ground rent mark is pegged to the US dollar with an exchange ratio of 4.2:1 and the ground rent mark to the old mark with an exchange ratio of 1:1 trillion. In order to psychologically isolate the ground rent mark from the old mark, a new "Rentenbank" was established. The ground-rent banks provided the Deutsche Reichsbank with new mark loans, and the Reichsbank in turn provided society with credit for the ground-rent mark. But the ground rent bank has never operated independently of the Imperial Bank, merely functioning psychologically as a firewall between the old and new marks. The Ground Rent Mark went into circulation on November

15, 1923. The new mark is not a French currency and does not have the ability to pay government debt and foreign debt.[96]

Schacht had already had 23 years of banking experience when he was entrusted with the heavy responsibility of stabilizing the Deutsche Mark. When Schacht invented the new ground-rent mark, it did not immediately stabilize the value of the mark; beating the currency speculation frenzy was the key turning point in stabilizing the mark's value, a struggle that went on for a year. It took a subsequent string of credit crunches to follow, before the goal of stabilizing the mark was finally achieved.

The first "New Deal" of the Schacht was to immediately stop all other private banks from issuing marks and to pay all old marks held immediately.

The second move was that the new ground rent mark was expressly prohibited from being lent to foreigners. Schacht understands that foreign currency speculators are a major speculative force in shorting the Deutsche Mark. This practice of his means that foreign speculators, after shorting the ground rent mark, will have a hard time getting the ground rent mark to close their positions in the foreign exchange market, so the willingness to speculate will be greatly impeded. With this single move, the initial defeat of foreign currency speculators was achieved, and stopping currency speculation was an important first step in German monetary reform.

These currency speculators are now beginning to realize that they can put an end to all speculation on the mark in the foreign exchange market if the central bank makes up its mind to do so. Schacht actually understood from the beginning how to deal with currency speculation, but a few months earlier, when the worst inflation was occurring, the Reichstag stood by and let foreign speculators destroy the mark.

Foreign currency speculators are still constantly attacking the new ground-rent mark, and the Schacht are finally getting riled up. At the end of November 1923, Schacht pointed out that

> *"speculation in the land-rental mark is not only very malicious to the economic interests of the country, but also extremely*

---

[96] Ron Chernow, *The Warburgs The 20th Century Odyssey of a Rememberable Jewish Family.*

> *foolish in itself. In the last few months such speculation (the required mark) has been obtained either through a very generous loan from the Deutsche Reichsbank or through the urgent printing of money by private banks in exchange for the Reichsbank mark."*
>
> *"But now three things have happened; emergency money (banknotes printed by private banks themselves) has lost its value; it (banknotes printed by private banks) has been forbidden to exchange with the Reichstag; the formerly generous loans of the Reichstag are now no longer issued; and the ground-rent mark is no longer available abroad. These reasons led to speculators not being able to get enough marks from the foreign exchange market to pay what they owed, and they incurred large losses."*[97]

The key message of the German mark's collapse has been leaked in this passage from Schacht. First, the massive shorting of the mark was "generously" financed by the Deutsche Reichsbank, since at the time these speculators could easily obtain large, low-cost loans from the German central bank, which were used to short the mark as a key measure to defeat it. In other words, central banks, controlled by international bankers, provide currency speculators with a sea of ammunition to short the mark. Secondly, foreign currency speculators borrowed large amounts of marks from private banks on German soil, which in turn "supplied" foreign currency speculators by printing their own banknotes, which were then converted into marks by the Central Bank, and the German private bankers were clearly accomplices to the foreign speculators. Schacht does not name some of the prominent German banking families that are still operating at the top even after the stability of his master Marc. Schacht made it clear that "some prominent banking institutions are also involved in currency speculation tricks, and the country is still full of currency speculators who can even take the family bank's good name and reputation for granted if they can make money". His punishment is that the central bank suspended the re-discounting of notes to these banks. Thirdly, national banks are also penalized for violating the prohibition on borrowing ground rent marks from foreign speculators.

Beginning on April 7, 1924, Schacht ordered the German Central Bank to refuse to issue new credit for a period of two months. This

---

[97] Hjalmar Schacht, *The magic of money* (Oldbourne, 1967).

move by the central bank was intended to restore stability to the German mark. At the same time, the Shah has adopted a severe credit crunch. He raised the interest rate on the then one-month loan from 30 to 45 per cent and the overdraft interest fee from 40 to 80 per cent. The move put all the foreign mark speculators in a bind, forcing them to hand over their foreign currency in exchange for German marks to pay for the money they lost shorting the mark. In this way, the German Central Bank significantly increased its foreign exchange reserves, which in April 1924 stood at about DM 600 million, and by August, after only four months of this policy, had more than doubled.[98]

After the strict implementation of the above measures by Schacht, the massive Mark Strangulation was finally cut off from the capital supply, thus ending in one fell swoop the speculators' frenzied attack on the German mark, after which the German mark regained its calm in the foreign exchange market.

In July 1924, when the German mark was restored to stability, the interest on borrowing began to fall. As a result of the severe credit crunch imposed by Schacht, many German government-owned post offices and railways formed their own banks. These institutions are large and powerful, and they quickly accumulate huge sums of money, and this accumulation is far faster than the private banking system. By the end of 1924, businessmen and other businessmen in German society, were treating the land rent mark and the Reichsmark equivalent. At this time, Schacht again converted the land rent mark into a mark issued by the German Central Bank.

The Schacht initiative is similar to the HKMA's "one-trick pony" measure in the 1997 Asian financial turmoil, that is, to raise the cost of money lending to currency speculators beyond their means, a move that will bring down the currency speculation frenzy in no time!

He did not have to reveal all this, but he did not want people to say that the Reichsbank was helpless during the hyperinflation in 1923. In addition, Schacht was a strong nationalist and advocated the stability of the German mark, which he also regarded as his sacred duty. As he watched the powerful Mark in his mind being destroyed by hyperinflation, there was an unnameable rage in his heart. In The

---

[98] Ron Chernow, *The Warburgs The 20th Century Odyssey of a Rememberable Jewish Family.*

Stability of the German Mark, published in 1927, Schacht was still defending the inaction of the Reichsbank, and by the time his 1967 book *The Magic of Finance* was published, he finally wanted to have a "say" in history. From 1923 to 1967, after 44 years of silence and a secrecy about the real causes of hyperinflation, he finally broke a certain subterfuge in Anglo-Saxon financial circles and gave an account of himself and history in an extremely obscure way, in a cold book about a long-forgotten 44-year-old history.

The Dawes Plan: Supporting the Beginning of Germany

Through hyperinflation, the international bankers were able to reap the benefits of the "shearing of the sheep", which not only swept Germany through decades of industrialized wealth, but also took massive control of the German financial and industrial system. At the same time, it provoked a strong anger among the German people against the Weimar Republic, thus disintegrating the popular base of the Weimar Republic. Next, it was time to strengthen Germany's industrial capacity and build up strength to challenge the hegemony of the British Empire.

In fact, the international bankers set the scene at the Paris Peace Conference: John Foster Dulles, a Wall Street lawyer who was a key figure in the Versailles peace talks and one of the drafters of the peace treaty, was responsible for drafting article 231 of the peace treaty, the German "war crimes" clause that laid the scourge of German vindictiveness. United States Secretary of State Charles Evans Hughes, who served as chief counsel for Rockefeller Standard Oil, persuaded President Coolidge to appoint Charles Dawes, a banker close to the JPMorgan consortium, to chair the Commission on Compensation. From 1924, when the Dawes Plan was implemented, until 1931, Germany paid a total of DM 10.5 billion in war reparations, but borrowed DM 18.6 billion from abroad; after 1923, the shadow of Jewish bankers, Rockefellers, and JPMorgan was everywhere behind, whether it was the German company IG Farben, United Steel, or the German Electricity Corporation, and Germany's post-war recovery was all controlled by Wall Street capital, which raised public funds through the sale of German bonds, from which the JPMorgan and Warburg families made additional large profits.[99]

In 1924, the Dawes Plan was launched on the American side. The point of the Dawes plan was to cut Germany's war reparations, from DEM 132 billion to DEM 37 billion. The United States used the money to issue loans to Germany, mainly to pay off Germany's debt to France and Britain. Britain and France get the money repaid by Germany and then give it back to the United States because both Britain and France owe the United States money. The result was that the Americans themselves lent money to the Germans to repay the Anglo-French, and the Anglo-French in turn returned a portion of the German repayment to the United States, so that the money went round and round again to the United States. In this cycle, it is the American taxpayer who loses. In the process, the German industry, controlled by Wall Street capital, which had already done the "bottoming out", reduced its debt burden and increased its profitability, while at the same time, all the bankers involved in the capital transactions gained a great deal. The Dawes plan was immediately welcomed by international bankers when it was proposed, as everyone had an equal stake in this circular repayment game. Dawes won the Nobel Peace Prize with Chamberlain in 1925 and later became Vice President of the United States.

Schacht and the international bankers also proposed a new compensation clause under which all profits generated by the German Central Bank would be divided, with 45 per cent of profits going to the private shareholders of the German Central Bank and 55 per cent to the Government. Eventually all the central bank shareholders agreed that half of the first 50 million marks of profits were taken by private central bank shareholders, and 25 percent of the second 50 million profits were taken privately, followed by 10 percent of the annual profits going to private shareholders.[100]

After Dawes's plan went into effect, huge US loans flooded into Germany, a large amount of foreign credit followed, and international bankers generally had a high level of confidence in Schacht. But the Schacht have adopted unusually strict restrictions on the use of foreign funds, stipulating that the money can only be used in the field of

---

[99] Carroll Quigley, *Tragedy and Hope* (MacMillian Company, 1966).

[100] Stephen Zarlenga, *Germany's 1923 Hyperinflation: A "Private" Affair.*

production and not for credit for luxury goods and consumption. Under such a policy, from 1924 to 1929, the German industrial production system under the control of Wall Street capital was rapidly built into the most advanced industrial system in all of Europe. The Schacht' credit support for production and policy orientation to severely restrict access to other similar stock, real estate and luxury consumer markets have been notably effective. Germany's industrial strength was quickly restored and it gradually became equipped to challenge Britain.

After taking control of German industry economically and financially, the next step was to foster a political leadership and political organization capable of fighting a world war against the British Empire. That's when Hitler and his Nazi party came into view of the international bankers. In the early stages of the Nazi movement, people on Wall Street and in U.S. State Department circles were getting their intelligence from multiple sources. Long before the beer hall riots of 1923, Robert Murphy, an official of the U.S. State Department in Munich, met Hitler personally through General Ludendorfff, a Murphy who would later become a central figure in the Bilderberg Club. It was through these secret contacts that a steady stream of Nazi ideas and organizational intelligence flowed into the secret decision-making circles of Wall Street and Washington for the attention of the inner circle of international bankers. And as early as 1926, Reichsbank President Schacht began secretly financing the Nazis. By June 1929, the bankers who controlled the Federal Reserve held a meeting and selected Sidney Warburg to further "interview" Hitler in Germany on their behalf, as well as to conduct cooperative negotiations. The Wall Street bankers offered the condition "to advocate an offensive foreign policy and foment revenge against France". Hitler didn't ask for much, giving 100 million marks ($24 million) for everything. In the end, the parties settled for $10 million. And Hitler's Nazi claims, which Sidney reported on upon his return, deeply impressed Rockefeller, and immediately after the New York Times began regular coverage of Hitler, special institutes for Nazi research were opened at universities.[101]

---

[101] Antony C. Sutton, *Wall Street & the Rise of Hitler* (GSG & Associates, 1976).

What the international bankers did not expect was that the street gangster Hitler had his own "grand plan" and took the international bankers' money for his own "private work".

CHAPTER VI

Hitler's "New Deal"

In the Second World War, the power of the military machine of Nazi Germany had long been known to the world, and Hitler was even more of a demon that everyone around the world cried out for. However, outside of academic circles, few people understand the workings of the monetary system and economic system in Nazi Germany. In the economic crisis that swept the world in the 1930s, Germany was the hardest hit, with a depressed economy and unprecedented unemployment. The fact that the Nazis were able to come to power legitimately through democratic elections is closely related to the economic crisis in Germany. At a time of social unrest and change in the minds of the people in Germany, the Nazis took the pulse of society and won the election by playing the New Deal card to save the economic crisis. If the Nazis had relied on mere slogans and propaganda, without real talent to govern the economic crisis, they would soon have lost the hearts and minds of the people and eventually collapsed like the Weimar Republic.

Hitler, who had just come to power in 1933, was faced with an economic mess. From 1929 to 1932, the utilization rate of German industrial equipment fell to 36%, total industrial production fell by 40%, the value of foreign trade fell by 60%, prices fell by 30%, iron production fell by 70%, shipbuilding output fell by 80%, unemployment reached 30%, the economic crisis exacerbated social class conflicts, and more than 1,000 strikes broke out in three years.

It should be said that Germany has been hit by an economic crisis far more severely than other capitalist countries in Europe and America. As soon as the Nazis came to power, they immediately devoted themselves to saving the economy, beginning what became known as Hitler's "New Deal". Under a series of strong economic measures, the German economy quickly recovered and began to grow strongly, with unemployment plummeting to 1.3 percent by 1938. From 1933 to 1938,

German pig iron production rose from 3.9 million tons to 18.6 million tons, steel production rose from 5.6 million tons to 23.2 million tons, and aluminum, magnesium and lathe production was even higher than in the United States. From 1933 to 1939, Germany's heavy industry and arms industry grew 2.1 times, production of consumer goods increased by 43 per cent and the gross national economy grew by more than 100 per cent, while the construction of the national highway network was completed, the basic system of heavy industry was reorganized and a modern army was equipped.

The Roosevelt New Deal, which began in 1933, only temporarily alleviated the crisis, and the U.S. economy entered a long period of so-called "special depression", under the strong stimulus of the so-called "New Deal", the U.S. economy is still weak recovery, 1937–1938, the U.S. fell into a serious economic crisis again, and it was not until 1941, after the U.S. participation in World War II, that the Great Depression completely emerged. Throughout the Roosevelt New Deal, the average unemployment rate in the United States was as high as 18 per cent and the gross national product did not return to pre-crisis 1929 levels until 1941. Had war not broken out and upwards of 10 million young Americans been drafted into the military, the unemployment problem would probably have continued for quite some time.

Germany was the country hardest hit by the economic crisis in the 1930s, but it was the first country to emerge from the Great Depression.

The history of the war crimes committed by the Nazis is already settled and is therefore beyond the scope of this chapter. However, monetary and economic policy in Nazi Germany is a little-known area, and we will look at the interaction between politics and money in Germany at the time from this perspective.

"Cynical Hitler"

One day in November 1918, Corporal Adolf Hitler of the Wehrmacht Liszt Regiment lay quietly in his hospital bed in the Army Hospital like the rest of the wounded, savoring the pain of temporary blindness due to the poison gas administered by the Allied Powers and the happiness of being awarded the Reich Iron Cross. Just then, a sudden news that struck Corporal Hitler from his hospital bed like a bolt from the sky, Germany announced its surrender to the Allied Powers! Anger and disappointment gnawed at the young Hitler like a viper, and what was it all about? Is this the bitter result of four years of fighting with countless comrades of war?

Shortly afterwards, the news came that the Government of the Weimar Republic had recognized the Peace of Versailles: Germany had lost about 1/10 of its territory and 1/8 of its population, lost all its colonies, demilitarized the Rhineland, made France occupy the Saarland and pay huge reparations (70 years to pay its debts until 1988), and above all the war crimes treaty: Germany had to recognize full responsibility for starting the war.[102] Like most of the old German people, Hitler was thoroughly enraged.

Prior to the November 1918 revolution, the situation in Germany, while not good, had not yet reached the point of complete defeat. On the battlefield of the Western Front, the Allies never occupied German territory, while German forces penetrated deep into northern France, and from March to July 1918, German forces launched five major offensives on the Western Front in succession. At the end of May of that year, the Germans launched their third offensive, which succeeded in breaking through the French line and pushing into a place only 37 kilometres from Paris, and on 15 July they launched their fifth offensive, which failed to achieve its strategic objectives, with the arrival of American troops in Europe and a significant increase in the strength of the Allied Powers. The Germans then switched to a strategic defensive posture in France. On the Eastern Front, after the Russian October Revolution of 1917, the Soviet regime first decided that the situation at home was so serious that the Russian army was so sick of war that it was impossible to continue the war. Lenin was determined to make peace with Germany, and in March 1918 Russia was forced to sign the extremely harsh Brest-Litovsk Peace Treaty with Germany, under which Germany would acquire nearly 1 million square kilometers of Russian land and nearly 50 million inhabitants. And the areas ceded to Germany owned 90 percent of Russia's coal mining, 73 percent of its iron ore, 54 percent of its industry and 33 percent of its railways. In addition, the treaty stipulates that the Soviet Government must demobilize the army, including the recently formed Red Army

---

[102] *The Making of the West: Peoples and Cultures*, 3rd ed. Vol. C. Boston: Bedford/St. Martins, 2009, p. 817.

unit.[103] On 27 March of the same year, three additional Soviet-German treaties were signed in Berlin, providing for the payment of DM 6 billion to Germany in various forms.

If Germany was able to stall and consume the Allied offensive on the French front in the west, and the war on the east was over, the German army would soon be able to concentrate its full strength on the west, and with the large tracts of land and abundant resources ceded by Russia, and the huge reparations of 6 billion marks, there would be a fundamental increase in German war power. Even if Germany ultimately struggles to win, the Allied Powers may not be willing to confront each other for a long time because of the massive human and material depletion and internal disputes, and it is indeed possible to end the war with dignity if Germany stalls.

Many Germans were convinced that the German army was invincible and would never be defeated. In other words, as long as the representatives of the government did not "sell out the country for glory" and the country did not collapse as a result of the revolution, the Germans would surely win. For some Germans, even if peace had to be sought, they believed that the Allies would be lenient with Germany according to the American Fourteen Points of Peace, that Germany could perhaps annex the German-speaking areas of the former Austro-Hungarian Empire, achieve a German-Austrian merger and create a Greater Germany according to Wilson's promised principle of "national self-determination"[104] – but the harsh reality gave the German population a pungent taste of being deceived and betrayed. Besides the Allied Powers, were there traitors within Germany who betrayed Germany? The people were united and almost immediately found scapegoats for the defeat: the weak Social Democrats who recognized the Versailles Peace Treaty and the "international Jews", who were called the "November sinners" and were considered guilty of selling out German interests.

With a bitter hatred of the so-called "November sinners", the cynical Hitler retired from the army with an old uniform and an Iron Cross. Unemployed, Hitler soon found a new job as a spy for German

---

[103] Liu Debin, ed., *History of International Relations*, Beijing: Higher Education Press, 2003, pp. 203–204.

[104] Ibid, pp. 206-207.

Army Intelligence to find out about the "German Workers Party", a small party of only 55 people at the time. Hitler had no theoretical foundation, but he was a man of great perception who, in his work of "spying", drew on the best parts of the impassioned orators of the various schools of thought and was able to quickly grasp the fatal flaws in their views while enriching his "theoretical system".

One day in September 1919, Hitler again came to the place where the German Worker's Party was meeting to find out what was going on. The content of one speaker quickly captured Hitler's interest, and the man whose views impressed him was Gottfried Feder. Hitler, in his Mein Kampf, published in 1924, specifically said:

> "After I first heard Feder speak, an idea immediately arose in my mind that I had discovered an important principle of our (Nazi) party."

It was at the behest of Feder that Hitler joined the German Workers' Party.[105]

Who was this Feder, and what kind of high-mindedness did he speak, that he was able to make Hitler get away with it, and thus find the principles on which the Nazi Party was founded?

Feder: Hitler's financial mentor

After Hitler joined the German Workers Party, Feder became Hitler's mentor in economics and finance. Hitler, inspired by Feder, took a keen interest in money, finance, employment, trade, economic crises and other issues.

Feder, who was not a student of economics and finance, began to "figure out for himself" the connection between money, the economy, depression, employment, war and the state in 1917, completely breaking away from the traditional academic mindset and coming up with a series of startling conclusions. He argued that the state must have the power to control the money supply, that the central bank must be nationalized and that private control of the central bank must not be allowed. For the biggest problem with private control of the central

---

[105] *Munich 1923*, John Dornberg, Harper & Row, NY, 1982. P. 344.

bank is that the interest earnings and other benefits it generates will be privately owned, rather than benefiting the state and the public.[106]

Originally, Hitler, who had no knowledge of economics and finance, had always thought that the defeat of the German "World War I" and the subsequent hyperinflation was a purely political issue. After Feder's advice, Hitler immediately and keenly grasped that finance was at the heart of all this, and was impressed by the essential difference between "creative industrial capital" and "greedy, predatory financial capital". When Hitler realised that finance and the power groups that controlled it were the real masters of Germany's destiny, his realm immediately leapt to a new level and he looked back on many of the questions that had confused him before, and immediately gained unprecedented insight and a new perspective. He gradually developed a clear logical framework for the future functioning of Germany and the "important principles" of the Nazi Party.

In 1920, Hitler proposed a system of philosophical principles for the Nazi movement after repeated and heated debates and reflections with Feder and others. Because of the philosophical level of the platform, Hitler believed that it would "never change". This system of thought was summarized in the 25-point platform, whose status was reaffirmed at the 1932 Nuremberg Congress of the Nazi Party.[107]

The 25 Point Platform contains all the basic ideas and policies of the Nazis. The demands and claims relating to the economy reflect the main economic ideas of Feder, the key points being.

Point 11: "Outlaw unearned income and break up interest slavery." This is consistent with Feder's consistent advocacy of the abolition of "interest slavery" and the distinction between "creative industrial capital" and "profit-eating financial capital". In his view, capital can only create value if it actually enters the cycle of the real economy, and "predatory" financial capital that is "rolling in and out of profit" only in the financial system is actually the result of the exploitation of other workers.

Point 12: "Suppression and confiscation of all illegal gains made possible by war." Hitler claimed that the German army did not lose

---

[106] *Hitler: A Profile in Power*, Ian Kershaw, Chapter I (London, 1991, rev. 2001).

[107] *Adolf Hitler*, John Toland, New York: Doubleday & Company, 1976. p. 94–98.

militarily in World War I, but that the soldiers at the front were "stabbed in the back" by the big bourgeoisie and Jewish financiers who "sold out the national interest".

Point 13: "We call for the nationalization of all enterprises (trusts) that have (so far) been put together." Feder proposed the establishment of an "aircraft carrier" of State-owned enterprises in order to achieve State monopoly of the main resources of society, thus avoiding the vicious competition and division of the rich and the poor caused by the excessive pursuit of profits by capital. He sees the nationalized torus as some kind of balance between reasonable profits for capitalists and stable employment for workers.

Point 14: "We are asking to participate in the big business dividend." Feder insists that big business must feed back to society and share economic prosperity with all segments of society.

Point 16: "We demand the establishment and maintenance of a healthy middle class, demand the immediate confiscation of big department stores and cheap leasing to small businessmen, demand special care for all small businessmen in the acquisition of goods by the State and the States." This view of Feder reflects the economic interests of the petty bourgeoisie and the common people of society, although it is no longer a so-called philosophical principle at all, but belongs to a specific policy level.

Point 17: "We call for a land reform that suits the needs of the nation. Call for a decree to confiscate land for the common good without cost, for the abolition of land rents and for an end to all land speculation." The most intolerable aspects of Feder's philosophy are "gain by doing nothing" and "speculation", and his desire to spend every social resource on tangible productive activities. He actually lives entirely in an abstract and idealized world, ignoring human nature. There is an old Chinese saying: "A gentleman is like water, a villain is like oil." The gentleman is of course very good, but to live with the gentleman for a long time can only be afraid that no one can stand that kind of eternal dullness and blandness; the little people certainly have problems, but the little people dig into their hearts to create all kinds of trouble, but also bring the ups and downs and changes of life. Creation and speculation are also the same thing, without creation, everyone has no food, but without speculation, life is inevitably too dull. The problem with Feder is that he tries to separate the spear from the shield, taking only the side he wants.

Point 18: "Death penalty for traitors, usurers and speculators."

In addition to this, Feder advocated reliance on the "authority of the State", the establishment of the Economic Construction Bank, the issuance of State securities and the financing of investments in social public projects. In view of the reality that the international bankers had long ago formed a monopoly over gold, he proposed to get rid of the gold standard, to let the State determine the amount of money in circulation, to use the production capacity of the real economy of the State as a backing for the currency, and to exchange commodities with other countries, thus escaping the control of foreign capital over German currency and foreign exchange.[108]

Hitler supported many of Feder's ideas conceptually, but he was a politician who could not speak of any interest in the theory itself, and theory was always a tool for him, used when it fit, thrown when it did not. The eternal law of statesmen is that power changes, by the pursuit of power, and by change, more power.

In order to gain more power, Hitler had to work with people who held "real power". In the view of Hitler, who was a soldier, the so-called real power is actually very simple, "violence + financial power", the two complement each other and are inseparable. It was unlikely that the poor, clanking Hitler would have been financed with large sums of money, but the "violent" support was already somewhat reliable.

Brewpub Riot: Hitler's Fame

If Feder provided Hitler with the theoretical weapon of economic finance, Rom (Ernst Rohm)'s contribution lies in providing the practical weapon of violence.

Rohm joined the Imperial Army at the age of 19 and was wounded three times in World War I, eventually becoming a junior officer. After the German surrender, Rohm joined the paramilitary organization "Freiheit" as deputy to Epp, commander of the Bavarian Freiheit, and became one of Munich's most powerful soldiers. "After the end of World War I, a large number of German officers and soldiers returned to their hometowns, and under the blow of the British "economic

---

[108] Ibid.

weapons", the shortage of supplies and the hopelessness of employment, these energetic veterans spontaneously gathered together and formed the Free Corps under the leadership of some officers. Secretly funded and equipped by the German military, the Free Legion was initially tasked with manning the long eastern border to address the Wehrmacht's immediate manpower shortage. In the system of the Weimar Republic, the army belongs to the state and is not allowed to participate in domestic partisan politics. After the political turmoil in Germany after the First World War, the Communist Party led a workers' revolution, and the Free Army, which was relied upon by the conservative forces represented by the government and the military, fought and suppressed revolutionary movements everywhere in blood.

In October 1919, Hitler made his first speech at a rally of the German Workers Party. Hitler fully demonstrated his true gift – an extremely incendiary eloquence, no matter how absurd and outrageous a point, which, after being processed by his paranoid brain, bursts forth again from his glib tongue with thunderous effect. He is no longer making a point, but rather stirring up an overwhelming force in intense, searing emotional catharsis and sharp, cold rational analysis. Perhaps the Germans were too thoroughly deprived, too ruthlessly humiliated, too nakedly betrayed, and the wild and extreme, subconscious inferiority and arrogance in the bones of the Germanic nation were suddenly triggered by Hitler's hot "truth flamethrower", and the remaining layer of rational protection was completely melted down, leaving only fanatical belief and the impulse for revenge.

Among the audience, which was overwhelmed by it, was Roma. Rom's admiration for Hitler was so great that he believed he had a great future and the potential to lead an ultra-nationalist movement. In the spring of 1920, he formally introduced Hitler into his own military circle. With the support of the violent groups, Hitler became ambitious and began to plan how to achieve the ideal of a rich country with a strong army.

In 1920, Hitler, with the help of Feder, ideologically developed the theoretical system of the 25-point platform and, with the aid of Rom, mastered the means of violence. At this time, he changed the name of the German Workers' Party to the National Socialist Deutsche Arbeiterpartei (National Socialist German Workers' Party), or Nazi Party. At Roma's instigation, the Bavarian military chief Epp was heavily involved in fostering the weak Nazi party, not only providing financial assistance, but also inviting Hitler to the barracks to recruit for the Nazis. Hitler was overjoyed that, in his words, the Free Corps was full of "energetic young men, organized, disciplined, and imbued in the military with an enterprising spirit of the world without difficulty". Under Roma's organization, the Nazis established their own armed force, the Charge.

In 1921, Hitler became the Führer of the Nazi Party, as he was expected to do. At this time, the Nazi Party had both ideological weapons and military backing, and with Hitler's unprecedented incitement, other far-right organizations in the Weimar Republic came to join in, and the Nazi Party's prestige was so great that by 1923, its membership had soared to 55,000.

In 1923, orchestrated German hyperinflation exploded, the mark plummeted, the financial world was in chaos, the wealth of the German middle class was bloodied, and France and Belgium marched again to take the Ruhr. All this stirred up the German population's fierce anger against the Weimar government and patriotic enthusiasm rose. On 8 November 1923, Hitler and Ludendorff led the charge and used Bavarian military and political leaders to stage a coup d'état on the occasion of a party at a beer shop in Munich. This is the famous beer hall riot in history.[109]

Although the riots ultimately failed, they caused shock to the world and gave the Nazis a rare opportunity for international propaganda exposure. Hitler's amazing eloquence in court and his unceasing outbursts of anger aroused the German public, and a large number of people spontaneously came outside the court in solidarity with the Nazis, and all major newspapers around the world published Hitler's picture on the first page.

Hitler tried to turn the debate into his own political speech during his court trial, but he was still sentenced to five years in prison. He spent nine months in prison and dictated the book *Mein Kampf*, which painted a shocking blueprint for a future Germany under Nazi rule. While in prison, Hitler realized that the Weimar Republic was full of wings, that the violent revolution had no chance of success, and that the only option was to "legally seize power". Immediately after his release from prison,

---

[109] *The Rise and Fall of the Third Reich: A History of Nazi Germany*, William L. Shirer, (Touchstone Edition) (New York: Simon & Schuster, 1981), P312.

he adjusted the Nazi Party's thinking and prepared to use parliamentary democracy to legally seize power.

The beer hall riots had the unintended effect that Hitler, originally a street thug, became an "international celebrity" overnight. So forces from all sides came to Hitler for all sorts of purposes to talk about cooperation. Hitler was busy with the reception and negotiation, a number of rounds down, felt that there were too many people to flirt with, the really powerful big players did not appear.

In fact, it did not occur to Hitler that his every move was attracting the high attention of certain circles of great energy.

Hitler was hit in the waist by the god of wealth

International bankers began looking for political agents in Germany as early as around 1920 who could carry the weight of history in the future. They have followed the various political parties that sprang up in Germany after the war, trying to find "super-primitive stocks" that would bring amazing returns, and Hitler's small party of a few dozen people has entered their radar.

The intelligence systems of international bankers are incredibly efficient. As early as February 1920, Morgan arranged for Donovan to make a secret visit to Europe, paying Donovan $200,000 to systematically examine all aspects of the postwar situation in Europe. It was during this trip to Europe that Donovan met Hitler in Berchtesgaden, Bavaria, Germany, and had a long night's talk with him, whom he considered an "interesting talker". This Donovan is the founder of the United States Strategic Intelligence Service (OSS), the originator of the Central Intelligence Agency (CIA).

Of course, this contact was only a very preliminary mapping exercise, as the political parties in Germany at the time were numerous and Wall Street's "venture capital" needed to further uncover the real potential of the original stocks from the large number of candidates.

The super-inflationary hurricane finally passed after the German mark speculative wave ended in 1924. After Wall Street copied the bottom of the German economy, the US Dow Jones plan was officially implemented, and the German economy quickly saw a strong recovery as a large amount of foreign capital flocked to it. As the economy recovered, the Nazis' influence quickly dwindled. In fact, the people of

Germany and the general public are the same, living in peace and happiness, rich food and clothing is the most important pursuit of the people, the fighting and killing in a chaotic world and the ups and downs of economic turmoil are not what the people desire. Once the world was at peace, the old German people quickly put the pain and disaster of the past behind them. From 1924 to 1929, Nazi activity in Germany went into a slump, and Hitler had to play by the book with parliamentary politics that he was not very good at.

While Nazi grassroots organizations sprang up all over Germany, voter support for the Nazi Party was rather pathetic. In the German elections of May 1928, the Nazis won 12 parliamentary seats with a pathetic 2.6 per cent of the vote. In the German elections that year, the left-wing coalition, represented by the Social Democratic Party and the Communist Party of Germany, won 40.4 per cent of the vote, the Catholic Central Party won 15 per cent, while several other right-wing parties, such as the German People's Party, split the remaining 42 per cent of the vote.

Hitler was a chaotic man who was never going to get out of trouble, with his country ruled and the world settled.

The Nazis were already like fish stranded on a beach that couldn't jump for days. At this point, however, the economic crisis that swept the world in 1929 broke out and the German economy took a sharp turn for the worse, with the number of unemployed in Germany reaching 2 million in 1930 and soaring to 6 million in 1932. The Nazis immediately seized this historic opportunity to blame the Treaty of Versailles and the war reparations for Germany's economic crisis, and the government's weakness and incompetence for trapping the people in deep water. The economic depression and social upheavals that had caused the German people to lose all faith in the Weimar Republic and the painful memories of seven years earlier began to emerge, only this time the crisis was far greater and longer than in 1923, and the Germans began to turn to the Nazis; in the general elections of September 1930, the Nazis received 18.3 per cent of the vote, overtaking the German Communist Party for the first time and becoming the second largest party in Parliament after the Social Democrats; in the general elections of July 1932, the Nazis received 37.4 per cent of the vote, overtaking the Social Democrats by 36.2 per cent to become the first party in Parliament.

Watching the Nazis soar, the international bankers finally decided to put their money on Hitler.

In November 1933, a pamphlet suddenly appeared in the Netherlands containing several conversations between a banker named Sidney Warburg and Hitler that revealed that the top American industrialists and financiers, including Rockefeller and Henry Ford, had financed Hitler before and after he came to power through the JP Morgan and Chase Manhattan banking group to the tune of $32 million. The book was censored in 1934, and the Warburg brothers, the American and German directors of Faber & Co. that it alludes to, have denied any connection with its contents, but the book's details are consistent with many real-life sources and are thus suspect and generally regarded as evidence that Wall Street's international investors were collaborating with the Nazis.[110]

Another international banker recognized for financing Hitler was Baron Kurt von Schroeder. The Schroeder family is also one of the "seventeen largest international banking families", with banks in London and New York. Schroeder and Rockefeller formed a joint venture bank in New York in 1936, with John Rockefeller's nephew as vice chairman and director.[111]

Schroeder graduated from the University of Bonn and joined the Reichswehr during World War I. After the war, he joined Stein Bank in Cologne as a partner. His right-wing political beliefs led him to sympathize with and fund the Nazi Party. He facilitated a meeting between German People's Party leader Barben and Hitler, which enabled Hitler to later become Chancellor of the Government.

Schröder was also a key figure in the Nazi inner circle, the "Circle of Economic Peers", also known as the "Kepler Circle", founded by William Kepler. Kepler is the quintessential red-top businessman with extensive contacts in politics and a keen political sense of smell. The "Kepler Circle" was first formed in 1931. Hitler had a deep conversation with Kepler about wanting a reliable group of entrepreneurs to advise the Nazis once they were in power, and Hitler

---

[110] Antony C. Sutton, *Wall Street and the Rise of Hitler* (GSG & Associates Pub 1976) Chapter 10.

[111] Richard Roberts, Schroders Merchants & Bankers (MacMillan, 1992).

said, "Find some business leaders who can now be non-Nazis and will serve us when we come to power."[112]

Kepler was true to his mission, and his circle of netizens to finance Hitler included.

- Fritz Kranefuss: Kepler's nephew and Himmler's assistant.
- Karl Vincenz Krogmann, Mayor of Hamburg.
- August Rosterg, Managing Director of the French subsidiary.
- Emil Meyer: Director of the ITT subsidiary and GE Germany.
- Otto Steinbrinck: Vice-Chairman, United Steel Corporation.
- Hjalmar Schacht, Chairman of the Board of Directors of the Reichsbank.
- Emil Helffrich: Chairman of the Board of Directors of Mobil Holding, German-American Petroleum.
- Friedrich Reinhardt: Chairman of the Board of Directors of the Commercial Bank.
- Ewald Hecker: Chairman of the Board of Directors of ILSEDER HUTTE.
- Graf von Bismarck: Executive Chairman of Steding.[113]

Kepler was elected to the Reichstag in 1933 and for a time became Hitler's financial advisor. In a few short years, he has made a fat living as a director of several companies, including the chairman of the board of two Farben Group subsidiaries. Farben and Mobil Oil have a close relationship. Farben had received the technology to produce synthetic gasoline from Mobil Oil, which had transferred more than 2,000 foreign patents to Mobil Oil on an emergency basis after the outbreak of the war in Europe.

The American International Telegraph and Telephone Company ITT was founded in 1921 by brothers Sosthenes Behn and Hernand Behn and was controlled by the Morgan family. The first meeting

---

[112] Nurnberg Military Tribunal Volume VI p. 285.

[113] Nurnberg Military Tribunal Volume VI p. 287.

between Penney and Hitler was in August 1933 in Berchtesgaden.[114] Later Benny and the Kepler Circle hooked up and met Schroeder. Seeing Schroeder's close ties to Hitler and the Nazis, Penney invited Schroeder to become the guardian of ITT's interests in Germany. Schröder helped ITT invest in lucrative military enterprises in Germany (including Focke-Wulf, which produced fighter jets) and served on the boards of these companies, into which ITT's profits were reinvested. In this way, Hitler was a key player in World War II when he fought the American and Allied forces with fighter jets produced with American investment. Not only that, but he also transferred ITT funding to the Gestapo of Himmler, the head of the secret service, whose contributions accounted for a quarter of the US corporate contributions to the Gestapo during the war.

The record of the interrogation of Kurt von Schröder by the Allies after "World War II" on 19 November 1945 shows the deep-rooted relationship between Schröder, ITT and the Nazis.

Q: In the previous record, you said you had dealings with several German companies related to ITT or Standard Electric, so did ITT or Standard Electric deal with other German companies?

A: Yes. Lorenz held a pre-war 25 percent stake in Focke-Wulf of Bremen, which built fighters for the Luftwaffe. I believe later Focke-Wulf absorbed more capital due to expansion and Lorenz dropped to just under 25%.

Q: So this happened after Colonel Penney held nearly 100 percent of Lorenz through ITT?

A: Yes.

Q: Colonel Penney approved Lorenz's purchase of the Focke-Wulf stake?

A: I am sure that Colonel Benny agreed before his representative in Germany formally approved it.

Q: In what year did Lorenz purchase a 25% stake in Focke-Wulf?

A: I remember just before the war broke out, before the invasion of Poland.

---

[114] Antony C. Sutton, *Wall Street and the Rise of Hitler* (GSG & Associates Pub 1976).

Q: Does Westlake know all the details of Lorenz's purchase of a 25 percent stake in Focke-Wulf? (Westerik acted as a German spy in WWI and WWII).

A: Yes. Know better than I do.

Q: How much does Lorenz invest?

A: Initially it was 250,000 marks. Then it was added quite a bit. Exactly how much I can't remember.

Q: Did Colonel Penney have a chance to transfer back to the United States the profits he had made in Germany before the war broke out?

A: Yes. The transfer back to the U.S. will be a little less profitable because of the exchange rate, but the vast majority will make it back to the U.S. Colonel Penney did not do so nor did he ask me to do so. He seems willing to keep the profits in Germany for plant and equipment and other military industrial enterprises. Haas in Berlin is one of them. Haas produces military radio and radar components. As I recall, Lorenz holds a 50% stake in Haas.

Q: You've been a director of Lorenz since 1935. During this time Lorenz and Focke-Wulf were engaged in the production of military industrial equipment. Do you know or hear of Colonel Penney or his representatives protesting against these businesses that are preparing for war for Germany?

A: No.[115]

The Kepler Circle and Himmler are getting closer and closer, also known as the "Himmler Circle". In a letter dated 25 February 1936 to his colleague Emile Meyer of the Himmler Circle, Schroeder described the aims and requirements of the Himmler Circle and the long-term objectives of the special "S" account opened at the Stein Bank in Cologne.

Circle of friends of the leader of the Third Reich

At the end of a two-day trip to Munich at the invitation of the leader of the Third Reich, the circle of friends agreed to open a special "S"

---

[115] Ibid.

account at the Stein Bank in Cologne at the disposal of the Reich leader. The funds are used for extrabudgetary missions. This way the leader of the Empire could rely on all his friends. It was decided in Munich that the signatories should set up and handle the account.

> *"At the same time, we would like to inform each participant that if he contributes on behalf of the company or the Circle of Friends to the above-mentioned mission of the Reichsleiter, the contribution should be deposited in a special "S" account (Reichsleiter account, postal checking account No. 1392) agreed to by the Circle of Friends at the Stein Bank in Cologne."*
> Heil Hitler!
>
> Kurt von Schroeder[116]

This letter explains why post-war Army Colonel Bogdan (former head of the Schroeder Bank in New York) went to great lengths to steer the investigation away from the Stein Bank in Cologne and onto the big banks of the Nazi era. Because the Stein Bank hid secrets about the collusion between American transnational corporations and the Nazi authorities in the "Second World War".

Schröder's support for the Nazis was richly rewarded after the Nazis came to power, with Schröder holding the following positions.

> ➢ German representative of the Bank for International Settlements.
> ➢ Chief private adviser to the German Reichsbank.
> ➢ Senior leader of the Gestapo, Iron Cross I and II.
> ➢ Chairman of the Board of Directors of the German bank Verkehrs-Kredit-Bank (controlled by the Reichsbank).
> ➢ Consul General in Sweden.

After the war, Kurt von Schroeder was found guilty of "crimes against humanity" by a German court, and the prominent international banker was eventually sentenced to three months' imprisonment.

"Crimes against humanity" is no small crime, and Schröder, who directly financed Hitler in World War II and was "caught in the act", received only a symbolic three months' imprisonment. Below, we will

---

[116] Nurnberg Military Tribunal Volume VII, p. 238.

also see the release from trial of the "God of Money" Schacht, who was the Nazi Minister of Finance and head of the Central Bank and was in charge of fund-raising throughout the war process. Looks like Schroeder has another reason to scream about his three months in prison.

In addition to Schröder, one of the "Seventeen International Banking Families", who was involved in financing Hitler, Max Warburg was also an important figure.

The Haavara Agreement

Hitler was mouthing off that he had two enemies and a world enemy. His primary enemy was the Bolsheviks, and in Hitler's view, Germany could not have been defeated without the Bolsheviks revolting and rioting in its rear, the first stab in the back. His second enemy was the international Jewish financial power, which, inspired by Feder, Hitler saw the power of the financial power and resented the Jewish bankers' financing of the Allies in World War I, which led to Germany's defeat and the betrayal of German interests by Max Warburg and others in the Versailles Peace Treaty, and the destruction of the economy by German hyperinflation, which Hitler blamed on the Jews. Hitler's blood feud was with France, the century-old enemy who forced Germany to sign the Treaty of Disgrace.

After the Nazis came to power, there was no immediate way to strike at the Soviet Union or France, but anti-Semitism was no barrier. His first programme was the "Haavara plan" to exclude the Jews.

The word "Haavara" means "transfer" in Hebrew, and the Haavara plan was signed in August 1933 by the Nazi Government of Germany and Jewish organizations in Palestine as a plan to encourage Jewish immigration to Palestine.

For the Nazis, the expulsion of Jews from German soil was a grand policy, but given Germany's strength at the time, it could not be too offensive to the international bankers, who held vast access to funds around the world. Most of these people were Jewish bankers, and many were Jews of German descent. Hitler's anti-Semitism was already notorious internationally, and the mass protests by European and American Jews against the boycott of German products had dealt a heavy blow to Germany's industrial exports, and it was in the interest of the Nazi government, which had just taken control of the regime and had not yet gained the upper hand, not to overstimulate the international Jewish forces in their counter-actions. As a result, the policy of exclusion and expulsion has been transformed into a policy of "encouraging emigration".

Germany's huge war reparations after the First World War were settled entirely in dollars and pounds sterling, so the German Government strictly controlled the outflow of foreign exchange and gold, which was tightened after the Nazis came to power by a 25 per cent penalty tax on capital transfers from Germany to overseas in 1931. All of this made the out-migration of money one of the biggest problems of the Jewish diaspora. Max Warburg is already one of the most important financial giants in Germany, with extensive contacts in the capital markets of London, Paris and New York, and it has become Max's duty to raise funds for the smooth implementation of the "Haavara Project".

After much deliberation between Max, the Jewish organizations in Palestine, and the Nazis, a model was finally formed that was beneficial to all three parties. Under this programme, Jews who were ready to emigrate handed over their marks and all immovable property in Germany to the Nazi Government, and after one year they received the same value of pounds sterling in Palestine, on the condition that the Jewish emigrants could not use the money, and that the entire amount would be used to purchase German industrial products, such as machinery, equipment, pipes, fertilizers, etc., which would be returned to the Jewish emigrants after the sale of those German products in Palestine. In fact, the Nazi Government did not really pay the pound sterling, which was transferred by the Warburg family and other international bankers to major bank accounts, and the Nazi Government ended up with these valuable "pounds" through the export of industrial products.

It's actually a three-pronged approach. For Zionists, the large number of new Jewish immigrants and the strong capital they brought with them gave a major boost to the development of the local Jewish community, laying a solid human and material foundation for the eventual establishment of a Jewish state. For their part, the Nazi government, while expanding exports of German products, creating jobs in Germany and gaining valuable international hard currency "pounds sterling", achieved its strategic goal of excluding Jews without using a single penny of government money, and at the same time was able to show favor to the international Jewish bankers' power bloc by mitigating the severe blow to German import and export trade caused by the worldwide boycott of German products they launched. It was also an opportunity for international bankers to make a fortune, and in order to supervise the implementation of the plan, German Jews set up the Palestine Trust Company, and 3/4 of the total funds required for the "Haavara Plan" and the credit for exports to Germany flowed to the Palestinian region through the channels of the Warburg family and other international banking families, where the Anglo-Palestinian Bank was set up to receive the funds, and from 1933 until the outbreak of the "World War II" in 1939, 52,000 German Jews (mainly wealthy) successfully emigrated to Palestine, and a total of DM 140 million was remitted to Germany through this channel, with the Warburg family receiving generous financial "service charges".[117]

The plan, simply put, was for Nazi Germany to pay German Jews who emigrated to Palestine with industrial products for their immovable property in Germany and their settlements in Palestine, and receive foreign exchange pounds, while allowing a portion of the funds to flow out of Germany. This plan does not conform to Nazi principles, but to Hitler's power-changing tactics as a politician.

In addition to their direct meddling in the German financial system, the international bankers cultivated an important agent, and that was the Schacht.

Schacht: the intermediary of international bankers

Horace Greeley Hjalmar Schacht was born in January 1877 in Teinlief (formerly Germany, now Denmark) to a German-American citizen father, and a Danish mother, Baroness Constance von Eggs. William's life has been a life of upheaval, working as a country teacher, newspaper editor, bookkeeper, and eventually settling down with American Life Insurance Company. William's most admired politician was the New York abolitionist and libertarian politician and journalist Horace Greeley, and in honor of this libertarian politician, William gave

---

[117] Ron Chernow, *The Warbugs* (Random House).

Little Yalma the American name Horace Greeley, thus showing the Schacht family's connection to America.[118]

Smart and industrious, Schacht Jr. specialized in literature, journalism, sociology, philosophy and political science, receiving the title of Doctor of Philosophy at the age of 22, before moving on to the financial world and working at the Bank of Dresden. Schacht had an intuitive perspective on the nature of finance, and his exceptional ability to work out of the box quickly made him a compelling financial elite.[119] In 1923, Schacht was ordered to save the devastated German mark by becoming president of the Reichsbank.[120] In 1930, due to problems with the revision of the Young plan, Schacht left the Reichsbank.[121]

Beginning in 1931, Schacht began active work for the Nazis, and in March 1933, when Hitler came to power, he appointed Schacht as president of the Reichsbank, the appointment document being signed by Hitler and President Hindenburg. Also signing this document were eight directors of the Reichsbank, including three Jewish bankers – Mendelssohn, Wasserman and Warburg.

In July 1933, Hitler established the "Commission on Economic Affairs" to begin planning the revitalization of the German economy. The 17 members of this committee were all big capitalists and bankers, including Krupp, Siemens, Bosch, Tyson, Schroeder and others, and the committee was headed by Schacht, who was elected by the capitalist group.

In August 1933, Schacht negotiated with the American Bankers Association on behalf of the Nazi German government for a loan. Wall Street readily agreed to a moratorium on Germany's previous loans and promised that in the future the entire proceeds of U.S. capital and industry in Germany would be used only in Germany and that the money would be used to build new arms industries or to expand old weapons manufacturing enterprises.

---

[118] John Witz, translated by Zhang Yujiu, *Hitler's Bankers*, Beijing: Guangming Daily Press, 2000, pp. 6–7.

[119] Ibid, pp. 14, 22, 30–31.

[120] Ibid, p. 74.

[121] Ibid, p. 108.

At a meeting in July 1934, Hitler asked Schacht what his opinion would be if Schacht were appointed Minister of Economy in Germany. Schacht pondered for a moment, cautiously offering to know how Hitler wanted him to deal with the Jewish people before accepting the appointment of Economy Minister. Hitler replied that as far as the economy was concerned, the Jews could do all the normal business activities that they had been able to do so far.[122] Schacht asked, of course, not about ordinary Jews, but to test Hitler's attitude toward Warburg and others. Hitler, who apparently could not move Warburg at the time, replied thus. In some ways, Warburg was actually Wall Street's eyes on Hitler's financial policies, planted alongside him.

On August 2, 1934, the day of President Hindenburg's death and Hitler's monopoly of power, Schacht was appointed Hitler's Minister of Economy.[123]

Schacht's relationship with Warburg is extraordinary and can be described as honorable and humiliating. On the one hand, Schacht deftly protected Warburg in front of Hitler, and on the other hand, Warburg was a touchstone for international bankers visiting Hitler. If Hitler had been dissident, then Wall Street's funding of Germany could have been interrupted, and the consequences would have been fatal for Hitler, who had just come to power in the face of a scorched-earth economic crisis. In addition, without Wall Street's support, Hitler's entire army would have faced serious difficulties in funding the war.

As the saying goes, "A little intolerance is a big mess." Hitler also knew this well. He used Schacht's financial brilliance to stabilize Warburg's Wall Street "through train" and, during the six years from 1933 to 1939, when Germany was preparing for World War II, he made full use of the DuPont and Chemical companies, the Rockefeller and Mobil oil companies, the JPMorgan and its Telegraph and Telephone companies, and the Ford Motor Company, all under the control of Wall Street capital, to hoist the pie of Germany's huge arms orders and lure greedy capital into the race.

---

[122] Shacht, *76 Years of My Life*, p. 404.

[123] John Witz, translated by Zhang Yujiu, *Hitler's Bankers*, Beijing: Guangming Daily Press, 2000, pp. 173–176.

Marx said that the capitalist could sell the noose that hanged him to the proletariat for profit, how wonderful! American car king Henry Ford was honored with the Iron Cross for his meritorious work with the Nazis, along with IBM General Manager and U.S. Chamber of Commerce President Thomas Ding Watson.[124] In the eight months of 1934, the number of United States exports to Germany increased more than fivefold from 1933 to 1934 for aircraft alone; there were more than 60 United States companies in the arms industry system in Nazi Germany. In addition to the sale of cutting-edge military products, the United States has generously transferred a variety of advanced military technology to Germany. DuPont sold neoprene and aircraft blast agent technology to Germany through IG Farben; Mobil Oil was active in marketing tank lubricant technology; the Luftwaffe's aviation gasoline was supplied by Mobil's aviation oil plant in Germany; and the International Telegraph and Telephone Company, under Morgan, was involved in the development of new German warplanes. Later in the war, even the U.S. Secretary of the Navy admitted that it was the United States that supplied Hitler with the most advanced aircraft engines.

Hitler's preparations for war would have been far from smooth without the help of Schacht and Warburg.

It was because of this layer that by 1936, three years after Hitler came to power, Warburg's family bank in Hamburg, Germany, was still making a profit. They paid interest and dividends to bondholders and other shareholders as usual, and the Warburg family banking business was largely unmolested by the Nazis. Even as late as 1938, the Warburg Family Bank was still profitable.

In addition to Warburg's close ties to Wall Street's Kuhn Loeb and Co., Schacht's experience has led him to have personal connections to the Anglo-American financial community. He had met JP Morgan himself as early as 1905 when he visited the United States with the Board of Directors of the Bank of Dresden.[125] One of his first acts after becoming Governor of the Reichsbank in 1923 was to visit Norman, Governor of the Bank of England, in London, where he formed a lifelong friendship with Norman, who later even became the godfather

---

[124] Ibid, pp. 212–213.

[125] Ibid, p. 33.

of one of Schacht's grandchildren.[126] Schacht spoke English so much more fluently than German that his trial decades later was conducted in both English and German. At the Nuremberg Tribunal, which tried Nazi war criminals after the war, only three of the defendants were acquitted on criminal charges and released on the spot, and Schacht, who had been Nazi Minister of Economy and Governor of the Central Bank and had raised funds for the entire war, was one of them, with the Soviet representative sharply accusing "capitalists will never be punished".

With the full implementation of Hitler's "New Deal", the German economy is improving, the unemployment population is declining, the military power is rapidly powerful, especially the 1936 Olympic Games held in Berlin, Germany, so that the German people "return to the heart of the four seas", Hitler's wings are gradually full.

After the German Olympic Games, Schacht began to feel vaguely that the situation was not good, not only because of the structural imbalance caused by the over-emphasis on military industry in the economy, but also because of the fact that Hitler's ultimate goal seemed "not simple". In the meantime, Hitler did not move to divide his economic power.

In the autumn of 1936, Hitler appointed Göring as the executor of the "Four-Year Plan" for the revival of the German economy and established new governmental bodies with specific responsibility for its implementation. Clearly, this new institutional set-up created a serious functional overlap with the Schacht' imperial economic ministry, which eventually inevitably led to a power struggle between the Schacht and Göring.

As the head of the liberal school in Germany, Schacht, who was theoretically uncomfortable with the economy under any state plan, and who saw that it was directly weakening his power, naturally resented the so-called "four-year plan" and immediately acted to resist and fight it. Hitler, however, kept making peace between Schacht and Göring, practicing tai chi pushers. Watching the large number of industrial and arms orders pouring to Göring, his own side is more and more "cold in front of the door and the horses are scarce", Schacht gradually realized that he had been played by Hitler.

---

[126] Ibid, pp. 78-80.

Thus, in August 1937, Schacht submitted his resignation to Hitler, who, after three months of "good words", formally removed Schacht as Minister of Economy in November. Not willing to concede defeat, Schacht, who is still the governor of the German Central Bank, also wants to use the currency-issuing power as a last-ditch struggle. Beginning in 1938, Schacht's refusal to re-discount the "job creation bill" finally intensified his conflict with Hitler. By this time Hitler had legally completed all preparations for the nationalization of the Central Bank, and in January 1939 Schacht was removed from the Reichsbank presidency and, while retaining the fictitious title of cabinet member, was in fact kicked out of the centre of power in Germany by Hitler. News of Shah's departure from the central bank position was kept under wraps for more than five months, until the final moments before the outbreak of the Great War. Hitler's political power tricks and Schacht's financial strategies were masterful, but in the end, politics trumped finance.

In 1944, Schacht was sent to the Dachau concentration camp on suspicion of involvement in the bombing of Hitler at Steffenberg.[127] Instead of fulfilling the important task of spying on Hitler, Schacht was played by Hitler without realizing it, and it was only natural that the idea of revenge would arise.

The Great Game of Chess

When Hitler, supported by international bankers, finally ascended to the throne of the German Führer in 1933, as he had hoped, several important power groups in the world were playing their own game.

The ruling elite of the British Empire is unquestionably convinced that the British system is the most perfect form of social organization in the history of the world, and that it should be implemented not only within the existing British Empire's boundaries, but also on a wider scale in all countries of the world, with a core interest in consolidating and strengthening the British Empire's system of global hegemony. The British Empire, by this time, had reached a sphere of influence unprecedented in history, and on the European continent, the greatest strategic challenger, Germany, had been utterly defeated, its economic

---

[127] Ibid, pp. 284-299.

and military potential radically suppressed under the Versailles system. West of Germany, the world enemy of France had Britain firmly tethered to its own chariot, and the huge losses of the war and the potential threat of Germany made France dependent on Britain for its survival.

In Africa, Britain's sphere of influence covers most of the African continent, with as many as 21 countries subjugated to the British Empire, and large quantities of raw materials and natural resources at Britain's disposal; in the Middle East, Britain controls most of the Middle East, from Palestine and Saudi Arabia to Iran and Iraq, and holds the source of oil in the Middle East; in Asia, Britain rules large areas from India and Malaya to Myanmar and Hong Kong, China, with vast human resources, natural resources and strategic corridors all under British control; in Oceania, it is supported by Commonwealth dependencies such as Australia and New Zealand as industrial raw materials; in America, Canada, Guyana, Jamaica, the Bahamas and others provide the British Empire with endless strategic supplies from naval bases to natural resources.

Britain also had the most powerful naval hegemony in the world, controlling all the world's major waterways, and the British Empire of the early 1930s looked around the globe with great ambition.

Of course, there are some hidden concerns in the UK, such as the amazing industrial potential of the US. But in the usual mindset of the British ruling elite, the United States remains a one-time British colony, lacking a global strategy. The financial center was in its infancy, with heavy speculation and regulatory chaos; severe overcapacity, indigestible to domestic markets, and heavily dependent on global market demand under British control; few overseas colonies, lacking pricing power over resources; and the U.S. military, then in the amateur segment, lacking a global military base.

So the way Britain controls America is very simple: Britain determines the world's cost of money, Britain has a monopoly on world resource prices, Britain controls the flow of global orders, Britain divides world market demand, and Britain protects trade shipping lanes. With these five strategic high points firmly at the throat of the United States, the United States will always be the global production plant of the British Empire, and the shareholders controlling the plant will be British capital. In a word, the UK positions itself as the organizer of the global market, while the US is merely the producer. As long as there is no large-scale war to subvert the whole world, Britain has nothing to fear from the United States trying to "usurp power".

The only thing that really worried the British was the potential of the Soviet Union. Although the Soviet Union in the early 1930s had only just recovered from the chaos of war and all sectors were still in disarray, the Soviet model of economic development caused great tension in the British Empire. If the socialist economic model is able to industrialize without colonial expansion and at the same time build up a strong armed force, this will not only pose a serious military challenge, but it is even more dangerous that the Soviet model will "mess up" the ideology of the world. If the Soviet Union had achieved its goal of being rich and powerful on its own, the British colonial model would have looked ugly in retrospect, unable to maintain its reasonable and legitimate order of rule. As a result, the Soviet Union was targeted by Britain as its most dangerous enemy.

In Britain's view, the rise of the German Nazis had both advantages and disadvantages; the disadvantage was that German rearmament created a threat to Britain, and the advantage was that Britain had a right-hand man to deal with the Soviet Union as a mortal enemy. Britain didn't take the Nazis too seriously, first and foremost a strong psychological advantage, the German economy was already fragile under the consumption of the Versailles system, the international bankers had complete control of Germany's central bank and financial system and the lifeblood of the heavy chemical industry, and Hitler was nothing more than a foreground puppet. As long as they can control the Nazi lifeblood, they will not be afraid to strike back. It would have been a joyous thing for Britain to have guided Germany to a strong position against the Soviet Union. Therefore, the British ruling elite was divided into two factions over the Nazi issue: the pro-German faction, represented by the famous "Duke of Windsor", and the other faction, represented by the later Chancellor Churchill, who had a fear of Germany and was firmly opposed to any ideas that would bring Germany back to power.

The emerging financial powerhouses in the United States, however, have their own set of strategic considerations. Long before the outbreak of World War I, with the explosive growth of American industrial power, America's ruling elite had been plotting how to replace the British Empire as the new world hegemon. After all, it's strength that determines mindset, mindset that determines vision, and vision that determines strategy!

Britain's greatest strength, in the eyes of the United States, is also Britain's greatest Achilles heel. The core problem with Britain's broad division of global production, resources and markets lies in the hollowing out of British industry at home, and Britain's complacent financial centre would be immediately vulnerable to disintegration if it left the solid real economy and attached itself to a loose community of interest in the global division of labour.

Thus, a large-scale war in which the United States could reap the dividends of war while significantly weakening British dominance and creating opportunities for its replacement is fully in line with the strategic interests of the emerging US financial power bloc.

On the other hand, the international Jewish financial forces, on the strategic idea of defeating the British colonial system and capturing Palestine in order to rebuild the Great State of Israel, and the emerging financial forces in the United States, have instantly cooperated with each other, and the two groups of forces on Wall Street have formed a high degree of tacit understanding.

At this time, the European landscape has a dramatic situation, Britain's primary enemy locked for the Soviet Union, the United States emerging financial forces target to replace Britain, the Jewish financial forces mainly attacked the restoration of Israel, these three forces have in common for different purposes to control a strong Germany can act as a gunslinger.

Hitler understood that all the forces were using him to achieve their own goals, but Hitler had his own agenda, he was totally unacceptable to being dominated and controlled, he was prepared to use all the parties to achieve his strategic goals, and Hitler was determined to play the leading role in the complex international strategic game landscape.

Social power platform in Nazi Germany

Many people mistakenly believed that the Nazi regime was a dictatorship with all the power to run society, that it could dictate all social resources as it pleased, and that Hitler could decide the fate of everyone. In fact, Hitler as a politician had to rely on the cooperation of the four platforms of power in German society in order to run his government.

Before the outbreak of World War I, the German social power platform was dominated by the army, the Junker landowners, the bureaucratic class, and finally the industrial capitalists. In the imperial era, the most important power was imperial power, and the emperor operated the regime on behalf of the four major power systems. And by the time of the Weimar Republic and before and after the Nazis came to power, despite the collapse of imperial power, the social power base was not fundamentally affected, only the order of power changed, the industrial capitalists became the bosses, the army receded to the second tier, the bureaucratic class remained in third place, and the Junker landowning class fell to the bottom. Arguably, the Junker landowning class became the biggest losers in the German power system after World War I.

The decline of the Junker landowning class in Germany began in 1880, and German agriculture was actually in a historical process of decline due to the rise of industry, the transfer of agricultural labor, various natural disasters, and the change in tariff protection in 1895. At this point the Juncker landlord class was on the verge of bankruptcy, and their slippage in economic status was bound to cut into their political influence.

When the Nazis came to power, control over agriculture was in the hands of the government and the Nazis. The key to so-called control is to have pricing power, and whoever can control pricing power in a field has the corresponding control over that field. When the Junker landowning class lost its pricing power in agriculture, it also lost its corresponding political power at the same time. Because of the deep historical ties between the military forces, with the Prussian officer corps at their core, and the Junker landlord class, Hitler had to defend the interests of the Junker landlord class in order to maintain military support for the Nazis. So, the Nazis compensated the Junker landowning class accordingly, making them financially profitable.

The main purpose of the agricultural programmes in Germany was to provide the Junkers with a stable market price system for agricultural products, in which their products were protected. At the same time, the basis for the social unrest caused by liberalism was eradicated due to the tight control of the Nazis over the whole society, and the whole market was excluded from the instability and price volatility caused by the political unrest. The Nazi government also imposed price controls on agricultural products, fixing prices within a margin that was not too high, but could guarantee sufficient profit for the Juncker landowning class. On top of that, the Nazis gave Junkers generous treatment and corresponding privileges. In terms of economic returns, Junker landowners enjoyed agricultural prices in 1937 that were only 3 percent higher than in 1933. The Government also provided them with guarantees and various incentives, such as not allowing agricultural unions to form, agricultural workers to go on strike or agricultural workers to demand higher wages. In effect, the Nazi government provided the Junker landowning class with a relatively stable income and profit margin by regulating trade unions, regulating strikes and regulating wage increases. In addition, the Nazis reduced the interest and tax on loans to the Junker landowning class, 1933 to 1936, the Junker landowning class of various loans of interest payments fell from 950 million marks to 630 million marks, three years after the Nazis came to power, the Junker landowning class of agricultural loans of interest payments fell by 320 million marks, taxes fell from 740 million marks to 460 million marks, can be seen for the Junker landowning class, the economic burden was greatly reduced.

In addition to this, the Juncker landlord class is completely exempt from the obligation to hand over unemployment insurance to the government and the state. The unemployment insurance system established in Germany at that time was the first social welfare system in the world, but the Junker landlords were exempted from this burden, and between 1932 and 1933 the Junker landlords received a total of DM 19 million in benefits from the reduction of the unemployment insurance burden. The biggest problem that has long plagued and threatened the Junker landowning class is bankruptcy for a variety of reasons. This threat of bankruptcy was "thoughtfully" eliminated by the Nazi government, and neither government nor private lenders were allowed to collect debts from the Junker landlord class, lest the Junker landlord class be forced into bankruptcy.

This set of agricultural policies pursued by the Nazis favored large farmers more than small ones, and the larger the Junker landowning class, the greater the benefits they received, and the greater the support of these people for the Nazis, which was consolidated through this set of policies.

One of Hitler's main aims in drawing in the Junker landowning class was to win the support of the army. The main essence of the Prussian officer corps was the Junker class, and all the generals in the German army with "von" in their surnames were descendants of the

Junkers, who were in the same boat as the army and had broken bones and ties.

The Prussian officer corps, the elite core of the German army, was far more influenced by the Nazis than by the Weimar Republic. In the days of the Weimar Republic, the officer corps would never have engaged in such a thing as the murder of some general, whereas in the days of Hitler, such things were frequent. This represents a gradual decline in military power, although this decline is more related to the state than to the Nazis.

In fact, the Nazis did not completely control the army. In the Third Reich era, the German army was still largely controlled by the government, and the Nazis did not directly control the army. It was because the Nazis could not directly control Germany's army that their own army, the SS, was formed, and there was always friction between the SS and the German regular army. In other words, the German military was not, to a large extent, under Hitler's complete control.

German law at the time clearly stated that armed members of the army could not also be members of the Nazi Party. Since the German army has a tradition of always obeying the head of state, when Hitler became head of state, he cleverly used such an opportunity to demand that the army pledge allegiance to him personally. And the main reason why the military allowed this to happen was that they largely identified conceptually with the policies pursued by the Nazi Party. In 1938–1939, there was hardly any opposition to Hitler among the German military generals because they had no reason to oppose him, and the results of Hitler's pursuit of his policy were exactly what these senior military generals wanted to achieve. But after 1939, some generals in the military began to question some of Hitler's decisions and to cast doubt on his judgment. However, the senior generals of these armies were unable to form a united front or a decisively influential force against Hitler.

In terms of the bureaucratic class, their power has been greatly diminished overall. Many Jews and anti-Nazis who worked in the government were asked to retire early. The hierarchical system of bureaucrats in the old German Empire included both bureaucrats with and without academic backgrounds. Bureaucrats with academic backgrounds belonged to the middle and upper echelons of the bureaucratic hierarchy, these people were academically certified and the Nazi rule did not hit them hard. But the lower bureaucratic classes were hit harder, especially some of the lower and unskilled bureaucrats, who were replaced in large numbers with members of the Nazi Party. By 1939, there were 1.5 million civil servants in Germany, of whom 282,000 were members of the Nazi Party.

The policy of exclusion of non-Aryans and politically unstable elements, established by the Nazis in 1933, affected only 1.1 per cent of the upper civil service. And the lower bureaucrats, especially the newly recruited staff, were mainly members of the Nazi party. Under the German Civil Service Act of 1937, civil servants are not explicitly required to be members of the Nazi Party, but are required to be loyal to the Nazi ideology. In the class of civil servants, however, their day-to-day work was not bound by the Nazi party charter, but by civil service law, which had a higher priority in the bureaucracy. On the whole, the lower civil servants were more influenced by the Nazis, while the upper civil servants largely maintained their previous working conditions and ways of working.

From this point of view of the German capitalists, by and large, they were not affected and disturbed too much by the Nazis. The capitalist class relied primarily on self-discipline, not on being regulated by the Nazis. Generally speaking, German industry and commerce at that time had a somewhat unusual status. First of all, the industrial and commercial capitalists were the class that gained power substantially after the Nazis came to power. Secondly, the class of industrial and commercial capitalists is not organized on a large scale, nor is it controlled and constrained according to a principle of loyalty to a particular leader. The Nazi government essentially did not interfere with the free operation of industry and commerce, and the Nazis did not have much control over the industrial capitalists in general, except in the emergency of war.

The traditional view that Nazi Germany practiced a state-capitalist and totally authoritarian political system was in fact inaccurate, since no such organizational model was really established in Germany at the time. It should be said that this system in Nazi Germany was an authoritarian capitalism, but not a dictatorial capitalism, whose main characteristic was the effective organization of society as a whole, under conditions in which various social acts and resources were mobilized primarily to satisfy capitalist purposes in the pursuit of profit.

The economic system of Nazi Germany

If traditional capitalism is a profit-centered economic system, then this system is not primarily concerned with production, consumption, prosperity, employment, national welfare, or anything else; its entire focus is on profit itself. This approach, which considers profit alone and ignores other factors, is bound to make enemies in all spheres of society, thus triggering a backlash from the rest of the social power hierarchy, and ultimately harming the bourgeois profit system itself when other social power platforms join forces against it.

The Nazi design of the economic system had to be built on the four platforms of power in German society, and it was designed to balance the interests of this profit-centric system with the enemies it established on all sides. On the one hand, the Nazis suppressed the extreme ego tendencies of the profit system in order to moderate the backlash of socially antagonistic forces brought about by the system; on the other hand, they maintained the functioning of the profit system by suppressing the underlying factors that threatened it.

In terms of the Nazi approach to governance, they mainly suppressed the various potential threats to the profit system in six ways: first, to suppress the government itself against the profit system; second, to suppress organized labour; third, to suppress competition; fourth, to avoid depression; fifth, to avoid commercial failure; and sixth, to suppress the development of other economic models in economic activity that are production-centred or non-profit-centred.

Since government action itself is not profit oriented, it poses a considerable threat to the profit system. In Nazi Germany, however, the threat of government was eliminated because the industrial capitalists supported and controlled the Nazis, who ran the government, and thus the Nazis effectively became agents of the industrial capitalists' indirect control of the government.

In fact, the ILO does not directly pose a threat to the profit system, since labour interests themselves are closely related to the profit system. But organized labor, especially labor with political beliefs, will directly threaten the capitalist profit system. So the Nazis had to control people's minds and labor groups if they were to control the destruction of the profit system by labor organizations. This control can be manifested in the control of labour's free time and recreation in such a way that when a person has a lot of leisure, he will always think about things and get a lot of distracted thoughts. The Nazi approach was not to abolish unions, but to regulate all organized trade union bodies. Under this Nazi regime, wages and other living conditions of labourers were actually in a state of gradual deterioration. However, for the exploitation of the workers, the Nazis took other means to compensate in some way.

The Nazis adopted, inter alia, a prohibition against industrial capitalists laying off employees and guarantees that workers would not lose their jobs. Looking at German employment figures, the number of employed people was 17.8 million in 1929, and only 12.7 million in 1932, the year before the Nazis came to power, when the economic crisis worsened. But by 1939, six years after the Nazis came to power, the number of employed people reached 20 million, at a time when unemployment in other European and American countries was high.

In terms of suppressing business competition, the Nazis mainly adopted a suppression of price competition. For the company's operations, there is price competition for market elements such as capital, raw materials, machinery and equipment, technology patents, and labor, and competition is an uncertainty that potentially plagues the company's stable operations and production plans and threatens the company's profits. In general, companies tend to work with competitors to agree on prices and then pass on costs to consumers together. The Nazis mainly used different institutional arrangements to suppress competition, firstly the monopolistic trade associations, secondly the trade associations, and then the employers' associations to coordinate the interests of the firm's competitors. Monopolistic trade associations set prices, organize production and divide the market; trade associations, mainly as political groups, effectively organize commercial and agricultural activities; and employers' associations control labour. As a result of thorough social control, the factors of commercial competition, such as drastic changes in the cost of capital, fluctuations in the prices of raw materials, workers' strikes and social confrontation, have been effectively controlled. In such an operating environment, business failures of companies become extremely rare and alternative business models that replace the profit system cannot survive.

Having eliminated these threats, German social operations attempted to enter a trajectory that would avoid depression altogether. But there is a greater danger that such a system of social production and operation will develop into a greater aberration, that the entire social system does not revolve around profit, and that such a system may well evolve into a greater aberration.

Indeed, in terms of how Nazi Germany operated, the Nazis themselves had to be attached to the four platforms of power in Germany, and on top of that attempted to develop a balanced and regulated profit system. Regardless of whether this system can function efficiently or not, it will not only fail to develop, it will not survive if the Nazis leave these platforms of power and systems of economic operation.

Hitler's "New Deal"

Hitler, who had just come to power in 1933, was faced with an economic mess. From 1929 to 1932, the utilization rate of German industrial equipment fell to 36 per cent, total industrial production fell by 40 per cent, the value of foreign trade fell by 60 per cent, prices fell by 30 per cent, iron production fell by 70 per cent and shipbuilding output fell by 80 per cent. The industrial crisis, in turn, led to a financial crisis, and in July 1931, the collapse of the German bank Darmstadt triggered a bank run, reducing German gold reserves from DM 2.39 billion to DM 1.36 billion and the nine major Berlin banks to four. The unemployment rate rose sharply, reaching nearly 30 per cent in 1932, and, together with the underemployed, the total number of unemployed and underemployed in Germany in 1932 reached half of the total number of workers. The economic crisis has exacerbated class conflicts in society, with more than L,000 strikes breaking out in three years.

Germany has been hit by an economic crisis far more severely than other capitalist countries in Europe and America. As soon as Hitler came to power, he immediately threw himself into the task of saving the economy. Particularly noteworthy is Hitler's "New Deal". Under a series of strong economic measures, the German economy grew rapidly and unemployment plummeted to 1.3 per cent in 1938. From 1932 to 1938, German pig iron production rose from 3.9 million tons to 18.6 million tons, steel production rose from 5.6 million tons to 23.2 million tons, and aluminum, magnesium, and lathe production was even higher than in the United States. From 1933 to 1939, Germany's heavy and arms industry grew 2.1 times, consumer goods production increased by 43 per cent and the gross national economy grew by more than 100 per cent, while the construction of the national highway network was completed, the basic system of heavy industry was reorganized and a modern army was equipped.

If you've seen Renee Riefenstahl's famous "Olympic" (Triumph of the Will), you'll be impressed with the combined strength and mental state of Germany in 1936. The cheers that resounded in the clouds, such as the standing arms of Lin, imposing buildings, athletes as beautiful as God, all implied the strength and dominance of the world. Hitler's personal prestige was also at its peak, and he no longer even had to show the "burning passion" of his earlier oratory talents, but simply showed his face in public, and thousands of people were automatically hypnotized like a drunk. German support for the Nazis was not based solely on brainwashing and indoctrination, and the Nazis' prominence in saving the economic crisis in the early days of their rule and the tangible economic benefits received by the German population were probably more convincing than the Nazis' own propaganda.

Compared with Germany, the United States "Roosevelt New Deal", which began in 1933, only temporarily alleviated the depression, the United States economy entered a long period of so-called "special depression", despite the "New Deal" and other measures to ease the crisis, the United States economy is still weak recovery. By 1937, the United States was again in a severe economic crisis, and it was not until 1941, when the United States participated in World War II, that it emerged from the Great Depression. Throughout the Roosevelt New Deal, the average unemployment rate in the United States was as high as 18 per cent and the gross national product did not return to pre-crisis levels of 1929 until 1941.

Hitler's "New Deal" created an economic miracle that, despite the inherent flaws behind it, was effective in saving the economic crisis.

Today, the world is once again facing a serious recession similar to that of 1933, and a careful analysis of the merits and demerits of Hitler's "New Deal" will be of some relevance.

Hitler's first fire of the New Deal: Nationalization of the Central Bank

As early as September 1919, Hitler was struck by the first time he heard Feder speak on financial money, and it was this speech that drew Hitler into the German Workers Party.

Hitler had no systematic theoretical basis in finance and, more specifically, was almost a financial illiterate. But Hitler, who was extremely enlightened and had no systematic knowledge, was able to grasp the essence of the problem at once. Such people learn in conversation, think in questioning, and have epiphanies in debate. Like all leaders, he doesn't need to be an expert in the field; what's necessary is a keen sense of discernment and a deep insight that catches the right voice in the midst of the multitude of rambling words.

In discussions with Feder, Hitler came to the fundamental truth that privately owned central banks reap enormous benefits by controlling the country's currency issuance, thus financing their control and exploitation of the entire population of society. Feder's theory is clearly an unorthodox fallacy that cannot be tolerated by orthodox academics, which attempts to explain phenomena in terms of the game of human interest, while the theorist only explores the "objective" facts after stripping away the human nature of the seven passions. Schacht contradicts Feder's views, especially when it comes to the principle of "right and wrong" in the central banking system. In fact, Shah's "theoretical views" and the "practical background" of his close relationship with Wall Street are inseparable, and the key issue is still one of interest.

Listening to the heated arguments between the two sides, Hitler was like a mirror in his heart, accepting Feder's ideas from the bottom of his heart and putting them into practice, but outwardly reusing Schacht and coldly dismissing Feder. Feder, who played a seminal role in Germany's pre-Nazi economic thinking, waited until the Nazis came to power, only to be sidelined to teach at universities. The reason is simple: the big industrialists and big bankers did not like Feder's theory, but enthusiastically supported Schacht, and these powerhouses were the very foundation on which Hitler's Nazi party depended for its survival. Hitler hated these "November sinners" from the bottom of his heart, but had to hang out with them and play along. Because he is a politician, he can only play by the rules of the game of interest and never put personal good or evil above the rules of the game.

However, Hitler did not compromise with Schacht and others on the important principle of nationalizing the central bank, and in 1933, as soon as his government came to power, the Banking Act was immediately revised to provide for: the abolition of the independence of the Reichsbank's Board of Directors and the transfer of the power to appoint the Reichsbank Governor and Board members to the Head of

State; the power to implement open market policy was given to the Reichsbank, but it was rarely used; and the Reichsbank could discount "job creation drafts" in order for the new government to finance job creation. This "bill of exchange for job creation" is the "Feder currency", first proposed by Feder, and later made a sweaty contribution in the realization of Hitler's "New Deal" miracle.

Of course, the aforementioned approach of the Nazi government, which was strongly opposed by the Reichsbank directors, was powerless to stop it. In February 1937, the Reichsbank's independence was completely stripped away when the Reichsbank New Order Act was enacted, which provided for the direct leadership of the Reichsbank Board of Directors by the Führer. By 1939, the Board of Directors of the Reichsbank was also finally dissolved. In the same year, the Nazi Government also promulgated the Reich Bank Act, which provided for the cessation of the exchange of gold for banknotes; that the provision for the issuance of 40 per cent gold and foreign currency could be replaced entirely by employment drafts, cheques, short-term Treasury bills, Reich Treasury bonds and other similar bonds; and that the amount of the Central Bank's loan to the Reich was ultimately determined by the "Leader and Reichsführer". This meant, in effect, that Germany had won its freedom from the Rothschild "golden cross" in the monetary system. By this time, the Nazi government had finally completed the legal and political nationalization of the central bank.

In order to avoid a strong backlash from the international bankers, Hitler had to slow down his progress and it took six years before he finally took the power of the central bank into his own hands.

"Federity": Germany's Lincoln Greenbacks

The theory that Feder has always adhered to is Georg Friedrich Knapp's theory of the nominal value of money, and his book The State Theory of Money proposes that money is a product of law, so the study of money theory must examine the history of law. An important milestone in the development of society is the legalization of the means of payment. There is only one criterion for determining what is money and what is not money, and that is whether such money can be used as a means of payment acceptable to the government. Under this theory, the government has the power to define the currency and no longer relies on gold that is controlled in the hands of international bankers. The government can designate a stone or a stick of wood as legal tender to pay taxes to the government at will. In other words, money would have no scarcity to speak of at all, nor would it serve as a store of wealth; it would simply be a circulating symbol used for exchange, without any intrinsic value.

In 1932, the Nazi Party's Economic Emergency Programme put this idea into policy terms by refuting the then-popular "capital scarcity theory" that if money was used only as a trading symbol, there would of course be no question of "scarcity". The programme states: "Our economic problems are not due to a lack of means of production, but to the fact that the means of production available are not being fully utilized. To reduce unemployment, the most urgent task today is to make use of idle means of production and to revive the internal market through a number of public labour programmes, such as the reclamation of wasteland, land reclamation, the construction of highways and canals, and the construction of worker settlements. In order to finance these programmes, productive loans should be invested. Twenty to thirty percent of this loan can be met by fundraising, and the remaining major portion can be met by savings in unemployment benefits, higher taxes."

Where does the money for "productive loans" come from? Feder's view is that, completely bypassing the constraints of traditional monetary theory and free from the constraints of gold and foreign exchange reserves, governments can create a new form of currency, the "Mefo Bill", for productive lending. Feder's ideas have a strong "wild card" overtone; in his view, there is a "lack of capital theory" on the one hand, and a large amount of "idle means of production" and labour on the other, while orthodox theorists emphasize that the lack of money creates idleness of means of production and labour. Their books say that money must be provided by "responsible" bankers, and now bankers won't provide it, so the economic crisis is over. For his part, Feder argues that such logic is utterly absurd; how can a living person be suffocated by urine? If bankers are reluctant to provide money, then Governments can create money directly, and once these "new job-creating currencies" enter the real economy, they can immediately revitalize the "idle means of production" and the labour force, thereby creating wealth and employment.

The Cobain-born Shaikh, who has repeatedly argued with Feder over the "new currency" proposal, and who represents the interests of the bankers, has an instinctive and extreme aversion to this way of bypassing the bankers and having the Government create money directly, even going so far as to denounce Feder's proposal as "a very crazy and extreme voice from interest groups whose aim is to completely destabilize our monetary and banking system". Schacht persuaded Hitler not to put into practice "the stupidest, most absurd and dangerous ideas, which often stemmed from the very stupid insights of the Nazi Party about banks and money".

Hitler, who had been a wise man, understood Feder's theories and Schacht's position. Hitler, who had just come to power, did not want to offend Schacht and the financial forces behind him, so on the one hand he "invited" Feder, the founder of the Party and the founder of Nazi economic theory, to take up certain idle positions, and on the other hand he appointed Schacht as his Minister of Economy, as a sign of his humility to the financial forces' group "taking orders". However, Hitler was determined that the practice of the "bill of exchange for job creation" must be carried out and ordered Schacht to come up with a programme as soon as possible.

Schacht could not bear Hitler's obstinacy and came up with an implementation plan. Schacht proposed the establishment of a "shadow company" (Metallurgische Forschungsgesellschaft) with a registered capital of only DM 1 million, which could be understood as a company that "purchases" goods and services on behalf of the German Government from companies capable of creating jobs, paid for by a "job creation bill", a short-term bill of exchange with an interest rate of 4.5 per cent for a period of three months, renewable over a period of up to five years. When the entrepreneur gets a "job creation draft", he or she can go to any German bank to "discount", obtain German marks in cash, and then hire workers, purchase raw materials and organize production. Banks that receive "job creation drafts" can either hold them themselves or send them to the Central Bank for "re-discounting" and receiving cash.[128]

The "bill of exchange for job creation" was a rather avant-garde "financial innovation" of the Nazis, and its effects were obvious. It is designed to address a number of important challenges.

First, the Allies, especially France, placed a legal cap of DM 100 million on the direct issuance of credit from the German Central Bank to the German government, in the name of preventing

---

[128] Ibid, pp. 163-164.

another super-inflation, but in fact severely limiting the German government's ability to spend and financially preventing Germany from renewing a massive military readiness war.

(a) The "job creation bill" is designed to bypass this legal restriction and help the German Government obtain more credit from the Central Bank.

(b) since the "job creation bill" was paid directly by the Nazi Government to job-creating companies through the MEFO company, it fulfilled a currency-like function. In this sense, the "bill of exchange for job creation" is equivalent to the "Lincoln Greenbacks" issued by the Lincoln administration during the American Civil War. But the "job creation bill" was used to create jobs, and the "Lincoln Greenback" was thrown directly into the fray. In essence, the Government has regained the power to issue money.

(c) Third, the "job creation bill" is paid directly by the Government to enterprises that can create jobs, thus enabling the Government to implement an economic policy centred on "employment", bypassing the "profit-oriented" lending by commercial banks, which inevitably leads to "loan scarcity" and deflation in times of recession, and ensuring that the new money goes directly into the real economy cycle, reorganizing idle means of production and workers into production, thus creating more wealth to match the credit for expansion.

(d) Fourthly, due to the severe shortage of gold and foreign exchange reserves of the German Central Bank, from 1929 to 1933, it fell sharply from 2.6 billion marks to 409 million marks, and by 1934, only 83 million marks remained, with a severe shortage of money supply. According to traditional classical monetary theory, Germany was already on the verge of bankruptcy and its strong productive capacity would be starved alive in a severe "capital shortage". The financial innovations of the "job creation bill", which freed gold and foreign exchange from constraints, and the Germans proved by practice that the so-called classical monetary theory was not sound.

(e) Fifth, the "job creation bill" fulfils the role of a clandestine rearmament that is difficult to detect by the outside world.

(f) Sixth, the 4.5 per cent annual interest rate of the "job creation bill" provides a convenient and low-cost way for businesses to finance themselves.

Although the actual implementer of the "bill of exchange for job creation" was Schacht, the idea and soul of it came from Feder.

"Financial innovation" saved the German economy

On 31 May 1933, the German Government announced the issuance of a "bill of exchange for employment creation" in the amount of DM 1 billion, the purpose of which was primarily to pay for special technical engineering projects. These renewable bills are paid by the Government to employers who will undertake large projects and employ large numbers of workers, so that everyone from business owners to ordinary households can benefit from the "job creation bill". When these instruments flow into the banking system, there is a constant amplification effect and they can be rediscounted at the German Central Bank, which means that the "job creation bill" together with gold, foreign exchange and long-term bonds form the basis of the German money supply.

One of the main reasons why most of the initial "job creation bills" were never re-discounted by the German Central Bank was that their interest rate of 4.5 per cent was more attractive and a large number of banks and other institutions chose to hold them rather than re-discount them. According to statistics, from 1933 to 1938, the issue of "job creation bills" rose year by year, and by 1938 the balance amounted to DM 12 billion, or 85 per cent of all government deficit spending. About half of this was used to finance direct job-creating enterprises, and the other half was used for Germany's clandestine military expansion.

A major advantage of the "job creation bill" is that it puts real purchasing power in the hands of newly employed German workers. As these notes became more liquid, the utilization of idle resources rose sharply, while the unemployment rate fell rapidly.

In public works, particularly in the construction of housing for the emerging middle class, the "job creation bill" played a key role; in 1932 there were about 141,000 housing units in Germany, and by 1934 about 284,000 housing units of all kinds had been built. Apparently the "job creation bill" doubled the number of dwellings under construction in Germany within two years. At the same time, the money was used to build Germany's road system, with thousands of kilometres of roads built by the "job-creation bill", creating a network of motorways covering all of Germany.

The economic policies adopted by Hitler, which to a large extent had a strong safeguarding effect on the German middle and poor classes, also incurred strong resentment and serious concerns from foreign bankers. Germany's proximate currency, the "bill of exchange for job creation", issued directly by the government, largely bypasses the control of the German economy by international bankers. Some economists believe that one of the root causes of the Second World War was the German government's complete freedom from Anglo-American control over it by issuing its own currency. Due to the shortage of foreign exchange and gold, Germany had to borrow from international bankers in the United Kingdom and the United States, and this debt relationship made Germany's politics, economy, policy and related vital interests, directly and indirectly influenced by international bankers. But if the link is given to Mai, Hitler holds the power to decide on Germany's economic development.

In the early years of Hitler's administration, he achieved great social acceptance and popular support, in large part because he freed Germany's economic development from the shackles of mainstream British and American economic theory and rebuilt the German economy. It is safe to say that the international bankers were clearly betting against Hitler as a treasure. Hitler would not willingly act as someone else's puppet.

Schacht's views on the "bill of exchange for job creation" are clearly ambivalent. In the beginning, when he was arguing with Feder, he had suggested that it was a very stupid and very bad idea, but then he also had to eat his own words. Decades later, many have repeatedly asked him whether this employment money order is a successful design or not, whether this substitution of central bank credit for capital savings whenever there is a savings shortfall is sustainable or not. Schacht also acknowledged the validity of the employment draft in theory, although he still put forward a series of constraints that the measure could only be effective in certain circumstances. At that time, Germany had no stock of raw materials, factories were empty, machinery and equipment were completely idle, and more than six million employed people were in a state of unemployment – only in such a situation, when credit was granted to the business owner, and the workers were allowed to repurpose the factory, to use the raw materials, to start production with the machines, could such a remedy save capital-generating power.

However, Schacht was still dissatisfied with this approach from the bottom of his heart, and his eventual ouster was directly related to his refusal to "re-discount" such employment drafts. According to himself, in January 1939, the German Central Bank submitted a memorandum to Hitler offering to deny further credit to the German government,[129] which had serious consequences.[130] on January 19, Schacht was fired by the government.[131] The next day, Hitler issued an order that the German Central Bank must grant all credit to the government, and this credit was to be granted whenever the government needed it.

After Schacht's dismissal, the German government kept it a secret from the public for more than five months, until the eve of World War II in July 1939. His refusal to extend further credit to the German government may have been a significant factor in his subsequent escape at the Nuremberg trials.

In 1948, after the war, a group of American professors again devised a monetary reform package for then defeated Germany: the Deutsche Bank mark was introduced, and at first everyone received a payment of 40 marks, while corporate employees received 60 marks and government departments received the corresponding mark for one month's salary. But all Reichstag currencies, whether savings accounts or debt amounts, are reduced to 10 per cent of their face value. On the other hand, stocks, assets and other tangible assets remain undervalued. This is an unprecedented act of "shearing", since the wealth of the poor is in savings accounts, while the wealth of the rich is mainly in assets. This type of "directional burst" currency devaluation actually created a huge process of wealth transfer that produced a major change in the social structure that was severe, even brutal, in the sense that it was as severe and widespread as the hyperinflation of 1923.

Rothschild and Hitler

On March 12, 1938, Hitler's army marched into Austria. Hitler held in his hands a list of captured heavyweight Austrian citizens. The name of Baron Louis Rothschild, head of the Austrian Rothschild

---

[129] Ibid, p. 243

[130] Schacht, *76 Years of My Life*, pp. 495.

[131] Ibid.

branch, is listed on this list. Among the family members, Louis Rothschild was the one whom the later great Victor of the Rothschild branch of England admired the most.

Three hours after Hitler entered Austria, German Nazi officers drove to the door of Rothschild's mansion in Austria, ready to arrest Rothschild. After they rang the bell at the door, they waited a moment before Rothschild's servant appeared at the door and opened it unhurriedly. The Nazi officer asked to see the Baron. The servants told them to wait outside the door and went inside to brief themselves. The Nazi officer waited honestly at the door. A long time passed before the servant came out again and said that Baron Rothschild was now at dinner and could not be disturbed. After saying that the servant took out a pen and politely said, "You want to see the Baron, make an appointment first." The Nazi officer was half dumbfounded and didn't know what to do, only to leave full of depression.

It follows that the Nazi persecution of Jewish bankers had not yet begun to take hold in 1938. The Nazi attitude towards the Jewish bankers was one of nominally shouting against them, and actually trying to exploit them, because everyone knew in their hearts that what Hitler lacked most in order to go to war was money. Thus, the Rothschilds did not take Hitler's initiatives to heart.

Hitler would never have gotten another penny from the financial markets if he had chosen to flip with the international bankers at this time. Hitler did not intend to break away at this point, at least not before he was ready in 1938. The next day, Victor called from England and told Louis not to stay any longer and to leave Austria as soon as possible. Louis promised, while unhurriedly packing his bags, and took half a day to get his bank clerk to pack his clothes too. The Nazi officer, who had spent the rest of his life in vain, once again came to the door and took Louis "without appointment".

Victor and other family members began to pressure the Nazi government to release Luis as soon as possible. The Nazi government made conditions that it was okay to let the people go, but only if all of Louis' assets in Austria were confiscated first. The Nazis were particularly interested in the large iron ore and coal mines owned by the Rothschild family in Czechoslovakia and other central European regions. The Nazis were preparing for war on a large scale and urgently needed to seize raw material bases to resupply the German arms industry. The Rothschild family's spies in Vienna and elsewhere immediately passed the information on to Louis Rothschild in prison.

Louis Rothschild got the news and started operations, transferring coal and iron ore assets in the Czech Republic and Austria to the Rothschild family branch in the UK. While in prison, the Louisians were still well informed and the "big transfer" of assets was not delayed, and the required set of legal documents were carefully completed, and control of the assets was smoothly transferred to the British United Insurance Company, the British Rothschild family.

This set of secret legal documents was signed without the knowledge of the gods, after being officially endorsed by Vienna and Portugal. After all the legal procedures for the transfer of assets had been put into effect, the Nazis discovered that the Austrian assets of the Rothschilds, which they had thought to be in possession, now belonged to the British Rothschilds and were out of their reach. Hearing of the outrage, Hitler instructed the Nazi government to threaten Louis with long prison terms if he did not turn over his assets.

Louis calmly told the Nazi officer that the assets were no longer his own and belonged to the British Rothschild. If the Nazis wanted to buy these assets, they should have contacted the London side directly. The Nazi government could do nothing but offer a quid pro quo that Louis would need to do some work for them if he was to be free. Without even thinking about it, Louis contemptuously rejected the Nazi government's request, telling Hitler that if the Nazis wanted to own the assets, they could only negotiate them through the Rothschilds in England. Hitler did not want to be in direct conflict with the British side at this time. Only to drop the price code again, offering to walk away as long as Lewis hands over £2 million.

The British side paid £2 million as soon as they heard the terms. Hitler signed the release order as soon as he got the money. That day, Louis had just had dinner and was resting when the Nazi officers came to the prison to release him. Louis stretched and told the Nazi officer that it was too late in the day and that he had decided to stay another night in prison and leave the next day. After saying that, he rolled over and went to sleep with him. The Nazi officers had no choice but to wait until Louis was well asleep in prison before moving on.

Hitler's power play

In terms of the way Hitler came to power and saved the economic crisis, Hitler was not the crazy and irrational person that people usually think of, on the contrary, as a politician, Hitler had considerable political power skills.

He relied on Feder's ideas and genuinely endorsed them, but ultimately chose the less like-minded Schacht as Minister of Economy because Hitler understood that Schacht was a "powerful man". When Hitler came to power and early in his administration, the economy was in decline, unemployment was high, social unrest was high, and the regime was unstable, he had to stabilize the international bankers and not reveal his true strategic goals too early, lest he end up "dying before he can get out". He took advantage of Schacht's financial brilliance, yet remained fiercely wary of him.

Although Hitler, who had just come to power, used anti-Semitism as a political banner, he often traded interests in the actual operation of his policies. This is true for the Haavara plan, it is true for the Austrian treatment of Rothschild's family, and it is true for the secret contacts with the Zionist organization told in the next chapter.

As Jews, the Warburg family should have been persecuted by the Nazis in Germany, but the Warburg family bank in Germany was still operating as usual in 1938, five years after the Nazis came to power, and was making huge profits. Not only that, Max Warburg held the position of director of the German Central Bank and of the IG Farben Group, Germany's largest industrial trust, under Hitler's watch until he emigrated to the United States in 1938. Hitler did not want to alarm the international bankers by prematurely exposing his attempts, and therefore remained unmoved by Max.

It was not until Hitler had taken control of the economic crisis and the Nazi Party was gaining ground and preparing to liquidate the power of the international bankers on the eve of war in Europe. He drove Max to the United States in 1938, fired Schacht in 1939, and dissolved the board of the German Central Bank.

Hitler, knowing full well that he was being used by the international bankers, would take advantage of the situation to buy time and conditions to quietly carry out his plan while giving the impression that he was obedient. In the process of building Germany's powerful war machine, in order to confuse the British ruling elite, he won Chamberlain's "policy of appeasement" by claiming to be inseparable from the Soviet Union, even as the Anglo-French Allied forces on the Western Front were quietly waiting for Hitler to take Poland and continue to attack the Soviet Union during the September 1939 attack on Poland. At the critical moment of the final destruction of the British and French forces, Hitler suddenly ordered the front line troops to stop their final attack and let the British and French forces live. This was one of the biggest unresolved cases of World War II, and many military historians believe that Hitler made a serious military mistake, when in fact Hitler was guilty of political childishness.

Hitler was a strong nationalist at heart, and he defeated France solely to avenge the Peace of Versailles. He did not want to and could not break with the international bankers, so he left 330,000 British and French Allies to live and set aside a piece of land for the Vichy Government in southern France. Hitler's idea was to avenge his great revenge while leaving room to spare, and then go east himself to destroy the Soviet Union, take control of the vast territory and resources of the western part of the Soviet Union, and then fight the British and Americans separately. The bombing of Britain was nothing more than a rogue's usual threat to increase his bargaining chips for a peaceful share of the spoils with the old colonial empire. Thus, on the eve of the war against the Soviet Union, Hitler sent his own crony, the Nazi Party's Deputy Führer Rudolf Hess, to fly to Britain for secret peace talks. Hitler's conditions were the return of all occupied territories of Western European countries, compensation for the costs of rebuilding them, a German police presence in those countries alone, and a peace treaty with Britain. Then attacked the Soviet Union, demanding assurances of strong British support. Hess was parachuting through the Scottish part of the UK in his latest warplane when he was captured by the local militia and the story was revealed to British public opinion.

Hitler had a good plan, but he had made a big mistake. In the view of the international bankers, Hitler was now completely out of control, and such a strong military force and a bottomless style of doing things had become a great danger, even more dangerous than the Soviet Union, that all forces had to be united to destroy Hitler.

As a result, Hess was "identified" as a psychotic lunatic in England, and Churchill described Hess's armistice conditions as a "subject for psychiatric study". The "psychopath" was kept under strict guard by British intelligence and was not allowed to be visited by any outsiders. In the post-war Nuremberg trials, Hess was found guilty of "crimes against peace", but not of "war crimes" and "crimes against humanity". However, the "psychopath" Hess was sentenced to life imprisonment, and even after the early release of most Nazi war criminals in the 1970s, Hess was still being held in tight custody. It was not until 1987 that Hess, at the age of 93, climbed to a height in prison, strangled his neck with an electric wire and committed a high and difficult "suicide". From then on, Hess, the Führer's closest secretary, who followed Hitler from prison through *Mein Kampf*[132] to Nazi power, closed his eyes forever.

---

[132] See *Mein Kampf – My Struggle*, Omnia Veritas Ltd – www.omnia-veritas.com

CHAPTER VII

Bankers and Intelligence Networks

Since its inception, the essence of finance has never been an empty and illusory theoretical exploration, but a cold and precise intelligence practice. The realm of the financier is to exploit information asymmetries to find, discover, and capture arbitrage opportunities in the market. Financiers, on the other hand, are at their peak by creating information asymmetries that interfere with, deceive, and confuse the thinking and judgment of other participants in the market, thereby creating opportunities for arbitrage.

The biggest thing a financier learns is not how to keep information fair, but how to achieve information manipulation. If the market is made up of people, and people are selfish by nature, then the uniform distribution of market information is a "utopian" fantasy that never has been and never will be. And all the theoretical systems based on "utopias" will always be a wonderful means of creating information asymmetry in the eyes of the financial super players.

Along the trajectory of information dissemination, the source of information generation is discovered, isolated information is centralized, cluttered information is classified, links are made between classified information, distorted information is reduced, and the product of information – intelligence – is obtained. The reverse execution of this process is counterintelligence. In the financial market, there is always a game of intelligence and counter-intelligence masters.

So, finance and intelligence will always be family.

The establishment and development of the international intelligence system is, to a large extent, an expression of the will of the international bankers, which starts from, revolves around, and eventually returns to, the interests. A deep understanding of the will of the international bankers and the pattern of their interests is of great value in putting into perspective the core functions of international intelligence agencies and the people they serve in the world today.

The KGB's "Cambridge Five"

I'm afraid no one who knows anything about international intelligence organizations is unaware of Kim Philby's big name. As a senior spy of the Soviet KGB, Philby undercover British intelligence for more than 20 years, and is the British senior liaison officer to the United States CIA (Central Intelligence Agency), responsible for coordinating the British and American intelligence systems of anti-Soviet spy operations, the key to its position, the long period of incubation, the British and American spy network of the destructive force, can be called the cold war.

I am afraid there is nothing more comical and ironic than the fact that the supreme head of Anglo-American espionage against the Soviet Union is himself a Soviet spy. Philby defected to the Soviet Union via Beirut in 1963 and was awarded the Soviet Red Flag in 1965, and in 1968 published his memoir My Silent War, which quickly reached the bestseller lists around the world. The Philby affair is perhaps the biggest scandal the British and American intelligence agencies have ever seen.

In fact, Philby was not alone within the Anglo-American intelligence system; he was surrounded by a well-known core group, the "Cambridge Five". Five Cambridge-era "henchmen" later became the backbone of the Soviet KGB's entry into Anglo-American intelligence circles.

The earliest of them to reveal their identities were Donald Duart Maclean and Guy Burgess. Maclean held key positions in British Intelligence Directorates 5 (counterintelligence) and 6 (external intelligence) before moving to the British Embassy in Washington, D.C., for intelligence duties. A great deal of critical information about the development of the atomic bomb and the progress of policy-making between Churchill and Presidents Roosevelt and Truman reached the Soviet KGB through the hand of Macklin. It is particularly noteworthy that McLean was the first to reveal to the Soviet Union the true intentions of the "Marshall Plan".

The "Marshall Plan" was essentially a bird-in-the-sky ploy, the core of which was to replace German war reparations and to deal a severe blow to the process of reconstruction of the Soviet economy while at the same time achieving the domination of European reconstruction by American financial power blocs. The Yalta Agreement and the Potsdam Proclamation made it clear that the Soviet Union would receive war reparations from Germany, which could be paid in the form of German machinery and equipment, industrial enterprises, cars, ships, raw materials, etc., at a time when the Soviet Union had suffered so much war damage that it had almost lost its ability to earn foreign exchange from exports, so that German war reparations would become the most important external resource in the process of Soviet economic reconstruction. The core of the "Marshall Plan" was the disguised abolition of German war reparations to the Soviet Union and its replacement by United States financial assistance to Europe. Although the aid was ostensibly open to both the Soviet Union and Eastern Europe, the Marshall Plan set out conditions for economic liberalization that were incompatible with the planned economic system of the Soviet Union and thus "forced" the Soviet Union out of the aid.

Another "beauty" of the Marshall Plan was the use of American taxpayers' money to "compensate" European international bankers for their losses in the war. The "Marshall Plan" was in fact a rehash of the American Dawes and Young Plan after the First World War, in which a whopping $13 billion was "loaned" to European bankers, who never repaid the money except in Germany. In fact, for international bankers, it doesn't make much difference whether the war is won or lost, it's just who pays the debt. Strangely but not surprisingly, the taxpayers of the United States, the victorious nation, became the biggest buyers of both world wars.

It was Macklin's accurate intelligence that enabled the Soviet side to see the Marshall Plan from the outset. Not only did the Soviet Union refuse to join the program, but it also forcefully prevented other Eastern European countries from joining and accelerated the removal of various heavy industrial equipment from Germany.

On 25 May 1951, Maclean's 38th birthday, Maclean, already suspected by British intelligence, defected to the Soviet Union with Burgess, another one of the "Cambridge Five", and was awarded the rank of colonel in the KGB.

At the height of World War II, Burgess, along with another of the "Cambridge Five", Sir Anthony Blunt, transferred a great deal of Allied strategic planning and foreign policy to the KGB while working in the

British Foreign Office. Burgess was also later sent to work at the British Embassy in Washington and lived with Philby. After defecting to the Soviet Union, he died of massive alcoholism.

The fourth of the "Cambridge Five" to be exposed was Sir Anthony Bronte. He worked as a counterintelligence agent for British Intelligence Five, leaking large amounts of deciphered German military intelligence to the Soviet Union. Before the end of the war, he was secretly commissioned by the British Crown to travel to Germany in search of confidential correspondence between the Duke of Windsor in England and Hitler, and between Queen Victoria in England and her German relatives. Queen Victoria was the grandmother of Kaiser Wilhelm II of Germany, and Anthony was knighted by the British Crown in 1956 and later became Professor of Art History at Cambridge University. After his Soviet spy status was revealed, his knighthood was stripped from him by Queen Elizabeth II of England, and then British Prime Minister Margaret Thatcher publicly named Sir Blunt as a Soviet spy. In 1983, Anthony Bronte died at his home in London.

However, the identity of the fifth of the "Cambridge Five" has never been revealed, which has become a major mystery in the world of intelligence. Over the years, there has been a great deal of disagreement and debate about who the "fifth person" really is.

The internationally renowned intelligence scientist Roland Perry has clearly stated, with a wealth of facts, that Victor Rothschild is the mysterious "fifth man".[133]

"The Fifth Man"

In fact, the Rothschilds are the originators of the international intelligence system. As early as the Napoleonic Wars, the Rothschild family had made a staggering profit on London's financial markets with intelligence on the progress of the Battle of Waterloo 24 hours before the market. For the large number of international banking families engaged in arbitrage in cross-border financial markets, accurate and fast intelligence is the "first productivity" of making money. Technological inventions have largely shaped the direction of intelligence systems. In an era where there was no telegraphic telephone, the Rothschild family

---

[133] Roland Perry, *The Fifth Man* (London: Pan Books, 1994).

pioneered the use of carrier pigeons to transmit data and trade orders in the financial markets. To prevent information from being intercepted during transmission and revealing secrets, the Rothschild family also created a suite of information encryption techniques. For the Rothschild family, intelligence is a long-established family tradition.

It was in this atmosphere that Victor Rothschild, the third-generation baronet heir to the Rothschild family, grew up. As heir to the English branch of the family, Victor carried with him a great deal of honour and a great deal of expectation. It seems that his father, Charles, was a weak link in the family chain, suffering from severe depression, and finally chose to take his own life because he could not bear the pain of insomnia for six years. At the time, Victor was only 12 years old. But as the successor to the family business, he took on a variety of unparalleled pressures.

The first pressure is on race. As a Jew, he had a highly sensitive complex of being discriminated against and at the same time an extremely strong sense of superiority. In spite of their exclusion and discrimination, the Jewish people are convinced that they are the only ones who are the chosen people of the biblical God, and that as rulers of the world, their power is inherently irreplaceable. Jews have an extremely strong sense of self-esteem, mixed with an extremely strong sense of being repressed. And a strong psychological fallout can often produce strong motivation and resilience.

The second pressure is the family reputation. Since Rothschild has been a major influence on the recent history of the world for over a hundred years, the pressures under his reputation have never been easy. Most of the students in the aristocratic school where Victor Jr. was enrolled were from prominent families. Still, all the classmates wore a look of awe when Victor Jr. revealed his family name. However, such a prestigious reputation and status is an added pressure, and with such a reputation, Victor Jr. must not be allowed to lose his poise and be inferior to others, he must and always will be first.

The third pressure is the intellectual challenge. Victor was a supremely intelligent man with an IQ of 184, an assessment later made by Nazi experts based on his performance in all aspects. Victor was indeed a very versatile man, a banker with an excellent track record, a renowned counterintelligence expert, a biologist, a master of atomic nuclear physics and a master of painting, art and music. Victor was constantly learning all kinds of new knowledge and had no free time in his life.

Young Victor, who entered Trinity College, Cambridge, is full of energy and loves adventure. At the time, he dabbled extensively in a variety of disciplines, including physics, biology, and psychology. He has always had a keen interest in the natural sciences, and also has a particular love of French. While learning French, he got an older student, three years older than him, to be an extracurricular tutor. This man was the later famous Sir Anthony Bronte, the fourth of the "Cambridge Five" to be exposed.

Bronte's relationship with Victor developed quickly, with Bronte often teaching Victor the pronunciation of French one-on-one.

In May 1928, during his sophomore year, Bronte joined the Cambridge Apostles, a well-known secret society at Trinity College, Cambridge. It was a secret society founded in 1820 by 12 so-called "apostles", 12 of the brightest undergraduates in the whole school, and not only that, but the 12 men had to be of noble origin, with extensive family connections in the English upper class. Such two requirements ensured that the members of the "Apostolic Order" would inevitably become the ruling elite of Britain in the future. Blunt later became Victor's "initiator" into the "Apostolic Order".[134]

On November 12, 1932, Burgess and Victor joined the Apostolic Society, forming a small group with Bronte, Victor, Burgess and others at its core.

The Circle of the Apostolic Council

The circle formed by the members of the "Apostolic Council" has a well-developed system of faith values, organizational forms, selection mechanisms and rituals. Their gatherings together are not a relaxed social affair where everyone eats and drinks, but a high level of rigorous training to "better" manage society in the future, based on deep historical roots, family ties, mutual admiration and high intelligence. What they have in common is a strong motivation for future social transformation. In other words, this is a circle of politically ambitious

---

[134] Ibid, p. 36–37.

people who are by no means just an academic group, nor a reunion, nor a mere secret society. This is especially important because of their extraordinary family background, wealth, intelligence and energy, and, most importantly, the "elite" complex that allows society to function according to their will. Such a group of people organized together and became lifelong allies who never betrayed each other, lifting each other up and encouraging each other to form an unbreakable community of interest, which is the tradition of the "Apostolic Church". The bond that can bring such a group of high-intelligence, high-energy people together is by no means more than interest; faith is a deeper force.

Introduced by friends of the "Apostolic Society", Victor became acquainted with Peter Kapitza, a very famous Soviet scientist at Cambridge at the time. Kapitza is a world-renowned physicist and Nobel laureate. Kapitza then accepted an invitation from the Royal Academy to work at the Rutherford Laboratory in Cambridge. As soon as Kapitza arrived in Cambridge, he formed the "Kapitza Club", which became quite famous in Cambridge. This club brought together some of the best physicists in Cambridge at the time to discuss the latest developments in physics. The Cambridge physicists joked that Kapitza had started the campaign so that he could get regular updates on the latest, cutting-edge advances in physics from the exchange of information between these eminent physicists, without having to read the boring papers himself. In fact, Kapitsa also had the little-known mission of compiling the latest information on the various advances in physics gathered from Cambridge, sorted into reports on the frontiers of physics and sent to Moscow regularly.[135]

The young Victor at the time was indeed attracted to the Kapitza set of ideas, the first socialist political system in the world developed by the Soviet Union. This political system, called scientific socialism, builds a complete social and economic system based on the theoretical foundation of strict scientific laws. Victor was most interested in physics and the natural sciences, so when he heard such an idea and experienced that it was a plan for the development of society using scientific principles, with the precision of an engineer, so that the entire political and economic system of society functioned entirely on precise, objective scientific theories and norms, his intuition immediately found

---

[135] Ibid, p. 37–38.

it to be a wonderful and masterful idea. This theory of thought not only fascinated Victor at the time, but also had a market in the elite "Apostolic" circles at Cambridge University.

The "Apostolic Society" regularly organizes discussions in which each person publishes a paper focusing on issues related to the functioning of society. Most of the topics submitted were focused on the Soviet model and the relevant experience of the USSR. In the minds of the members of this small group, it was generally agreed that such a model of the Soviet Union could solve the crises and problems of the world.

The numerous papers submitted by Victor revolve around the logical thread of exploring the role of banking in the functioning of society. One of his important articles was entitled "Communism and the Future of Banking".[136] This article is full of all sorts of novel flashes of wisdom and interesting and actionable proposals, but the Apostolic Church has not responded to it with much enthusiasm. Because most of these apostles did not have the appropriate knowledge in the field of finance and were not very knowledgeable about business operations, they were inclined to be academic when discussing issues. They are more concerned with social change, the functioning of society and the underlying institutions of society.

Among them, Bronte was a "pioneer" who had fully embraced the theoretical system of scientific socialism. At the same time, he tries to lead Victor down the same path. In daily conversation, he often subtly asks Victor what he thinks of his own family bank. This question inevitably puts Victor in a difficult position. On the one hand, he feels that his family's entire banking operation is a meaningless movement of money from one place to another in order to profit from it, and believes that the financial system constructed by the international banking family does not bring more benefits to society; on the other hand, he does not want or want to be on the opposing side of the powerful group of international bankers that his family represents.

Victor, who was in his twenties at the time, was undergoing a tremendous shock of ideas and values. Bronte repeatedly instilled in Victor the idea that the banking monopoly system constructed by the international bankers was not without benefit and could also be of great

---

[136] Ibid, p. 45.

benefit to society if a revolution broke out and the entire banking system was fully nationalized and controlled by the state.

Victor is not a mere "white bunny" in the eyes of Bronte and Kapica. Thanks to his precocious personality and deep-rooted religious beliefs, as well as his innate family imprint, Victor was already a man with an active and complex mind, a strong will and great ambition at a very young age. His most important characteristic is extreme subjectivity, and he will never be radically changed by persuasion and theoretical influence from outside. His mind is consistent, thoughtful, deep, hidden and pointing to clarity. He clearly had his own considerations and intentions, and this is the way of thinking that has been handed down through generations of families.

In his mind brewed a far more ambitious goal, even a social development plan far beyond ideology. As he embraces the ideas of those around him, he also ponders how he can use those people to serve his goals. Active in Victor's nature were the genes of the businessman, whose desire to acquire profit always overrode his interest in theory.

In the Apostolic circles, there was another big name: the famous British economist, Keynes. Victor and Cairns walked very close. Cairns was an early member of the "Apostolic Order" and taught at Cambridge University in the 1930s, where he had a private office at King's College. Keynes was not a believer in communism, but he was interested in the idea that the government should be involved in the workings of the economy and had been closely observing a series of economic reforms and dynamics in the Soviet Union, where the world economic depression that began in 1929 threw the capitalist system of thought into a major crisis, and where social thought of all kinds was trying to find a way out of social development, and economists were no exception. It can be said that Keynes at that time was also influenced by the Soviet idea of a planned economy model.

Victor often went to Cairns' office at Cambridge University to talk to Cairns. Every time he visited Cairns' office, he saw Cairns sitting in a rocking chair, reading a philosophical work by Locke or Hume. Victor almost never saw Keynes focusing on economics. The two meet to talk about their common interests and hobbies – book collecting – and there is no end of things to say. But there was always a question in Victor's mind as to when Keynes was going to do what he was supposed to do.[137]

Cairns was in his twenties older than Victor, but the age and experience gap didn't prevent them from becoming close, forgettable friends. Victor Cairns never needs to make an appointment in advance, so he can come to the door whenever he wants. There are always endless topics to talk about when the two meet, from philosophy, society and literature, to theory and practice in social transformation, to the big question of how society should really work. Another major topic that Victor and Keynes often explored was the perception of the British gold standard. The Rothschild family's special place in the world of gold cannot be ignored, and Victor naturally had an unusual interest in the role of gold in the British banking system and the world monetary system.

The most popular of the "Apostolic Council" seminars were Keynes' speeches and papers. Cairns was nearly fifty years old at the time, and his social experience and insights, as well as his first-hand knowledge of socio-economic, political, and diplomatic information and materials, certainly made these undergraduate students in their early twenties look up to him. He has both theoretical depth and a wealth of insight and experience in social practice. Keynes gave a paper entitled "Government Intervention" at a seminar of the "Apostolic Council", which inspired and shocked most members of the "Apostolic Council", including Victor. Victor's focus of interest was never purely theoretical or abstract; he was actually more concerned with practical operational details. In a letter to a friend, Victor refers to this Keynesian treatise and complains that

> *"'The Apostolic Society' gang is always banging on about what a communist society should look like, a topic that is actually quite boring. Burgess, Waterson, and Richard Davis all talk about such theoretical problems with both eyes, giddy and sweaty, but to a large extent they all say things that lack an inherent logical coherence, at least to me."*[138]

---

[137] Ibid, p. 43.

[138] Letter from Victor Rothschild to Keynes, *Keynes Papers*.

Another of Victor's arguments was vague and pretentious, and his paper entitled "Communism and the Hope of Science" received great praise and unanimous acclaim in the "Apostolic Council".[139]

In the meantime, a new member of their clique was added to the group, a student of sociology at Cambridge University, who was Philby, the third exposed KGB spy in the "Cambridge Five".

Philby's father

Philby's father, John Philby, was also a legend. John Philby was also a graduate of Trinity College, Cambridge, and his classmate Nehru was later the Prime Minister of India. Although less famous than his own son, as a Jew, John Philby was highly concerned with the situation in the Middle East and Palestine, and he played a crucial role and influence in the geopolitics of the Middle East. John Philby was an officer in the British Colonial Intelligence System who was involved in planning the Great Arab Uprising against Ottoman rule and protecting the oil fields in the Basra region, the only source of oil for the British Imperial Navy at the time. John Philby pledged his support to the Arabs for the establishment of a unified Arab federal state. John Philby was also involved in the Arab uprisings along with the famous "Lawrence of Arabia" (Thomas Edward Lawrence), but the two sides supported different Arab leaders, with John Philby favoring Ibn Saud, an Arab tribal sheikh, and Lawrence supporting King Hussein of the Hejaz.

The House of Hashemite, a direct descendant of the Prophet Muhammad, has been the legal guardian of the holy cities of Mecca and Medina for the past 700 years in the region of Hejaz. King Hussein was universally respected in the Islamic world as the great sheikh of the Arabs, and in October 1915, the British representative McMahon struck a deal with Hussein promising him that he would win independence after the war if the Arab tribes launched an uprising to join the war.

Neither Shad nor Hussein knew that Britain and France had secretly agreed on the post-war division of power in the Near East, and in May 1916 they signed the Sykes-Picot Treaty, which provided that of the Arab provinces of post-war Ottoman Turkey, France would get

---

[139] Roland Perry, *The Fifth Man* (London: Pan Books, 1994), p. 43.

Syria and Lebanon, and Britain would get Jordan, Palestine and Iraq.[140] In November 1917, the British issued the Balfour Declaration, which singled out Palestine as the Jewish homeland,[141] in exchange for the military research of the Jewish scientist Chaim Weizmann, the first president of Israel. The Great Arab Federation promised by Britain is nothing more than a scam. Britain's treachery cast a lingering shadow over relations between the Arab world and the West for many years to come. Philby and Lawrence are nothing more than pawns for the British government. In the end, Ibn Saud, backed by John Philby, became King of Saudi Arabia, while Feisal, son of Hussein, backed by Lawrence, became King of Iraq.

In 1921, John Philby was appointed by the British government as the supreme head of intelligence for the British Greater Palestine region, whose jurisdiction encompasses the entire territory of present-day Israel, Palestine and Jordan. It was here that John Philby developed a long-standing relationship with Allen Dulles, later director of the U.S. CIA. This is a big reason why Kim Philby was able to lurk in the CIA for a long time without raising suspicions.

At the end of 1922, John Philby returned to London to participate in policy discussions on the Palestinian question. Key players included, King George of England, later Prime Minister Churchill, Rothschild and Weizmann, leader of the Zionist movement. Thereafter, John Philby began working as a senior advisor to the Saudis, helping him expand and strengthen areas controlled by Saudi Arabia, becoming one of the most powerful figures in the country.

In 1933, John Philby brought American oil power to the Middle East when he signed a 60-year exclusive right to exploit the Hasa region of the Persian Gulf with Standard Oil Company. In fact, John Philby is the most important channel of contact for the U.S. special relationship with Saudi Arabia.

In 1936, the Arab-American Oil Company (ARAMCO) was formed as a joint venture between Standard Oil Company of California and East Suez Company, with John Philby representing Saudi interests.

---

[140] Liu Debin, ed., *History of International Relations*, Beijing: Higher Education Press, 2003 edition, p. 275.

[141] Ibid, p. 277.

In 1937, John Philby began planning a mass Jewish emigration to the Palestinian areas, with Saudi Arabia providing secret protection. John Philby simultaneously negotiated with Nazi Germany and fascist Spain that if war broke out, the neutral Saudis would sell their oil to neutral Spain and then transit Germany from Spain. The U.S. Justice Department's Nazi Special Investigative Team had determined that Adolf Eichmann, head of the Jewish section of the German Gestapo, had met John Philby in the Middle East in the mid 1930s.

In 1935, Adolf Eichmann became the main architect and implementer of the SS anti-Semitic policy, and after the German annexation of Austria in 1938, Eichmann was responsible for the forced relocation of Jews in Austria and worked with the Zionist "Aliyah Bet" agency to make the process of forced relocation more efficient and solid.

In February 1939, John Philby was in London to discuss Jewish immigration in Palestine with Ben Gurion (Israel's first prime minister) and Weizmann. John Philby proposed that Weizmann's Zionist organisation pay the Saudis £20 million to resettle Palestinian Arabs, to which Weizmann replied that the matter needed to be discussed with US President Roosevelt. In October, the Zionist organization promised the "Philby Plan", but the Arabs were firmly opposed to it because of leaks. Given the religious sensitivities of Palestine, this plan was shelved for three years, and on 3 August 1940, John Philby was arrested in Bombay on charges of Nazi sympathy (Defense Regulation 18B) and subsequently remanded to England. He was released seven months later thanks to the rescue of Cairns et al.

In August 1943, Harold Hoskins, President Roosevelt's envoy to the Middle East, came to Saudi Arabia to revive the "Philby Plan", stating that the cost of the 20 million pounds was "guaranteed by President Roosevelt of the United States". The Saudi King is in great difficulty in the face of this huge sum of money, since it has long been leaked that if he accepts it and then moves the Arabs out of Palestine, he will undoubtedly be considered a "bribe" by the entire Arab world. On second thought, the Saudi king finally gave up on this hot brick.

Kim Philby and Victor Rothschild

In June 1933, Philby had just finished a course in economics at Cambridge University and received a scholarship to Trinity College with full marks. Philby used some of that money to buy the entire Karl Marx collection and used the rest of the money to buy a used motorcycle. Philby was ready to travel all over Europe on his used motorcycle. It was John Philby's son, after all, who was surrounded by an impulse for adventure.[142]

This undoubtedly created a strong irritation for Victor Rothschild. His family background, special status, wealth and fame weave invisible strings that bind him to never be able to "go back in style" as Philby did. The temptation to be so near and far forms an even stronger attraction for Victor. Victor couldn't resist asking Philby if he could take him along. Perhaps because this wish was unlikely to come true, Philby's departing figure was filled with extraordinary swagger and poise in Victor's eyes.

In May 1934, when Philby finished his European tour, which had taken about a year, and saw Victor again, he was surrounded by an additional fiancée, Rietz Friedman, an Austrian Jewish underground Communist. This excursion played an important role in Philby's life. During his time in Austria he befriended Ritze and was involved in a number of secret underground jobs, including rescuing Jews who were being persecuted by the Nazis at the time, covering up the underground activities of the Communists, raising funds against fascism, rescuing trapped workers from Nazi persecution, transmitting secret letters and even disguising himself as a journalist to find out Nazi secrets.[143]

From Philby, Victor saw a life he had never been able to try in his life, and deep down he couldn't wait for days of such adventure and excitement.

Once after a meal, Philby tested Victor's willingness to do something more immediate than donating money to support Jewish immigration. Victor already knew that a great deal of Philby's experience involved a Soviet background, and he knew in his mind that if he promised to help Philby more directly, then he himself would become a supporter of the Soviet Union.

This was a major life choice for Victor. He chose to help the Soviet Union not only for purely theoretical reasons of good and evil, but also

---

[142] Roland Perry, *The Fifth Man* (London: Pan Books, 1994), p. 47.

[143] Ibid, p. 49.

because of his deeply hidden "private" schemes. Coming from an intelligence family, Victor has a pretty deep understanding of the value of intelligence. In a world increasingly close to war, the loss of intelligence would mean a major crisis for the family's century-old foundation, and the provision of intelligence to the Soviet Union would accumulate bargaining chips for the Rothschilds' dealings with the Soviet Union, the future world superpower. The most overwhelming truth of the Rothschild family for a hundred years is to bet on both sides and always stand with the winner.

After gauging this truth, Victor is determined to play a game of balance between the world's superpowers and be the final winner.

"The Cambridge Five" penetrated British intelligence

As the Rothschild family had already built up a large network of contacts in the UK, when the Apostolic Friends graduated and began to look for work and prepare to enter the British upper class, Victor was obliged to lend his energy and play a decisive role in their advancement in the workplace. First he used connections to introduce his good friend Burgess to George Ball, a heavyweight in the British Conservative Party at the time. George Ball was the principal officer of British Intelligence Five and the founder of the Tory intelligence agency. Later, on the recommendation of Victor and George Ball, Burgess entered the D section of British Intelligence Six, where his first assignment was to study the Jewish question in Palestine. The specific job arranged by the superiors was to create an antithesis among the Jews to the Zionist organization under Weizmann in order to decentralize the Jewish lobbying power against the British Parliament in favor of a compromise between the British government and the Arabs. The government suggested that the opposite side should preferably be led by Victor. In fact, Victor was a staunch supporter of Zionism, and because of the traditional low profile and tactics, the Rothschild family was generally seen by outsiders as taking a more moderate position.

As a result of his excellent work, Burgess introduced Philby to Intelligence VI's D section as well, and Burgess also introduced Guy Liddell, Executive Deputy Director of Intelligence V's B section, to Victor, setting the stage for Victor's later move to Intelligence V.

The Rothschilds also had an unusual relationship with Churchill. Churchill had been a regular seat in the family since the days of Victor's grandfather, Neti. Churchill was one of the predecessors who had watched Victor grow. Churchill's signature in the Rothschilds' guest book spanned 40 years, from 1890 to 1930, and even forged an extraordinary friendship with Victor's uncle Walter. Churchill has always been a strong supporter of Walter's ideas for the establishment of an ultimate Jewish state, Israel, in Palestine. It was also because of this that Churchill became the object of the Rothschild family's strong support in British politics.

In 1939, Victor presented Churchill with an analysis of the German banking system in which he pioneered an unorthodox but highly visionary line of thinking. The diverse financial transactions collected by the Rothschilds in their branches in various countries contained key data and information on all types of purchases and transactions of goods in Germany, and all purchases of goods by the Nazi government, as long as they were made through bank transactions, were under the control of the Rothschilds. Through a careful analysis of these financial data, Victor arrived at a projection of Germany's future purchases of military materiel and weaponry, concluding that the Nazis were carrying out a military expansion plan. Churchill's war office applauded the young man's novel research ideas. It was this article that paved the way for Victor's smooth entry into the British Intelligence V Bureau, Part B, in 1940, primarily for commercial counterintelligence work.[144]

Victor's excellent work and performance at British Intelligence V helped him to bring Bronte into Intelligence V's D section and recommend Maclean to Intelligence VI.

By this time, the "Cambridge Five" had fully infiltrated British intelligence and foreign policy-making, playing a crucial role in the course of the war. Victor Rothschild was actually the most central member of the "Cambridge Five", from whom all the connections were spread and gathered.

---

[144] Ibid, p. 89-90.

Between Sumerian and American, the two sides of the same coin

In 1937 Victor's uncle, Sir Walter, died. Walter himself had no children, so the title of knighthood was inherited by the 26-year-old Victor, who became the third Sir Rothschild. As a hereditary Lord of England, Victor automatically became a member of the British House of Lords, and his social activism energy was greatly enhanced.

The Soviet physicist Kapitza, who was in England at the time, had returned to Moscow, and Victor had been in close contact with Kapitza, sending him regular reports on the progress of research in various disciplines, including the latest developments in atomic physics, as well as important results and data from other disciplines published in internal journals. These data and information are of a high level of sensitivity and confidentiality and are not available from ordinary international scientific research channels. These areas include research on biotoxins, the results of which can be directly applied to the manufacture of biological weapons. Such up-to-date information and data, in the hands of Soviet scientists, are invaluable.[145]

A hardworking man with a surprisingly high IQ, Victor reads research papers in a wide range of disciplines and delves deeply into them, except for banking, which is his ancestral specialty. For example, in biology, which seems to be as far removed from him as a mountain, he has specialized in the analysis of the laws of sperm movement, trying to discover the mystery of why only one sperm can enter the moment the sperm egg meets, and how the "winner" sperm has an exclusionary effect. With regard to atomic physics, he requires himself to read all the scientific literature and various open and confidential papers, and has reached a fairly professional level of depth in his study of nuclear physics.

Victor's first job at the UK's Intelligence5 was to analyse whether the operations of all German commercial and industrial companies operating in the UK posed a security threat to the UK. In the early 1940s, he had already discovered that numerous German business establishments in disguise were actually working behind the scenes for the Nazi government. In particular, his report notes that these agencies

---

[145] Ibid, p. 77.

are likely to spy on the UK and that the network is so widespread and yet so obscure that it is difficult to screen the complex and vast network of commercial espionage organized by normal means.

At the time, the UK machining industry relied heavily on German suppliers for the production of a wide variety of moulds. The situation caught Victor's eye. He proposes to transfer the entire supply chain of all German suppliers to American companies. The United States officials were so elated to hear Victor's proposal that they busily invited him to the United States Embassy to discuss specific transfer matters. This action allowed Victor to fly in and build an important relationship of trust with U.S. officials.

Because of Victor's excellent work in counterintelligence, he was asked by the OSS (Office of Strategic Services), the CIA's predecessor, to train future US intelligence officers. The counterintelligence material written by Victor became an official textbook for the US intelligence services. For this, Victor received the Special Medal of Honor from the U.S. Army, as well as the George Iron Cross from the United Kingdom, and President Harry S. Truman specifically honored Victor Rothschild for his contributions to the U.S. Army.

The Rothschild family established a close relationship with Haganah early on. Haganah was a secret Zionist intelligence organization founded in 1920 as a precursor to the later Israeli Mossad. Haganah's main mission was to establish Israel, and the organization, heavily financed by the Rothschilds, established a vast spy network and surveillance system throughout Europe, secretly monitoring all anti-Zionist political organizations in the major cities.[146]

In his efforts to raise the "asset value" of his political and military intelligence, Victor was most concerned with creating greater bargaining chips to pave the way for future plans. He has already succeeded in holding American interests in check by choosing American manufacturers as a means of operating against commercial espionage. At the same time, he paid more attention to research advances in cutting-edge military technology, ready to appease the Soviets by providing them with the military technology intelligence they needed most. With a grasp of U.S.-Soviet intelligence dynamics, at the heart of British intelligence and close ties to the Zionist

---

[146] Ibid, p. 79–80.

intelligence network Haganah, Victor became the most important information and intelligence hub of the Second World War.

Core Confidential

Victor used his Cambridge connections to secure a key research position for himself at Porton Down, a British defense science and technology laboratory. The work carried out in Borden's laboratory is a top-secret project, mainly biological and chemical weapons research, which will eventually be used in the manufacture of bacteriological warfare weapons. The goal of the biological weapons research programme is to be weaponized and mass-produced within three years, and will be used as a weapon of last resort against Germany. Once Hitler had truly developed the strength to fight a landing on British soil, Britain would not hesitate to use killer biological weapons against Germany.

Of course this research work is in the process of inventing poisons, but also creating antidotes, and the development of biological and chemical weapons goes hand in hand with the development of vaccines. Victor paid close attention to both of these critical data, while motionlessly collecting data from the Bacteriological Warfare Research Institute in Maryland and the results of actual tests conducted in Mississippi, USA. The work carried out at the Laboratory was one of the most top secret projects of the entire war. Within four months of Victor's arrival at the laboratory, the Soviet KGB had received a large amount of experimental data, and the pace of Soviet biological and chemical weapons research had followed closely. Victor's "intelligence assets" appreciated rapidly on the Soviet side.[147]

During the war, Victor's scientific interests were mainly focused on the field of weapons of mass destruction research. In terms of the value of "intelligence assets", the more weapons capable of mass destruction of an adversary in war, the more difficult and potentially influential they are to study and the more States seek them at all costs, and this information constitutes a "good asset" with the potential for significant added value. Victor was never short of money, and financial gain was not something he pursued. He had in mind a far-sighted

---

[147] Ibid, p. 95.

attempt to turn these "good assets" into important international geopolitical leverage, in exchange for support for Israeli statehood in Palestine.

The atomic bomb is a much larger "good asset" than a biological weapon, and Victor certainly doesn't discount its value.

In the early days of World War II, Victor discovered the strategic value of the atomic bomb in future wars. At the time he strongly recommended that Churchill intensify his research on the atomic bomb, so Churchill prioritised the British research of the time: firstly, the development of radar to address the immediate need for early warning of German air attacks, and secondly, the development of the bomb.

During the development of the atomic bomb, Victor was an important player in the entire project.

The clandestine development of the atomic bomb in the United Kingdom was carried out by Sir William Axe at Imperial Chemical Industries (ICI) under the codename "Tube Alloys".[148]

In October 1941, Victor entered the Core Committee to monitor all steps in the development of the atomic bomb and used his influence extensively in Britain to help Sir William Axe secure government funding for research. Throughout World War II, Victor was the most knowledgeable, knowledgeable and informed expert in the Anglo-American intelligence system about the atomic bomb.

In late 1941, shortly after the outbreak of Pearl Harbor, two top American Columbia University scientists came to the United Kingdom and proposed that the United Kingdom and the United States should integrate resources for nuclear weapons research. It was agreed that the atomic bomb had to be developed before the Nazis. Prime Minister Churchill followed the progress of atomic bomb research so closely that he had to listen to Victor's presentation almost daily on the progress of atomic bomb research.

At the moment, Victor was in a special and advantageous position, having been granted access to all confidential papers and experimental data. While studying at Cambridge University, he became very knowledgeable about nuclear physics. While carefully reading the

---

[148] Ibid, p. 113.

confidential papers, he constantly asked some heavyweight scientists to make sure he fully understood all the detailed issues involved. Victor quickly became a top authority in the field of atomic bomb research. When he had figured out all the details, he had even begun to suggest direct modifications to the various experimental problems in the development of the atomic bomb.

Victor not only knew the details of the research, but also had a comprehensive and systematic grasp of the overall progress and coverage of the British and American atomic bomb programs. This puts him in a very good position in the entire field of atomic bomb research and analytically integrates other information into a comprehensive report detailing the overall progress of the bomb. The "intelligence assets" in Victor's hands at this point were sufficient to have a vital impact on the entire course of the war.

Rudolf Peierls, a Jewish nuclear physicist who immigrated to Britain in 1933, had already demonstrated in theory that atomic nuclear chain reactions were possible, and therefore it was feasible to build reactors to make fuel for the atomic bomb. Pierce first suggested that one kilogram or so of U235 being separated was enough to make an atomic bomb. Until 1940, all scientists believed that a tonne of U235 would have to be used to make an atomic bomb, but Pierce's calculations shattered everyone's expectations. Immediately afterwards, Peirce and Sir Mark O'Riffin of the University of Birmingham worked together to validate the feasibility of their technology and come up with a set of design solutions. The scheme was quickly accepted by Victor, who subsequently carried out a detailed analysis and study of it.

The plan was quickly transferred to the Soviet Union. The Soviet Union expressed a high degree of interest and interest in the progress of the atomic bomb. At the time, Hitler's pressure on the Soviet Union was growing. After the Battle of Stalingrad, the Soviet-German battlefield was in a state of stalemate, and information on the course of the development of the atomic bomb was a deadly temptation for the Soviet Union.

The Soviet physicists such as Kapitschka were at a standstill in their research in the field of atomic bombs, when new ideas from Victor, such as the rains after a long drought, inspired Kapitschka and others to speed up the development of atomic bombs with immediate effect. On the American side, Fermi proposed that plutonium could be used in atomic bombs based on the Pierce chain reaction theory in the 1942 Chicago experiment, and built the world's first nuclear reactor.

Fermi's thinking has been challenged in the UK by the likes of Pearce. Under these circumstances, Victor had to conduct extensive field trips to almost every research branch of defense science and technology, interviewing a wide range of researchers from all walks of life in order to understand the key technical aspects of the entire atomic reactor, in order to fully understand whether plutonium could be used as fuel for the reactor. But such a high-profile investigation into the details of the atomic bomb is bound to raise suspicions.

Who is Victor? He quickly and calmly devised a perfect solution.

Victor began by writing a report to Guy Liddell, the British Deputy Minister of Intelligence V's B Division, in which Victor suggested that security awareness throughout the national laboratories and cooperative agencies in the commercial sphere was weak and ineffective in preventing infiltration by German spies. He recommended that security management be urgently strengthened to firmly establish a sense of alarm. Liddell felt that Victor's report made a lot of sense and put Victor in charge of security for the entire defense cutting-edge scientific research program. This position is exactly what Victor had in mind, and with the imperial sword, he was able to legitimately check the "security situation" of the progress of all the projects he was interested in. Victor becomes the "safety inspector" for all sensitive projects in the UK.

In 1942 he visited the University of Birmingham to check "at random" on the progress of work in the Pearce and Furyk laboratories, and "on the way" to another office to check on the work of Orion. At the time, Orion was doing research on radar. In his 1994 memoirs, Oriffin notes,

> *"This was the only meeting I had with him (Victor), and Victor wanted to know everything about the progress of the project, and he visited the whole laboratory, read every research report and absorbed all the detailed information in them, and he was not an expert, but he also did not pretend that he knew everything, but kept asking lots of questions, taking notes again, and then having long discussions with me. Discuss the various issues*

surrounding scientific experimentation. He is a very intelligent man and I like Sir Rothschild very much."[149]

In fact, this kind of security check by Intelligence 5 goes well beyond the scope of general security protection. Victor is actually learning the specifics of all the project progress, especially the technical details. He took advantage of Orion's inattention to take a three-inch diameter magnetron tube from Orion's office, which had three magnetic poles used to generate short waves and was a cutting-edge device for radar. That evening Victor had all the details and components of this device precision mapped at his home in Cambridge. Victor's drawing skills are excellent, and his three-dimensional drawings, based on his own observations and understanding, are far more understandable than the photographs taken by a camera. Soon, a picture of this beautiful three-dimensional diagram appeared on the desk of the KGB.

The next morning, Victor sent the magnetron back to Orion with a note that read,

"Perhaps you should step up your security management. Very happy to meet with you. Your faithful friend, Victor Rothschild."[150]

Orion received the stripes and broke out in a cold sweat because the magnetron was missing and he surprisingly didn't notice. Orion had no doubts at all about this move by Victor, and in a sense, he was even grateful, because with Victor's position and responsibilities, he was perfectly capable of typing reports criticizing the security breach in Orion's team, which would have caused a lot of trouble in Orion's lab, but Victor had only written a note of kindness as a reminder, which was a tall order. Orifin didn't dare to slack off and replied immediately, immediately stepping up security management to ensure that all lab equipment was not taken away without registration.

In early 1943 Victor again visited Professor Thomson's laboratory at Imperial College London, again in the name of security checks. Professor Thomson explained to Victor the details of how to make an atomic bomb from plutonium. But the Thomson team, while correctly

---

[149] Ibid, p. 116–117.

[150] Ibid, p. 117.

understanding the principle, misused heavy water as a neutron decelerator in the reactor, which caused the experiment to fail.

Victor quickly took Thomson's team's research progress again, drew it up again in precise three-dimensional diagrams, and forwarded it to Bronte, who in turn sent it to the KGB. Soviet physicists later reflected that these were the data they were searching for, and Victor's intelligence helped them to cut down on the research time considerably. The Soviet Union admitted years later that the first atomic bomb exploded in 1949 was just a rehash of the American design, a design that was an unprecedented new way of thinking for them and helped Soviet nuclear physicists understand the most basic principles of atomic reactors. I am afraid that none of the senior government officials and chief scientists in the whole of Britain and the United States, including even Churchill, knew as comprehensively and meticulously as Victor did about all aspects of the atomic bomb.[151]

Victor had by this time become an indispensable source of strategic intelligence information for the Soviet Union. He finally made an offer to the Soviet Union.

Victor's Price: The Secret Exchange of Atomic Bombs for the Establishment of the State of Israel

Beginning in 1947, the Soviet Union abruptly changed its consistent position on the issue of Israeli statehood and explicitly supported Israel's re-establishment in Palestine.

In international historiography, there has been a great deal of confusion about this. Be aware that Marx was firmly opposed to Zionist thinking from the beginning. Marx made it clear that the establishment of the Jewish state was an illusion. He was firmly critical of Zionism. Stalin took this same critical attitude towards Zionism. After the establishment of the Soviet Union, its negative attitude towards Zionism in politics did not change. The official position of the Soviet Government was clear, Zionism was described as a reactionary ideology used by Jewish capitalists to exploit Jewish workers, while the idea of establishing a Jewish national home in Palestine was considered a historical step backwards and contrary to the proletarian

---

[151] Ibid, p. 118.

internationalist movement, and in May 1939 Britain published a White Paper against Zionism.[152] After the outbreak of the Soviet-German War in 1941, the Soviet Union eased up on its opposition to Zionism, but its overall position did not change.

To everyone's surprise, in April 1947, when the United Nations convened a special session on Palestine, the Soviet position took a big 180-degree turn and expressed support for the partition of Israel and Palestine.[153] Gromyko, the representative of the Soviet Union to the United Nations, made a lengthy speech at the United Nations in which he expressed sympathy for the "extreme misfortune and suffering" suffered by the Jews during the war. Therefore, the desire of the Jews to establish their own state cannot be ignored. On behalf of the Soviet Government, he proposed "the establishment of an independent, dualistic, democratic and Arab-Jewish State of the same nature" in Palestine. If this option cannot be implemented, consideration should be given to "dividing Palestine into two independent, autonomous States, one Jewish and one Arab". He said that it would be "unfair" to refuse to consider or deny the Jewish people's claim and right to have this wish fulfilled. When Israel was declared a state on 15 May 1948, the Soviet Union recognized it immediately, established an embassy in Israel on 26 May, and supported Israel in many ways thereafter, and on 11 May 1949, the Soviet Union and the United States jointly supported Israel's full membership in the United Nations. It is extremely rare for Israel to be born with the joint support of two superpowers.

An analysis of the time period shows that Victor Rothschild provided the Soviet Union with a great deal of important intelligence, particularly strategic intelligence on the design of the atomic bomb, which had a clear temporal correlation with the change in Soviet attitudes towards Zionism.

The first atomic bomb of the Soviet Union was successfully exploded on August 29, 1949. In other words, the timing of the Soviet Union's sudden policy adjustment towards Israel coincided with the

---

[152] Paul R. Mendes-Flohr, Jehuda Reinharz, *The Jew in the modern world: a documentary history* (Oxford University Press US, 1995).

[153] Roland Perry, *The Fifth Man* (London: Pan Books, 1994), p. 176.

timing of the Soviet Union's active preparation for the atomic bomb test.

Nuclear weapons were undoubtedly of great strategic importance to the Soviet Union. The United States had the world's first atomic bomb in 1945, while the Soviet Union had to live in the shadow of American nuclear weapons. This lingering sense of oppression has left the Kremlin restless. Only the possession of the atomic bomb could establish the Soviet Union as a superpower. It should be reasonable to infer that vital information was exchanged for the establishment of the State of Israel. Dissecting the time period in which the two events occurred, there is clearly an intrinsically linked consistency.

As reported in the American professional journal Atomic Scientists News Briefing, archives in the KGB archives show that the first atomic bomb intelligence received by Soviet agencies arrived in the Kremlin in October 1941, a copy of a memorandum from British nuclear physicists calling on Churchill to build nuclear weapons. It caused a panic in the Soviet hierarchy, and Stalin thought it was disinformation. Victor "happened" to join the core committee of the British atomic bomb project "Alloy Tubes" in October 1941, overseeing all steps in the development of the bomb.

The Bulletin of Atomic Scientists also reported: "In early 1943, he (Stalin) appointed physicist and patriotic youth Kurchatov as head of the Soviet atomic bomb project. Unlike the Americans who had started from nothing, Kurchatov had mastered the essence of Western nuclear research in the hands of Beria's spies. The couriers transported the secret information to Moscow, where it was then transferred to the Saru nuclear weapons manufacturing site, 400 kilometres away. Under strict secrecy, Soviet scientists began imitating parts of the atomic bomb." Victor, in turn, "happened" to visit Professor Thomson's laboratory at Imperial College London in early 1943 under the guise of a "security check". Professor Thomson explained to Victor every detail of how to make an atomic bomb from plutonium.

Victor not only had the most comprehensive and in-depth knowledge of the development of the British atomic bomb, but he was also extremely familiar with the American bomb. Victor is close friends with U.S. Atomic Energy Commission Chairman Lewis Strauss. Strauss is also a senior partner at Kuhn, Loeb & Co. and has strong ties to the international banking family.

The value of Victor's "intelligence assets" in the Soviet Union was heightened by the Rothschild family's prominent position in the international financial community and by Victor's core secrets in the British intelligence community in relation to a large number of atomic bombs and biological and chemical weapons, as well as by his strong influence and contacts in the British political circle.

At this point Victor made an offer for the Soviet government to loosen its control of Jewish immigration to Palestine and to support the establishment of Israel in Palestine.

After the end of the war, Victor called more and more openly and strongly for the return of Jews to Palestine to establish the State of Israel. At the time, he made a series of speeches in this regard in the British House of Commons, calling public attention to the issue, which attracted widespread attention from all sectors of British society.

There is a fierce conflict of interest between Jews and Arabs over the establishment of the State of Israel, and all Arab countries are firmly opposed to the establishment of any form of Jewish state. From the perspective of the Arab states, these land generations are Arab roots and it is impossible to allow Jewish immigrants to re-establish a state of Israel.

In the intricate and delicate game of international politics, Victor dances with his long sleeves and displays great political skill. He used the media to portray himself as a neutral and moderate Jewish rationalist through the family group's special influence in the media, and he was portrayed as the most pro-Arab political figure in the entire Jewish world.

On July 31, 1946, in a polemic against the status of Palestine, Victor came to the fore. The controversy was sparked by a series of terrorist acts that erupted in the Palestinian area, highlighted by the massive bombing of the King David Hotel by Jewish terrorists, which killed a number of British soldiers.

In his speech, Victor for the first time explicitly responded to the US proposal to partition Palestine.[154] After first denying that he was a Zionist or had any connection with the Zionist organization, he began to recount with emotion the persecution and oppression of the Jews in

---

[154] Ibid, p. 152–155.

Europe over the centuries. He then spoke of the famous British White Paper issued by the British Foreign Office in 1939, which explicitly opposed Jewish settlement in Palestine. This was considered by the Jews of the world as a violation of the British "Balfour Declaration" of 1917 and a shameful betrayal. Victor also quoted Churchill's view of the White Paper that "this is a clear betrayal of a previous promise, which was another Munich Agreement". In response to the United States zoning proposal, Victor responded that the first condition of the proposal was the cessation of all terrorist acts and the complete disarmament of the armed forces distributed in Palestinian areas, which was a prerequisite for the immigration of new Jews to Palestine. In his view, the current situation was clearly unfavourable to the Jewish people, as a number of Arab States were ready to use force in the vicinity of Palestine. In other words, Victor believes that Jewish armed groups in Palestinian areas should reasonably and necessarily exist and develop.

In this part of the historical review, Victor movedly notes that after more than two thousand years of wandering, the Jews were finally able to return to their own land and the homes they once lived in. He denounced the Nazi persecution of the Jews and stressed that the extreme horrors suffered by the Jews during the "Second World War" made it necessary and urgent for the Jews to have a true sanctuary of their own, thus preventing any future persecution. His speech attracted the attention of the world. For the Rothschilds, the war was not over, and their determination to establish a state of Israel would never waver.

At this point, the deck of cards before the Soviet Union was becoming clearer and clearer, and if the Soviet Union wanted to continue the cooperation of Victor and other Jewish scientists in the development of the atomic bomb, it would have to compromise diplomatically and support the idea of Israeli statehood.

Soviet support for Israel's statehood, which began in 1947 and lasted only 20 years until 1967, was followed by a return to centuries of tradition.

The "Cambridge Five" were also exposed during the same period of time, and Victor himself stopped working with the KGB in the early 1960s. Faced with numerous "rumours" questioning his relationship with the KGB, Sir Victor Rothschild deliberately published an open letter in a British newspaper in December 1986: "I am not, and never have been, a spy for the Soviet Union."[155]

"Target Patton"

In November 2008, a book with explosive content was published in the United States – *Target Patton*. The book argues that General Patton, the famous American general of World War II, was not actually killed in a car accident, but was murdered.

Similar claims have long been made in American military and historical circles, boiling down to several speculations about the motive for the murder: one claim is that the German Nazis did it. But the war is over, the Nazis in Germany are basically falling apart, and the murder of American generals has no meaning to affect the course of the war, which is not very likely.

Another way of saying it was done by the Soviet side. Since Patton's attitude towards the Soviet Union was always hostile, and at the end of World War II he even arrogantly demanded that the United States release the German SS, which he would lead along with his men in an offensive against the Soviet army, the Soviet Union had a motive to murder Patton.

There is another way of saying that Patton is a master of merit. The latter part of World War II played a key role in the process of liberating Europe and aroused the jealousy of the US military hierarchy, especially Eisenhower and Bradley. The argument advanced by this assertion was that Eisenhower and Bradley at the time had taken measures of delay and resistance to many of Patton's military operations, distributing vital material equipment and gasoline to Montgomery but not to Patton. It is presumed that Patton's superiors, out of cynicism and jealousy or to prevent Patton from stabbing their incompetence and malfeasance out, ended up killing the man.

The book "Target Patton" makes another shocking claim that the US strategic intelligence agency OSS (the predecessor of the CIA) was the real mastermind behind Patton's murder, and that it was the founder

---

[155] Ibid, p. 365.

of OSS, Bill Donovan, who the international intelligence community called "Crazy Bill", who dominated the whole affair.[156]

The book mentions the assassination of one of Patton's confidants named Bazata. During the Second World War, Bazata was a spy for the Allies, a marksman who claimed to be one of his clients, and one day in April 1945, near the end of the war in Europe, Donovan met with Bazata and said that a mission "concerned some complex American interests" and "required your patriotic qualities of courage". This mission is the murder of Patton. Donovan instructed Bazata to find his own helpers when acting, and no agency would admit to it, much less have official support. In the fall of 1945, he signed a contract with Donovan for the murder of Patton for $10,000. Donovan claimed, "I was taking orders from above and a lot of people wanted this done."[157]

On the morning of December 9, 1945, Patton and his entourage were traveling in his Cadillac limousine on a two-lane highway. It was a Sunday and there were few cars on the road, the road was straight and the view was up to half a mile away. Barton was looking out the window when the crash happened. At this point, a military truck came in the opposite lane and, less than six meters from Patton's car, suddenly drove straight over with a sharp turn of nearly 90 degrees, and the truck came sideways in front of the Cadillac. The driver only had time to slam on the brakes while trying to hit the car to the left, but it was too late and the Cadillac slammed head-on into the truck. Barton was thrown from the back seat to the front seat, bleeding from the bridge of his nose to the top of his head in a gaping gash. Barton said his neck hurt, then added, "I couldn't breathe. Help me move my fingers." At 12:30 p.m. that day, Patton, who was seriously injured in the emergency vehicle, sped toward the nearest 130th Resident Hospital in Heidelberg.[158]

Barton was life-threatening for days, and paramedics resuscitated him day and night. With such a serious injury, he's actually recovering quite quickly. The doctor said there was a miracle, and the cloud of sadness on the faces of the family and ministers slowly dispersed. By the 10th day after the accident, on December 18, Patton's injuries had

---

[156] Robert Wilcox, *Target Patton* (US: Regnery Publishing, Inc. 2008), p. 25.

[157] Ibid, p. 92–99.

[158] Ibid, p. 20, 167–170.

stabilized and he was ready to return to the United States for Christmas, and on December 19, the day before Patton left, his condition suddenly worsened and he developed a blood clot. For a very short time his condition took a sharp turn for the worse, and on the afternoon of December 21, Barton died. The body was not dissected.

The book reveals that the murder plan did not intend for Barton to die in a car accident, but instead used drugs. The use of "cyanide extracts that can cause blood clots, heart failure, etc." in the hospital resulted in Barton's death. The drug was manufactured in Czechoslovakia and, with just a little, could kill in "18 to 48 hours".[159]

All records related to the Barton crash, such as official accident reports, eyewitness testimonies, and other records are missing in the Barton crash. Barton's Cadillac, afterwards, was hastily towed away without any accident records or inspection, and has never been seen since. If one assumes that the Soviets poisoned Patton in the hospital, it would be difficult to systematically destroy all relevant archival information in the hands of only the US military.

It was once revealed to Barton that "one of his own" was going to hurt him. Barton replied then, "Come on, they can run fast enough to catch me." Barton may have had a vague hunch that someone was preparing to plot against him, as he had been in three bizarre car accidents in a month.

It would also be puzzling if the mastermind was Bill Donovan, the founder of the CIA. As the founder of the U.S. strategic intelligence system, he was once highly regarded by President Harry S. Truman as "a man who has made significant contributions to the United States". Besides, Donovan and Barton have no personal history. Why would he murder Barton? There are no real answers given in this book. Who the hell is Bill Donovan? What exactly was his real motive for murdering Patton?

---

[159] Ibid, p. 16-7, 202–204.

Donovan's Origin[160]

Born on January 1, 1883, in Buffalo, New York, Donovan graduated from Columbia University Rothschild School, where he was a classmate of later President Franklin D. Roosevelt, and from 1903 to 1908 he was favored by a famous professor at Columbia Rothschild School, Harlan F. Stone, the famous Justice of the United States Supreme Court.

One of the students Professor Harlan Stone particularly admired, in addition to Donovan, was John Edgar Hoover, the later head of the US FBI. Hoover is no slouch either. Harlan Stone, then as U.S. attorney general, appointed Hoover as the first director of the FBI, a news that shocked Washington. Hoover served as the first director of the FBI from 1924 until his death in 1972, and remained in office for 48 years, making him the most powerful and intimidating head of the intelligence community in American history.

Another of Donovan's "honored guests" he met while at Columbia was Professor Jackson E. Reynolds. He became the president of the First National Bank of New York and was a strongman in the J.P. Morgan consortium, and it was with his support that Donovan became the head of the U.S. Strategic Intelligence Service OSS.

Donovan's social directory is full of notables, including the famous actress Eleanor Robson, the daughter-in-law of August Belmont, the Rothschild family's agent in New York.

Donovan opened a law firm in Buffalo, New York, and befriended Ross Romsey. Rose Romsey came from an illustrious and wealthy family; her father, Dexter Romsey, and uncle Bronson once owned 43 square miles of land in Buffalo, and by 1890 the family had more than $10 million in assets. Rose Romsey's mother was also the daughter of a wealthy family with thousands of slaves owned by her ancestors, probably the most slave owners in American history. After a few twists and turns, Ross Romsey ended up marrying Donovan.

Donovan was sent to Europe by the Rockefeller Foundation to join the "War Relief Corps" during World War I in 1915, after being

---

[160] *Wild Bill Donovan: The Last Hero*, by Anthony Cave Brown, New York: Times Books, 1982.

promoted by friends at Columbia University and Wall Street. Herbert Hoover, then a colleague sent by the Foundation to run the project, became the 31st President of the United States.

After the United States entered World War I, Donovan was on the front lines and was honorably wounded. The war credit sheet records that he once captured a German machine gun squad on October 15, 1918. Donovan was thus awarded the Congressional Medal of Honor. His courageous deeds were widely publicized in the American media and appreciated by Wall Street bankers, and in 1919 and 1920 Donovan undertook secret Wall Street missions to China and Siberia.

After the end of World War I, JP Morgan formed the Overseas Business Corporation to prepare a $2 billion bond issue to finance post-war Europe, and in February 1920 Morgan invited Donovan again for a $200,000 salary for a secret visit to Europe, primarily to obtain secret information about the European bond market. Donovan was entrusted with this task because he had experience in the battlefields of Europe, lived in Europe for many years, and had built up a network of contacts and intelligence. It was during this trip to Europe that Donovan met Hitler in Berchtesgaden, Bavaria, Germany, and had a long talk with him overnight. He thought Hitler was an "interesting talker".

Donovan was appointed to the New York District in 1922, and in 1924 he was called to Washington by former Columbia Rothschild School professor Harlan Stone. Donovan's first request when he met his teacher was to have Edgar Hoover's FBI director removed. Stone is both Donovan's protector and Hoover's backer, so Donovan doesn't get what he wants. As can be seen from this incident, there was an obvious feud between Donovan and Hoover, which may have been one of the reasons why the CIA and FBI consistently stumbled in their later cooperation.

Between 1924 and 1928, Donovan became a close associate of the later President Hoover. Hoover recommended that President Coolidge appoint Donovan to take full responsibility for the organization and coordination of Hoover Dam. While Hoover was moving smoothly into politics, Donovan served faithfully for four years as a top-level strategic advisor. Hoover even invited Donovan to be his running mate during his presidential campaign, but because Donovan was Catholic, Hoover, fearing that running with him would lose a large portion of the non-Catholic vote, dropped Donovan after several considerations. After President Hoover's successful campaign to take over the White House, it was natural to reward meritorious men. And surprisingly, Donovan, who was a core member of the main campaign team, did not get a seat in the cabinet. Depressed, Donovan is ready to withdraw from the political scene in Washington.

From 1936 to 1937, Donovan's friends in the Nazi government in Germany invited him to visit the progress of the Spanish Civil War. In Spain he met Kim Philby of the "Cambridge Five".

In 1937, the Rothschilds' bank in Vienna ran into trouble as the Nazi annexation of Czechoslovakia had a negative impact on the Rothschilds' loans in the country. Donovan happened to have quite a few contacts in the Nazi inner circle. So Rothschild asked Donovan to step in and poke around inside the Nazi government. With this help, Donovan's relationship with the Rothschilds was further deepened and consolidated.

OSS – "Oh So Social"[161]

On 29 May 1940, William Stephenson, who had worked with Donovan in the 1915 "European Relief Corps", arrived in New York with a letter from General Brinker Howe, a former European acquaintance and then British intelligence officer, recommending that the United States establish a strategic intelligence service as soon as possible.

Donovan took the letter to a friend on Wall Street and fellow Columbia Rothschild School student – President Franklin D. Roosevelt – to lobby. Roosevelt then ordered Donovan to London to prepare for the establishment of the US strategic intelligence agency OSS, and although it was a so-called covert operation, many in the US media speculated that Donovan's London trip was on a secret mission from President Roosevelt. Donovan also stopped by southeastern Europe to learn about the land under German occupation, and although the German side knew he was on a mission to set up an American spy agency, it didn't bother him at all, in part because Germany didn't want to mess with America.

---

[161] *OSS: The Secret History of America's First Central Intelligence Agency*, by R. Harris Smith, University of California Press, 1972.

Donovan returned to Europe and presented the information he had learned to President Roosevelt, who officially appointed Donovan as Director of the OSS on June 13, 1942. From then on, Donovan was referred to by Roosevelt as "my secret leg" and mainly helped Roosevelt carry out secret plans.

In the OSS under Donovan, JP Morgan's son Niels was the chief financial officer, Paul of the Mellon family held key positions, and his brother-in-law David Bruce ran the London branch of the OSS and later became US Ambassador to France. The son of Paul Warburg of the Warburg family, "the architect-in-chief of the Federal Reserve", Jamie Warburg, is Donovan's personal assistant. Not to be outdone, the Vanderbilt, Dupont and Lane families have placed family members in important positions in the OSS. No wonder some people call OSS "Oh So Social" ("It's all about relationships"). In terms of connections, the U.S. Strategic Intelligence Agency is nothing short of an international banker's social circle, primarily serving the heavyweight financial families of Rockefeller, JPMorgan, Rothschild, Warburg, Vanderbilt, Mellon, DuPont and Ryan.

Intelligence and finance will always be family.

The motive for Patton's murder

After learning about Donovan's connections with the OSS, we return to the book Target Patton. If Donovan and Patton have no personal vendetta, then who is Donovan's "superior" when he claims, "I took orders from above, and many people want this done"? Is it his name that leads the President of the United States, or is it his substantial "top" and "many" family of international banks?

Patton was an extremely hostile general to the Soviet Union, and his constant creation of friction with the Soviet Union threatened to spark a military conflict between the United States and the Soviet Union, or even trigger a war, if he could not be contained. It would have been totally in the interest of the international bankers to see the US and the Soviet Union at war at this time, especially during the period 1945–1948, which was a critical time for Israel to prepare for statehood. The Zionists had been preparing for nearly a century of greatness in one fell swoop.

Through World War I, the Ottoman Empire had fallen and the Palestinian region had finally seceded; through World War II, large numbers of Jewish immigrants had arrived in Palestine. When Nazi Germany was completely destroyed, Britain and France were still panting in the ruins of the war, the United States, out of the pressure of gold power, the Soviet Union could not resist the desire for the atomic bomb, the great powers for different reasons just appeared in the issue of the establishment of the State of Israel, a consensus on the issue of a hundred years rare, if we let Patton, who has a strong reputation in the United States, rich contacts and military loyalty, make the United States and the Soviet Union to engage in hostility or even war, the Zionist dream of a hundred years will be complicated and may even be completely and permanently killed, this price is in any case unbearable. It is absolutely intolerable for one Patton, but ten Patton, to come out and stir up trouble at such a critical juncture!

The gaze of a handful of elite decision-makers, deep and cold, projected toward the common end goal of their faith. Any obstacle or disturbance on the road will be eradicated in an instant.

CHAPTER VIII

The Ruling Elite and the "Invisible Oligarchs"

> *"Wealth alone cannot quench the cravings and lusts of the super-rich. Instead, many of them used their abundance of wealth and the influence that that wealth brought them to seize greater power. Such power flourished in a way that the tyrants and despots of the early years could not even have dreamed of. It is a power that governs the world, not only the wealth of the world, but also those who live in it."*[162]

This passage describes very accurately the ultimate "grand scheme" of the international bankers, which is the establishment of a world government with the "Anglo-American" power group at the top of the pyramid. This is not a fanciful speculation or wild conjecture, but a strategic process that has evolved over generations of development.

From the early British Rhodes Society to the later American Foreign Relations Association, the ruling elite from Britain and the United States conducted a full range of theoretical explorations and practical exercises, from theory to practice, in order to achieve their strategic goal of world domination. The implementation of this massive and organized plan cannot be carried out without the financial support of the three powers.

The Western society we see today is ostensibly democratic, free and pluralistic, and the financial oligarchs of the past have been successfully driven out of power by the sacred democratic system. The powerful and super-rich families have disappeared into thin air and are nowhere to be seen. Has history been changed? Does capitalism no

---

[162] Gary Allen, *The Rockefeller File*, Buccaneer Books, Inc. 1976.

longer serve a minority power group? Have the international bankers really taken the initiative to give up their supremacy and go back to the mountains and live the life of ordinary people?

Human nature actually does not change, and the desire for greed and control has never changed from the beginning of man's life until modern society, and will never change in the conceivable future. Change is simply a form of greed and control. From commercial capitalism to industrial capitalism, from financial capitalism to monopoly capitalism and today's so-called pluralistic capitalism, the nature of the domination of the majority of society by a powerful minority has never changed, except that the means and forms of domination today have changed considerably. The direct, visible, naked financial oligarchs have hid behind the scenes and in their place are the emerging and vast system of foundations that have become an important part of the ruling power of the Western world today, while their controllers are still the former gold power families.

The mysterious crash of Korean Air KAL007

In the early morning hours of 31 August 1983, an unidentified large aircraft was seen on a Soviet air defense radar screen on the island of Kupai, entering the air defense identification zone of the Far East intercontinental missile launch base, and two Soviet air defense SU-15 fighter jets were ordered to take off urgently to intercept it; five minutes later the Soviet pilot requested operational instructions from the base and the base commander issued an order to "destroy the invading aircraft". On that day, news agencies around the world sent out the news that the Boeing 747 of Korean Air KAL007 was shot down by a Soviet plane over the island of Kochi, killing all 269 people on board. The news immediately shocked the world and became one of the most serious events of the Cold War.

According to the statement from the United States side, the misdirection of flight KAL007 from Anchorage, Alaska, to Seoul in the airspace of the Soviet Union over Kamchatka and Kupala Island in the early hours of 31 August was an accidental mechanical failure that was not deliberately arranged and therefore could not have been foreseen and stopped in time. As a result, at 3:27 a.m., KAL007 was shot down by Soviet Air Force missiles over Khuppa Island, with none of the 269 passengers and crew surviving. The then President of the United States, Reagan, dismissed the incident as a cold-blooded massacre of unarmed civilians that was inexcusable and deserving of international sanctions and condemnation. On the contrary, the Soviet side pointed out that the invasion of KAL007 into its airspace by a premeditated spy mission to spy on military installations on the Kamchatka peninsula and the Kusai islands, and therefore the Soviet forces were ordered to shoot it down only in order to defend national security, was an appropriate act of self-defense that was forced upon them and therefore did not deserve undue misunderstanding and purposeful condemnation.

For more than 20 years, the controversy surrounding the mysterious air crash of Korean Air's KAL007 flight has been unbroken, with the most powerful claim being that top-secret inside information obtained from the Soviet Union by Mossad agents of the Israeli intelligence agency in 1992 stated that KAL007 did not explode immediately after being hit by an air-to-air missile, but continued its flight for about 12 minutes and finally succeeded in landing on the island of Khuppa or in adjacent waters. After the forced landing of KAL007, the Soviet authorities dispersed the passengers to the Lubyanka prison near Moscow and the Frengel shelter in the Far East, and a similar revelation was made on Korean television on 15 January 1996, in which it was stated that KAL007 had not crashed and that most of the survivors on board were still being held in two Russian shelters. In the 38-page document, the CIA asserted that Korean Air flight KAL007 was successfully landed at sea after being attacked by Soviet air force warplanes with missiles, and that most of the crew on board were spared, but their whereabouts are unknown.[163]

Among the 269 passengers on Flight KAL007 was one very special person, U.S. Congressman Lawrence Patton McDonald. Congressman McDonald is the cousin of the famous American World War II General Patton. The two cousins have in common, without incident, one of the most striking features, which is their firm opposition to the idea of the so-called "New World Order" and all attempts to destroy national sovereignty in the name of "internationalism" and "globalization", and both have great influence and appeal in the United States, where MacDonald is preparing to represent the Democratic Party in the 1988 presidential election. At the time, McDonald was the "loudest" and most destructive politician in the United States, attacking

---

[163] Schlossberg, Bert (2000). *Rescue 007: The Untold Story of KAL007 and its Survivors*. Xlibris. ISBN 0-7388-5775-0.

the American Foreign Relations Association and the Trilateral Commission.

After the KAL007 flight incident, Macdonald was left alive and dead. Jerry Falwell, a major evangelical leader who has had a major impact on American society, shares the same basic ideas as MacDonald and falls into the American right-wing category. His instinctive reaction to the KAL007 flight crash was: "What really bothers me in my mind is that the Soviet Union shot down KAL007, which killed 269 people, and their main target was MacDonald."[164] As with the speculation about the murder of General Patton, were the Soviets really the culprits? There may be other possibilities.

The political forces, represented by MacDonald, belong to the traditional rightist group in America. Their basic philosophy is to uphold the Constitution and founding spirit of the United States, to support the Bill of Rights, to believe in individual liberty and democracy, to oppose excessive government interference in civil rights, to advocate a thorough market economy, and to take a firm stand against all international forces that override sovereignty. This faction has a strong public opinion base in the United States, especially the historical legacy of the American War of Independence against British colonial rule, leading them to believe that the people can own guns and have a right to armed uprising in the event of tyranny and dictatorship imposed by the government. They believe that small government serves the people, while big government rules the people. They have limited the power of the federal government in every way possible, not to mention allowing a "world government" that exceeds "American sovereignty" to rule over the American people.

This political belief clashes sharply and sharply with the general policy approach of "globalization" and "world government", with the interests of international bankers at its core.

In November 1975, Congressman MacDonald launched a public challenge to the international bankers, writing in his preface to a book called *The Rockefeller File*.

---

[164] *Who killed congressman Lawrence Patton Mcdonald*, by Todd Brendan Fahey (fargone@disinfo.net) – July 01, 2001.

> *"Wealth alone cannot quench the desire and greed of the super-rich. Instead, many of them used their abundance of wealth and the influence that that wealth brought them to seize greater power. Such power flourished in a way that the tyrants and despots of the early years could not even have dreamed of. It is a power that governs the world, not only the wealth of the world, but also those who live in it.*
> *For more than a hundred years, from the days when John D. Rockefeller built an oil monopoly empire by unscrupulous means, books about the Rockefellers have been swarming enough to fill a library. I've read a lot of these books about Rockefeller, and none of them have dared to expose the most important part of the Rockefeller story: that Rockefeller and his allies have spent the last 50 years carefully planning to use their economic power to seize political power, first to control the United States and then to control the world.*
> *Am I talking about a conspiracy? Yes, that's it. I am convinced that there is a conspiracy: it is an evil plan of international proportions, conceived for generations and inherently unquestionable."*
>
> November 1975[165]

While the mainstream media in the United States has turned a blind eye to such a challenge, MacDonald has even personally stood in the street with propaganda material and preached it loudly to any interested pedestrian, with an obsession that goes far beyond the subliminal bottom line of American political circles to the point where it is intolerable to the international ruling elite.

To make matters worse, MacDonald is actually preparing to run for president. In his campaign speeches, he will speak about the plans of the international bankers to take control of the world, and millions of people will hear these "harsh" statements live. Macdonald's hard work was never lost on his cousin, General Patton, who would never admit defeat, and the two brothers are known to the American people as "heroes" who are not afraid of heaven and earth. If he does run in the presidential election, God knows what dramatic changes will occur and the situation will most likely spiral out of control. While President Kennedy's loss of control was evident, McDonnell was a greater threat than Kennedy, who not only had a broad civilian appeal, but also,

---

[165] Gary Allen, *The Rockefeller File*, Buccaneer Books, Inc. 1976.

through the authority of General Patton, had the support of a large number of senior military generals who had pledged their permanent allegiance to the national interests of the "United States of America", a group that did not buy the idea of a "world government" that transcended "American sovereignty". What's more, MacDonald and his allies have even built their own secret intelligence network to counter the forces of the CIA and FBI. If we continue to unite the masses of people who are "armed and reasonable", the United States may really "change color".

Who were the allies in McDonnell's alleged "generations of Rockefeller and his allies" plan? How has the plan evolved over the generations? To figure all this out, we have to start at the source of the plan.

The Diamond Empire and the Elite Fathers

John Ruskin told the students of Oxford that the upper class in which they lived had a great tradition of education, art, legal norms, free will, grace and self-restraint. But these traditions must be extended to the lower classes in England, and throughout the world, and only then can the lower classes be and deserve to be saved. If Britain's upper classes cannot spread their valuable traditions out, they will soon be swallowed up by an inferior class far larger than themselves, and those traditions will be discarded. To avoid such dire consequences, they must channel their traditions to every corner of the world as quickly as possible.

Ruskin's "moving" speech was recorded by a student, Cecil Rhodes, who kept the notes with him for the next 30 years.[166]

"A diamond lasts forever, a diamond that lasts forever." Behind this popular advertising slogan is the world's largest diamond giant, the De Beers Group. The group holds 40 per cent of the world's diamond market today, a figure that at one point was as high as 90 per cent.

The founder of De Beers, Cecil Rhodes, was born in 1853 and was a British politician and prominent businessman, colonizer of Rhodesia (old name for Zimbabwe), after whom Rhodesia was named. By

---

[166] Carroll Quigley, *Tragedy and Hope*, GSG & Associates, 1996.

plundering the natural resources of southern Africa, Rhodes acquired a great deal of wealth and established the Rhodes Scholarship after his death.

As the son of a suburban preacher, Rhodes is considered a single-handed "hero" of British colonial expansion. Rhodes made his fortune in South Africa by mining diamonds, building the De Beers diamond empire that once controlled 90 percent of the world's diamond industry. But his ambition went far beyond that, and even the British believed that "he not only wanted the whole earth to be British, but he wanted to bring the moon under British rule".

Rhodes attempted to reach the Rhodes family as early as 1882 through an agent sent by the Rothschilds from San Francisco to Africa to supervise diamond mining. At the time, South Africa's diamond mining industry was on its last legs in a fierce competition. Rhodes accurately judged that whoever could get financial backing from London first would come out on top in the battle for diamonds. He wisely decided to fall in love with the big tree of the Rothschild family. Finally, in 1885, on a ship bound for London, Rousey met another American engineer in charge of diamond mining in the Rothschild family and offered him the position of General Manager of the De Beers Company. Through his introduction, two months later, Roz was able to make a formal acquaintance with Nathan Rothschild, the head of the Ro family in London.[167]

Niti was so bullish on De Beers that he first bought 5,754 shares of De Beers for himself and immediately became the largest shareholder. With the support of the Roz family, Roz's De Beers ate the big fish, swallowing up the more powerful diamond companies in one fell swoop, and eventually establishing the world diamond empire.

Rousey had a high degree of trust in Rothschild, and at a meeting in 1888, Rousey confided in Nathan, "With your support behind me, I believe that everything I say can be done." This trust soon made the two companies close business strategic allies, and in 1889, De Beers issued £1.75 million in corporate bonds, with the Rothschild Bank of London buying 17.8 per cent, and in 1894, the Rothschild Bank of London simply issued a further £3.5 million of its own bonds for De Beers.

---

[167] Niall Ferguson, *The House of Rothschild*, Penguin Books, 1999.

With the support and encouragement of the Roz family, the expansion has grown in stride.

The De Beers Diamond Company grew rapidly in a series of successful mergers and its annual dividend was £1.6 million (40% per share) from 1896 to 1901 and £2 million from 1902 to 1904.

In 1900, Nathan spoke highly of Rhodes:

> "You have made De Beers a myth. You've established a monopoly on diamond production, you've single-handedly controlled the diamond sales market, and you've managed to set up a whole set of mechanisms to perpetuate that business model."

Rhodes and Nathan coincided on the political philosophy of colonialism and imperial expansion, and the two were increasingly like-minded. In 1889, when Rhodes founded the British South Africa Company, Nietzsche was a founding shareholder and investment advisor, and in June 1888, Rhodes amended his will to give Nietzsche all of his shares in the De Beers Company, which he had intended to pass on to his siblings. In the letter accompanying his will, he instructed Nathan to use the money to establish "a society chosen for the benefit of the Empire". Rousey identified Rothschild as the only "nobleman" capable of supporting him in achieving his vision.[168]

While Rothschild's eyes were firmly fixed on the immense commercial value of the diamond industry in De Beers, Roz's gaze crossed over Neti's shoulder to the vast fertile ground of Africa and the world. The diamond in Rhodes' eye is more symbolic of his tireless quest to achieve political influence. In his letter to Neti, Rhodes said that De Beers must become "another East India Company" and build "the framework for the ultimate realization of the ideal" from Africa.

The Lodz Club, the "Whampoa Military Academy" of the British ruling elite

> "No country that values its security will allow the Milner group to fulfill their ambition that a small group of people can wield so much power over government and politics, can exert so much

---

[168] Carroll Quigley, *Tragedy and Hope*, GSG & Associates, 1996.

> *influence over the channels of information that create public opinion, and can have a complete monopoly on the writing and teaching of the history of their time."*
>
> —Caroll Quigley[169]

The right to write history is perhaps the highest power in politics, for posterity can never fully experience the lives and feelings of previous eras, and they can only rely on the refraction of history books for what happened in the past, and the taking, cutting, editing, and commenting on historical material can dramatically change the way people see things. Whoever has control over the writing of history books will have the final "imaging effect" of the mirror of history, which can turn ugliness into beauty and the devil into an angel. History shapes people's consciousness, and history shapes today's judgments.

Clinton's college mentor, Professor Carroll Quigley, in his 1949 book, The Anglo-American Power Bloc, noted that the Rhodes Society, founded in 1891, would "rule the world through propaganda," a little-known secret organization that had a huge impact on world history in the 20th century.

In his first will and testament, written in 1877 at the age of 24 at Oxford, Rhodes set out the "noble" aims of the secret society:

> *"To extend the dominion of the British Empire over the whole world; to perfect the system of outward expansion of the British Empire; to colonize by British nationals all that was viable ... to reintegrate the United States of America into the British Empire; to unify the whole Empire; to introduce colonial representation in the Imperial Parliament, and to unite the scattered members of the Empire, thus laying down a world free from war and compatible with human welfare."*[170]

By Rhodes' design, this goal is best achieved through secret associations of a number of people who are mutually loyal and willing to dedicate themselves to a common cause. The means of implementation are to exert political and economic influence from behind the scenes, while "manipulating the press, education and information agencies". To achieve this goal, Rhodes, by will, used all his property to establish a secret organization of "propagandists" in the

---

[169] Carroll Quigley, *The Anglo-American Establishment* (GSG & Associates, 1981).

[170] Ibid.

service of the British Empire, the Rhodes Society, throughout the world, similar to the Church of Christ.

The Rhodes Society consists of 3 concentric circles. The inner circle was dominated by Rhodes himself, and its members were all wealthy men with vast personal fortunes who shared the idea of a permanent British Empire, forming the Rhodes Secret Society (known as the Milner Group after 1901); the second circle was the Cecil Bloc, made up of powerful political figures dominated by the Marquis of Salisbury (Robert Cecil); the outermost circle was dominated by Arnold Toynbee, uncle of Arnold J. Toynbee, author of The Study of History, and Lord Milner, financier, and was made up of intellectuals of all stripes, known as the Toynbee Group.[171]

The second of the three groups of the Rhodes Society was responsible for influencing education and propaganda in the British Empire, controlling the Times for half a century, and exerting significant influence over Eton Public School and All Souls College, Oxford, through scholarship. The three circles are united and mutually reinforcing, with the "Toynbee Group" providing ideological support, the "Cecil Group" exerting political influence and the "Milner Group" providing financial backing, and the Trinity forming a clandestine organization to influence the fate of the British Empire and the world.

By 1938, the Rhodes Society had absorbed a large number of wealthy upper-class people, forming the most influential political force in Britain.

The core members of the Lodz Club are brought up through a standard selection process: the best students from Oxford are selected for admission to All Souls College, and the "seeded" students are then tested and eliminated for selection to the Royal Institute of International Affairs, The Times, The Round Table Magazine, the Foreign Office or the Colonial Office. Of course, these people have at best reached the second circle, where they occupy key positions in academia, and guide and influence public opinion through the news media, such as the great Isaiah Berlin, and Arnold J. Toynbee, author of Historical Studies, who entered the Royal Institute of International Affairs from an early age.

---

[171] Ibid.

The Rhodes Society's strategy is to brake more people by influencing a critical few elites, targeting the elite in society.

The following historical events show how the Lodz Society, which boasted of "world domination through propaganda", has influenced recent history.

> - Instigated the "Jameson Raid" of 1895
> - Leading to the Boer War of 1899–1902
> - Founded the Union of South Africa 1906–1910
> - 1910 Founding of the British Empire periodical, *The Round Table magazine* (mouthpiece of Rhodes Society)
> - 3 colleges that have long influenced Oxford University: All Souls, Balliol, New College
> - Control of *The Times* for over half a century
> - Control of the British delegation to France for the "Paris Peace Conference" in 1919
> - Principal designer and manager of the League of Nations
> - Established and controlled the Royal Institute of International Affairs in 1919.
> - 1917–1945 dominated British policy towards Ireland, Palestine and India
> - Influenced the policy of appeasement of Germany from 1920 to 1940

Still controls the sources and writing of historical information on the internal and external policies of the British Empire since the Boer War

The concept of the "Commonwealth" is the one that came about and was widely publicized and thus made a reality.

The Rhodes Company has offices in the United States, Canada, India, Australia, New Zealand and South Africa, as well as in the colonies and former colonies of the British Empire. The prestigious American "Council on Foreign Relations" (CFR) is the American branch of the Rhodes Society. The Lodz Club met in secret from time to time in the autonomous territories of the British Empire, planned and deployed in a unified manner, influenced the formulation and implementation of political and economic policies from behind the scenes, and manipulated the press, education and propaganda institutions, with the primary goal of unifying the English-speaking countries in the form of a federation, and eventually establishing some form of world government and achieving "one world". The world government, the world currency, the world taxation, etc., which are popular in the world, are all based on this club.

The Marquis of Salisbury, the central figure of the "Cecil group", was a three-time Prime Minister who reigned for 14 years, more than any other Prime Minister in recent British history. He exerted his influence by, first, infiltrating the three directions of politics, education, and journalism; second, recruiting talented individuals (primarily from the All Souls Academy) and linking these individuals to the Cecil group by association, reputation, or position of power; and third, placing core members in important positions of power to influence public policy in as discreet a manner as possible.[172]

Other core members of the "Cecil Group" are: Balfour (Foreign Secretary), Viscount Lyttelton (Viscount Cobham), Baron Wyndham (Barons Leconfield), Duke of Grosvenor (Dukes of Westminster), Earl of Palmer (Earls of Selborne), Duke of Cavendish (Dukes of Devonshire), Earl of Gathorne-Hardy (Earls of Cranbrook).

"Milner Group"

The "Cecil Group" continued to exist for a considerable time after the death of the Marquis of Salisbury, leader of the Cecil family, in 1903, but the lack of ambition and determination of its new leader, Balfour, slowly loosened the organization and was gradually replaced by the "Milner Group". Milner has no shortage of ambition and determination, sacrificing his own personal happiness and social life to achieve political goals, which the pleasure-loving Balfour cannot accept. Acutely aware that it was impossible to continue to rely on family ties to consolidate the group, Milner turned to ideology. Salisbury sought to build a clique out of friends and relatives, playing politics to preserve the old England they loved. Milner, on the other hand, was not a conservative; he had his own ideals: to expand and

---

[172] Ibid.

integrate the social welfare system of the British Empire, which was essential to the British way of life, and to bring to the world "the British way of life, the best and most capable of mankind". However, the world has changed and he has since placed more emphasis on advocacy and conceptual unity within the "Milner Group".

The influence of Arnold Toynbee's ideas on the Milner Group was threefold: first, English history represented the great moral idea – the evolution of freedom of thought, most conducive to the complete unity of the British Empire; second, the sense of duty and obligation to serve the country should be of paramount concern to anyone; and third, the necessity for working people to do social service work in English society, especially education.

The Times was an important part of the elite influence of the "Milner Group", which targeted an influential elite minority rather than the general public. It and the other autonomous branches of the "Milner Group" work closely together to influence readers and increase the influence of each branch. The outside world seems like different sides of the same truth. For example, a Member of Parliament (panelist) announces a policy to publish a study on the same subject almost simultaneously with the Royal Institute of International Affairs, a researcher from All Souls College (panelist) publishes a volume on the same subject (through the relevant publisher of the panel), an "editorial" in The Times analyses the Member of Parliament's policy critically but ultimately endorses it, and two publications are reviewed at the same time in the newspaper's "literary supplement" (the most influential literary criticism journal in Britain) (same review). The reviews of the "editorials" and "literary supplements" were written anonymously by the panel members. Finally, an anonymous Roundtable article strongly advocates the same policy. While each ploy and step only affects a portion of the population, the cumulative effect of these strategies is significant. If necessary, the secretary of the Rhodes Trust could travel to the United States to conduct a series of informal interviews with former Rhodes Scholarship recipients, while persuading a retired prominent politician (such as the former Governor of India) to say a few words at the unveiling of a plaque in memory of the deceased Chancellor at All Souls College or New College, Oxford. It is a curious "coincidence" that both the American interview and the Oxford unveiling speech emphasized the same topic.

The first issue of The Round Table was published on November 15, 1910, without the publisher's and five article authors' signatures on it. This tradition has continued. The magazine argues that anonymity is for greater independence and freedom. The real reason is much more practical. The editors and writers of the magazine were mostly unknown and would have made readers laugh if their names were signed. When certain authors become "big shots" and editors feel the need to protect their political reputation, it is common practice to keep authors anonymous until they die, and even then not to publish their published articles. The Round Table is the primary propaganda tool of the Rhodes Society or the "Milner Group". The editors and authors of the Round Table are known as the "Round Table Group". Their firm belief was that freedom, civilisation and human dignity could only be best developed through the British Empire.

The panelists' views are usually unanimous, with the biggest differences coming from the weakest and most conservative economic areas of this group. Until 1931, the panel's financial perspective came from Robert Brand, a partner at Longhey Brothers. The Lange brothers are also one of the "Seventeen International Banking Families", representing the view of the international banking families of the late 19th century that the key to economic development and prosperity is banking and finance. A sound currency, a balanced budget and an international gold standard will lead to economic prosperity and improved living standards. This is in opposition to Milner's point. Milner insists that finance should be subordinate to economics and that economics should be subordinate to politics. If deflationary policies on financial grounds have adverse economic or political consequences, it should be abolished. Milner argues that the financial policy implemented by the British Empire for 12 years, advocated by Brand in 1919, was disastrous because it caused unemployment, recession and the destruction of exports. He advocated separating the British Empire from the world through tariffs and other barriers, encouraging economic development through government spending, self-regulation of capital and labour, and social welfare.

In fact, the views of the "Milner Group" represent a major change in the thinking of mainstream international bankers about gold and money, as gold's restrictions on government spending and war financing no longer meet the needs of bankers, and the idea of large-scale cheap money gradually becomes the new mainstream.

Milner's views are based on "monopoly capitalism" or even "state capitalism" rather than the outdated "financial capitalism" advocated by Brand. This view was accepted by most members of the "Milner

Group" after 1931. The abolition of the gold standard in the same year completely proved the complete failure of the financial policy advocated by Brand in 1919. As a result, after 1931, the "Milner Group", which advocated monopoly capitalism encouraged by the Government, prevailed. In fact, Milner and Toynbee have never believed in economic individualism.

In fact, it does not matter what Milner and Brand disagreed about, what matters is that Brand's views dominated the "Milner Group" between 1919 and 1931, while Milner's views prevailed after 1931. These facts prove that the financial policy of the British Empire between 1919 and 1945 coincided perfectly with the policy of the "Milner Group" during the same period. And the "Milner Group" has dominated the Conservative Council since the "First World War". This shows the extent to which the Milner Group has influenced British domestic policy.

From 1919 to 1939, members of the "Milner Group" made up one fifth to one third of the Cabinet, which explains the British Government's policy of "appeasement" towards Germany advocated by the "Milner Group".

German policy of the "Milner Group" is based on two core points[173]

On the one hand, they see history as the result of the struggle between good and evil. The Germans were divided into "Prussian dictators" and "good people". If the Prussian dictator loses his power and influence and the latter is granted clemency, Germany will permanently leave the "Asian dictatorship" and return to "Western civilization". Framework-wise, the theory is reasonable, but difficult. For there can be no objective criteria for distinguishing between "good" and "bad" Germans. The fact that an overwhelming majority of Germans participated in World War I, and the December 1918 issue of The Round Table held the same view, but the "Milner Group" did not remember that they still considered the "bad" Germans to have been driven out with the Kaiser in 1918. The German Kaiser is just a representative of the other four major power groups. The four major

---

[173] Ibid.

power blocs in Germany included Prussian officers, Junker landowners, government bureaucrats, and industrial giants who, to save themselves, abandoned the emperor who had become a burden. Their power and influence is still there, even greater. The army bigwigs can order the government prime minister in a more direct tone than the emperor. In short, there was no revolution in Germany in 1918 and the "Milner Group" turned a blind eye to it. Brand is largely responsible for this, arguing that chaos and social unrest can only be avoided if the German economy recovers as quickly as possible. In the view of traditional bankers, economic prosperity cannot be achieved without the industrial capitalists and bankers in power. In addition, Brand is convinced that the old industrial blocs will be quickly revived if payouts are eased and credit is extended to Germany.

Panelist Philip Kerr, on the other hand, advocated the balance of power policy customary in Britain since the 16th century, which is to support the second power in continental Europe against the first. The "Milner Group" found from its experience at the Paris Peace Conference in 1919 that it was impossible to export autonomous or parliamentary government to the European continent. Because of France's insistence on the use of force as the basis of social and political life, in particular its insistence on a German military presence and the establishment of an international police force under the direct authority of the League of Nations, the divide between the Group and France has deepened. According to the Christian philosophy of the "Milner Group", force is ineffective on moral issues and can only corrupt those who possess it, and the real basis of social and political life is custom and tradition. Thus the balance of power had a double objective: to make Germany a redeemable sinner by compromise, and a regenerated and purified Germany against the "evil" Soviet Union, and to weaken the overburdened France of national feeling.

While Hitler's rise to power took advantage of the misjudgment of the British ruling elite and saw through the idea of the emerging power bloc in the United States trying to replace the global hegemony of the British Empire, and the Jewish international bankers' eagerness to defeat the colonial system of the British Empire in order to regain the dream of Israel's restoration in Palestine, Hitler organically integrated the two political forces and financial support that encouraged Germany's aggressive expansionist policies, accelerating Germany's economic recovery and military reconstruction. It can be said that from 1933 to 1938, Hitler made full use of the collusion between the major powers in Europe and America and the Jewish financial forces to achieve his own strategic objectives, and played the major powers into the hands of a few of them, showing great political skill.

"Anglo-American power bloc"[174]

From the 1920s onwards, the Lodz Club worked to establish a special Anglo-American relationship that would eventually lead to Anglo-American unity. In Tragedy and Hope: World History in Our Time, Quigley describes the existence of an "Anglo-American power bloc" between the United States and Britain to achieve the above-mentioned strategic objectives.

The five newspapers with the greatest influence on American public opinion – the *Boston Evening News*, Christian Science Monitor, New York Times, New York Herald Tribune and Washington Times – are all in the hands of this power group. And these mainstream media handlers are "recommending" each other, such as the editor-in-chief of Christian Science Monitor, who was the American liaison to the British magazine The Round Table, and the original editor-in-chief of The Round Table, Lord Lotta, who was a contributor to Christian Science Monitor when he was British Ambassador to the United States and was Secretary General of the Rhodes Trust. Several Wall Street financiers of great renown have served as U.S. ambassadors to the United Kingdom.

Quigley notes that, at least in the early twentieth century, decision-making power in important American universities was in the hands of the "Anglo-American power bloc". Until the 1930s, JPMorgan essentially controlled decision-making power at Harvard and Columbia Universities; Yale University was under Standard Oil's Rockefeller Group; and Princeton University was under the Prudential Life Insurance Company. At the beginning of the twentieth century, the United States Government, under the pressure of the "progressive movement", passed several tax laws that were unfavorable to the group, especially the inheritance tax, and the group gradually transferred huge amounts of private property from Wall Street to tax-exempt

---

[174] Carroll Quigley, *Tragedy and Hope*, GSG & Associates, 1996.

foundations, successfully completing an invisible and magnificent transformation of wealth.

Walter Lippmann, an American political commentator and government advisor who was a member of the Rhodes Society, had a profound influence on 20th century American society and foreign policy. He first drafted the famous "Marshall Plan" for the reconstruction of Europe, chaired the development of American psychological warfare strategies during World War I, World War II and the Cold War, and was a key liaison between the Association for Foreign Relations and the British Rhodes Society. As a key strategist for successive U.S. presidents from Wilson to Nixon, he founded the Association for American Foreign Relations while accompanying President Woodrow Wilson to the Paris Conference after World War I.

Regardless of the background and mission of its members, the way in which they influence public opinion and the policies of the United States and abroad, the Council on Foreign Relations has been described as the "shadow government" of the United States and the British Lodz Club in the United States. The Council's flagship publication for influencing United States foreign policy is Foreign Affairs, the "organ newspaper" of the Council on Foreign Relations and a key voice of the United States Foreign Policy Group. The leading contributors to Foreign Affairs magazine include almost all the heavyweights of American foreign policy, including Lippman, George Kenan, Brzezinski and Kissinger, and Huntington's The Clash of Civilizations was first published in the magazine.

When the Paris Peace Conference was held in 1919, both Britain and the United States wanted to take advantage of their victorious position to establish a system of international society dominated by them. "After the Paris Peace Conference, Lippmann and other Americans who attended, most of whom were members of the Rhodes Society, founded the "Royal Institute of International Affairs" in a hotel in Paris.

As a branch of the Rhodes Society, the "Foreign Relations Society" first entered the United States under the name of the "American Section of the Royal Institute of International Affairs", and in 1921 the "American Section of the Royal Institute of International Affairs" merged with the "Foreign Relations Society", an organization founded in 1918 by bankers and lawyers in New York to discuss wartime business and banking issues, under the old name of the "Foreign Relations Society", which is what we see today.

The American Foreign Relations Association, which has existed for more than 80 years to date, has undoubtedly long since departed from Rhodes' earliest desire for England to reassert its rule over the United States of America, but is gradually realizing the dream of Anglo-American interests to become world leaders. As China cheered globalization, I wonder if anyone saw the cold face and smug smile of the Rhodes Society behind this huge social machine?

The idea that the world is being manipulated by a handful of secret societies is not a novelty, nor is it uncommon. As one British scholar put it, "It should have occurred to us long ago that the powerful and the rich act according to their own interests, and that is called capitalism."

The Western world we see today is ostensibly a democratic, free and pluralistic society, where the financial oligarchs of the past have been successfully driven out of power by the sacred democratic system. The powerful and super-rich families have disappeared into thin air and are nowhere to be seen. Has history been changed? Does capitalism no longer serve a minority power group? Have the international bankers really taken the initiative to give up their supremacy and go back to the mountains and live the life of ordinary people?

Human nature actually does not change, and the desire for greed and control has never changed from the beginning of man's life until modern society, and will never change in the conceivable future. Change is simply a form of greed and control. From commercial capitalism to industrial capitalism, from financial capitalism to monopoly capitalism and today's so-called pluralistic capitalism, the nature of the domination of the majority of society by a powerful minority has never changed, except that the means and forms of domination today have changed significantly. The direct, visible, naked financial oligarchs have hid behind the scenes, and in their place are the emerging and vast system of foundations that have become an important part of the ruling power in the Western world today, while the people behind the controls are still the financial families of old.

The Foundation: The Invisible Rothschild of Wealth

"The Great Way is invisible" and "the Great Hidden Dynasty", the Chinese have long insight into the mysteries of the human heart. The most profound truths are often found everywhere, and the highest level of any ruler is to make his opponent visible but not himself, so that he can always remain invincible.

At the beginning of the twentieth century, when financial monopoly capitalism was at its peak, international bankers were rich in family assets and powerful in political influence, but the side effects were also severe. The greater the power of the financial oligarchy, the wider the antagonism, the stronger the resistance, the greater the discontent and the more obvious the sense of hatred. The most frightening thing is that the financial oligarchy is in danger of falling into a state of collapse when the various opposing forces of society join forces.

When the international bankers finally got to know this, it seemed that everyone had agreed and the big families disappeared from the public eye almost simultaneously, before and after the First World War. In response, they gave a consistent low-profile explanation, stating that the descendants of the family were no longer interested in property control and were each pursuing diversified interests and careers, and that the family property was mostly structured as investments. With the rapid development of new industries and high technology in modern society, the family traditionally accumulated property has been greatly reduced. The feng shui wheel, the world has been a completely different world, people are also completely different people, the old family is forever declining, the traditional rich family in the present day has withdrawn from the historical stage, the spotlight turned to the "rising stars".

Is that really true?

In fact the fortunes of the major wealthy families have not shrunk at all, but have been legally and reasonably hidden away. The super-rich have just "turned around" in front of everyone and have succeeded in being "invisible". The actual control and dominance of wealth never leaves their grasp. Instead of leaving, their grip on wealth was magnified. Only, the property labels of the past were written directly and clearly on your heads, while the modern rich have long since removed them. They are invisible, silent, ubiquitous and omnipotent, and their ruling strategy has gradually reached the realm of the "Avenue of Invisibility", relying mainly on agents to put on a show in the front office, while they themselves are deeply hidden behind the scenes, controlling the functioning of society.

This perfect new rule of the wealth game is the vast system of foundations that now actually manipulate society in Europe and America.

In the first half of the 20th century, financial capitalism completed its transition to monopoly capitalism, and the financial power blocs moved from direct control of industrial capitalism on the front lines to a behind-the-scenes model of indirect control. At the heart of the emerging corporate operating structure is the separation of ownership and control, the widespread mobilization of social public capital, the aim of which is to control the mega-social wealth with minimal capital through maximum leverage, to control to the widest extent the backbone leaders in all sectors of society, forming the base of the pyramid of monopoly capitalism, without revealing itself externally as the true controller. The company is ostensibly run by professional managers, but the board of directors and key equity controls are entirely concentrated in the hands of very few financial families. At the heart of the rules of the game is the vast system of foundations and other investment groups controlled by financial families, which enforce "discrete" key equity and board control through ostensible surrogate institutions. The holding institutions are the well-known financial institutions and asset management companies (Street Names), which function as a "firewall" for foundations and investment groups controlled by financial families to keep the public eye out of the actual circle of shareholders. The more we reach the era of pluralistic capitalism, the more widespread this phenomenon becomes.

But to participate in this new kind of game, rich families must first make "sacrifices". As the saying goes, "If you want to practice your divine powers, you should draw the sword from the palace." How can you get it if you don't? Give up the name and get the substance. The "initiation" of the Great Rothschild of Wealth Stealth is donation, and the theoretical basis for donation is the legal concealment of property by giving up ownership and extending control. What the tycoons have lost is simply the chains of being "barbecued" in the charts and in the media spotlight, and what they have gained is the cool freedom and multiplied control of their wealth behind the scenes.

The Foundation avoids the estate tax, income tax, gift tax and, even better, the capital gains tax on the Foundation's investments, which the wealthy hate most. With full tax exemption, the foundation's assets are growing like a snowball. U.S. Congressional reports show that as much as 2/3 of total annual U.S. income is tax-free thanks to the foundation.

Correspondingly, the pressure of the state's tax burden is being placed more and more heavily on the middle class, who will never be able to establish their own foundation. The foundation assets of the super-rich are expanding rapidly like cancerous cells that are constantly feeding off the family wealth cells of the middle class, and the distribution of social wealth is even more inequitable.

According to statistics, in 1969, the net income of 596 foundations in the United States was more than twice the net income of the 50 largest banks in the United States. Since the establishment of the first foundation in 1790, there have been an increasing number of foundations in the United States.

- 18 before 1900)
- 76 from 1910 to 1919.
- 173 between 1920 and 1929.
- 288 from 1930 to 1939.
- 1,638 between 1940 and 1949.
- 2,839 between 1950 and 1959
- By 2002, as many as 62,000[175]

Foundations only need to "contribute" 5 per cent per year to their philanthropy, and the means by which international bankers make their money is more than a mere 5 per cent return. What's more, this 5 percent philanthropic investment can also be used to achieve social impact and academic research control, earning itself a better social climate and legal policy tilt for greater profit.

Nowadays, the rich and famous have learned the same game. Why make the Fortune list? Why write wealth in one's own name and not in someone else's name when it is under one's actual control? The main purpose of having wealth is not to satisfy vanity, but to achieve control that lasts forever! This allows the actual controllers of the listed company to avoid exposure, often through stock surrogacy. The difference between China and Europe and the United States is that there is no "legal", "perpetual", "tax-free", "inheritable", "financial secrecy",

---

[175] David Rivera, *Final Warning: A History of the New World Order-Illuminism and the master plan for world domination*, 1994.

"interlockable", "derivable" legal vehicle similar to Europe and the United States to help the rich to hide their wealth, in order to achieve a major "upgrade" of the wealth control strategy of the transition from direct to indirect control and explicit to implicit control.

The Chicken Soup of the Heart says: the more you give up, the more you have

The story of Rockefeller's later years has been told over and over again as a classic in Chicken Soup for the Soul books: the old Rockefeller lived his life on money, saving as much as he could, but at the age of 53 he was diagnosed with an incurable disease, his medicine was ineffective, and he could barely survive on less than two dollars worth of cookies and yogurt when he was netting millions of dollars a week. When he came to his senses, he began to donate most of his possessions to establish scientific institutions and charitable organizations, thus giving his life a new lease of life and living happily to the age of 98.

So Chicken Soup for the Soul tells everyone: the more you give up, the more you have. This is actually true, and Rockefeller's did have more through donations. And the vehicle for this "miracle" is the Foundation.

The old Rockefeller had a notorious reputation for using cruel, unforgiving and widely criticized tactics in his beginnings. He was once the most hated man in the American public. To revolutionize the public image, Rockefeller Sr. takes a consultant's advice to go big with philanthropy.

In fact, Rockefeller Sr.'s move was far more effective and meaningful than just improving public image.

He made substantial property donations, but the "donated" property was not out of his control. Through a series of strategic operations, such as foundations, Rockefeller has achieved greater and stronger control over its "donated" property. This is the Rockefeller "scientific principle of giving": the more you give, the more you control.

The first foundation established by Rockefeller was the Rockefeller Foundation, which was established in 1910.[176] By 1910, most states in the United States had adopted the 16th Amendment, which imposed an income tax on progressive income. The Rockefeller Foundation is arguably the most successful and effective "pre-tax plan" that legally and reasonably avoids progressive income tax in one fell swoop. During the same period, Standard Oil was spun off by order of Justice Kenesaw Landis, and the Rockefeller consortium immediately responded with the creation of four tax-exempt foundations, and then donated the vast majority of the consortium's shares. It's the equivalent of taking money out of your left pocket and putting it in your right pocket, but the money shakes itself out and the fame is different. So the various oil companies that were spun off were able to get the money they needed, while avoiding taxes on their earnings and assets. The addition of the family's descendants to the Foundation's charter will continue to "serve" the Foundation for generations, with a crucial veto vote, and all that remains is the inexhaustible benefit. The Rockefeller consortium's replacement of control with ownership of the property not only achieved a tax avoidance function, but also the miraculous effect of significant wealth appreciation. Because foundations can buy and sell a variety of assets, including real estate and marketable securities, and do not have to publish financial statements, they can achieve invisible influence on the market.

The money is donated into the foundation, reinvested into multi-level corporate enterprises in different industries, and when the size of the investment is sufficient, the board of directors of all entities receiving investment must be appointed and delegated by the foundation. Thus, although the money is no longer in the name of a particular family, the actual manager and the right to use the money remain firmly in their hands. Note that at this point the money has been changed from nominal to last name. In this way, first of all, the personal income tax that would have been levied on all of Lo's money disappears; secondly, the gift tax that would have been levied on Lo's money if he had given it to "Zhong Lo", "Little Lo" and "Little Lo" is also saved; and thirdly, the estate tax, which is almost the only tool that can restrict the inheritance of wealthy people's property, is up to 50%

---

[176] Ron Chernow, *Titan: The Life of John D. Rockefeller*, Sr., New York: Warner Books, 1998, (p. 563–566).

in the United States, and since the money is no longer in Lo's name, the estate tax is naturally eliminated. Through donations, Lao Rothschild legally and reasonably left money to himself and "Zhong Rothschild", "Little Rothschild", "Little Rothschild", and "his children and grandchildren are in endless need".

Since then, Lowe's has contributed half of its annual income to the Foundation, significantly offsetting its taxable income. Older Lowe's eliminates income tax, Middle Lowe's, Little Lowe's and Little Lowe's will avoid estate and gift taxes, and even better, the gains from the investments of these foundations will also be exempt from capital gains tax. Thanks to the benefits of the tax exemption, the Foundation's assets have been able to grow by leaps and bounds. What is called non-profit is essentially non-taxation.

Rockefeller Sr. donated millions of shares of Titanic Oil Corporation stock he owned to a foundation called the Do Good Foundation, a Rockefeller-controlled organization. The "sublimation" of his property was easily accomplished by simply transferring the shares in his name to the Foundation. Foundations and charities such as the Do Good Foundation are numerous and multi-layered, and they do contribute to numerous research and medical projects and to poverty alleviation, but these expenses pale in comparison to the hidden assets of the wealthy and the taxes avoided by the foundation system. Coupled with the fact that investment income from property donated to the Foundation is also tax-free, the Rockefeller consortium is the true controller of the property on the one hand, and exempt from investment income tax on the other, which makes its wealth grow even faster.

The Washington Post has reported that, after two generations of careful family management, the vast majority of the Rockefeller consortium's assets were transferred to foundations at various levels and levels, as well as to their derivatives, subsidiaries, and companies under direct and indirect control, resulting in a vast network of foundations. The financial reports of each Foundation network node "unit" are not audited, are not subject to public disclosure, and all investigations involved are politely and legally rejected, thus falling off the radar of the accounting and regulatory systems. This is actually the Rockefeller family's invention of the great law of wealth stealth, which today's super-rich are all following suit. Gates and Buffett's game of wealth donation is nothing more than a continuation of the Old Rothschild family practice of the early 20th century.

After sixty or seventy years in business, the Low family controls as many as a few hundred or even thousands of foundations and affiliates, a network that no one can sort out clearly. The Rock family's disclosed wealth to the public is about $1 billion to $2 billion. Using the tip of the iceberg to describe it all may not be the case. The actual wealth of the super-rich is completely beyond measurement, verification and tracking.

This is the mystery of the more you give up, the more you control.

The Rockefellers, the "family down the road"

The mass media has been conveying to the public for years that today's Lowe's conglomerates have long since fallen from grace and are nothing more than middle-class rich people. If the decline of the Rothschild family from the leading position of the wealthy in Europe is attributed to the successive wars in Europe and the implication of the Rothschilds in the general situation, then how can the disappearance of the Rothschilds' wealth be reasonably explained? The Rockefeller consortium has always controlled the U.S. oil, chemical, and pharmaceutical industries, operating the top banks for more than a century, and the U.S. economy's history has not been interrupted by successive wars. To this day, the Rothschild family's total wealth is a mere $2 billion, comparable only to the wealthy Chinese who have made a fortune in the last 20 years? Might as well see if the international bankers are really at home.

During Nelson Rockefeller's presidential campaign in the 1960s and 1970s, the U.S. Senate routinely held hearings on his property status. Nielsen first announced that his personal fortune was about $33 million. After a preliminary investigation by the Senate, and after repeated consultations with Nielsen, Nielsen changed his tune and admitted that his personal assets were $218 million, six times more than initially claimed. At this time, when the dollar was still in the US dollar era, one dollar corresponded to 0.88 grams of gold, and his personal assets amounted to 191 tons of gold, which at the current price of gold ($900/oz) are now worth 25 times what they were then. The figure of $218 million Nielsen provided to the Senate is already quite staggering, far more than the personal fortunes of the first 37 U.S. presidents combined.

However, these personal assets were already the Rockefeller family's foundation that had "donated" most of the assets to its own family, with the remainder being Nielsen's own share after being distributed among the 84 family members.

In the course of the Senate's investigation of Nielsen's personal assets, he had to face, but could not reasonably explain, the fact that in the 1970s, Nielsen had not paid a penny of personal income tax for several years. The reason is simple: in 1970, Nielsen's team of financial advisors and attorneys made a "scheduling and adjustment" of his assets in his name, with the immediate effect that Nielsen was not subject to income tax at all for several years after that. It is estimated that the last thing the staff involved in the investigation wanted to do at the time was to leave the phone number of Nelson's dedicated tax accountant and call it when they filed their own taxes.

During the Senate's property inquiry into Nelson, he spoke eloquently, and if you question whether our family manipulates some kind of vast economic power, my answer is that it does not exist. We are simply investing, not controlling. Family members are not interested in controlling property. Whether it's a family member or an asset management team, everyone's goal and expectation is to get a return within reason. So, what is the size of the Loh family's asset management team?

The asset mastermind of the Lowe's consortium is Richardson Dilworth. He joined the Lowe's consortium in 1958 and became the master manipulator of the family's asset management. Prior to joining Lowe's, Richardson Dilworth was a principal partner at Kuhn, Loeb & Co., the early 20th century equivalent of today's Goldman Sachs, the most prominent Wall Street investment bank that played a vital role in the financial operating system. Its principal partners include Leibow, Kuhn, Warburg, the Schiff family and other Jewish financial families, all of whom are top investment bankers of great repute. Kuhn, Loeb & Co. has a deep relationship with both the Rockefeller Consortium and JP Morgan.

Richardson Dilworth's vast estate under management includes about $1.033 billion in personal assets listed in the names of 84 Lowe descendants. The assets were held primarily in two complex trusts created by John D Rockefeller Junior, one for children in 1934 and the other for grandchildren in 1952. There are more than 200 foundations of all types under the Low family name, and the number of foundations and trusts that are controlled directly or indirectly through layers of shareholding is far greater, conservatively estimated to be in the thousands. All foundation organizations and trusts are international in nature, and their operations and funds flow freely around the globe with little regulation, making attempts to sort out their true financial flows and volumes completely impossible. The only names we see are Merrill Lynch or Goldman Sachs, as well as other wealthy consortia that don't give out real names in their massive investments and projects.[177]

These foundations and trusts exploit and exploit modern commercial institutional holdings in all their forms and nomenclature, with intricate, interlocking and disorienting layers and connections, and with a strong team of star managers and lawyers at all levels, of whom it is feared that only a few senior asset lawyers have any idea of the true number and extent of assets. Under the principle of protecting private property and the confidentiality of information, the financial status and details of such institutions are never disclosed or made public and are completely opaque. From the point of view of structural design, such an institution can be established without any limit at the level of hierarchy, subordination and subordination, so that the true state of the institution is well and tightly concealed.

The Senate's publicly released findings do not disclose the number of assets of each member of the Low family, but only a total number. Again, the reason is that personal privacy should be fully respected. The minutes and documents of the Low family's financial meetings are permitted to be withheld from public disclosure. The banner of private information obscurity immediately obscures the right of the entire public to know.

The public can only learn from a small amount of publicly disclosed information, such as.

One of the Low family's properties in New York was worth more than $50 million in 1930 for land alone.[178]

Nielsen's son Steve's estate has 70 miles, or the equivalent of 100 kilometers of private roads, on more than 4,000 acres, and earlier information revealed that the estate covers 7,500 acres (about 45,000

---

[177] Gary Allen, *The Rockefeller File*, Buccaneer Books, Inc. 1976, p. 11.

[178] Ibid, p. 13.

acres). In 1929 there were 75 buildings in which more than 100 families lived. The collection of intra-family documents on the estate alone is worth $4.5 million.

Referring to the "lavish renovation" of the estate, Rockefeller Sr. paid $700,000 to Amtrak to have a section of the railroad on the "territory" of the estate demolished and another $1.5 million to a college on the estate as "moving expenses".

This is just one of the Lowe family's estates in 1930, another mansion in New York with 32 rooms, a castle in Washington, several more estates in Maine, and here's not counting the several plantations owned in Central America such as Venezuela, several farms operated in Brazil...

In 1975, Nielsen purchased 18,000 acres of land in Texas for the sole purpose of using it as an "outdoor event site".

At Pocantico Hill, there are more than 500 on-call domestic workers of all kinds, including cleaners, security guards, cooks and gardeners, 45 ready servants at a resort estate in Seal Harbor and 15 hired servants at a private home in Nelson. The incomplete count of the servants of the Rothschild family had exceeded 2,500. All the estate's premises are kept in perfect condition, ready for any visit the hosts may wish to make.

In addition to real estate, Low's deep-pocketed moneybags also hold stocks held by consortia, just to take the example of Exxon Oil Company, the renamed New Jersey Standard Oil Company, which was part of the Standard Oil Company after it was spun off. The value of Exxon shares held directly by the Lowers was $156 million (1974), a figure that does not include shares held indirectly by the Lowers in the form of foundations and trusts, etc.

The famous Rockefeller Center, with its published valuation of $98 million, is a ridiculous figure, and an article in the Los Angeles Times of September 30, 1974, addressing the issue of the Rockefeller Center's accurate valuation, stated that various experts had concluded that it was impossible to estimate. The market generally agreed that this asset should have been worth $1 billion in 1974.[179]

---

[179] Ibid, p. 15.

Roughly counting the investment assets operated by the Rockefeller Consortium in 1975, the stock class includes $85 million worth of California Standard, $72 million worth of IBM, and over $10 million worth of company stock: Chase Manhattan, Mobil Oil, EaMac, General Electric, Texas Instruments, Minnesota Mining & Manufacturing, etc.

The Rockefeller consortium holds significant stakes in the 50 most important companies in the United States. An incomplete count shows that there are 154 full-time staff members at the Lowe's consortium managing these assets, and that the direct assistants to Big Money steward Richardson Dilworth are 15 top financial professionals. These asset management staff also serve as directors and managers at various types and levels of foundations and trusts, and they manage $70 billion in assets. Again, to draw the reader's attention to the fact that this is $70 billion in 1974!

This is true of the Rockefellers, and it is not true of the Rothschilds and other international banking families.

In addition to their wealth, the Rockefellers also expanded their social influence by forging closer strategic alliances with the most powerful families in America through extensive intermarriage. According to incomplete statistics, the Lowe's family has a "top-down" marriage relationship with half of the 60 richest families in the United States. Chief among them are Stillman, Dodge, McAlpin, McCormick, Carnegie and Aldrich.

Leverage and wealth control

Exxon replaced General Motors as the top-ranked largest industrial company in the 1974 Fortune magazine list of the largest publicly held companies. Rockefeller holds $324 million worth of oil stock, roughly representing a 2 percent stake in each of the four largest oil companies, and information disclosed in the 1966 Patman Congressional Inquiry shows that nine Rockefeller family foundations collectively hold about 3 percent of the companies under Standard Oil. At this figure, the Rockefellers actually hold an effective stake of about 5 percent in the Big Four oil companies. Combined with the substantial oil company holdings of trusts, banks, insurance companies, and university funders under their umbrella, the Low family has direct and absolute control over the U.S. oil industry.

In the banking industry, the banks controlled by the Lowers include First Nation City Bank and Chase Manhattan Bank. Chase Manhattan Bank is the third largest banking institution in the world, and this third is in terms of size, it is actually the most influential bank in the world. Chase Manhattan Bank is a merger of Chase Bank and Manhattan Bank, controlled by a prominent Jewish financial family. This merger has brought significant commercial success and benefits to both partners. Later, this bank was merged into what is today JPMorgan Chase.

That is not all of its assets.

The *New York Times* report argues that much of Chase Manhattan Bank's business operations are conducted through its overseas institutions and are not disclosed on the published statements.

In 1975, Time magazine revealed that Chase Manhattan Bank had 28 overseas branches and more than 50,000 affiliated banks worldwide. Assuming a branch bank has $10 million worth of assets, then Chase Manhattan Bank has the power to dispose of up to $500 billion in potential property. Influence and dominance on this scale can instantly cause huge shocks in the global currency, foreign exchange and gold markets, and then take advantage of the shocks to create panic situations and profit from them, which is a typical shearing operation.

Nielsen declared at a hearing to run for vice president: I myself do not own any shares of Chase Manhattan Bank.

This statement is technically impeccable and there really isn't a single share of Chase Manhattan Bank under his personal name. However, the Low family owns 623,000 shares (equivalent to 2.54%) of Chase Manhattan Bank, the Rockefeller Brothers Foundation owns 148,000 shares, Rockefeller University owns 81,000 shares, and the Rockefeller family and related institutions together own the equivalent of 4% of the controlling stake in Chase Manhattan Bank.

Chase's 1974 annual report disclosed total assets of $4.2 billion and the Low family's annual net income of $170 million.

The control and ownership of a business by a wealthy family is a carefully guarded secret, and when asked to disclose relevant information, they hand over the names of a number of financial escrow agencies (Street Names) to get by easily. The holding information of financial intermediaries is in fact very vague and very different from the real situation, and some intermediaries are so fictitious that the so-called custodian information does not reflect the identity of the real holders and beneficiaries at all.

In addition to Chase Manhattan Bank, the Lowe's consortium also controls New York's largest bank, National City Bank (NCB). The bank's chairman, Stilgman, was a business partner of William Rockefeller and one of the managers of Standard Oil Trust Company. His two daughters were married to William Rockefeller's two sons, respectively. Stilgemann was also married to the wealthy Carnegie family. This "top-down" relationship adds to the Rockefeller family's power.

The third bank controlled by the Lowe's consortium, Hanwha Bank (Chemical Bank), is primarily controlled by the Harkness family. Edward Harkness, a long-time partner in close business relations with Rockefeller Sr. and one of the administrators of the Standard Oil Trust Company, was the second largest shareholder in Standard Oil in 1939, just behind Rockefeller Sr.

Outside of the banking system, the Rockefeller consortium further amplifies its de facto control of the business through the insurance system. It is well known that commercial banks are the main channel for granting short-term credit to enterprises, while insurance companies provide long-term credit. Holding commercial banks and insurance companies in parallel is the equivalent of holding the lifeblood of a business' capital in two hands.

As a result, the overall control over the enterprise by the Rockefeller consortium has increased significantly.

The Rockefeller consortium forms director-member interlocking relationships with three major U.S. insurers: Metropolitan Insurance, Metropolitan Life Insurance and New York Life Insurance. It is estimated that the Rockefeller consortium controls 25 percent of the assets of the nation's 50 largest commercial banks and 30 percent of the assets of the 50 largest insurance companies.

Through high multiplier leverage, the control of the Rockefeller consortium over socio-economic and wealth is unprecedentedly amplified.

According to a 1974 Senate Banking Committee report, the Lowe's consortium held 5 percent control over a large number of publicly traded companies. Indeed, through other financial institutions, such as banks and insurance companies, the control of the Rockefeller consortium over these companies, in the form of 5% direct equity plus 2% other equity plus management shareholding, has been significantly strengthened. Such companies include ExxonMobil Oil, Standard Oil of California, Standard Oil of Indiana, etc.

In addition to the big three banks and the big three insurance companies, the Rockefeller consortium has achieved deep control of the business by controlling the bank's trust department. The bank trust department plays a vital role in both stock ownership and voting rights. A large number of large investors entrust their shares to the bank's trust department, and at the same time entrust the corresponding voting rights to the bank's trust department to exercise decision-making power over the enterprise on their behalf.

There is a popular saying that any company is squeamish about the trust department of a bank. Significant and critical decision-making power rests largely in the hands of the bank trust department, which in 1967 owned $35 billion in bank trust assets, or 14 percent of the nation's trust assets.

Through these direct and indirect holdings, the Rockefeller Consortium has gained strong and efficient control over companies in a variety of industries.

Chase Trust Investment Management is the single largest shareholder in 21 of the most important companies in the United States. Those companies directly under the control of the Lowe's consortium include United Airlines, Northwest Airlines, Long Island Power, National Steel, American National Airlines, and 16 other major companies.

Companies that have been included in the Rockefeller consortium's kingdom through highly magnified control include IBM, AT&T, Central Railroad, Delta Air Lines, Motorola, Safeway, Hewlett-Packard and others.

Companies that are controlled through the influence of bank credit and the interlocking of board seats in major companies include DuPont, Shell and others.

Summarizing the information on the various clues, we were amazed to find that the Rockefeller consortium actually controls 37 of the 100 largest industrial companies in the United States, 9 of the 20 largest transportation companies, all of the largest electric, water, and gas companies, 3 of the 4 largest insurance companies, and countless small and medium-sized investments, loans, and retail businesses.

Economic control of this magnitude and magnitude beyond imagination is bound to produce a corresponding political influence. It has become difficult to tell who is in charge of decision-making between the super-rich conglomerates and the government, and the two sides have become deeply interpenetrated and fused into one whole.

The Washington Post writes that once Nielsen was elected vice president, he would encounter interests associated with the Rockefeller consortium in almost every issue of public economic resolution, creating a clear conflict of interest.

In addition, there is management interlocking and mutual control among the major foundations, as is the case with prominent large foundations such as the Rockefeller Foundation, Ford Foundation and Carnegie Foundation. The Carnegie Foundation is an important part of the Rockefeller Foundation, whose principal operators are members of the Association for American Foreign Relations, controlled by the Rockefeller Foundation, and two of the six principal members of the Financial Management Board are directors of the Rockefeller Consortium Financial Institutions. The Ford Foundation's president from 1953 to 1965 was chairman of the Manhattan Bank, and his successor was also a director of the Bank of Manhattan and served as president of the World Bank. Several of the principals and operators of the Ford Foundation are members of the American Foreign Relations Association.

Congressional Inquiry

Such a strong control of wealth and political influence by the Rockefellers certainly caught the attention of the US Congress early on.

In 1950, Congressman Peterman launched an investigation into the Foundation's assets to investigate whether the Foundation was using various asset portfolios to disguise market manipulation. The findings of this investigation read, in part, "The economic life of our entire country has become intertwined with the business practices of a large number of foundations. Unless action is taken immediately, every aspect of American life will be under the control of the Foundation."[180]

The report was submitted without any further action, and no action was taken, and it ended without a trace.

In 1952, Congressman Eugene E. Cox led the second congressional investigation of tax-exempt foundations in an attempt to thoroughly ascertain whether such foundations were using their resources for purposes contrary to American national interests and traditions. From the day the investigation was launched, the Rockefeller consortium used its long-established Democratic Party faction to obstruct it in every way possible. First of all, it "spared time like gold", and only six months were approved for this huge investigation, which took several years to complete, then it repeatedly delayed the availability of funds, set up numerous obstacles, and repeatedly delayed the time by discussing the details of the investigation process.[181]

After months of persevering in the face of many setbacks and difficulties, Senator Cox was finally unable to withstand the obstacles of his opponent, and in the course of the investigation, he became ill and finally died.

Since then, Congressman Carroll Reece (R-Ky.) has filed a third investigation with the intent of furthering and continuing the investigation over time. The move immediately provoked a fierce backlash from the Lowe's consortium. It is clear to everyone that if the conclusions of the investigation reveal the nature of the foundation's operations, the foundation system will be strongly challenged and opposed, and will most likely be terminated.

The Washington Post, which has close ties to Low, immediately jumped in and, in a rarely harsh tone, accused the investigation of being thoroughly stupid, useless and a waste of public resources.[182]

The major mainstream media, unwilling to be left behind, have been attacking Reese and the investigation, labeling it a "conspiracy

---

[180] Ibid, p. 40.

[181] David Rivera, *Final Warning: A History of the New World Order – Illuminism and the master plan for world domination*, 1994.

[182] Gary Allen, *The Rockefeller File*, Buccaneer Books, Inc. 1976, p. 43.

theory" and doing everything in their power to smear, attack and ridicule Reese, portraying him as a "McCarthyist".

The investigation is being conducted almost in a state of total shutdown. As the investigation progressed with extreme difficulty, Reese discovered that four of the five members of the investigation committee were all agents of Lowe's, except himself. Of those members, Rep. Wayne Hays (R-Ky.) was the most vocal in his opposition, obstruction and confrontation of the investigation. Hayes regularly went to a Washington hotel for lunch every week, during which time he met with representatives of several major foundations to discuss the response.

Hayes's ability to interrupt was so prominent during the investigative case hearing that he interrupted 264 times during a hearing that lasted 185 minutes. He also refused to comply with the hearing system, constantly attacking, abusing and belittling witness testimony, interrupting without interruption and finally causing the hearing to be suspended.

Hayes also revealed that he was contacted by the White House side to discuss how to terminate the commission's further investigation.

The Rees Commission had no choice but to narrow the scope of its investigation again and again, eventually focusing on the three largest foundations. However, this has finally come to an end due to increasing pressure and obstruction, as well as time, financial and personnel constraints.

On August 19, 1954, Reese summarized this investigative activity by saying,

> *"The Foundation is second only to the federal government in power... Perhaps Congress should recognize that the Foundation has become more powerful in certain areas, at least more so than the legislative branch of government."*[183]

Since then, there has been no more organized government and congressional resistance against the Foundation.

---

[183] David Rivera, *Final Warning: A History of the New World Order – Illuminism and the master plan for world domination*, 1994.

Foundations, elite groups and governments

The height of monopoly capitalism is the suppression of rivals and the elimination of competition. In order to achieve this, cooperation with the Government becomes necessary. And achieving greater control over industry, commerce, capital, technology, manpower and resources in a broader sense will require the synergy of government until world government is achieved.

The influence of international bankers on politics and government is achieved largely indirectly through the initiation and funding of the American Foreign Relations Association. The American Foreign Relations Association has been under the control of the Lowe's Consortium from its inception until now.

Every socially influential person in American society, from lawyers, bankers, professors, and generals to journalists, editors, and officials, almost invariably heavyweights who have some influence on the political decisions of the U.S. government, especially foreign policy, have been recruited by the Council on Foreign Relations.

The vast majority of successive presidents since President Roosevelt of the United States have also been members of the Council on Foreign Relations. Presidents rotate by term, and government officials are running water soldiers, but the gold lord standing behind the president, the family power group behind the government, the gold power behind the three powers, has never changed.

The Rockefeller family's influence on the White House, which began to emerge during the McKinley presidential election of 1894, carried over into the Roosevelt era, where Low's influence gradually played a decisive role. The Roosevelt New Deal was actually the Rockefeller New Deal. Most of the measures introduced by the New Deal are a direct reflection of the business interests that benefit the Lowe's consortium.[184] The key agent that Rockefeller arranged around Roosevelt was Harry Hopkins. Hopkins ran a social service agency that received funding from the Rockefeller Foundation for ten years. Hopkins was Franklin Roosevelt's alter ego and their relationship was like that of Colonel Howes and President Wilson. "Hopkins' actual

---

[184] Antony C. Sutton, *Wall Street and FDR*, Arlington House Publishers, 1975.

power during World War II was second only to President Roosevelt and the second most powerful figure in Washington. Hopkins admits that Low has helped him a lot and that he owes Rockefeller a lot.

Nelson Rockefeller's relationship with Roosevelt goes back a long way. During his tenure as U.S. Secretary of Commerce, Nelson Rockefeller was a key executive in Roosevelt's New Deal.[185] An article in the *New York Times* of May 20, 1960 stated that Rockefeller was a very close and good friend of Roosevelt's relations. They spent the holiday together at Shangri-La, today's Camp David.

Eisenhower's first Secretary of State, Dulles, was a cousin of Rockefeller, and the second Secretary of State, Chris, was a member of the Council on Foreign Relations and a key executive of Standard Oil. Eisenhower's attorney general was a member of the Foreign Relations Association and a former Rockefeller employee. Upon taking office, Eisenhower selected hundreds of federal and district court judges and barristers, as well as senior government officials, all of whom, along with 17 key government officials in the Eisenhower administration, were members of the Foreign Relations Association.

President Kennedy himself was a member of the Foreign Relations Association, and his Secretary of State, Dean Rusk, was an agent of Rockefeller's direct arrangement. Kennedy had not even met this Secretary of State until he appointed him. It is not unusual that Presidents such as Reagan and Jimmy Carter, when they appointed Secretary of State and Chairman of the Federal Reserve, had never met these people. Rusk's official position as Secretary of State was also that of the Rockefeller Foundation, and he actually took a "leave of absence" as Secretary of State of the United States Government. Kennedy's Assistant Secretary of State is also a member of the Foreign Relations Association and an administrator and director of the Rockefeller Brothers Foundation. His Assistant Secretary of Commerce, Alexander Trowbridge, is a member of the Council on Foreign Relations and an administrator of Standard Oil. He was promoted to Secretary of Commerce during Kennedy's administration, and the Executive Deputy Secretary of Defense, who was promoted at the same time, was a member of the Council on Foreign Relations.

---

[185] Gary Allen, *The Rockefeller File*, Buccaneer Books, Inc. 1976, p. 156.

President Nixon's attorney general was Rockefeller's royal counsel. He was Nixon's general national coordinator and advisor during the election.[186]

Nixon's first vice president, Spiro Agnew, who was chairman of the Rockefeller Board of Elections during the 1968 election, opposed Nixon during the general election and was later placed beside him as a political adviser. Nixon's most prominent adviser was Kissinger, who served as Nelson Rockefeller's personal foreign policy adviser for 10 years.

Kissinger immigrated to the United States from Germany in 1956, and in less than 20 years, he went from a quiet Harvard professor to the soul of American politics precisely because he had a powerful Rockefeller push behind him. Kissinger and Nixon disagreed on a number of political platforms, and the two had met only once before Nixon appointed Kissinger as assistant for national security, and Nixon had no favorable feelings for Kissinger. But Kissinger was personally named by Rockefeller, and Nixon could only "do as he was told" in the appointment process.

All 115 officials at all levels of the Nixon administration were members of the Foreign Relations Association, most of whom remained in key positions during the Ford administration. During the Republican presidency, Nelson Rockefeller placed a number of key candidates in key positions such as the various House and Senate policy committees.

As for the influence of the Lowers on the White House, someone made an estimate in 1975 that more than 5,000 officials in high federal government positions were candidates for the Rockefeller powerhouse.

The Rockefellers have a major interest in international affairs, especially foreign affairs, and have made sure that the two key positions of Secretary of State and head of the CIA are in the hands of the Rockefellers in successive administrations. With Rockefeller's cousin, Allen Dulles, as its first director and staffed with a full squad, the CIA is, from the standpoint of personnel, almost the overseas law

---

[186] Ibid, p. 157.

enforcement arm of Standard Oil. Low's other cousin, John Foster Dulles, was Eisenhower's Secretary of State.[187]

The Rockefeller Group and successive U.S. administrations have truly become one family, not one of us.

Rockefeller said that the State Department in Washington was our greatest help, with numerous ambassadors and ministers helping us open up new markets in the farthest corners of the world. The U.S. government serves the interests and pursues the policies of the Rockefeller Group at every level. Washington Post reporter Jack writes that the U.S. State Department's policy decisions are, in a sense, centered around oil company interests. When an oil company can't get a certain benefit overseas, the U.S. State Department steps in to help fix it. In many countries, the U.S. Embassy functions as the overseas office of an oil company. The shadow of the seven major oil companies is everywhere in the policies of the State Council.

> Rockefeller also has a firm grip on the Treasury Secretary pick to ensure that the Treasury functions as the banking arm of JPMorgan Chase.
> Robert Anderson, Eisenhower's treasurer, is a member of the Council on Foreign Relations
> Douglas Dillon, Kennedy's treasurer, is a member of the Council on Foreign Relations and a trustee of the Rockefeller Brothers Foundation
> Johnson's treasurer, Henry Fowler, is a member of the Foreign Relations Association
> William Simon, Ford's finance minister, is a member of the Foreign Relations Association.

In recent years, however, that power has gradually been grabbed by Wall Street's investment banks.

---

[187] Ibid, p. 159.

Foundations and the education system

In 1890 Andrew Carnegie published a collection of eleven of his essays in a book entitled The Gospel of Wealth. In his book, he assumes that the free market system has come to an end before the industrial and financial giants of their generation, who not only have absolute wealth, but also control the government. But he was afraid that the next generation of people would grow up, realize the seriousness of the problem and rise up against this system that was beneficial to them. His conclusion is that the education system must be controlled.

Recognizing that the regional fragmentation of the United States education system is unlikely to be "wiped out" on a case-by-case basis, the super-rich continue to adopt a "channel king" strategy, focusing on investing in teachers' associations and the development of educational materials that can effectively control the education system as long as they have firm control over teachers and the content of education. So the Rockefeller Foundation invested heavily in the General Education Board, the premier teachers' association in the United States.[188]

Rockefeller once said that we have unlimited resources to make people obey and that the current way of education is long out of date.

The Rockefeller Foundation and the Carnegie Endowment are simultaneously funding the development and distribution of textbooks on a large scale, effectively exerting influence on the education system by indirect means. When two or more generations are brought up under the educational influence of the same ideology, the thought patterns of several generations will gradually assemble in one direction. The Rockefeller Foundation and the Carnegie Foundation have been fully funding the textbook industry in schools and educational institutions at all levels throughout the United States since the 1920s and 1930s, without interruption.

Besides the channel, another focus is to control the high end. 2/3 of Rockefeller Foundation and Carnegie Foundation education funds are directed to higher education. In the 1930s, 20 percent of all U.S. higher education funding came from the Rockefeller Foundation and the Carnegie Endowment. They actually functioned in part as the U.S.

---

[188] Ibid, p. 44.

Department of Education. The influence these two foundations have exerted on American higher education has been effective.

The National Education Association, the largest teachers' association in the United States controlled by the Rockefeller and Carnegie Foundations, said in a 1934 report that the dying free market model must be completely destroyed and all should submit to greater social control.

This view fully supports Rockefeller's idea. Roche suggests that "competition is a sin" and should be eliminated. Such an idea is intended to stifle and eliminate competitors, achieve monopolies and complete greater control over society.

Public opinion shaping

Influence on political and public opinion cannot be achieved without control of the media.

The Rockefeller Foundation's influence on the media is also based on the core principle of "Channel is king". First of all, the control of news sources through the control of the three major news agencies, the three major news agencies are the source of news for all local print media, the layout content and editorial ideas of the major local media, the three major news agencies are the first priority. With the three major news agencies in its hands, the Rockefeller Foundation has brought together print media such as books, newspapers and magazines.

In addition to the "channel is king", the media also needs to control the high-end. Based on the principle of "catch the thief before the king", Lok first took down the New York Times, the guiding light of the major media. The position of the New York Times editorial will serve as a benchmark for the perspectives and attitudes of all mainstream media coverage, all of which remain consistent as the New York Times instantly adjusts its coverage.

Low also held the Washington Post in high regard. Published in the nation's capital, The Washington Post is a daily desktop necessity for politicians. Its director, Katharine Graham, is a member of the Foreign Relations Association. Franklin Murphy, who runs the largest newspaper in the West, The Los Angeles Times, is also a member of the Foreign Relations Association. Low coordinates the interests of the major media gatekeepers by initiating and funding the Foreign Relations Association.[189]

In television media, William S Paley, the CBS helmer who owns more than 200 television stations and 255 radio stations, is a member of the Council on Foreign Relations and the principal administrator of the Rockefeller Foundation.

NBC is a television station affiliated with the RCA. Its director, David Sarnoff, is a member of the Council on Foreign Relations.

ABC has 153 TV stations and is biased towards entertainment programming. Chase Manhattan Bank has a 6.7 percent stake in ABC.

Through bank and trust holdings, Rockefeller holds a 14% stake in CBS and an RCA 4.5% stake.

These TV media giants are actually all under the umbrella of the Rockefeller consortium. Some have jokingly called whether it's ABC, CBS, or NBC, it's actually RBC, or Rockefeller Broadcasting Company.

There is another area of the media that cannot be ignored, and that is advertising. Ad revenue accounts for 2/3 to 3/4 of total print media revenue and is certainly the golden chicken that the media values. The biggest customers for advertising are chains and malls. Media editors are not going to let the voices against the goldmasters amplify openly.

The largest chains and specialty stores in the United States, such as Macy, JCPenny, Sears, etc., have at least one of their board members who is a member of the Foreign Relations Association and interlock with the board interests of banks and corporations controlled by Foreign Relations Association members.

In addition, oil companies and financial institutions are major advertisers in the media. What kind of media has the guts to pick and choose what the big golds don't want to hear?

The Foundation also values the orientation of religious voices; the United States is, after all, a religious power, and the influence of religious power on society cannot be underestimated. The Rockefeller Foundation and the Carnegie Foundation fund the New York

---

[189] Ibid, p. 68.

Theological Seminary and the Federal Council of Churches. The voice of social "mainstream" theology has gradually shifted to advocate for the development of social planning and control, as well as control over money and economic activity. The Federal Council of Churches has over 40 million members in the United States. The power effect of such a potential ideological influence is immeasurable.

World government: the goal of the "Anglo-American power bloc"

> *"Some even believe we are part of a clandestine group that seeks to jeopardize the core interests of the United States by portraying my family and myself as "internationalists" conspiring to create a global political and economic structure – a single world (government) – in cooperation with some people in various countries (with the same ideals). If this is an accusation, then I plead guilty, but I am proud of it."*
> —David Rockefeller[190]

Rhodes' ultimate vision was for the United States to return to the bosom of the British Empire and then to build, with the British and Americans at its core, mechanisms that would spread the gospel of their "good social system" throughout the world and dream of a "world government" based on that. Of course, this is not a fair pyramid of power, and the Anglo-American "upper class", with its "great tradition" and "elegance", will unashamedly sit at the top of the pyramid to dominate the world "on a much larger scale than their lower class".

For this "great ideal", Rhodes established a Rhodes Fund to encourage and fund young Americans to study in Europe and to educate American youth to work toward the goal of a unified government worldwide. For decades, large groups of American elites, influenced by the Rhodesian mindset, have embraced and followed the idea of a world government. Former US President Clinton was awarded the Rhodes Scholarship.

"After the end of World War II, Britain had irretrievably lost the possibility of putting the United States back into its own orbit, and there had been a fundamental change in the strength of both sides, while they

---

[190] David Rockefeller *Memoirs*, Random House, 2002, p. 405.

shared a far more serious threat than Nazi Germany, namely the Soviet Union.

Thus, a move towards a complete integration of the two sides to overcome the challenges of the Soviet Union and other powers and to try to establish a "world government".

When it comes to world government, the elites are divided into two major factions: progressive and radical.

The progressives advocate a world government through the organization of regional alliances, gradual expansion, and then union with each other.[191] The formation of the Atlantic Alliance is a case in point. The Atlantic Alliance essentially violates the spirit of the U.S. Constitution and betrays the autonomous purposes of an independent and sovereign nation, but this organization and the ideas it espouses are shared by a large number of wealthy individuals. The Atlantic Alliance has 871 wealthy members, 107 of whom are members of the Foreign Relations Association. By the mid-1970s, the membership of the Atlantic Alliance reached over 2,000. An important resolution sponsored by the organization is the "Atlantic Alliance Resolution", which advocates the repeal of the United States Declaration of Independence and the creation of a new Anglo-American union beyond the principles of the United States Constitution.

In 1949, the "Atlantic Alliance Resolution" was formally introduced into the United States Congress and, of course, was not adopted by Congress, a proposal that was too shocking for the vast majority of its members to accept immediately. Every year since then, the proposal has been brought up for consideration and has been endorsed and supported by heavyweights such as Rockefeller, Nixon, Eisenhower, the Dulles brothers, Kissinger and McCarthy, and in 1975 it was reintroduced to the House of Representatives, where it was supported by 111 members of the House. For years, the Atlantic Alliance had the secret support of the Rockefeller family. Nelson Rockefeller is offering a free office building at 10 East 40th Street in New York for use by the Atlantic Alliance.[192]

---

[191] Clarence K. Streit, *Union Now*, Harper & Brothers, 1940.

[192] Gary Allen, *The Rockefeller File*, Buccaneer Books, Inc. 1976.

The radical wing of the world government is represented by James Warburg, son of Paul Warburg of the "Seventeen Great Banking Families". Paul was the architect-in-chief of the Federal Reserve, a partner at the prominent Wall Street investment bank Coon Rapo, and James was a financial advisor to President Roosevelt. The United World Federal (UWF), which James founded in 1947, was heavily funded by the Rockefellers. James Warburg's famous slogan is "One World or None". Among other things, the very radical Professor Milton wrote an article in 1949 claiming to tear down the American flag and spit on it.

One of the main sources of spiritual strength for the radical wing of world government was the detonation of the first atomic bomb in human history by the United States in 1945, and by the time James Warburg founded the "World Federation Movement" (UWF) in 1947, no second country had possessed nuclear weapons. Weapons of mass destruction are psychologically giving the "World Federal Movement" elements a great deal of arrogance, and those who follow me will prosper and those who oppose me will perish, and those who dare to oppose the world government will be wiped off the face of the earth. This is what James Warburg proposed in 1954:

> "We should have a world government, whether people like it or not. The only question is whether this world government comes about through (peaceful) consensus or (forceful) conquest."

"The idea of the World Federal Movement is that world peace will be achieved through a unified world organization and system. A large number of young people in the United States have been influenced by this trend, believing that such a system would fully guarantee individual freedom, freedom of religious thought and world peace. "The World Federal Movement has been working for decades to bring about the establishment of a world government, without making visible progress.

The Rockefeller Group has heavily funded the actions of both progressives and radicals in various forms, but getting the American public in general to abandon the traditional notion of an independent state in favor of a world government is by no means going to happen overnight. Progressives and radicals have worked tirelessly for decades, but they are a long way from their ultimate goal.

Thus, the advancers of the idea of world government created a third organizing body, the Trilateral Commission, to shift perspectives and approaches and continue working towards their overall goal. The Trilateral Commission was led by Brzezinski, who advocated a different view from both the Atlantic Alliance and the "World Federal Movement". Brzezinski argues that asking Americans to abandon the idea of an independent state, which has formed a century-old tradition, altogether is not intuitively or emotionally acceptable. The advancement of world government should gradually achieve the ultimate goal of "saving the nation on the curve" by indirect, slow, euphemistic, ingenious and tortuous ways and means.

The ideas put forward by the Atlantic Alliance are too narrow to meet the challenges of the gradual multipolarization of the world since the 1970s, including the cold war situation and more complex international gaming relations. Therefore, instead of directly and openly advocating a simple concept of world government, public attention should be directed and drawn to the common problems facing the world and to the search for coherent solutions, such as the economic crisis, the deterioration of the ecological environment, energy depletion, etc.

It is clear that this process will not move forward if Governments and the public are only concerned with localized issues and internal affairs.

The establishment of a global world government can only be truly approached when all countries of the world, from national leaders down to the general public, have to focus on the same issues together and gradually reach consensus and unity of thought.

The proponents of the idea of world government are laid out in four main directions.

(1) The establishment of a new world monetary system.

(2) The worldwide resource and ecological crisis.

(3) Promote integration and consolidation of world trade.

(4) Energy crisis.

Its general idea is to integrate plus crisis, to advance consensus in integration, to wait for conditions while advancing, to create crisis while waiting, to bring about action in crisis.

Any country that does not follow such a course and focuses only on its own internal and local problems is bound to face three great challenges: the food, energy and financial crises. The scale and destructive power of these crises would be comparable to that of the Great Depression of the 1920s and 1930s. Leaders have had to sit down together to discuss the urgent need to compromise and compromise with each other in the intricacies of the game and to give up part of their economic and monetary sovereignty in order to build an effective consensus.

At this point, some people may have a smile of triumph on their face. One wonders why international bankers, who have achieved tremendous influence and control over the United States, are committed to seeking to abolish American independence and sovereignty and establish a world government.

This is the ideology shared by more than 95 per cent of the members of the American Foreign Relations Association, which in some way dismantles and abrogates the independent sovereignty of the United States in order to achieve a broader and deeper global control and to realize the "ambitious vision" of world government. This ambitious goal went through various forms of process, sometimes radical, sometimes slow, sometimes circuitous, but this general platform never changed.

At a time when the worst economic crisis in eight decades is sweeping the globe, a seemingly unattainable ideal is approaching. The financial tsunami of 2008 may have been the long-awaited godsend!

CHAPTER IX

After the Financial Tsunami

Roosevelt famously said,

> "None of the major historical events occurred randomly and naturally, and all of them are without exception the product of careful planning."

Or did Roosevelt see through the lens that people operate behind all events, and that if an event occurs without benefit to all parties involved, it will not evolve into a major event. The more far-reaching and complex the event, the greater the need for strong organizational coordination and the difficulties that must be overcome to make it happen. It is hard to imagine that anyone would be willing to do something so laboriously unappealing without a significant interest as a motivation.

So it is with political events in history, and so it is with financial events. Behind the financial markets remains the game of human interest, and the whole purpose of people's participation in financial market activities is to gain profit. As is the case with other games of interest, participants must abide by the rules of the game, including all potential rules. The difference in financial markets is simply that people's interests have been standardized and packaged and priced in such a way that they are better "liquid", less costly and faster to transfer. As a result, major financial events will likewise reflect the interest landscape of super-weight participants, and these high-energy super-players, often play a decisive role in influencing the market at major turning points.

The 2008 global financial tsunami was nothing more than a repetition of human nature, with a similar pattern of human greed and fear, and super-winners who see human weakness and exploit it to the fullest and reap the greatest rewards, compared to the crises of history.

The heart of the game of interest is a zero-sum game, and as long as the legality of private property remains in force, there can only be a single owner of the same asset, tangible or intangible, at some point. What is traded in financial markets is the ownership of standardized interests (embodied in assets or rights to the proceeds of assets), which can never be shared and which is typically exclusive.

The essence of this financial tsunami is that financial derivatives create the illusion of multiple ownership on top of the same underlying asset, and when the underlying asset fails to consistently generate sufficient returns to fill the benefit ownership created and is eventually discovered by market participants, the manifestation is a crisis of benefit ownership crowding out. Financial assets such as CDOs are, by their very nature, iterative and multiple reproductions of ownership of asset proceeds, and these virtual ownership transactions are typical of "Ponzi schemes".

The question is, do international bankers really not understand the obvious truth that such an obvious "Ponzi scheme" is bound to end in a financial disaster? There is nothing "unforeseen" new about such scams, which have been repeated many times throughout history. The crisis was actually predetermined and predicted long before they did.

The fact is, Buffett called financial derivatives a "weapon of mass destruction" as early as 2005; Paulson told President Bush in Camp David as early as 2006 that the financial derivatives crisis was about to erupt; Fannie Mae and other companies also began to lay off workers on a large scale in the summer of 2006; the cover of the January 2007 issue of the British magazine *The Economist* already clearly depicted Greenspan holding the "detonator" of the U.S. economy about to explode to his unlucky successor Bernanke;[193] the managers of major hedge funds in 2005 blogged about how to sell CDOs and other "asset toxic junk" to "stupid" Asian investors. Even when Currency Wars was finalized in the second half of 2006, it clearly pointed to the major crisis in financial derivatives and the inevitable emergence of the "two-room" problem, as well as the major risks to the United States dollar and United States treasury debt, and predicted that the subprime mortgage crisis would inevitably evolve into a global financial tsunami that would eventually lead to a severe recession in the world economy.

---

[193] *The Economist*, 2006.

And is it true that Greenspan, the head of US monetary policy, still did not perceive the approaching crisis as of 2006? Was his indulgence in financial derivatives unintentional or intentional? Is it true that such a global financial crisis, which has not been seen in a century, is "random" and "unforeseen"?

To understand all this, we must first go into the spiritual world of Greenspan, who is so responsible for the crisis, and experience what he and the world ruling elite he represents may really think, and what strategic ends they are trying to achieve, where the world is going and how the crisis will evolve.

What China lacks most is not an expert in a particular field, but a strategic thinker who can break down barriers between fields. Under the conformist educational system, most professionals in various fields have been molded into "bookcase" scholars whose brains are primarily used to store information and process it along inherent patterns. In fact, asking the question correctly means solving half the problem. What does it mean to be creative? At the heart of creativity is the ability to ask questions that are different from the norm, and the perspective of the question determines the breadth and depth of the ideas that constitute the "central processor" that collects, processes and processes the vast and complex information resources. Research that fails to ask the right questions is as soulless as a walking corpse, and research that lacks strong ideas can only scratch the itch.

We know what we know, and we know what we don't know, but we don't know what we don't know.

Greenspan: Engineer of the economic machine

The greatest mathematician of the 20th century, Greenspan's name, I'm afraid, has no place in the rankings, but among economists, he is absolutely genius for his super-sensitivity to numbers and models.

While attending NYU School of Business, Greenspan took major courses in finance and accounting. In his autobiography, he mentions an internship at an American business organization during his school years. That institution is the Brown Brothers, which made a big name for itself on Wall Street.

One of the first things Greenspan did at Brown Brothers was to collate and adjust some of the data information released by the Federal

Reserve, particularly the big supermarket chains, on a weekly basis. The task may seem simple, but it is cumbersome and arduous. Since there were no computers at the time, it was not easy to do statistics purely by hand. A lot of manual calculations, constant charting with pencil drawings, and a process of adjusting a set of data in one stroke. It's a super boring job that Greenspan does with a lot of interest. He seems to be born with a high degree of sensitivity to numbers, and in the face of dull and uninteresting numbers, he is able to spot things that others cannot see in their eyes. Through this work, Greenspan mastered the solid basics of statistics. Most importantly, his super-sensitivity to data, guided by the scientific method, has reached the realm of "letting the data tell its own story".

After college, Greenspan worked in statistics at The Conference Board, a New York-based think tank,[194] an institution that served precisely the Federal Reserve Bank of New York. The NIA's vast library of books became the most important part of Greenspan's life. Through these books and statistical reports, Greenspan began to understand the mechanism by which the American economy works,[195] understanding how various industrial sectors operate and link and together form the overall national economic system. In Greenspan's mind, the evolution of industrial systems since the beginning of the Industrial Revolution, from steam engines to textiles, from railways to metallurgy, from shipping to shipbuilding, from machinery to military industry, from telegraphs to telephones, from coal to oil, from automobiles to airplanes ... countless socio-economic screws were screwed together in his mind to run the huge machine of the national economy.

The NIA's library also presented Greenspan with a vast array of statistics. Most of these statistics are "old", and many date from around the Civil War in 1861, when the Society compiled a complete and complete collection of detailed statistics on almost every important industry and trade in the United States. Greenspan, in the NIA's library, is like a mouse dropped into a rice bowl, and is simply enthralled with these statistics. If he got into the cotton industry, he spent his days studying all kinds of cotton, from ingredients, grades to categories,

---

[194] Martin, J. (2000) *Greenspan: The Man Behind Money*.

[195] Greenspan, Alan (2007) *The Age of Turbulence*. Penguin Press.

production processes, including different kinds of cotton in the industry will be how to use, how to process, which cotton processing machines need to be used and the whole production process, until the market sales, these data in Greenspan eyes, is a colorful world. Data on the importance of the United States, such as national railroad transportation, the U.S. rubber industry, and the 1890 U.S. demographics, are even more compelling to Greenspan.[196] These boundless figures and information would have trapped others, but kept Greenspan reading too much to release. Immersed in a sea of data, Greenspan quickly gained a deep and comprehensive understanding of American statistics across all industries.

Over the years, Greenspan had gained an understanding of the overall mechanics of the U.S. economic machine, and with his painstaking study of historical data from various industries, the young Greenspan had become a skilled "technical worker" in the economic machine field. He is well versed in the principles of the machine, knows the various operating parameters well, and has accumulated considerable "historical experience" with the dynamic data of each component and its linkage effects.

His brain is equipped with a software that quickly analyzes the current state and trends of industry in the United States as a whole, taking the exact pattern and pulse of economic activity from the data. Through intensive reading and accumulation of data over a period of years, the "Geiger model" has succeeded in creating a unique and accurate data flow and data module for the analysis of the operating state of the overall economic machine and of local industry components. If a set of basic parameters of a firm's economic activity is entered, a report predicting the macroeconomic cycle can immediately be generated in Greenspan's brain, automatically accompanied by a full histogram and line graph.

Like engineers in other professions, Greenspan was not much interested in economic theory, because engineers are interested in how to solve the various problems that arise in practice, not in abstract theoretical exploration. In the autobiography Greenspan also mentions that he was not very interested in Keynes's macro studies and that his excitement was at the technical level, especially with data and models.

---

[196] Ibid.

Greenspan is more concerned with how the economic machine actually works and less concerned with how economic theory is explained.

Of the theoretical studies, the only one that impressed Greenspan was a course he had taken in 1951, taught by Jacob Wolfowitz, which combined data statistics with economic theory.[197] The professor was the father of Wolfs, who later served as Deputy Secretary of Defense for the United States during the Bush Jr. Wolfs Jr. was one of the main architects of the Iraq War, a leading representative of neoconservatism after retiring from the Defense Department and later serving as president of the World Bank.

In the course taught by Wolfs, Greenspan first embraced the entirely new idea of constructing variables between economic structures using mathematical statistics. Before coming into contact with the theory now known as econometrics, Greenspan had already equipped himself with a primary "Greystoke model" developed by himself to form a complete and mature analysis of the overall economic development and dynamic trends, but had not yet formed a relatively clear theoretical system and lacked mathematical tools for accurate representation.

When Greenspan first heard about Professor Wolfezy's econometrics concepts, he was immediately enlightened, and felt that he would stand out in the field. "Once the data is imported into the mathematical model of econometrics, it can immediately output predictions of future economic trends. Because Greenspan's data comes from the front lines of production practice and has been accumulated over a huge span of years, the mathematical template of the "Greystoke model" combined with the super database in his brain produces results that are far more accurate and realistic than purely theory-based economic models.

The database in Greenspan's brain is not only rich and comprehensive, but also unique in that it covers a vast amount of historical information. Over the course of a long history, industries have undergone constant development and change, and various data have formed dynamic data flow paths as economic systems have evolved. "The theoretical framework and model system of the Gertrude model is not static and isolated, but has a considerable degree of self-

---

[197] Ibid.

evolutionary and self-learning properties. His grasp of the laws of economic operation gained in essence when he gained the support of mathematical tools.

Greenspan's brain presents lucid macroscopic images that mimic the laws of nature and the celestial bodies as seen by Newton. In his mind, the world can be constructed entirely into a complex mathematical model, and as long as the data accumulates long enough, it is logically feasible to predict future economic trends through this model. With the right initial variables input, the future economic trends output from the Greco model will be very close to reality.

By this time, Greenspan had climbed Mount Everest in his heart, and he was able to look at the world economy with a sense of grandeur and courage. He tries to make sense of the world with his own model, using his data to verify this speculation.

The Korean War made Greenspan an overnight success

Greenspan's obsession and confidence in data and mathematical models reached its peak with the outbreak of the Korean War.

During the war, information related to the military industry, such as data on the manufacture of fighter jets, bombers and other new types of aircraft, was blocked as a military secret due to the massive preparedness efforts of the US Department of Defense. Many links in the chain of economic activity are closely related to aircraft manufacturing, such as manufacturers of special metals, aluminium, copper and steel, special craftsmen and engineers, and these industry groups are in urgent need of information on military production. The socio-economic impact of the military aircraft manufacturing industry on the whole is enormous, especially in the fiscal year 1953, when military expenditures amounted to 14 percent of GDP, which is quite alarming. In the absence of data on the military industry, analysts on Wall Street and in many industries are in the dark about the impact of acts of war on future economic development.

It was at this juncture that Greenspan stepped forward. Believing that the continuation of the collective blindness of Wall Street and allied industries would adversely affect the U.S. economy, he volunteered to project his own information on military production, which was tightly blocked and kept secret by the military. Greenspan's move is based on his overconfidence in the "Greystoke model", based on statistical data accumulated over the years on various industries in the United States, supplemented by the mathematical tools provided by econometrics.

Greenspan first searched through public sources of information and immediately discovered that the military secrecy bureau was not a vegetarian, and that all information related to the manufacture of military aircraft, from aircraft types, materials used, aircraft configuration to the number of aircraft planned to be produced, had been blocked by the military to the nth degree.

Greenspan had to stop at public sources of information and instead search for data from the "World War II" period. Because in 1940, the U.S. military had not kept this military-industrial data secret. Greenspan searched the Congressional records of the 1940s for the limited data on hearings and official releases in the relevant industries, using the data collected in the 1940s records as a benchmark, and through as many avenues as possible, tried in every way to accumulate the data and information publicly available on all aspects of the aircraft industry. At once, the engineers' operating manuals, the production statements of the various companies involved, the management statements, and the voluminous federal statistical statements, as well as the order data of the peripheral industries accessible by the U.S. Department of Defense, piled up on Greenspan's desk.

The "Gertrude Model" is up and running.

Based on data benchmarks from the "World War II" period, with limited public information, such as the weight of a particular type of aircraft, the "Greystoke model" begins by calculating the proportion and quantity of aluminium, copper and steel in the materials used in the components of the aircraft, and gradually calculates the material used in each aircraft, and then consolidates the total, and in turn extrapolates the economic impact of the United States military industry on the components of the entire economy, such as copper, steel, metallurgy, rail transportation, electricity and other industries.

In 1952, Greenspan's research came to light. The article, entitled "The economics of the United States Air Force", caused an instant "earthquake" in the Pentagon. The military's first gut reaction was that Greenspan must have been a high-ranking spy, because the statistics he published were so close to the secret data held by the United States military that the Pentagon immediately concluded that "this man must have had our secret data, otherwise it would not have been so accurate".

But Greenspan can indeed assure, with all sincerity, that "this one really isn't." He said that these results were entirely derived from the "Greco model".

The Pentagon was stunned and speechless.

Throughout the American economics community, Greenspan has risen like a rising star to the attention of many.

In the 1950s, Nova Greenspan had good reason to believe that he had risen to the position of Newton in physics. The basic laws and universal rules of the world economy were firmly in his hands. With the slightest push of God's hand, he can calculate with precision all the directions of the world economy.

Just as Greenspan was rising like a star, another bright star in the night sky came crashing down on him. Her dazzling light shot straight into Greenspan's heart and didn't fade again.

Ayn Rand: Greenspan's Spiritual Director

> *"The giants of thought you admire so much have taught you that the earth is flat and atoms are the smallest matter. The whole process of scientific history is the process by which fallacies are continually poked through, not by which anything is achieved. Only the most ignorant and ignorant will still believe that old-fashioned statement of seeing things as they are. What you see is what needs to be doubted in the first place."*
>
> —Ayn Rand[198]

If there is anyone who does not know Ann Rand's name, then this person certainly cannot be called an American Pass. Ann Rand's writings have deeply influenced the worldviews of elites in the United States and throughout the Western world since the 1950s.

Ayn Rand is a writer of Soviet Jewish beauty who lived in the Soviet Union in her early years and immigrated to the United States as a young man. She has close and unusual ties to the international banking family in Europe and America. Her *Atlas Shrugged*, published in 1957, had 1,168 pages and a circulation of 80 million copies, making it the second most widely distributed book in the Western world after the

---

[198] Rand, Ayn (1957), *Atlas Shrugged*, 50th Anniversary Edition.

Bible. It has been said that the book "could derail a train if it were put on the tracks". Before publication, an editor at Random House suggested she cut parts, to which Ann Rand replied, "Would you cut the Bible?" As a result the novel was published word for word,[199] and it subsequently triggered a super-spiritual earthquake in the American intellectual class. Over the past half century, the book has received a great deal of critical acclaim and has been very polarizing.

In 1952, at the age of 26, Greenspan, who was already well known for his talent, joined the "Ann Rand Circle"[200] through a friend. The serious and slightly dull Greenspan has just approached glamorous beauty writer Ann Rand and is adoring her to the nth degree. For the next eight-plus years, Greenspan made almost weekly trips to Ann Rand's residence to discuss issues with her. It is somewhat puzzling that the "Ayn Rand circle" is concerned with "high-end" philosophical and ideological issues, while Greenspan is clearly "out of touch" with this circle, as he is an expert in mathematical models and data statistics, and has mentioned that in his youth he did not have much macro thinking habits, lacked interest in theoretical issues, and that the excitement is mainly focused on the practical level of skill or data. What on earth made him so interested in Ann Rand's little salon?

Of course, we all love beauty, but Greenspan didn't seem to go for beauty, but rather the man who introduced Greenspan to Ann Rand eventually became the lover of the beauty writer.

Imagine going to a discussion for a few hours a week for eight years in a row, something that is undoubtedly not easy to do for modern people with busy lives. Even living in the same city as a loved one or parent, the vast majority of people can't make it to a weekly meeting, let alone the busy man Greenspan. Clearly Greenspan was not a novelist, much less a philosopher, or someone interested in macrotheory. He lasted so long that it was evident that Ann Rand's little salon had a super "mental magnetism" that fascinated Greenspan with its extraordinary appeal.

In fact, it was Ayn Rand's ideas and worldview that attracted Greenspan, a major soul challenge he had never encountered before, a

---

[199] Martin, J. (2000) *Greenspan: The Man Behind Money.*

[200] Ibid.

spiritual realm he could never have imagined before, an intellectual sublimation to rediscover the mechanisms of the world economy!

The period from 1952 to 1957 was the climax of Ann Rand's creation of Atlas Shrugged, and it was also the five years when Greenspan's understanding of the world underwent a major transformation. This book not only gave Greenspan a permanent "concussion" but also made Ann Rand a lifelong spiritual mentor to Greenspan.

The Atlas Shrug is the Greek god Hercules, who carried the tilted heavens with one hand and sheltered the multitudes, but the humans who received the benefits did not appreciate him as much as they should have and were disrespectful of Hercules' selfless devotion.[201] At the heart of the book is the fact that only a few elites in the world are the "Hercules" who "carry the sky", the elites who drive the development of human history and are the source of social progress. But these elites have been treated socially unjustly and have not been empowered enough. Since the vast majority of the asylum-seeking ordinary people without minds or souls can strike or put up a fight at any time, what will the world become if the elites strike one day too?

Ann Rand raises the unusually poignant question of historical perspective and worldview: who is the main driving force of history? Throughout thousands of years of long human history, this question has been repeatedly and fiercely debated as to whether it is the masses of people or a few elites that are the main drivers of historical development.[202]

The "eye of the book" is that money is the most central spindle of the various mechanisms that make up the functioning of society, and that the whole socio-political, economic, military, cultural, artistic, historical and other aspects of society actually revolve around money. The idea of this book is to not recognize any morality, but to think that money is the only measure of morality. Those who have money are far more capable of creating wealth than normal people and are bound to become socially powerful. Ann Rand believed that for society to gain

---

[201] Rand, Ayn (1957), *Atlas Shrugged*, 50th Anniversary Edition.

[202] Rubin, Harriet (2007). "Ayn Rands Literature of Capitalism". *The New York Times*.

progress, it must encourage the strong and not sympathize with the weak.

This viewpoint is very much in line with the basic approach and thinking of the rise of the gold powers. In other words, after thousands of years of repression, once the power of gold has become dominant in society and the power of gold has been greatly unleashed, the international bankers who hold the power of gold will rightfully become the masters of the whole world and become the role models and embodiments of morality.

This book is highly regarded among the top echelons of American society because it speaks to their own hearts. The book's bestseller is in large part the result of a concerted push and concerted effort by the world's elite, the ruling elite, to use the book to conduct a thorough moral brainwashing of society at large.

The Atlas Shrug was introduced to China in 2007, but many people don't really understand the spiritual content of the book, treating it more as a philosophy book, or a novel, and readers treat it as a book that represents a rebellious mindset. In fact, the most important thing about the book is that it vividly portrays the spiritual world of the super-elites who rule this world. By reading this book, the reader can touch the living soul of the "Anglo-American power bloc" of amazing energy.

Who is the Hand of God?

> *"There are many people in this world, but in the end, there are only two kinds of people, one who leads and the other who follows. Meaning, not being the protagonist is a dragon set."*
> —Folk tale

At the age of 26, Greenspan was convinced that the laws of the world economy were already in his "Greystoke Model", and that, given the right initial variables, his "Greystoke Model" would be able to calculate the laws of the whole economy, just as Newton had done in the world of classical mechanics.

But the question is, who set the initial variable? This is something that Greenspan hadn't even thought about before. In fact according to Newton, God's hand pushed the world, and the rest is about as far as Newtonian mechanics can handle. But in economic activity, who is God? Whose hand has pushed the economic system and whose palm holds the key to the economic machine? The issue first confronted Greenspan head-on.

After meeting Ann Rand, Greenspan first realized the importance of the "Hand of God". It was Ayn Rand who started Greenspan's "brainstorming" and it was Ayn Rand who gave Greenspan an epiphany of answers.

In his biography, Greenspan emphasizes that he did not realize the importance of human beings in economic activity until he met Ayn Rand, and as his relationship with Ayn Rand grew deeper, it suddenly dawned on him that human beings were in fact the most important object of study in the economic field.[203] Of course, the man Greenspan was referring to was not the old lady selling popsicles at the door, nor the old man playing tai chi on the street; he was referring to the very ruling elite that Ayn Rand had done so much to praise.

It is they who determine the direction in which economic activity operates, it is they who push it, and Greenspan used to just see the state of socio-economic operation after being pushed by them, and correctly describe that state, and that's all. And he had never before paid attention to the setting of initial conditions and who was setting those initial conditions, who was making the economy go in one direction and not the other, who was the initial driving force of the economy, who was the hand of God.

It was this series of thunderous question marks that drew Greenspan down the path of visiting Ann Rand for eight years, starting at the age of 26. That mysterious and powerful magnetic field is not philosophy, nor art, much less fiction. As Greenspan moved closer and closer towards the center of the magnetic field, he wondered how the hand of God would strike.

Ann Rand became Greenspan's guiding light, completely rewriting the trajectory of his life. Greenspan's epiphany lifted him out of mathematical models and data limitations. Greenspan has since gone from strength to strength.

---

[203] Greenspan, Alan (2007). *The Age of Turbulence*. Penguin Press.

Ayn Rand's Pseudo-Proposition

Ann Rand is a staunch critic of all forms of social justice policies and government intervention in the economy, accusing it of being an act of robbing the rich to help the poor. She expresses extreme disdain and firm opposition to these social ideas that emphasize equity, arguing that the amount of money measures a person's ability and that only the strong can create more wealth and be of greater value to society, so they should not be punished. The existing social system is largely about whipping the fast cows, punishing the strong and forcing the strong and wise to support the useless and weak, and in Ann Rand's eyes, this is certainly a sin.

Whether the government plundered the wealth created by the strong with violence and power, or the weak begged the strong to give with weeping and pity, or other social morals and public opinion put pressure on the strong to give, or all kinds of despicable people stole and plundered the money and wealth of the strong, these acts seemed to Ayn Rand to be extremely wrong and absurd.

In China's current society, her ideas may be supported from the heart by a section of people with great wealth and material advantages.

Ayn Rand's idea cannot, by its very nature, be inferred to be an error; it merely embodies a disposition. Who is right and who is wrong depends on which side of the issue the observer and judge is on. As a member of the social elite, one would obviously identify with Ann Rand's judgment and philosophy and would heartily praise this book by Ann Rand. By the same token, the underprivileged, those who do not have access to great material wealth in society and who are poor themselves, are naturally negative and resistant to Ayn Rand, who defines them as incompetent, incompetent and born "parasites" of the general public.

Ann Rand also presents a unique challenge to the concept of parasites. While conventional wisdom holds that capitalists and the bourgeoisie are parasites that exploit the proletariat, Ann Rand makes a series of poignant rhetorical questions in her book, why are elites accused of being parasites when they have created more wealth? The elites bring jobs, why are they considered exploitative? Why is it that the elite, who are the driving force behind all sorts of inventions, are judged by society to be unproductive? Why is it that the elite, who know how to run a social economy and are thus in a key position, are accused by the masses of being too powerful and too well paid? In a word, these people have the money and control the wealth, and that's what they rightfully deserve because they put in the greater effort. The general public, on the other hand, is full of food, useless, vile, low-morality, short-sighted, resentful, incompetent and jealous of the strong. So the conclusion is that the elite few are the driving force of historical development, and the general public is the infallible parasite.

Her words and ideas are indeed intensely stimulating and challenging.

No government would openly support Ayn Rand's views, even in a country as typical of elite dictatorships as the United States. The government, too, can only remain silent in the face of such a naked moral preaching of the sacred supremacy of the Golden Power by Ann Rand. Because the United States also needs to consider the morality of maintaining superficial social harmony. In any society, the extremely intelligent and the extremely capable are, after all, the minority at the top of the pyramid, while the vast majority of people of mediocre ability and average intelligence make up the bulk of society. Any government is aware of the fact that if it stands clearly on the side of the very few and opposes the political posture of the majority, it is bound to cause great shock and unrest in the mindset of society and public opinion. So neither the U.S. government nor the mainstream media can side with Ann Rand's views. And so the controversy grew more and more intense.

A significant number of people in the American intellectual class were opposed to Ann Rand's views. Ann Rand also has a series of diatribes against them, calling these people hypocritical and useless. On this point, Ann Rand's assessment is not entirely wrong, but no society could be in such a state of contrasting, black and white, as she insists. The intellectuals' criticism of the book stems from their discomfort with Ayn Rand's extreme rhetoric, which may have a pretentious and false element, but more from the fact that Ayn Rand's theory of the supremacy of the rich challenged the basic bottom line of human nature, that is, the basic values of what is good and what is bad were thoroughly challenged and subverted, and the intellectuals, who have the world as their business, naturally refused to sit back and watch. The notion that money is moral is also unacceptable to many, and if money is used as the only criterion for judging a person's success, or whether or not a person has any existential value, then there is no doubt that international bankers are the most valuable people in society because they know best how to make money and control the source and flow of money creation, and it is their natural right to rule the world, what about everyone else? Are slaves destined to be born? Such a view is dangerous and threatens the stability of the overall structure of society.

In fact, the debate over whether money represents morality or sin is not the point; the central issue is whether the distribution of money is reasonable and just. Money represents wealth, and wealth represents the common contribution of the elite and the general public. The injustice of this society is, in the final analysis, in the money distribution system. An unreasonable monetary system, which institutionally ensures that the distribution of benefits is biased towards a few elites and constitutes a gross injustice to the general public, is the root of the evil.

Thus, what Ann Rand is proposing is simply a pseudo proposition. There is no need to judge whether money is beautiful or ugly, that is not the essence of the problem, the real essence and core is how money is distributed rationally. Ann Rand evades the crux of the matter with a gigantic essay, which is that it is the unjust distribution of wealth and the unjust division and appropriation of wealth that is the watershed between morality and sin.

In this book, Ann Rand attempts to justify the money view, the morality of the elite minority, and thus the general public's acceptance of the rationality of a society ruled by a minority elite. This book by Ann Rand has been designated as a must-read extracurricular book for elementary and secondary school students in the United States. Whose rules are these? The ruling elite, of course. The ruling elite systematically inculcates this idea into the young generation of the United States by controlling the educational institutions and the American Teachers Association, including the selection of teaching materials, and different schools assign different age groups to different abridged versions and different stages of the Atlas Shrug. 80 million is not a marketable amount, but a report card "promoted" by the elite through a thorough brainwashing of the social population. This is the reason why the book is selling so well, but not the real reason why it is a world famous book.

The mentality that Ann Rand represents as the self-righteous master of the world, the chosen group of God, the inevitable and natural ruler of the world, stirs up the discontent of the majority wherever it is put. Because by human nature, the general public seeks by nature a society of equality and true goodness, and no one wants to be a slave, and Ayn Rand's book openly challenges people's basic values and moral bottom line. She emphasizes and inculcates an unjustified rationality, and more emphatically and repeatedly reiterates the special importance of money and the hypocrisy of social ethics, both in direct conflict with human common sense and intuition.

"If Hercules strikes"

In the book, Ayn Rand tells the story of a massive systemic crisis of "Hercules' collective strike" that the ruling elite orchestrated and perpetuated to gain greater power.[204] In one period of time, all the elite forces of society, such as the chairman of the banking industry, the owner of the railway transport industry, the oil tycoon, the king of the metallurgy industry, and the century-old founding families with vast mining resources, together with the famous politicians, scientists, artists, inventors, etc., the core ruling elite that controlled all the important components and designs of the entire socio-economic machine and ran this huge machine, suddenly disappeared without any signs. They follow a predetermined sequence of steps and timetables to disengage from all key parts of society and hide in the deep mountains to escape. What will happen to the Red and Cloudy World represented by the general public that they have abandoned and punished at this time?

In Ayn Rand's design, when this social elite is withdrawn from the key sectors, they will deliberately adopt a "self-destructive" approach. The protagonist of the copper mine in the novel personally destroys the foundation of his family's business, which has been handed down for hundreds of years, and destroys it so completely that after he destroys it, no one will ever be able to dig another kilogram of copper out of its ruins; when the railroad company withdraws, it scraps the entire railroad, which has taken generations of work; and when the bankers withdraw, it causes the complete paralysis of the financial system of the whole society. The economic system of the United States is falling apart, society is gradually plunging into serious chaos, and the fire of civilization will gradually dim until it is extinguished. As the world plunges into darkness and turmoil, all the common people finally wake up to the fact that they can't leave the elite, and their only option is to

---

[204] Rand, Ayn (1957), *Atlas Shrugged*, 50th Anniversary Edition.

beg the elite to come out of the mountain and save the world again. The elites make conditions that they must monopolize more power, that they must exert the necessary control over society, and that society must function according to their ideas. In a nutshell, the elite must achieve the supreme goal of ultimately monopolizing all social resources.[205]

If one compares the chaotic situation described in this book with today's financial crisis, one finds a high degree of similarity between the two. Is the current deconstruction of economic entities and the collapse of the financial system really spontaneous and inevitable? Is it possible that the elites are on strike? Is it possible that it was designed and engineered by the "Anglo-American power bloc" to gain greater social control and more power over the functioning of the world?

According to Roosevelt, no political event is completely disorderly and random, and there is careful planning behind every political event. Political events are like that, so are economic events, major changes in the financial system, all random? If not, there must have been a major plot and careful planning behind these events.

The elite, with Ayn Rand as their spokesperson, believed themselves to have intelligence and abilities far beyond those of "mortals" and that they had been chosen by God out of "natural selection" and were destined to be a special group. And the "regulars" other than them, the "Gentiles" as the Bible calls them, are supposed to submit to a hopeless predestination to accept and submit to the government of God's chosen people.

In this way, the "Gentiles" can never be the true elect of God. If we accept the indoctrination of such ideas and ideologies, there is no doubt that there is no choice but to obediently be a slave and be governed according to the rules designed by the Anglo-American elite. Deep-rooted differences at the spiritual level cannot be reconciled under the political guise of so-called democratic freedoms. What the elites allow "mortals" to participate is not an equal game, nor is it an equal life, let alone an equal society.

When you finish The Atlas Shrug, you will have a deeper understanding of the social reality of absolute objective rationality, but at the same time, of desperate regret, and a deeper appreciation of why

---

[205] Ibid.

these people think they are the rulers, why they think the way they do, and why they do. When you lift the curtain of this understanding, all the wars, coups d'état, social upheavals that are happening in the world today will reveal a different picture before your eyes.

Do we need to see the world "with a different eye" and find the truth behind the curtain? Do we still accept without question the message conveyed by the Western mainstream media?

And in whose hands is the international media? It's also an international banker. If these people have transplanted the intelligence battle between the KGB and the CIA into the media, how much of what we see as "real information" is a gross distortion of the facts and how much is a magician's prop?

The question of how one can see the truth and understand, with what attitude, the true state of affairs in which the world operates today is an important one that every member of a real society with the ability to think independently must face and think seriously.

Gold: the ideal currency for the elite

In Ayn Rand's story, when the elite quietly "strike" from every important position in society, they all take refuge together in the Colorado Mountains as they prepare to rebuild a paradise country.[206] What is most interesting in this worldly paradise is that the currency they use is not American money, nor any form of paper money, but actual gold money. In fact, whether it is Greenspan's exposition of gold in Gold and Economic Freedom, written in 1966,[207] the Rothschild family's nearly century-long control of gold pricing power, or the underhanded manipulation of gold by the world's heavyweight central banks and superbanks, there is no denying the special interest of international bankers in gold.

The supremacy of gold in the heart and true spiritual world of international bankers explains why these people hold onto it firmly

---

[206] Ibid.

[207] Greenspan, Alan (July 1966). "Gold and Economic Freedom". *The Objectivist*.

while brainwashing others into thinking it is not important. The book twists and turns and subtly gives a clear answer.

In Atlas Shrugs, Francisco is the soul of the entire story, and in explaining what money is and what wealth is, he repeatedly presents an important criterion, which is that money must be based on a standard value, and that this value must have real meaning in order to be an objective measure of the value of economic activity. An objective price scale requires that its benchmark be a commodity, say a unit quantity of gold. Gold is a store of wealth and value and accurately reflects the recognition of the value embodied in different goods and services.

In Francisco's phrase, the value standard role of money is being eroded by inflation. Francisco believed that the devaluation of the currency was mainly achieved through the substitution of paper money for gold, which he believed was an important and essential cause of the moral decline of society.[208] Thus, in the eyes of the world's ruling elite and international bankers, gold is an honest currency that represents an objective, just and fraudulent act of exchange, the solemn and unspoiled promise of transactions between the various members of a society, and it represents that the wealth you have today can be exchanged for goods and services equal to today's in tomorrow, in the next year, in the distant future.

Gold acts as a fair and objective social contract that integrates all parties involved in the transaction, closely and equally, without deception or falsification, and Francisco believes that gold acts as a fair and rational yardstick and store of wealth in the middle of the entire monetary system. And a rational monetary system is in fact, in turn, a system for distributing wealth in society, and whether it is just and reasonable or not determines how high or low the moral and ethical level of society as a whole is. A reasonable monetary system would give social justice and equal treatment to those who work hard, strive to create wealth, and are good at saving and accumulating. Those who are skulking and speculating are curbed and restricted under such a rational monetary system, which is therefore an important cornerstone of social ethics.

Since the monetary system determines the way wealth is distributed, it also ultimately determines the bottom line of social

---

[208] Rand, Ayn (1957), *Atlas Shrugged*, 50th Anniversary Edition.

morality and ethics, and while a rational monetary system stimulates wealth creation and discourages speculation, an unreasonable monetary system conversely encourages speculation and discourages real wealth creation. Under an unreasonable monetary system, the bottom line of social morality will eventually disintegrate, the entire ethical system will collapse, and social civilization will inevitably go into obscurity and extinction. From the perspective of Francisco, a representative of international bankers, an irrational monetary system is a means and a conspiracy to scavenge wealth.

Greenspan's 1966 essay "On Economic Freedom" is a thorough and clear articulation of ideas that are fully consistent with Francisco's views and theoretical connotations. Francisco's distaste for devaluing money and inflation is equally visceral and profoundly expressed in Greenspan's essay. It is clear that this group is collectively opposed to the so-called loose monetary policy and the so-called legal tender system, and is convinced that neither the United States Government nor the Federal Reserve, among others, should interfere in the functioning of the economy. They are staunch advocates of a thoroughly laissez-faire capitalist economy.

This leaves us with no room for doubt. Greenspan was 40 years old when he published this article in 1966, and his personal views, values and worldview had long since been set. But when he took the chair of the Federal Reserve, he let loose on the flood of the dollar, which led to a prolonged period of easy monetary policy in the United States, which eventually led to the financial tsunami that is sweeping the world today. What exactly was Greenspan thinking? What he actually did was very different and even incompatible with his own beliefs.

The fact that Greenspan's words and actions in policymaking and implementing monetary policy are in such stark contrast to his consistent beliefs and insistence gives us all the more reason to put an additional question mark on the financial crisis that is currently unfolding. Couldn't Greenspan really see that the economic crisis was coming? With Greenspan's ability, his level of competence, his mathematical modeling, his precise grasp of data and his high sensitivity to macroeconomic measurement, he was able to predict the economic crisis of 1958 six months in advance in 1957, when he was consulting for U.S. steel companies, and accurately predicted that the economic crisis was imminent, while in 2002 he implemented monetary easing, injected large amounts of money into the economic system and raised fish, but turned a blind eye to the continued expansion of the housing bubble. Does he really not see the storm coming that will eventually lead to a financial catastrophe?

Greenspan spoke until early 2007 that the subprime mortgage crisis would not be much of a problem.[209] If his level of judgmental decision-making were true, he would not be called Greenspan.

Is there a possibility that Greenspan is consciously destroying the value of the dollar, destroying the credit of the dollar, destroying the basis of its existence? Note that the collapse of the dollar in no way means a collapse of the United States; on the contrary, after getting rid of all dollar debt, the United States has been able to mount a light attack. The United States, based on its strong military power, scientific and technological innovation capabilities and abundant resources, has completely freed itself from debt entanglements and changed the rules of the world currency game through "bankruptcy protection". In the end, the United States will take out the bottom of its 8100 tons of gold reserves and 3400 tons of IMF gold, at this time, in order to "save the currency credit", the United States has to link the "new currency" and gold, in order to win the world's credit. Of course, the countries of the world that lack gold reserves will be the biggest losers. At that point, the dollar would lose a "chain of debt" and gain a whole new world of gold.

Are we going to have a repeat of the 1923 German hyperinflation? If it will, then the very few who start shorting the dollar on a large scale are a dangerous flare.

The distorted dollar and the "debt lagoon"

> *"The dollar does not solve the problem, the dollar itself is the problem."*
>
> —Wise Men of the People

If we think of a country as a corporation, then the country also has a balance sheet of its own. Under the assets of this balance sheet is the wealth of a country, that is, the goods and services created through labour, and under the liabilities are the "receipts", that is, money, of the

---

[209] Greenspan's Bubbles: The Age of Ignorance at the Federal Reserve.

fruits of these labour. Money is not wealth per se, but merely a "right of claim" to wealth and a "right of distribution" to wealth.

If the real economic part of a society is mainly "making the cake", then the central role of the monetary system is to "cut the cake". The monetary system determines the value orientation of a society's distribution of wealth and thus forms the basis of a system of rewards and penalties for wealth creators and owners. A rational monetary system works by "rewarding hard work and punishing laziness", which is systematically protected and systematically rewarded by efforts to create wealth and honestly save the fruits of labour, thus encouraging people to create more wealth and enjoy a fair distribution of the fruits. On the contrary, an unreasonable social system will inevitably have the effect of "rewarding laziness and punishing attendance", which will viciously stimulate wealth speculation and gambling, seriously distort the mechanism of social wealth distribution, severely punish honest wealth creators, and cruelly exploit wealth savers who have shared their share. Why do people need to work hard if they can make a fortune by speculating in stocks? Who would go to the hard and tedious work of the real economy if everyone was taking it easy and making huge profits in the financial markets? With the growing trend of conceit and hard work, and the declining spirit of thrift, thrift and hard work, the enthusiasm of the whole society for wealth creation will be seriously eroded, and eventually, the country and even civilization will decline. The famous monetarist Franz Pick famously said, "The fate of money will eventually become the fate of the nation as well."

The monetary system is the moral and ethical cornerstone of a society and even a civilization. From this point of view, Greenspan and others have long had a thorough insight into what an honest monetary system really means for human civilization. This is the fundamental reason why they are bound to eventually abandon the existing economically indebted and morally flawed dollar system.

The financial crisis that has swept the globe is not the result of a series of fortuitous and coincidental events, but rather a long-awaited total liquidation of the serious structural imbalances in the economy on a global scale. The most important factor that has contributed to such a severely distorted economic structure, rare in world history, has been the excessive issuance of the dollar since the collapse of the Bretton Woods system in 1971. The crisis has finally erupted, after more than three decades of slow deterioration and the inevitable near-unsustainability of the dollar, which has been amplified year by year and has gradually brought together potentially dangerous elements in the world economy.

The essence of the crisis is a major crisis of the dollar system, unlike the previous recessions since the 1930s, and no matter how this crisis ends, the world will never return to its previous pattern. From the world economic development model to the division of labour in international trade, from the global monetary mechanism to the reconstruction of financial markets, from the balance of power in international relations to the geopolitical map, from the new energy revolution to the dawn of the green era, the impact of this financial crisis on the existing world pattern will be no less than a world-class war.

In 1971, the United States unilaterally abolished the Bretton Woods system. Henceforth, the issuance of the dollar is neither subject to the rigid constraints of gold nor the soft oversight of international institutions. The United States has embarked on a path of indulgence in the issuance of the dollar, using its privileged position as the world's reserve and settlement currency to reap the staggering benefits of a mint tax on the world.

Beginning in 1959, dollar issuance consistently outpaced the growth of the real economy in the United States GDP, and this over-issuance of dollars entered a new phase of rapid climbing after 1997,[210] the gap between the two lines reflecting, to some extent, the "mint tax" that the United States has been imposing on the world for decades through the excessive issuance of dollars. In particular, the United States unilaterally abolished the Bretton Woods system in 1971, which was a major international default on the US dollar's US currency stock and real GDP. The Bretton Woods system is a legally binding international convention jointly signed by the major countries of the world, and the United States Government abruptly and unilaterally abolished the peg of the dollar to gold without consultation, amounting to a serious default on the dollar. Since the dollar has a history of such a default "history", it is not inconceivable that there will be another sudden default and bad debt in the future.

If it is said that absolute power necessarily leads to absolute corruption, this statement applies equally to the dollar. While the

---

[210] Batra, R X (2005), *Greenspan's Fraud: How Two Decades of His Policies Have Undermined the Global Economy*.

privilege of the dollar has brought great benefits to the United States, it has also brought increasingly serious side effects.

On the one hand, the printing of dollars to enjoy the fruits of other people's work, the pleasure of gaining something for nothing is like an addiction to drugs, which has gradually dismantled the Puritan spirit and the social moral and ethical system of thrift and hard work that the United States has been upholding since the founding of the country; it goes against the spirit of the "American dream" of working hard to create wealth; it breeds and indulges the whole society's vicious notions of encouraging speculation, worshipping luxury, indulging in consumption, eating everything that comes in handy and expanding oneself; it corrodes the enthusiasm of the new generation of society to create real wealth, and it increasingly empties the social wealth that the United States has accumulated for 200 years.

On the other hand, in the process of exporting dollar bills for world commodities, it is bound to accumulate large deficits and debts, the increasing scale of debt and the cost of interest payments, fundamentally weakening the national strength of the United States, in order to make up for the deficit can only increase the scale of printing money, thus leading to the growing imbalance in the distribution of social wealth, the middle class debt pressure increases year by year, while the income level is far behind, the financial situation of households is increasingly fragile, and the payment crisis has just taken shape.

It is the chronic over-issuance of the dollar that has led to the severe distortion of the global economic structure. The extreme imbalance between over-indebtedness and consumption in the United States and over-production and savings in emerging countries would have been impossible to maintain without the unjustified system of the dollar. No other country in the history of mankind has been able to remain in a trade and fiscal deficit for more than 30 years, as the United States has, and to keep its national economy under heavy debt pressure without systemic collapse, for the very reason that, after the dollar was divorced from gold, the United States did not actually have to make any effort to pay its debts and could have reduced them substantially by simply firing up its money printing machines, while spreading the consequences of inflation evenly over the world. The absurdity, depravity and injustice of such a monetary system are unprecedented in the history of the world.

Even so, the dollar system cannot be sustained forever.

As of 2008, the total size of the national debt, local government debt, corporate debt, financial debt, private debt of the United States has reached 57 trillion dollars, and in recent years has been rising at an annual rate of 7% to 8%, increasing in a profitable manner, while the annual sustainable GDP and national income of the United States increased at a rate of only about 3%. Because the cost of debt has always grown above the average national income growth rate of 3 percent, starting in 1980, the total U.S. debt (not just the national debt) as a share of GDP has climbed for nearly 30 years, soaring from 163 percent to the current 370 percent. The size of the increase in total U.S. debt becomes more and more staggering the further into the future it goes because of the profit-taking effect. At present, the total debt of the United States has created a dangerous "debt lagoon".

The total debt of the United States has increased by an average of 6 per cent per annum since the United States dollar left gold in 1971, and has risen by 7 to 8 per cent since 2000. If we calculate at a conservative 6% growth rate, then in 41 years, the total debt of the United States will be a staggering $621.5 trillion! While the national income of the United States from its current size of $11 trillion, at a long-term sustainable growth rate of 3 per cent, will be only $37 trillion after 41 years, the debt of $621.5 trillion will be as large as $37.3 trillion in interest payments if calculated at an average interest cost of 6 per cent.

In other words, 2051 will be a pivotal year in which the total interest payments on the entire debt of the United States will exceed the total national income of the United States, meaning that the United States will be economically bankrupt for good!

These debts do not include the hidden liabilities of the Medicare and Social Security funds, which currently exceed $10 trillion.

American society is already operating under high leverage. The entire national economy will eventually be unable to withstand such heavy debt servicing pressures, leading to a final collapse.

Thus, it is not a question of whether the dollar crisis will or will not erupt, but only of when. The greater likelihood is that the collapse will have occurred before the big dollar limit arrives in 2051. Perhaps the financial tsunami of 2008 kicked off the disintegration of the dollar.

The Future of the World Economy: 14 Years of the "Great Depression"

What we need to focus on is no longer what happened in the financial tsunami, but what will happen in the world after it.

Looking at the current economic fundamentals, the panic over the financial crisis seems to have subsided for the time being, and the light of hope for economic recovery seems to be on the horizon, as the world's stock markets have seen an unexpected rally since 2009, is this the beginning of a new bull market or a terrible bear market rebound? Is the world economy really about to recover?

The plunge in the US stock market in 1929 merely kicked off the Great Depression, and a very similar bear market rally in the US stock market in 1930 sparked an equally strong sense of hope. But what followed was a much larger financial meltdown in 1931 that completely undermined confidence in the financial markets and triggered a 10-year-long Depression.

Greenspan, who had described the financial tsunami as a once-in-a-century event, naturally did not deserve a fundamental shift in thinking after the outbreak of the crisis, from a "leap of faith" that completely ignored the enormous risks of the financial crisis to a stern statement that the crisis would be even worse than in 1929.

In fact, there should be many people who already see a very bleak economic future for the world, and the economic depression of the 1930s is actually not that far from today's world. It has always been taken for granted that the world of today has changed in an indescribable nature from its past, that mankind seems to have ascended a plateau of permanent prosperity, that all decline is short-lived, and that every recovery is rapid. Central bankers seem to have found the panacea for the Great Depression, monetary policy can create wealth out of thin air and stop the spread of all crises, and governments are convinced that fiscal policy can turn the tide and achieve permanent prosperity at will. If there are indeed inherent laws in the economy, then the role of human beings must go with the flow, recognize the laws and navigate the ups and downs, which is important for investors.

After the thrilling rapids, the people rejoiced and came to a wide lake where everything seemed to have calmed down. At this point, only those who were standing on high ground suddenly realized that just downstream, not far in front of the lake, was a chillingly large waterfall.

This is the beginning of the "Great Depression Era" for the 77 million "baby boomers" in the United States.

The "Baby Boomer" generation in the United States refers to the "4664" phenomenon in the United States after the Second World War: from 1946 to 1964, 77 million people were born in the United States during that 18-year period, representing a quarter of the United States population, and this group is the backbone of American society today. With the growth of the baby boomers, the U.S. economy entered a period of dazzling prosperity; in the 1960s and 1970s, the U.S. baby boomers drove the growth of toys, cartoons, and popular music; in the 1970s and 1980s, the baby boomers who were active in marriage drove the growth of real estate and the automobile industry; in the 1980s and 1990s, the baby boomers who were in the golden age of consumption drove the growth of personal computers and the Internet. During this period, the "baby boomer" population created the largest stock market gains in history, home price increases, and demand for international aviation, personal computers, computer networks, and sports and leisure tools.

The final inflection point in the peak time period for the birth of the "baby boomer" generation was 1962, a demographic curve that has been adjusted for the immigrant population, considering that the United States is a large immigrant nation. Note: Remember this figure for 1962.

According to the U.S. Department of Labor, Americans peak spending in their lifetime at age 47, when they are in their prime, in their prime years and in their prime income. After the age of 47, people begin to think about retirement and old age, and their bodies are getting older, and they have to prepare for medical appointments and medicine, from this point on, people's expectations of future income decline, consumption begins to gradually slide, and life becomes increasingly frugal. As we get older, various desires start going downhill in sync.

The "baby boomers" in the United States have never been in the habit of saving, and the first half of their lives were just in time for the United States to become a hegemonic empire that dominates the world, and there is a general feeling of super-optimism about the future in their mindset. They don't have the grizzled memories of the Great Depression of their fathers, or the brutal baptism of World War II where you die and I live, everything is so smooth and everything is so brilliant.

After 47 years of extravagant living, children born at the turning point of the "baby boom" decline in 1962 came to the turning point of the American nation's fortunes, 2009. The world suddenly became bleak, economic prosperity abruptly disappeared, financial tsunamis were rattled and a wave of unemployment swept in. At this time, they suddenly found that they had lost nearly half of their pension invested in the stock market, while the bank account deposits were never "as thin as cicada wings" due to their year-round big hands and feet, at the same time, indulgent lifestyle habits and reckless spending ahead of schedule, making them long in debt. In such a scenario, their consumption will plummet off the normal aging consumption curve and must tighten the belt of their pants faster and harder to cope with the brutal economic cold spell ahead.

2009 will be a turning year for the world economy, and we can see in the chart that the Dow Jones stock index is surprisingly highly consistent with the population's consumer age curve. The logic is obvious, the stock market reflects the performance expectations of listed companies, and a company's performance depends on product sales, which naturally come from people's consumption, which pulls 72% of GDP in the US.

Historically, from 1966 to 1982, the U.S. stock market experienced a nearly 16-year stock market bear market (inflation-adjusted), a bear market cycle that coincided perfectly with the last wave of the population aging cycle curve. After the 1980s, the "baby boom" in the early 1960s, the peak of the population graduating from college and entering the labor market, this large group of young people vigorous, risk-taking, entrepreneurial, daring to spend, stimulated the U.S. economy, greatly boosted consumption, creating an unprecedented era of economic prosperity, the stock market followed by a bull market for nearly 20 years.

And 2009 is exactly in the population consumption curve represented by the cliff edge, one step forward is the "consumption waterfall" of the inflection point. As the last "baby boomers" born in 1962 slip past the peak age of 47 in 2009, a dramatic downward spiral of consumption will follow, lasting until 2024. It's going to be a 14-year-long cycle of consumer decline, and with a high level of debt, the U.S. consumer market will be in a long ice age comparable to the 1930s!

Note that neither monetary nor fiscal policies will have a noticeable effect on an aging generation, after all, they will not return people to childhood. It is not very realistic to encourage older people to borrow boldly to spend, and the year-on-year contraction in consumption will deprive the "green shoots" of the current seemingly bright economic recovery of fertile soil for credit. After all, consumption drives 72% of U.S. economic growth!

Japan reached the peak of population consumption in 1994, followed by more than a decade of economic depression, the Japanese government lowered interest rates all the way to zero, the total national debt caused by fiscal stimulus amounted to 160% of Japan's GDP, and the Japanese economy still cannot start. This is closely related to the inability of the government to force the elderly to borrow heavily for consumption that only the young are interested in.

More seriously, Europe's demographic cycle coincides with that of the U.S., and both economic sectors in Europe and the U.S. will simultaneously fall into a long-term consumption ice age. This will be a major change in the economic ecology for all emerging countries with serious overcapacity in the European and American markets as their main export targets. Countries that cannot adapt to this catastrophic level of change will be eliminated from the scene and the road ahead will be extremely difficult.

As a fundamental law of the economy, the elites who rule the world have long seen it coming, and all they have to do is to use it to achieve their major strategic objectives, for which they have been waiting for a long time. Again, readers are reminded that 2024 will be a crucial year for the world. This is the year that the international banker's century-old dream will likely become a reality!

CHAPTER X

Back to the Future

Back to the Future is an American science fiction blockbuster that depicts a high school student, Martin, in an unexpected escape from life, traveling from 1985 to 1955 in a time warp machine designed by Dr. Brown, which unfolds a series of thrilling and bizarre stories.

In this chapter, we will also take a time warp ride from 2009 to 2024, 14 years later, when the world will have a world central bank and a world unified currency.

The sense of national sovereignty and nationalism has always been the mortal enemy of the idea of world government, and the whole point of a unified world currency lies in the abolition of sovereign currencies. The question of the right to issue currency is not a purely theoretical one at all, but a question of real interests. If currency is not a power, then I can't imagine it has anything to talk about at all.

If the trend towards a unified world currency is irreversible, the question is who will dominate it. Currency implies the right to distribute the wealth of society, which is the most central interest of any State's power, and the introduction of a world currency inevitably requires sovereign States to surrender their right to distribute wealth.

In a game of interest for a world powerhouse where China is not yet in a dominant position, joining a game of currency control dominated by others will be a matter of China's national fortunes for the next 50 years, with the wealth of 1.3 billion Chinese people at stake – the most important but most insignificant of all Chinese strategic decisions.

Dominate or be dominated, that's the question!

On January 1, 2024, the world single currency is launched

> *"Control of money is a great struggle, and control of its issuance and distribution is about controlling wealth, resources and humanity as a whole."*[211]
> —Jack Weatherford, famous American anthropologist and historian of money.

On New Year's Day, 2024, the official launch of the world's single currency by the World Central Bank in Basel, Switzerland, was carpet-bombed 24 hours a day on the Internet, on television, in newspapers and magazines around the world through rolling news reports by the world's major news agencies. A New Year's Day editorial in the British *Financial Times*, entitled "The world enters perpetual prosperity", enthusiastically praised:

> *"The people of the world have finally learned the benefits of the world's single currency, and at their behest, governments have abandoned sovereign currencies that have been in place for centuries. This is a great moment in human history, and it signifies a new phase of permanent prosperity for human society."*

For its part, the British magazine *The Economist* commented with authority and professionalism:

> *"With the use of the world's single currency, markets will no longer need cumbersome currency exchanges or expensive hedging to cope with exchange rate fluctuations. Currency speculation, the risk of currency failure, and imbalance problems would all disappear. This exchange of currency for real value will be more effective when political winds are not taken into account."*

The *Wall Street Journal* represents America's attitude of "taking the good as it comes":

> *"America cannot stand in the way of the inevitable trends of history. Indeed, abandoning the dollar and supporting the world's single currency would not exclude the legitimate interests of the United States, but rather highlight its dominant role and power of engagement. It is particularly important that the United States' own best interests lie precisely in the removal*

---

[211] Weatherford, Jack, *The History of Money* (Crown Publishers, 1997).

> *of monetary privilege and the return to fair competition, which is the only way to fundamentally break the spell of the dollar's sinking destiny, as pointed out by Trayvon's paradox, and that the United States will be in a unique position to revive the real economy's strong power in the global marketplace, continue to maintain its position as a central power in the world political and economic order, and play its historic role of leading the world's progressive tide."*

China's Sina.com published a chorus of applause from mainstream economists:

> *"Thanks to the joint efforts of all the countries of the world, we have finally ushered in a new spring of globalization. China would be one of the biggest beneficiaries of a more just world financial order. Although our foreign exchange reserves have suffered a certain amount of losses and uncertainty as a result of the withdrawal of the dollar from circulation, in the long run, this is the price that China must pay for its smooth integration into the mainstream international society. In the long run, China is still the winner of globalization."*

In stark contrast to the supportive, lopsided attitude of the international media, the worst anti-globalization demonstrations in the 21st century have erupted in the United States. Unemployment in the United States has reached a high of 15 per cent under the weight of a prolonged recession, and discontent with the Government has reached a breaking point with the large number of Americans who have lost all their property and pension health benefits. Large mass demonstrations by millions of people in New York and Philadelphia, United States of America, to protest the end of the circulation of the United States dollar, with people dressed in a variety of dollar-style costumes and gathered around the Liberty Bell, the symbol of the American Revolution, hundreds of thousands of people chanting "The Star-Spangled Banner will never fall", the leaders of the demonstrations reciting the Declaration of Independence and the United States Constitution, and their determination to defend the dollar to the death against the dictates of the World Central Bank, which was above the United States Congress. On the Great Lawn of the Washington Monument, half a million demonstrators from the east angrily chanted slogans such as "The White House has betrayed America" and large slogans such as "Stop the betrayal", "Hang the traitor", "To hell with the world's currency" and "Defend the Constitution" covered the entire Pennsylvania Avenue and 7th to 14th blocks. As the battle between legislators on Capitol Hill intensified, police and protesters in front of the Lincoln Memorial clashed bloodily, traffic on the 495 Beltway came to a complete standstill, and the eight-lane road became a base camp for the demonstrators to sleep rough. Bomb threats were made against the buildings of the World Bank and the International Monetary Fund, right-wing organizations such as the American Association of Gun Owners were secretly conspiring to launch an "armed uprising" to overthrow the traitorous Government, and there was a treacherous situation within the Pentagon, where some military generals in the military who were firmly loyal to the interests of the United States of America met in secret to plot a coup d'état. (Richard Kubo, source: Harvard University official website)

Paris, France, was plunged into a state of anarchy, with banks smashed, shops looted, cars burned, public transport cut off and mass strikes leading to a declaration of military control. Protests in London have gradually turned into riots, the Financial City of England is almost dead, major financial institutions have announced all employees without pay leave, the army into the city to maintain order. Cities such as Berlin, Frankfurt, Rome, Vienna, Moscow, Tokyo and Seoul were also hit to varying degrees.

The internationalists have clearly underestimated the determination and strength of the nationalist resistance. The rise of the Internet has broken the monopoly of mainstream media channels of information, and more and more of the general public is beginning to realize that the loss of the state's right to issue currency means total enslavement. In a democracy, general elections are one of the effective means for the general public to exert influence over political leaders, and at the national level, the right to issue sovereign currency remains relevant to voters. But if the sovereign currency is abolished, the world's central bank becomes a super financial monster over all democratically elected governments, independent of government, unmonitored, unelected and without any democratic process that can effectively constrain it.

The issuance of the world's single currency will be the historic moment in human history when gold power reaches the pinnacle of its power. This moment did not come about by "chance" or "randomly". It even has a precise schedule. An organization called the World Single Currency Association plans to,

> "*Program schedule through 2024. In line with the realist strategy, the progress of this plan will ensure that the goal of a single world currency is achieved by 2024. When Professor Richard Cooper proposed a monetary union in industrialized countries in 1984, he devised a 25-year timetable for advancing it, and that timetable took us to 2009.*"[212]

- New member of the euro area in 2009: Slovakia

- 2009 Five West African Monetary Area countries: Ghana, Nigeria, Sierra Leone, Gambia, Guinea, using common currency: ECO

- 2010 Gulf Cooperation Council (GCC) countries plan to launch a new common currency, including: Baring, Kuwait, Oman, Qatar, Saudi Arabia, UAE

- 2011 50th anniversary of the publication of Mondale's paper "The Theory of the Optimal Monetary Zone" in American Economic Journal

- New members of the euro area in 2012: accession by Estonia

- 2012 Five East African countries implement a common currency: Burundi, Kenya, Uganda, Tanzania, Rwanda

- 2012 International Conference on the Preparation of the Global Monetary Union

- 2013 New members of the euro area: Latvia, Lithuania, Bulgaria

- New members of the euro area in 2013: Czech Republic, accession by Poland

- New members of the euro area in 2014: accession by Hungary

- New members of the euro area for 2015: Romania

- 2016 South African Monetary Union of 14 (SADC): Angola, Botswana, Congo, Lesotho, Madagascar, Malawi, Mauritius, Mozambique, Namibia, South Africa, Swaziland, Tanzania, Zambia and Zimbabwe

---

[212] Cooper, Richard N., "Is there a Need for Reform." (Speech at a Federal Reserve Bank of Boston conference, May 1984).

- 2017 Selection of a global currency name worldwide (the euro was named in 1995 and implemented four years later)
- 2018 Economists predict world single currency implementation, at least in most industrialized countries 1988 Economists predict world single currency implementation 30 years later
- 1 June 2020: World Central Bank established, partially or fully modelled on the International Monetary Fund or World Bank
- January 1, 2021: New world single currency ready for electronic transactions
- 2021 The African Union, established in 2001, sets the goal of establishing a pan-African monetary union
- 1 January 2024: worldwide transactions are processed through the new world single currency; 1 May: thereafter, all old currencies will no longer be used for transactions and can be converted into the new world single currency at designated banks in member countries, currency risk ends and asset values continue to appreciate.

The single currency: the end of history

We look forward to promoting world monetary policy at a time of crisis like this. The current financial crisis is the only possible time, because you can only do things like this to build a new system when there is a crisis.[213]
    - 13 November 2008, "Father of the Euro" Mondale

The global economy needs a global currency.[214]
    —Paul Volcker, former Chairman of the Federal Reserve

---

[213] Mondale: The promotion of a world currency can only come at a time of crisis (CBN, 13 November 2008).

[214] Bonpasse, Morrison, *The Single Global Currency* (Single Global Currency Association, 2006).

> *Control of money and credit can strike at the heart of national sovereignty.*[215]
> — Alden W. Clausen, President of the Bank of America and President of the World Bank

> *Once a country's currency and credit are partially controlled, it doesn't matter who is making that country's laws.*[216]
> —W L Mackenzie King, former Prime Minister of Canada

There are always smart people in this world who read the money game, and Kiyosaki, author of Poor Dad, Rich Dad, is one of them. Shortly after the onset of the financial tsunami in September 2008, he mentioned in a November 24, 2008 article,

> "In 1910, seven men, estimated to own 1/6 of the world's wealth, held a secret meeting on Jekyll Island off the Georgia coast. Six of them are Americans, and they represent JPMorgan, Rockefeller and the U.S. government. The other came from Europe and represented Rothschild and Warburg, and the establishment of the Federal Reserve in 1913 was a direct result of this secret meeting. Interestingly, the Federal Reserve Bank of the United States is neither federal nor a reserve nor a bank ... they control the banking system and money supply in the United States. The Bretton Woods system in 1944 led to the creation of the World Monetary Fund and the World Bank, which were created to control the world's banking system and money supply, just as the Federal Reserve did for the United States. In 1971, President Nixon announced the abandonment of the dollar peg to gold, which meant that the first step in controlling the world's financial system was complete. In 2008, the world economy was in crisis and the rich would eventually get richer, but most of the poor would get poorer. Much of this crisis stems directly from these secret meetings decades ago. In other words, a large part of the financial tsunami was orchestrated."[217]

---

[215] Clausen, A. W., in a 1979 interview with the Freeman Digest, "International Banking".

[216] Mackenzie King, William Lyon, in a radio address, August 2, 1935, Quote printed in Walter Stewart's book, *Bank Heist* (Harper Collins, 1997).

[217] Kiyosaki, Robert, *How the Financial Crisis Was Built Into the System* (Yahoo Finance, November 24, 2008).

Does the world need a global central bank? If a single world monetary system is to be achieved, it will require a monetary policy of unprecedented scale to arm the international financial system. In essence, a single global currency would allow banks to have power over nations, races and languages. Former Canadian MP Paul Hellyer commented on the world's single currency in 1994: "In such a global monetary/banking system, the interests of citizens, individual states, would be subordinated only to the interests of the international financial system ... states would no longer be able to make any independent policies."[218] The most powerful financial system above sovereign States will be operated by world power groups that are not accountable to anyone.

It is not a one-day project; it has to be conceived, accumulated, planned and theoretically researched over a long period of time, and wait for the right time to launch it. Of these, timing is the most critical, and launching too early and too late can be equally harmful. The theoretical exploration of the world's single currency reached a fairly advanced stage as early as the 1960s. Among them, some important statements about the world's single currency have clear relevance.

1969:

> "Let me move from nitpicking objections to some more active discussions, and start with the best and worst international monetary systems. The best monetary system, in my judgment, is a world single currency with world financial authority."[219]
> —Charles P. Kindleberger, professor of economics, Massachusetts Institute of Technology, speaker at the Boston meeting of the Federal Reserve

1984:

> "I have proposed a radical option for the next century: a single currency for all industrial democracies based on a common monetary policy, with a joint money-issuing bank to determine monetary policy... This proposal is indeed too radical in the

---

[218] Hellyer, Paul, *Funny Money* (Chimo Media, 1994).

[219] Kindleberger, Charles P., speaking at a Federal Reserve conference.

> *short term, but could provide a vision or goal to guide the next steps...*"[220]
> —Richard N. Cooper, Professor, Harvard University, United States of America, speaker, Federal Reserve Boston Conference

1998:

> *"For the world as a whole, the speed of the transition to a single world currency may surprise many, the world may have evolved from over 200 currencies today to just one in 10 years (2008), and 25 years from today (2023), historians will wonder why it took so long to purge a currency that has existed for 20 centuries."*[221]
> —Bryan Taylor, Chief Economist, Global Financial Data, Inc.

(This is a pretty good level for a public figure to say such things more than 10 years ago. (Rather than being a prophet, it would be more accurate to say that he was a planner.)

2001:

> *"When VISA was founded 25 years ago, its founders saw the world as a system that required a single currency for exchange, and everything we do is based on a global vision and an effort to achieve our global vision step by step."*[222]
> —Sarah Perry, Head of Strategic Investment Planning, VISA

2004:

> *"If the global market economy is to flourish in the coming decades, the emergence of a global currency seems logical."*[223]
> —Martin Wolf, Chief Economic Commentator, Financial Times, Senior Economist, World Bank Annual Meeting

On 5 January 2007, Ben Steyer, Director of the International Economics Department of the Foreign Relations Association of the United States, published an article in the Financial Times of the United

---

[220] Cooper, Richard N., "Is there a Need for Reform." (Speech at a Federal Reserve Bank of Boston conference, May 1984).

[221] Bonpasse, Morrison, *The Single Global Currency* (Single Global Currency Association, 2006).

[222] Ibid. p. 7.

[223] Wolf, Martin, writing for the *Financial Times*, August 3, 2004.

Kingdom entitled "Digital gold and the shortcomings of the monetary system", which compared the advantages and disadvantages of floating and fixed exchange rates and repeatedly stressed that the monetary system of today's world is the weakest link in the process of globalization and that the solution is the remonetization of gold, using electronic gold as a means of payment under modern technological conditions. He concludes,

> "(A monetary system for digital gold) may sound radical and unattainable, but electronizing a gold currency that humans have experienced for 2,500 years of practice may ultimately prove that this monetary system is more sustainable than a sovereign currency with only a brief 35-year trial period."[224]

On 9 May 2007, Diplomacy magazine, the mouthpiece of the American Foreign Relations Association, published another article by Ben Steyer, entitled "The End of National Sovereign Currency". In his article, Stahl states, "In order to globalize safely, countries should abandon monetary statism and abolish unnecessary currencies, which are the source of much of today's unrest." In Steyr's view, the root cause of the financial turmoil in the world today is the interference of "sovereign currencies". He said: "Why has the problem of a series of currency crises in recent decades become so serious? Beginning in 1971, President Nixon officially decoupled the dollar from gold, so that the currency that moved around the world was no longer a claim to anything physical. The world's currencies are now purely sovereign appearances that governments magically conjure up... The myth of linking currencies to sovereignty is costly and sometimes dangerous. Monetary statism is incompatible with globalization." It is certain that Mr. Steyer is about to introduce the concept of a "single world currency", so the sovereign currency must be deposed. Mr. Steyer further stated,

> "Over the past few decades, the dollar has become the undisputed global currency, with countries around the world holding dollars to trade in various markets, especially oil. The privileged status of the dollar today is not divinely given, the dollar was also initially backed by another currency of integrity (gold) and others are willing to accept the dollar because they

---

[224] Steil, Benn, Digital gold and a flawed global order (*Financial Times*, January 5, 2007).

> believe that what they bought in the past can be exchanged for an equivalent commodity in the future. This puts a huge burden on the U.S. government to ensure that integrity. Unfortunately, those institutions have failed to shoulder that burden. Reckless U.S. fiscal policy is weakening the dollar's global currency position."[225]

And what is the solution that Mr. Steyer proposes? Again, the re-monetization of gold and the world's single currency. He said:

> "But private gold banks already exist, so that account holders can make international payments in the form of real gold bars as shares. While the gold and silver industry is still a small business, it has seen significant growth in recent years as the dollar has declined. It would certainly sound outrageous to talk about a new gold-based international monetary system. But so was a monetary system without gold in 1900. Modern technology has made it possible to restore gold money through private gold banks, even without government support."[226]

It is this paragraph that is the highlight of the article, and it is the whole point of the article. In other words, the elimination of sovereign currencies, even without the support of governments, and the implementation of a single world currency with gold at its core!

It is clear that the values of gold money of Steyer, Ann Rand, and Greenspan, which are closely related to each other, stem from the financial ideas of many banking families in old Europe, especially the Rothschilds, and are very different from the monetary views of the emerging power groups in the United States. The Rothschild family's main means of cleaning up after their opponents for two hundred years is "to be invincible first, in order to wait for the enemy to be invincible". If there are two major forces in the financial world today, they are the "gold environmentalists" with the Roche family at their core and the "oil war faction" with the Rockefeller as its banner, a dollar-issuing vested interest group. The two sides agree on a strategy for future control of the world's single currency, but there are major differences at the level of interests and monetary philosophy.

---

[225] Steil, Benn, "The End of National Currency" (*Foreign Affairs*, May/June 2007).

[226] Ibid.

"Gold environmentalists" attach more importance to the moral attributes of money, emphasizing its inherent fairness and reasonableness, and firmly occupy the moral high ground, believing that the future world currency is bound to include two basic elements, gold and environmental protection, in order to meet the honesty and flexibility of money. The "oil war faction", on the other hand, values the violent factor behind the currency, believing that as long as they control the oil supply in the Middle East, they will not be afraid to keep their heads down, coupled with a strong military and war deterrent, no one in the world will dare to reject the dollar easily. Even the abolition of the dollar and the rejection of dollar debt, the new world currency is a "credit" that can be fiddled with under the bayonet. These two power blocs compete at the international level in the United States versus old Europe, or the dollar versus the euro, and at the domestic political level in the United States in the tug-of-war between the environmentalist Democrats and the oil war Republicans.

How to leverage between these two factions to maximize China's strategic interests will be a major issue that will test China's diplomatic wisdom.

On January 7, 2008, the UK's *Financial Times* published a commentator's article "Gold is the new global currency", one of the most outspoken calls for the remonetization of gold in the mainstream European and American media in recent years. The article argues that the recent spike in gold prices reflects investor nervousness about the current international financial situation, and that once gold eventually becomes a form of currency, then it will appreciate not only against the dollar, but also against the pound and the euro. The article argues,

> "A better view of gold may be that the central banks' understanding of gold before the U.S. abandoned the gold standard was that it was not a commodity, but another currency."

If we understand the masterful and skilful manipulation of the media and public agenda by the "Anglo-American power blocs" from the days of the Rhodesians, we cannot easily ignore the "personal views" expressed by iconic mouthpieces under the direct control of the world's ruling elite such as Diplomacy, The Economist, The Financial Times, and heavyweights such as Ben Steyer, because they are by no means mere expressions of personal views, but are important indicators of the will of the interest groups and are part of an elaborate and massive propaganda offensive. If this is not to be expected, then as the crisis deepens, more and more Western media and market participants will gradually develop a "coincidental" interest in gold. Ultimately, the soaring price of gold will become the "stab at" the dollar system's "wrestling cry".

Immediately after the May 17, 2009 Bilderberg meeting, Rogers and Soros, among others, began warning frequently that the coming crisis would be a currency crisis, and they were not kidding. A serious currency crisis, to be marked by a dollar crisis, is intended to serve two main purposes: first, to help the United States to carry out a complete reneging; and second, to shake up the existing world monetary system and create momentum for the concept of a world single currency. This should be fairly comparable to the crisis of 1907 that led to the creation of the Federal Reserve in 1913. One would see how fragile the world economy would be without a world central bank and a unified world currency.

The crisis has come at the right time

> *["International monetary reform is usually only possible in the face of global crisis responses and threats."] The Nobel laureate also pointed his finger at possible crisis triggers, saying that "the global economic crisis will definitely involve the dollar" and that a unified world currency will be seen as "a fluke" of the global dollar disaster.*[227]
>
> —May 2007, "Father of the Euro", Mondale

> *"In my entire career, I have never seen a central bank (the Federal Reserve) explore (monetary) theory with such distortion over the past six or seven years. From the eulogies of the 'new economy' in the late '90s to the current (advocacy) of new theories of current account adjustments, the US central bank has led attempts to rewrite traditional macroeconomics and try to convince market participants of these 'corrected' theories... I myself have never been a believer in conspiracy theories, but*

---

[227] Mundell, Robert, "A Decade Later: Asia New Responsibilities in the International Monetary System", presentation given in Seoul, South Korea, May, 2–3, 2007.

after witnessing what the Fed has done since the late '90s, I have had to change my opinion."[228]

- 25 April 2005, Stephen Roach,
Chief Economist, Morgan Stanley

Note that the timing of Mondale's speech was in May 2007, three months before the US subprime mortgage crisis broke out, and even earlier, two years before the crisis broke out, in April 2005, when Stephen Roach, in his article "Original Sin", had already described exactly how and why the financial crisis developed! Those who argue that there are no signs of a financial crisis or that the world is unprepared are untenable. The "harem" of the Federal Reserve has "3,000 beautiful" economists, with the most comprehensive data and statistics, while the head of Greenspan is a genius in data and models, saying that he still has no sense of the impending financial crisis in 2006, is in any case not convincing.

Historical experience has shown that crises are opportunities to implement major reforms, and as financial magnate Alden Clawson put it, "New comprehensive political-economic systems, across racial lines, always arise from conquest or from a common crisis."

In crisis-like thinking, Mr. Steyer seems to offer an "altruistic" solution. In order to avoid a crisis, all countries have to do is give up their monetary sovereignty before the problem is irreversible. Governments must move beyond the fatalistic notion of sovereignty that national independence must be the issuance and control of a common currency on their own territory. "National currencies and global markets cannot simply be mixed together or they will breed deadly currency crises and tense geopolitical situations and use this as an excuse to create destructive protectionism." Just wait and see, Mr. Steyer's "prophecy" will be "self-fulfilling". (Alden Clawson, source: World Bank official website)

So how should one get rid of monetary sovereignty? Steyer said frankly that the world needs to restructure into three regional currencies: the dollar, the euro and a new Asian currency. This proposal echoes the work of Robert Mondale, who has been travelling the world teaching a new international monetary unit based on the dollar (Dollar), the euro (Euro) and the yen (Yen). According to Mondale's plan, on the

---

[228] Roach, Stephen, Original Sin (Global Economic Forum in Tokyo, April 25 2005).

basis of these three currencies, a "world monetary unit" called the "drop" (DEY) would be formed, and the International Monetary Fund would be the managing director of this currency.[229]

> "The question now is not whether the world will adopt a single global currency, but when, and how smoothly and cheaply, rather than crudely, costly and confusingly. For internationalists, national sovereignty is the overriding obstacle, and in order for a global central bank and a world single currency to exist, some political arrangement must be formed."

In a 2003 lecture entitled "The International Monetary System and the Case for a World Single Currency", Robert Mondale responded frankly to the political obstacles: "A world single currency without a world government is not possible. Enforcing a single currency would have significant organizational implications." (Morrison Bumpas, source: www.itp.net)

In May 1999, economist Judy Shelton formally recommended to the U.S. House of Representatives Banking and Finance Committee that North America achieve a unified North American currency, the American dollar (Amero), and other scholars have been studying this intercontinental currency option with the goal of creating an increasingly binding new regional currency system covering Canada, the United States and Mexico.

But how will regional currencies evolve into a single global currency? Morrison Bonpasse is president of the Single Global Currency Association (SGCA), a group of economists who work with the world's single currency. Bumpas argues that

> "the monetary unions of the 21st century, and those of the 20th century that have survived, are milestones on the road to the future and a global monetary union. Thanks to the success of European and other monetary unions, we now know how to create and sustain a third generation monetary union: a global monetary union with a global central bank and a world single currency. The world is preparing to start preparing for a single global currency, just as Europe is preparing for the euro and the Arab Gulf countries are preparing for their own common

---

[229] Mundell, Robert, "A Decade Later: Asia New Responsibilities in the International Monetary System", presentation given in Seoul, South Korea, May, 2–3, 2007.

currency. With the establishment of a global single currency target by a representative group of countries with a significant share of the world's GDP, the project can move forward like the regional currencies that preceded it."[230]

"In short, the regional monetary model is the stepping stone to the world monetary model. Yet nationalism prevails now." Bumpas writes, "This can be illustrated quite simply: how to go from the current 147 currencies to 1. The evolving remnants of nationalism and political will are the main challenges to moving towards a world single currency."[231]

Perhaps from 2009 to 2024, the world economy will enter an era of unprecedented turbulence. This era of crisis will lead to a complete dismantling of many of the important economic rules we know today, most likely including major changes in the world monetary system. Unfortunately, by that time we may suddenly find that there is little gold in our hands other than a large amount of increasingly devalued flashy dollar bills. In a scenario where the rules of the game are changing dramatically, China is likely to lose the opportunity to participate in setting the rules of the currency game. Without gold in hand there is no voice in the future world monetary system and no leverage in the negotiations of the future rules of the currency game. In China's foreign exchange reserves, people with gold are ruled by people, and people with dollars are ruled by people.

Here, 2024 is not an impromptu slap in the face. With the way international bankers have operated for centuries, though they have miscalculated, rigorous reasoning and scientific calculations have been important reasons for their repeated successes. In chapter IX, we have talked about that, starting from the end of 2009, Europe and the United States will experience a 14-year-long cycle of severe consumption contraction, in this consumption-led economic growth of nearly two thirds of the two world's largest economies at the same time into the state of consumption decline "resonance", the world economy full recovery will be a "painful and extremely long" process, and in this period of time, the conditions for a new currency crisis is readily

---

[230] Bonpasse, Morrison, *The Single Global Currency* (Single Global Currency Association, 2006).

[231] Ibid.

available. In a long cycle of decline in the European and American consumer markets to produce strong trade protectionism is an extremely natural phenomenon, in a trade war of beacons and wolves, the scenes of national currencies competing to devalue to promote exports can be clearly imagined without much brain power. The consequences of currency devaluation will naturally lead to worldwide inflation and, above all, a rapid rise in commodity prices, especially oil, will push up production costs in all sectors, triggering an increase in the price of the final product, leading to the realization of inflationary expectations. The massive release of liquidity by Governments to bail out the financial crisis, which had been in a state of sedimentation and slow-moving money, was like a huge reservoir of calm waters, when an abrupt reversal of inflationary expectations would be like blowing the embankment of a dam, and the raging torrent of liquidity would release an amazing inflationary energy that central bankers would not have time to recover. The fight against hyperinflation would last at least a year, just as it did from 1923 to 1924 when Germany experienced hyperinflation.

In the aftermath of the currency crisis, Governments have not yet dried their sweat, and world-renowned economists and international think tanks will offer their advice, arguing that sovereign credit currencies, led by the United States dollar, are the culprit of the currency crisis, and that the lack of timely and effective coordination of monetary policy will be the second major cause of the currency crisis, with central banks acting on their own. The conclusion would be that the crisis of globalization requires global cooperation, that sovereign States alone will not be able to solve it, that the world single currency is clearly the "panacea" for it, and that the world central bank that issues the world currency must be "independent" of "interference and obstruction" by national Governments. Of course, Governments will not willingly relinquish their power over the distribution of their wealth, and bargaining is inevitable and will continue for many years, ideally around 2020. This is the year that the United States, with a potential shortfall of $100 trillion, and the full implosion of its Social Security and Medicare systems, will have to undergo a complete "bankruptcy protection" in order to emerge completely from the threat of a debt-ridden lake. From 2020 to 2023 after several years of trial operation, 2024 will be a good starting point, Europe and the United States new generation of population consumption peak is precisely in this year to start. With the shining of the world's single currency, the world will "definitely" experience an economic boom in the coming decades.

The world's central bank would be like a joint-stock company, with shares in every country in the world, except that Britain and the United States would have the privilege of a controlling shareholder, or a veto. Henceforth, the dominion of all the wealth created by all human beings on earth will effectively fall into the hands of a very small number of people. The distribution of the world's wealth, which will undoubtedly be the greatest power that humankind has ever imagined, and from which the vast majority of those who created it will be deprived of the right to distribute the fruits of their labour autonomously, will be an important turning point in the history of human civilization. Darkness and light, freedom and slavery will cut history in two at this moment.

The fate of money and the fate of nations

If the world's single currency is ultimately unavoidable, what kind of currency can honestly assume the responsibility for the equitable distribution of wealth under all circumstances?

The essence of wealth is the product of people's labour, and money represents the "right to claim" the fruits of that labour. Everyone in society should have the "right to claim" the fruits of others' work by selling the fruits of his or her own work. When such a "right of claim" is transferred, it acts as a "means of payment"; when a "right of claim" is generally accepted, it becomes a "medium of exchange". If the holder of the "right of claim" chooses to delay its fulfilment, it fulfils the function of a "store of wealth"; ultimately, when this "right of claim" is demanded, it is able to obtain the fruits of someone else's labour intact, and this "right of claim" is a good "measure of value". Together, these four factors form a perfect correspondence between money and wealth.

In fact, of the four major functions of money, the most central is the function of "wealth storage", the more intact the delayed cashing ability of wealth, the more money can achieve the important role of "value scale", the more popular in the market, and the easier to circulate, thus becoming a high-quality "medium of exchange" and "means of payment".

At the heart of the "store of wealth" is the fact that the "right to claim" wealth now must be able to obtain the fruits of others' labour in the future without loss and "fairly". This "fairness" is not the principle of equivalence as we commonly understand it, and in fact it is difficult to make a valid value assessment in the actual exchange process. Equitable access is when both parties involved in an exchange assess the fairness of the transaction based on their different priorities of needs, and it is because different people have different definitions of what they "need most" that the transaction can be achieved in a complementary manner.

"Expectations" become an important component of money because of the time lag between the exchange of the fruits of present and future labour. Historically, primitive currency represented a "right to claim" without "expectation", all transactions had to be carried out on the basis of the fruits of labour already performed, society did not have a surplus of products for future exchange, and the function of the "store of wealth" was not obvious. With the development of productivity, there exists in society a surplus of the fruits of labor that can be used for future enjoyment, and with that comes the advent of money and interest. Interest acts as an "expectation" of more surplus labour in the future, thus constituting a "reality + expectation" money supply.

When maritime trade rose, the advent of the bill of exchange took the expected component of money to a new level, and if interest represented a reasonable expectation of an agricultural harvest in a self-sufficient economy, the bill of exchange extended monetary expectations to reasonable expectations of commercial trade.

The era of the industrial revolution saw the emergence of the banking industry's "fractional reserve" system, which effectively extended the expected component of money further to underpin the massive expansion of industrial production.

The advent of the information age has given rise to the proliferation of financial derivatives, a process that transforms the wealth of the virtual world into the money supply of the real world, thus infinitely amplifying the "expected" component of money to the brink of unsustainable destruction, and ultimately leading to the financial crisis.

Historically, the expectation component of money is inherently rational, but when it is excessive, it triggers the contradiction that past expectations cannot be met by reality.

If the core elements of the "store of wealth" include "real labour outcomes + expected labour outcomes", then the "real labour outcomes" reflect the commodity attributes of money, while the "expected labour outcomes" reflect the credit attributes of money. The complete abolition of the commodity nature of money would lead to the dysfunction and dysregulation of the "store of wealth", and any historical currency, once removed from the commodity nature of money, would eventually be subject to constant devaluation.

The "wealth storage" function of money determines not only its endogenous self-sustainability, but also its external acceptability, i.e. its circulation domain.

The rise and fall of major civilizations throughout history is, in essence, a comprehensive reflection of the efficiency of that civilization's integrated allocation of natural resources and its ability to integrate social resources under its control, while the strength and weakness of the currency are external manifestations of both. The rise of a strong civilization is naturally accompanied by a strong and robust currency and an expanding currency circulation, which, by ensuring its stability and reliability, builds a strong system of social trust to form a solid contract for multilateral interests. Under a strong monetary system, society operates under a "monetary legal system". On the contrary, an inflection point at which civilization flourishes and declines is mainly reflected in the inability of the wealth-creating capacity to meet the ever-increasing consumption of expenditures, and the problem of a diffuse deficit that induces currency devaluation and progressively worsening inflation, which in turn suppresses the wealth-creating dynamics of society, leading to a shrinking of the currency circulation area and weakening the capacity and efficiency of social integration and resource allocation, thus accelerating the deterioration of fiscal problems. At the same time, the devalued currency undermined the contractual relations of common interest that had been formed among the various strata of society, and the "monetary rule" was replaced by the "money-man rule", resulting in the disintegration of social centripetal forces, moral degradation and, ultimately, the overthrow of States and the decline of civilization.

It is in the history of the rise and fall of ancient Rome that the history of its monetary boom and bust is well represented. During Julius Caesar's reign, he single-handedly established the strong gold and silver monetary system of ancient Rome, which, along with the expansion of the Roman army into the vast area around the Mediterranean Sea, in turn greatly strengthened the Roman Empire's ability to integrate resources into the surrounding area, thus strengthening the Empire. During the heyday of the centuries-long Roman Empire, the Roman Empire had a prosperous economy, stable prices, moderate taxation, advanced trade, and commercial lending rates in the normal range of 4 to 6 percent, the lowest level in the entire Roman Empire.

From the time of the Roman Emperor Nero in 54 A.D., as the country's coffers became increasingly stretched while its expenses grew larger, the Emperor Nero began to cover the fiscal deficit by devaluing the currency. From A.D. 54 to A.D. 68, the silver content of Roman silver coins dropped from 100% to 90%, to 85% by A.D. 117, and to 75% by A.D. 180. After two more emperors, by 211 A.D., only 50% of the silver content of Roman silver coins remained. The cycle of gradual currency devaluation that began in Nero's time lasted more than 150 years, a period that also coincided with the turn of the Roman Empire's heyday. But the inflationary nightmare soon entered a period of accelerated deterioration, and from 260 to 268 AD, the silver content of the Roman silver coin quickly fell to just 4 percent. The Roman Empire at this time was already in economic difficulties, with more than one rebellion at home, and years of use of soldiers abroad, the high denomination of the currency but the very low silver content led to soaring prices, higher taxes, and finally provoked a mutiny of soldiers, and King Origen was assassinated in 275 AD.

His successor, Emperor Diocletian, wanted to follow the example of Caesar and Augustus and revive the Roman currency. To counter inflation, he even announced the reissue of full-value silver coins, but he mistakenly demanded that the new coins be "equated" with the old ones, which had been severely devalued, and as a result his new coins were quickly collected and withdrawn from circulation. The only way to combat inflation was to control prices, which led to the famous "Edict of 301 A.D.", which set maximum prices for thousands of goods and services, varying according to the quality of the goods and the type of service. As interest rates continue to soar, the law limits interest to between 6 and 12 per cent, depending on the level of risk taken. The shortage of certain products has led to a ban on exports of goods such as various foodstuffs and "strategic goods" such as iron, bronze, weapons, army equipment and horses. Control over these aspects has essentially been extended to the hierarchy. Constantine the Great demanded that the son of every soldier remain a soldier unless he was unfit for military service. Likewise, agricultural workers are required to work in agriculture permanently and for generations to come. This trend was later extended to all sectors that were considered essential or followed by none. The consequence of price controls is that the creators of wealth are unable to make a profit under such a price system, so large quantities of commodities are diverted to the underground black market. In response, the Roman emperor severely cracked down on black market transactions, and the crackdown eventually had its effect, but at the cost of the wealth creators simply stopping any creation and the Roman Empire's economy was on the brink of extinction. By this time the monetary system of the Roman Empire had completely collapsed and the government had to stop collecting taxes in currency and instead collect goods and services directly. The powerful Roman Empire was completely reduced to bartering for goods.

By about 350 AD, Roman silver coins were worth only $1/30,000^{th}$ of what they were in Augustan times, and the Western Roman Empire had finally come to its final breaking point.

In contrast, Constantine the Great reestablished a new monetary unit in Eastern Rome, a new strong monetary mechanism based on the pure gold coin (Solidus), which became an important guarantee for the continuation of the Byzantine Empire for thousands of years. Its credibility is so good that such gold coins are circulated in neighboring hostile countries and as far away as Africa and Western Europe. Some historians believe that the key fulcrum of the Eastern Roman Empire's millennium-long existence in a dire situation surrounded by enemies on all sides was its economic structure and financial system based on a golden currency. The purity of the Byzantine gold currency was maintained until 1034 A.D. and then accelerated from 1081 onwards, when a strong gold currency system that had maintained its purity for nearly 800 years finally collapsed, followed by Byzantium's status as a world trade centre and the centripetal force and moral ethics of a great empire.

The alternation of strong and weak currencies has been repeated not only in Western history, but in Chinese history as well. During the Northern Song Dynasty, the general lack of copper in the Sichuan region necessitated the heavy use of iron money in commercial transactions. At that time, it cost 20,000 iron dollars to buy a piece of cloth, weighing about 500 pounds, which needed to be transported by car, the transaction cost was very high, which severely restricted economic development. To alleviate this problem, some local merchants in the Chengdu area created the world's first banknote issuing institution, and they issued the world's first paper currency,

"Jiaotzu", against iron money. Later the Northern Song government in 1024 years began to issue "government-run Jiaotzi", collateral is called banknotes, generally iron money, is nearly 30% of the amount of banknotes issued, that is, roughly three times more than the fractional reserve banknotes issue mode. During the first 100 years of the issue of the Jiaozi, the volume of Jiaozi was still relatively restrained and the socio-economic development did take place, but by 1160, the proportion of banknotes had dropped to $1/60^{th}$ of the volume of paper money issued, and later the government simply abandoned the banknotes and issued Jiaozi at will. By the end of the Southern Song Dynasty, inflation was 20 trillion times higher in 150 years! In fact, the Southern Song monetary system collapsed before the Mongolian army's iron-footed invasion. The collapse of the monetary system, the shrinking of government taxation, the collapse of the country's ability to mobilize for war, and the collapse of the Song dynasty were in fact the result of the collapse of the paper money system.

The end of the Jin dynasty was rather similar to the Song dynasty, where severe inflation caused by a weak currency finally killed the kingdom. The Golden State issued paper money for more than 70 years, the price of goods rose 60 million times, until the people's hearts were in turmoil and wealth creation was extinct, the same monetary system before the collapse of the empire.

By the Yuan Dynasty, although the Yuan government tried to learn the lessons of the collapse of the paper money system in the Song and Jin dynasties, and made extensive reforms in policy measures to create the world's first monetary system similar to the silver standard at that time, but war, famine, and excessive spending of extravagance could not be restrained by means of self-discipline. The Yuan Dynasty began to issue banknotes for more than 20 years, the currency was drastically reduced to 1/10 of its original value, at the end of the Yuan Dynasty the price of rice rose to more than 60,000 times in the early years of the Yuan Dynasty, the banknote system completely collapsed, and the public refused to accept official banknotes. With the loss of the currency circulation area, the meta-government is no longer able to control finances and taxation, and the country is declining in strength and eventually collapsing in currency.

The Ming experiment with the paper currency system lasted for another 150 years, and by 1522, the Ming Bao banknotes were devalued to 2 per cent of their original value, and inflation was rampant. The Ming government was finally forced to abandon the paper money system in favor of a return to the metal money system. After nearly 500 years of experimenting with paper money systems from the Song to the Ming, history has finally come to the lesson that paper money, an unfettered and weak monetary system, cannot be stable in the long run.

From a historical point of view, whether it is the Song Dynasty, or the Yuanming banknotes, including the "colonial vouchers" in the American War of Independence, the "Lincoln Greenbacks" in the Civil War period, and the "Feder money" in Nazi Germany, these banknotes, although they can play a role in stimulating economic development within a certain historical period, can only be used as a means of emergency, but by no means the way to long-term peace and stability. Any paper currency that loses its commodity attributes will repeat history.

Since the disintegration of the Bretton Woods system in 1971, when the dollar was completely decoupled from gold, human society for the first time came together into an era of a purely credit monetary system without commodities as a backing. The existence of a credit currency presupposes that the person who creates it must keep his or her word in order for a currency based on it to have value. The essence of the financial crisis in the United States was the inability of debtors to honor their credit, so the dollar, which was derived from such debt, was bound to depreciate dramatically. The problem with credit currencies is that there is a permanent risk of default on the debt, and a currency based on that risk cannot truly function as a "store of wealth".

Historical experience has shown that the four functions of money – "store of wealth", "medium of exchange", "means of payment" and "scale of value" – must work together in order for the mechanism of currency operation to be stable and sustainable. A pure credit monetary system, without the core function of a "store of wealth", would eventually lose its "scale of value" function. After only 38 years of operation, the pure credit money table, which carries the world economy, is already severely out of balance and shaky under the four legs of the money table with two missing. With the U.S. debt stock currently at a massive $5.7 trillion, and debt pressure increasing at an average rate of 6 percent, the total debt will reach an appalling $10.2 trillion in 2020, just 10 years from now, and its total GDP will be only $18.8 trillion at a potentially sustainable growth rate of 3 percent, with interest payments on the debt alone eating up one-third of all U.S. GDP, and this interest payment pressure will continue to grow hopelessly fast. If the United States was playing a fair game of money, it could not have had a second choice but to declare "bankruptcy protection".

In 2020, the United States Government's potential deficit in Social Security and Medicare will "contribute" another $100 trillion in hidden liabilities. The US will have no choice but to print money on a large scale to ease the pressure of debt payments. But can the countries of the world, which were completely disappointed with the dollar in 2009 and are ready to flee its assets, continue to tolerate the pain and helplessness of holding the dollar when they face a much larger dollar depreciation trend by 2020?

If the dollar eventually heads towards collapse around 2020, there will be no more sovereign currency in the world that can replace the dollar and the credit monetary system will face final liquidation. At that point, the re-monetization of gold will be inevitable. Re-monetization of gold would restore the "wealth store" function of money and rebalance the four legs of the money table. However, gold alone as the pillar of the modern monetary system, but there are great shortcomings, the biggest problem is that the increase in gold production can not catch up with the speed of world economic growth, so gold in the strengthening of "wealth savings" function at the same time, but curbed the "value scale" function of effective play. So, under a full gold monetary regime, the entire world economy would still develop unevenly. As the future of the world's single currency, gold must be a strong complementary element in order to constitute a monetary system that can "long-term stability".

The Perfect and Deadly Combination: World Single Currency = Gold + Carbon Currency

Corresponding to the rigidity of gold, the new monetary elements must have "elasticity", which can compensate for the mismatch between gold and economic development, making the four major functions of money complete and adequate.

This is the root cause of the CO2-emitting currency that will eventually shine on the world monetary stage.

Things are more precious than they are rare. For the CO2 concept favoured by the "golden environmentalists" among international bankers to have value, it must become "scarce". What can be done to make carbon dioxide, which could have been emitted freely, scarce?

Then there must be a "saying" of scarcity, and that is environmental protection. The underlying logic is that the protection of the environment is a matter of human survival, and that carbon dioxide emissions are at the heart of environmental protection, and that, therefore, carbon dioxide determines the fate of humanity. Since CO_2 is so critical, there must be a "cap" on its emissions, and as long as there is a cap, there can be an artificial "scarcity". Thus, there is the Kyoto Protocol.

At the heart of the Kyoto Protocol is the establishment of a "cap" on carbon dioxide emissions, which would then require the world's countries to undertake corresponding emission reduction obligations. If the respective emission reduction targets are not met, the excess emission targets of other countries will have to be bought from the CO_2 emissions market, and for the first time the potential financial value of CO_2 emission allowances has been given in the form of an international treaty. In the future, carbon dioxide emission allowances as a tradable financial product will be freely listed and transferred, like all bonds and stocks, and can be mortgaged in banks, and eventually become an integral part of the central bank's base currency.

Carbon dioxide emissions are a wonderful concept in the extreme, with a high degree of "resilience", since their emissions can be controlled and adjusted by human beings, thus ensuring the "scarcity" that money must have. It is also a reliable "proxy variable" for socio-economic activity and, like electricity consumption, CO_2 emissions can be used to assess the level of economic growth, thus allowing for the inclusion of a reasonable "expected" component of money in the total money supply.

Of course, carbon dioxide is not the only "elastic" monetary element, but, as things stand, it has the greatest potential to become one of the components of the world's single currency. This is not just because it makes theoretical sense, but more fundamentally because the strategic interests of the world's ruling elite can be best served by using CO_2 as a monetary element. The developed countries of Europe and the United States, as the game changers of the world currency, are bound to choose the monetary elements that are most advantageous to them, they have a strong advantage in high technology, their socio-economic structure has already been transformed from an industrialized society to an information and service society, a large number of traditional industries have been or are accelerating their transfer to the emerging developing countries, whose carbon dioxide emissions are trending downwards at a time when the emerging countries are industrializing on a large scale and their carbon dioxide emissions will be inevitably rising for the foreseeable future.

The monetary system, as the supreme power in a society, will always be at the "eye of the wind" at the heart of the game of various power groups. The choice of a monetary system that maximizes its own benefits while effectively curbing the rise of potential competitors will undoubtedly be the focus of much brain-teasing and contemplation by various interest groups.

If a "perfect" combination of "gold + carbon emissions" currencies is eventually introduced, the West will clearly be the biggest winner, while developing countries such as China will be the biggest losers. Obviously, the West has more than 30,000 tons of gold reserves, while China has only 1,000 tons, and the vast majority of China's foreign exchange reserves are concentrated in dollar assets. If gold is remonetized and the dollar collapses at the same time, the U.S. will rely on the vast majority of its debt. With the Treasury's 8,100 tons of gold reserves and the 3,000 tons of gold under IMF control, the U.S. economy will be lightly loaded and will soon be rejuvenated after being completely freed from its massive debt burden. Most of the fruits of China's 30 years of reform and opening up have been consumed by the United States on the one hand, and the trade surpluses saved on the other hand have been borrowed by the United States, leaving only the United States debt in the hands of white notes. The re-monetization of gold will completely loot the $2 trillion in wealth that China has accumulated over 30 years of reform, the equivalent of 30 years that China's 1.3 billion citizens have worked for the West for nothing.

If carbon dioxide emissions are monetized, then China's environmental "fines" for the next 30 years will also quietly arrive, which means that in the future the Chinese people will have to continue to do nothing for another 30 years. The world's single monetary system of "gold + carbon emissions" currency combinations would have cost China's 1.3 billion people 60 years in the West!

What does it mean to be a financial strategy? That's the power of financial strategy! China is not short of experts, what China is short of are strategic thinkers!

As the saying goes, it's too early for no gain. The strategic West of environmental monetization has been plotting for 40 years, who would spend so much time and money promoting the idea of CO_2

emissions without a strong interest drive? Where have these "compassionate" world ruling elites ever really done anything to save human lives when there are so many forms of altruism, far more immediate threats than carbon dioxide, such as poverty in the third world, hunger and disease that kill thousands of children every day in Africa? If even the imminent saving of lives is being ignored by these people, how can people believe that there is no significant interest driving the concepts of carbon currencies, carbon trading, carbon tariffs, etc., that are all over the map in the West?

What is fatal is that these people are so clever that, under a massive and prolonged propaganda campaign, the issue of carbon dioxide has been "shaped" into the world's most pressing public agenda, and indeed, the issue of carbon dioxide emissions has even been raised to the strategic level of the survival of the planet. They have a firm grip on the moral high ground of the world. Anyone who opposes CO_2 reduction will be labeled as anti-human, even anti-Earth. Countries that resist CO_2 emission limits will become public enemies of humanity and will be damned in every corner of the world. Governments and civil society groups will rise up and attack, for example, by imposing a staggering tax on carbon emissions from international trade, which will squeeze the products of the "enemies of humanity" out of the world market; the punitive consensus in international financial markets will put the overseas mergers and acquisitions of the "enemies of humanity" completely on hold; and the punitive "environmental tax" will be imposed on all international raw materials and commodities necessary for the economic development of the "enemies of humanity", leading to severe cost inflation and significantly weakening the country's economic development potential.

The heavy price of this hat is one that China absolutely cannot afford, and this day may not come in a year or two, but it will most likely be the harsh reality that China must face in 10 years.

To this end, preventive strategic research is urgent, and China is already facing a currency war that cannot be seen.

End of the Dollar

America's existing $57 trillion debt weir, which is growing profitably every hour of every day, combined with the huge burden of hidden health care and pension liabilities over the next 10 years, has long been a heavy shackle for the U.S. economy to continue to grow. The United States will in fact never be able to pay off these debts. It will only get deeper and deeper in the swamp of debt as time goes on. The credibility of the dollar has been seriously shaken and it is only a matter of time before it is completely abandoned by the world. The makers of dollar policy know this well.

The implementation of the basic national policy of "controlled zeroing" of the dollar is already the only way out and the best option for the long-term interests of the United States, in order to deceive the people of all countries, including China, to the maximum extent possible before the total collapse, and to cleverly rely on the debt of several trillions of dollars in order to change the face of the future, to reassemble lightly. But abolishing the dollar is something that the American people at large and investors around the world can't say yes to, so only a big crisis can bring about big change. This is one of the reasons why the current financial crisis in the United States has erupted.

In a normal economy, the currency can only depreciate little by little, and it takes a long time and journey to get the dollar to zero completely. Over such a long period of time, the growing debt burden of the United States is bound to completely stifle its economic development and provide ample time for other countries to abandon the dollar. To do so, the dollar must reasonably and legally accelerate its depreciation while leaving investors in the dollar unsuspecting and even supporting the Fed's policy of abusive currency issuance. Thus, the regulations prohibiting bankers from speculating wildly were lifted, a variety of financial weapons of mass destruction – financial derivatives exploded, the interest rate policy to encourage subprime mortgages came out, with extreme risk quickly engaged in the large financial enterprises of the bosses of the super high rewards appeared, a century-old financial crisis suddenly erupted, the Federal Reserve hundreds of billions of dollars of money printing crime was legal, foreign investors expressed support and understanding and even continued to buy. In an effort to allay the fears of foreign investors, the dollar has inexplicably stopped falling and surged again. All sorts of strange things, and it all came together!

Dollar interests numb the nerves of the world by boiling a frog in warm water. Unlike the straight-line appreciation of the yuan, the tactic of the dollar devaluation is a big drop and a small rise, a sudden drop and a sudden rise, with more and more and more and less, so that those who are short the dollar cannot see the timing and do not dare to act rashly, so that the holders of the dollar and the United States treasury bonds around the world have always had illusions about the dollar, but they cannot make a prompt decision and get out of it quickly, so that the dollar can continue to hold investors in deep, so as to achieve "controlled zero" in accordance with the timetable and manner most favourable to the dollar interest group.

However, neither Europe nor the United States is likely to let the Chinese fishermen get rich in this financial crisis and get big while they can. They'll make sure to cram as many Chinese passengers as possible on the titanic ship of dollars. And Chinese passengers are feeling good about owning discounted tickets to this luxury cruise ship and heading to the Yellow Springs. A possible scenario for the future is that the dollar's "a thousand corpses passing by the side of a sinking ship, most of them Chinese".

What is particularly noteworthy in this process is the US government's bailout show, which is really brilliant and wonderful! Among the most dramatic of these was the extraordinary scene in which Paulson knelt in Congress begging for passage of the $700 billion rescue bill, which pushed the big drama to a tragic climax. These bailout shows are designed to show the world that I, the US government, have done everything in my power to save the dollar and the US economy. You can see that I am trying desperately to "bail out" the market with 100 billion in three days and 1 trillion in five days. I can't be blamed if I can't be saved again. When all was ready, suddenly one day, Anglo-French and German simultaneously announced that they would no longer accept dollars. No one saved the stock market from plunging, no one cared if the dollar plunged. Overnight, all of America's debt disappeared, along with the Chinese savings and most of its foreign exchange reserves. The American people's pensions are in the soup, health insurance is gone, the U.S. national debt is turned into water, the dollar reserves as hand paper, all these will eventually explode the anger do not come at me the U.S. government. I've done everything I can, I've done everything I can, I've done everything I can, I've done everything I can, I have a clear conscience. The Western theoretical community will take aim at the "evil sovereign currency", with the "unfortunate" dollar as the bull's-eye. Finally, the world's ruling elite can only express their most sincere sympathy and condolences to the vast number of dollar victims, including the hardworking and kind-hearted Chinese people. Their eulogy will end thus: "Let us, living ones, rise from the ruins of sovereign currencies and embark on the new journey of the world's single honest currency! Amen."

"The world under Hercules"

In the film *Back to the Future*, Martin, who stumbles back to Martin 30 years ago, finds that his young father and mother by mistake don't seem to be in love anymore, and is horrified to see that the image of the siblings and himself is gradually disappearing from the family photo taken 30 years later! Martin, who was so busy, finally ignited the spark of love between his father and mother, and in the moment when the parents of the teenage girl and boy kissed happily for life, 30 years later the crystals of love finally reappeared in the family photo. Martin snapped to his senses and realized that all his actions in returning to the past would change the course and outcome of his future life.

He sprinted up to the time machine Dr. Brown had made and set the time to a few moments before departure. After a thrilling race against time, Martin "ran" back 30 years to the moment when Dr. Brown was about to be killed by the criminals, in the moment of the bullet fired at Dr. Brown, Martin flew up, changing the ending of the death of the doctor.

At this point, it finally dawned on the audience. Why is it called "Back to the Future" when the story is about "Back to the Past"? It turns out that "going back to the past" is precisely to change the future, and the future can be rewritten "back".

The grand finale scene of Ayn Rand's Atlas Shrug is the triumphant return of each of the "world's best" ruling elites who went on a "collective strike" and succeeded, flying advanced private jets. As they tower over the masses, at a time when the red world is gradually plunging into chaos, decline and destruction in full accordance with their carefully crafted timetable, the group of greedy, shameless and foolish government officials who once fought them have been utterly defeated and are powerless, and the true essence of the world – wealth, wisdom, thought – is concentrated only in the hands of this elite group flying high above the sky. They smiled triumphantly and proudly as they watched the world beneath them go on the "right track of wisdom, rightness and excellence" according to their design.

Throughout the story, the government chiefs who try to restrain these ruling elites are the antithesis of their hypocrisy, stupidity, shameless greed, bravado, and untouchable ugliness. And all the other "little people" of the general public have been a virtually negligible part of it from the beginning. They are incompetent, ignorant, weak, cowering beside the broken railroads, abandoned mines, and at a loss for words in the bankrupt banks, chaotic towns, and hungry countryside. Ann Rand simply doesn't bother to give names to these dispensable minor characters in the story – they're just a blur of background color anyway, a cloud of difference from the elite heroes, waiting to be placed as pawns in a whole new world of chess in the future.

The "Hercules" have single-handedly thrown off the old, inefficient and restrictive patterns on the ground and will reconstruct society with "the greatest wisdom and ingenuity, the greatest talent and design". They have been preparing and planning for this for many years, and they are moving the whole social system step by step towards the "blue sky of dissolution", just as Keiji Yokomichi did in the Japanese film "The Hunted", according to the steps and rhythms they have precisely designed. Yes, what a blue sky, the ignorant masses are walking through, walking through...

Will "Hercules" really have the last laugh? Is it true that the "future" they have created cannot be changed?

Hercules are confident that they hold the golden key to the future and have designed a destined destination for all people. But what Hercules overlooks is that the fundamental driving force behind the whole of human history is the people! Water can carry a boat, but it can also overturn it. This has been the case in the past and in the present. The righteousness of mankind is the vicissitudes of the world.

If all the beings under the sky knew their fate would be "arranged" by the "Hercules" in the future, would they still be indifferent today?

Perhaps "Hercules" overestimated himself and underestimated others.

What will the "Hercules" see when they look down on the vast expanse of the earth?

Perhaps they will see that countries such as Russia and Brazil are strategically and decisively getting rid of huge amounts of US bonds.

Perhaps they will see Middle Eastern countries tenaciously changing their petrodollar-dominated settlement system.

Perhaps they will see that developing countries, represented by China, are not following the financial crisis script they have compiled and playing by the book.

They will also see the developing countries planning their own future monetary system to compete with the "Hercules" single world currency. When the general public is informed of the future end, their actions now will change the future!

Let's wait and see.

Acknowledgements and Reflections

The year back home, which was also the final writing time for *Currency Wars 2 – The Power of Gold* , saw many life changes. These changes not only made this book, but also made a new of me. Before writing the preface to this book, I couldn't help but feel a lot of emotion.

In 2009, life left me with an irreparable regret – my mother, Ms. Ren Yunqing, left the world due to illness as the pen of "Currency Wars 2 – The Power of Gold " closed. When my mother was seriously ill, I was unable to do my filial duty by her side due to my intense workload. Although she is still saying, "Don't let him come back because he is busy", I do not know how much she misses me. In her heart, I am a banner that she hopes her son will always fly high, even in heaven, and she will be glad and proud of it. Dear mother, your little triplet will work hard and live happily, and I am sure your heavenly spirit is watching me every moment, praying for me and giving me strength! My two brothers took care of my mother when she was seriously ill, which made me sigh with regret. I think that although my mother has left, the three of us will definitely be more united in our lives, and we will be able to help each other in the future until we die.

When it comes to my mother, I can't help but think of my youngest daughter who is far away on the other side of the ocean. Baby, have you grown up? Got fat? Are learning outcomes getting better? Maybe you are too young now to understand why Daddy would stay away from you to go back to your homeland and start a business, but please believe that you will always be Daddy's little angel and that the happiness of your life is my greatest wish! Daughters, listen to your mother, who has worked so hard to educate and care for you, and take good care of yourselves while I am not with you, and your gratitude will be etched in your hearts this life.

2009 was the beginning of my 40th year, and what a difficult process it was for someone who was so passionate but who hadn't been close to his country for years. It was at this time that I was fortunate to meet Ms. Ren Wen, the publisher of Global Finance magazine, Mr. Xiang Song-jo, the chief economist, and Mr. Peng Xiaoguang, the deputy editor-in-chief, and we founded the Global Finance Institute because of our common vision and belief. In my opinion, Ms. Ren's wealth of business experience, business acumen, and graceful demeanor are the key to the rapid emergence of the Global Institute of Finance and Economics as a major force in China's private think tank in a short period of time. And Song Jo and Xiao Guang are using their extensive contacts in the financial and economic circles at home and abroad, thick and thin knowledge, for the Global Institute of Finance and Economics built a bridge to the world. The cooperation with you has made me feel the spiritual power of the new generation of Chinese elites. If it wasn't for your help, my vision wouldn't have come to life so quickly, and I wouldn't have the strong team of Global Finance Magazine, Global Finance Research Institute and Beijing Jinquan Investment Company Limited standing behind me today.

My brothers and sisters in my career, give me confidence when I'm at a loss, give me warmth when I'm lonely, we have no complaints and no regrets, we're united and we love each other, all the struggle is just because I love the moment of success!

Many people say that success is for those who are prepared, but many who are prepared do not have the opportunity to succeed, and on July 4, 2009, after all our work as one of the organizers of the Global Think Tank Summit was successfully completed, the young Global Finance team finally stood on a new career path. Even the days of fatigue and toil were no longer enough, as we set a farther course for the future. I would like to express my special gratitude to the elders, namely, Mr. Zeng Peiyan, President of the China Center for International Economic Exchanges, the organizer of the Summit, Mr. Zheng Xinli, Executive Vice President, Mr. Wei Jianguo, Secretary-General, and Mr. Chen Yanbing, Deputy Secretary-General. During the intensive preparations for the Conference, your trust and support made the younger generation unforgettable, but in fact, there is no need to talk about gratitude in your realm.

In addition, I would like to thank Mr. Tang Shisheng, Chairman of Hongyuan Securities, for the kindness he extended to me at the beginning of my return to China. You have made many valuable suggestions and comments on the origin and role of credit, the relationship between credit and money, and the root causes of the financial crisis. With your encouragement and guidance, I have read parts of *The Complete Works of Max Engels* on credit and money and the financial markets of 19th century Europe and have been greatly inspired.

In addition, I would like to give special thanks to Ms. L.H., the principal research assistant and writing assistant for two copies of The Currency Wars. Her heart and wisdom coalesce in every one of my creations.

There are so many people to thank: Mr. Robert Mondale, who is easy to talk to, Mr. Chen Jian, who is quietly supportive, Mr. Li Jun, who is the general manager of the Institute, Mr. Liu Congxing, who is strict and meticulous, Mr. Shi Weidong, who is a true friend, Mr. Yang Wei, who gave up his superior life in the United States and returned home to fight with me, Mr. Sheng Jie, who is my assistant, all the members who gave me unparalleled support at the beginning of the Institute, all the experts on the editorial board of Global Finance and Economics, all the loyal readers who look forward to the publication of *Currency Wars 2 – The Power of Gold* every day, Mr. and Mrs. Niu Zhang, who have given me a lot of care in their lives, please forgive me for being unable to thank all those people for various reasons. And at this point, all words of gratitude seem too pale, because I know in my heart that the support and commitment of all of you has been my greatest asset in this life. What do I regret about this life?

Allow me to dedicate this book to all those who love me and those I love, and may you always be healthy and happy!

Afterword

This book was not written to teach you how to invest, how to allocate assets, or to teach a typical set of currency hedging methods. This book is intended to answer the question that has puzzled us for so long and remains unanswered: why do currencies conflict?

A very gifted scholar in the field of world economics, Song spends a great deal of time exploring history, studying reality and trying to decipher the future. By the time Song wrote his second book, *Currency Wars 2 – The Power of Gold*, he had flipped through more than 100 books and traced them back 300 years to explore the origins of the current financial system. In his book, Mr. Song opens the "Pandora's Box" about how 17 families ruled the world's financial system from the beginning of the 19th century to the present and how they controlled the banking system, crude oil, the industrial industry and the defense industry by creating financial instruments and creating major events so that they could master the world skillfully and effectively from the beginning to the present. They sit at the top of the pyramid and hide all their secrets under their thrones. Mr. Song tried to urge his country, China, to understand the trends of globalization. When you read this book with great interest, you will feel that time has passed like an arrow and history has changed. I personally rate this book as one of the best of all works that depict such topics. The takeaway from reading this book is 10 times that of reading his first book, *Currency Wars*, and I can't wait to read the third book he is beginning to work on. I am very grateful to Mr. Song for providing us with such valuable thoughts and perspectives and for sharing his passion and persistence with his readers.

Dr. Mohamed Abdul Haq

President and CEO of G6 Group and
Chairman of Fortune Nest Group

Beijing, 28 June 2009

Other titles

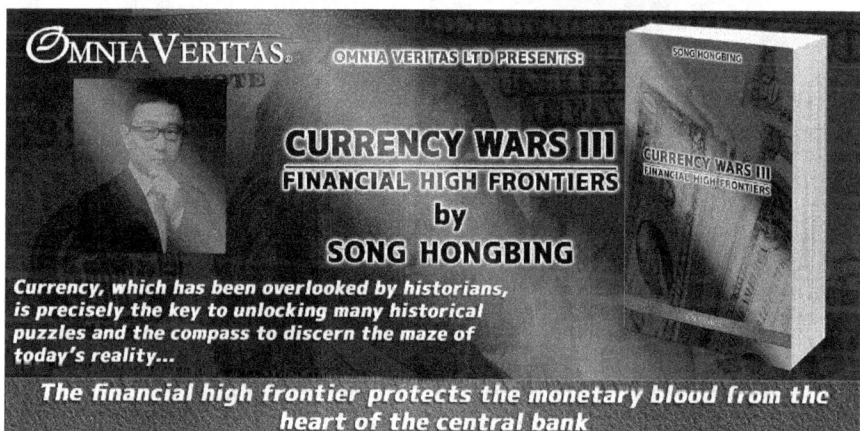

THE POWER OF GOLD

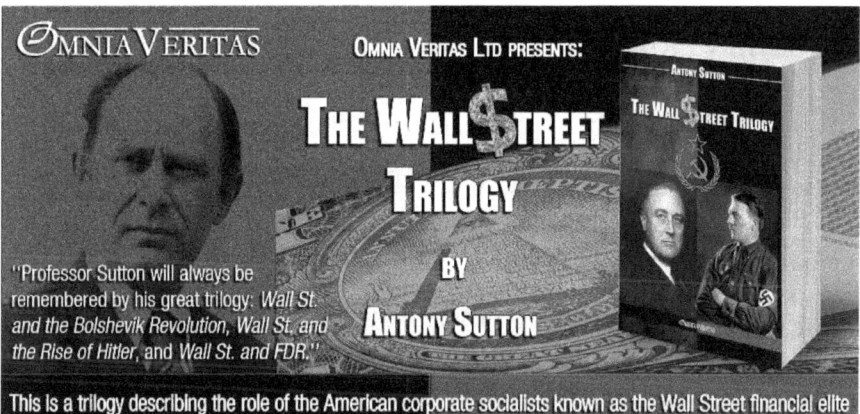

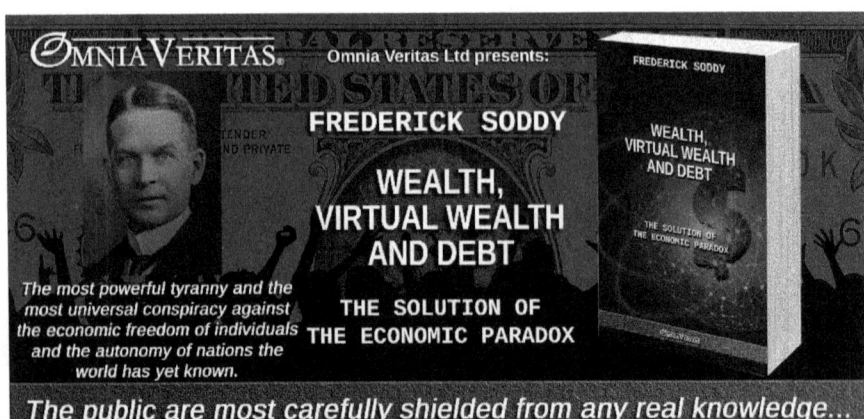
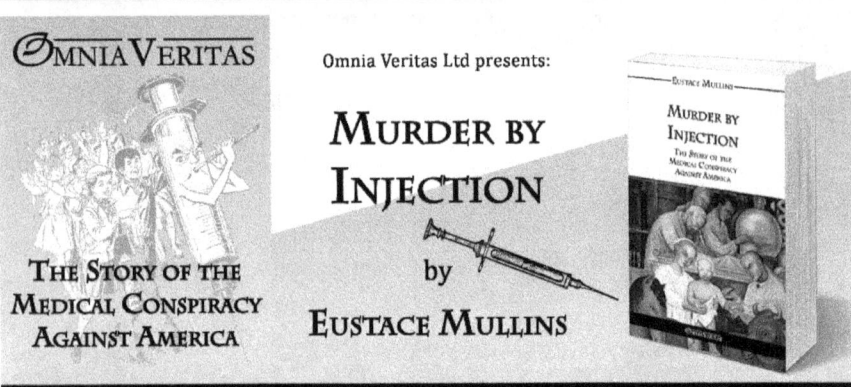
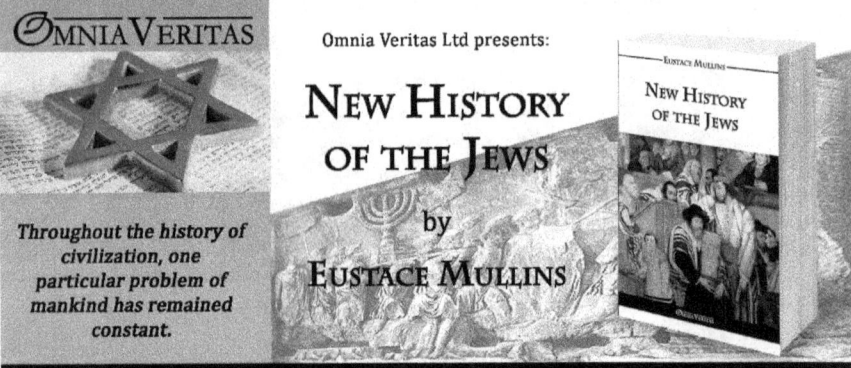

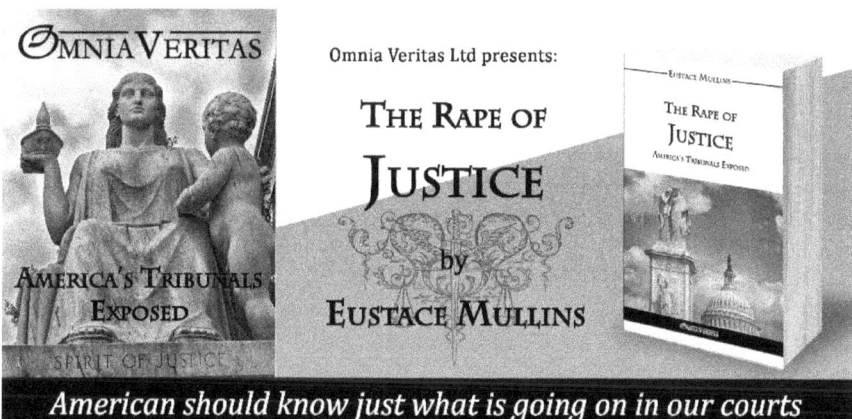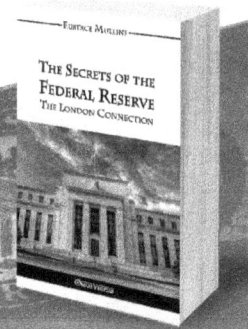

www.ingramcontent.com/pod-product-compliance
Lightning Source LLC
Chambersburg PA
CBHW071310150426
43191CB00007B/574